Shakespearean Comedy

Shakespearean Comedy

By THOMAS MARC PARROTT

NEW YORK
RUSSELL & RUSSELL · INC
1962

TO MY FELLOW MEMBERS OF
THE SHAKSPERE SOCIETY OF PHILADELPHIA

Preface

IN THE year 416 B.C. the Athenian tragic poet Agathon gave a banquet to celebrate his winning of the first prize in a dramatic contest before thirty thousand spectators. Among the guests were Socrates and Aristophanes, and they alone survived the long discussion on the nature of Love and the drinking bout that followed the irruption of a band of revelers into the so-far sober party. Aristodemus, the reporter of the discourse and the doings, fell asleep on a couch, but woke at cock-crow to find Socrates drinking out of a large goblet with the two poets and discussing the genius of tragedy and comedy. He maintained, in opposition to the accepted opinion, that the genius of the two was essentially the same and that a poet should be able to compose both tragedy and comedy. His hearers, convicted rather than convinced, fell asleep in their turn, and Socrates departed to bathe at the Lyceum and return to his house.

Nothing of the work of Agathon remains, and Aristophanes never, so far as we know, wrote a tragedy. The thesis of Socrates that one and the same poet could write both tragedy and comedy had to wait for centuries until it was demonstrated in the work of Shakespeare.

Shakespeare, however, did something more than exemplify the argument of Socrates. Notwithstanding the separation of his plays by the editors of the Folio into Comedies, Histories, and Tragedies, as in common practice today, he did not write sharply distinguished types of drama. On the contrary, he united, to quote Dr. Johnson, 'the powers of exciting laughter and sorrow in one composition,' and this 'mixing of comick and tragick scenes,' for which he was condemned by neo-classic critics, extends, says Johnson, 'to all his works.' There is hardly a Shakespearean tragedy in which the sound of laughter is not heard, hardly a comedy in which there is not at least the shadow of impending disaster.

It would, of course, be absurd to spring at once from Socrates to Shakespeare and to imagine the English poet a sudden genius born in fate's due time to fulfil the prophecy of the Greek philosopher.

Shakespearean drama, like Elizabethan literature in general, is founded on a long tradition in medieval and early Renaissance literature, where the sharp distinction between tragedy and comedy maintained by the classicists was either unknown or ignored. Shakespearean drama has a double aspect; it is indeed for all time, but it is also of its age, truly Elizabethan. This is, perhaps, particularly true of the comic element in his work where contemporary color—manners, modes of thought and speech, and topical allusions—is everywhere apparent. Fully to apprehend and enjoy Shakespearean comedy the reader should have some knowledge of its literary background.

Strangely enough, no historical and systematic treatment of Shakespearean comedy exists; the English histories, tragedies, and Roman plays have received fuller and more satisfactory treatment. Why this should be is not at once apparent. One need not agree with Johnson's marked preference of Shakespeare's comic to his tragic scenes to accept his dictum that Shakespeare's comedy seems to be 'instinct,' that in his comic scenes he 'produces without labour what no labour can improve.' And if his comedy is indeed instinctive, it is possible that we may learn more of Shakespeare's very self from his comic than from his tragic scenes. And since a strain of comedy permeates practically all his work, it seems inevitable that a study of Shakespearean comedy should survey the entire dramatic corpus of Shakespeare. To limit this study to his so-called comedies would be to lose sight of his greatest comic character, Sir John Falstaff, and would overlook the extraordinary interplay of comic and tragic strains in his supreme achievement, *King Lear*. It is the purpose of the present work to examine all [1] Shakespeare's plays, grouping them by genres in approximately chronological order, and testing them one by one for the presence and the quality of comic gold, accounting also, if possible, for the thin vein and the low value of this ore in certain plays.

Yet since Shakespearean comedy is Elizabethan as well as perennial, it seems necessary to prefix to this examination of Shakespeare's plays a survey of the comic element in the medieval drama from which it springs: the Miracles, the Morals, and the Interludes. This is followed by a study of the impact of the New Learning of the Renaissance upon the native English drama and by a scrutiny of the achievements in

---

[1] Two omissions may be noted: (1) *King Henry VIII*, a late play in which Shakespeare collaborated with Fletcher; there is no trace of comedy in the Shakespearean scenes; (2) *The Two Noble Kinsmen*, in which a Shakespearean fragment seems to have been prepared for the stage by Fletcher, who contributed all the comic scenes.

comedy of the playwrights who held the stage when young Shakespeare came to London. In each case an attempt is made to estimate the nature and extent of their influence on Shakespeare's early work in order that we may realize at once his indebtedness and his originality. Only so, it would seem, can we rightly appreciate his success when he attained complete independence.

There are three dominant characteristics of Elizabethan drama, especially of Elizabethan comedy: a native, often naive, realism; a striving toward the classical idea of form and order; and a recurrent urge to express in verse something of that beauty which lies beyond the reach of all the pens that ever poets held. All three find expression in Shakespearean comedy; at times one, at times another predominates; in his best work they blend in a harmony that lifts them high above the rank and file of Elizabethan plays and makes them a possession for all time. After every allowance is made for Shakespeare's debt to his predecessors we still must acknowledge that it was his own peculiar and native genius which enabled him to create such work as this.

It is a commonplace of criticism that Shakespeare wrote his plays to be acted rather than read, acted on his own Elizabethan stage, before an Elizabethan, not a modern, audience, and acted by a company of whom he was one, for whom, indeed, he wrote all his parts. We know now enough of Shakespeare's stage to be able, in imagination at least, to visualize a performance at the Globe or Blackfriars. We no longer, it is hoped, think of Shakespeare's audience as composed mainly of the lower classes of Elizabethan London, with a solid core of rowdy apprentices fighting for bitten apples. In fact his audience represented a cross section of London life: solid shopkeepers, like the Citizen in *The Knight of the Burning Pestle;* scholarly, drama-loving members of the Inns of Court; and gay, sophisticated courtiers. Shakespeare's plays were repeatedly commanded for performance at Court, and we have Ben Jonson's word for it that they 'took' (i.e. enchanted) the pleasure-loving Elizabeth and the pedantic James. We do not know enough about Shakespeare's fellow-actors to assign their respective roles in the plays he wrote for them. Attempts to do so have been largely guess-work, based on the supposition that each actor had his own peculiar 'line'; but this fails to make allowance for the recognized versatility of the professional actor in Shakespeare's day as in our own. It is, however, possible in a few instances to allot a role to a certain member of the company, and it may be that Shakespeare composed the role in question with that particular one of his fellows in mind as its inter-

preter. This work will treat, as far as possible, each play of Shakespeare's as one primarily destined for performance by his fellow-actors
on his own stage.

Such treatment, however, is not always possible, and even if it were
it would hardly satisfy the reader. After all, Shakespeare's plays have
come down to us in printed form; the printed stage directions, which
give a clue to the performance of the play on his stage, are often so
scanty and so terse as to afford little help. In some plays, indeed, they
are almost altogether lacking. The reader is likely to be more interested in other matters than the original performance of the plays: in
Shakespeare's choice of theme, in the sources he used, and in his treatment of these sources, his faithful fidelity to some, his free adaptation
of others. Accordingly, in every case where the source of a Shakespearean play is known, a summary of the original is given, and an
effort is made to account for Shakespeare's handling of what we may
call his raw material. Only thus, it seems, can we get a glimpse into
Shakespeare's workshop, see him at his desk with Holinshed or North's
Plutarch, an old play-book, or an Elizabethan romance open before
him, while he turns over in his mind how he can best transmute what
he reads into a play suitable for presentation by his fellows at the
Globe, or Blackfriars, or, as in the case of *Macbeth,* directly at the
Court.

The manner of the original publication of Shakespeare's plays also
calls for some attention. Only sixteen of them, less than half the whole
number, were published during his lifetime, and of these some five or
six were printed from what his friends, the editors of the Folio, called
'stolen and surreptitious copies.' The other twenty plays appeared in
print for the first time in the Folio of 1623, seven years after his death,
ten years or more after his connection with his company as actor and
playwright had come to an end. It is apparent, of course, that in this
interval there was time and opportunity for the alteration of Shakespeare's text by excision, revision, and insertion of new matter. In certain plays some such alterations are practically demonstrable: the
character of Hecate in *Macbeth* and the doggerel chant of the ghosts in
Cymbeline are not from the hand of Shakespeare, but are interpolations added for the purpose of securing a supposedly more striking
stage effect. In this matter of publication, minute bibliographical details have been avoided and the opinion of modern scholars has been
briefly presented.

In the discussion of sources and of the text, the author has endeavored to present the known facts as accurately as possible. Having done so, he has at times allowed himself the liberty of indulging in an hypothesis that might clarify and explain the facts. It is to be hoped that such hypothetical explanations will not be taken as dogmatic statements, but rather as honest, if perhaps mistaken, attempts to interpret Shakespeare's purpose, method, and results.

Quotations from Shakespeare embodied in the text of this book have been drawn regularly from the one-volume edition of *The Oxford Shakespeare,* edited by W. J. Craig.

As this work is intended for the general reader rather than for the scholar, the apparatus of footnotes and references to authorities has been reduced to a minimum. During long years of experience as student, teacher, and editor of Shakespeare's plays, the author has sought to familiarize himself with the best of Shakespearean criticism in German, French, and English. To list the authorities to whom he is indebted would only cumber the page with names, unfamiliar probably to most of his readers. Yet a tribute of thanks must be paid to President Lowry of Wooster College, at whose suggestion this work was undertaken; to Professor William W. Laurence, late of Columbia; to Professor O. J. Campbell of Columbia; and to J. Dover Wilson, late of the University of Edinburgh, for generous assistance and advice; also to my friend Professor Hubler of Princeton for frank and penetrating criticism.

THOMAS MARC PARROTT

Princeton University
February 1949

Contents

Shakespearean Comedy

1

The Medieval Background

ENGLISH drama, like the drama of Western Europe in general, begins within the Church, as a recognized part of the liturgy. It is natural, then, that in the search for the beginning of English comedy we should turn to the oldest remaining church plays to discover, if possible, any germs of comedy within them. The search is not immediately or greatly rewarding. The primary purpose of the liturgical drama was edification. As a twelfth-century churchman once put it: 'the old fathers of the church in order to strengthen the belief of the faithful and to attract the unbeliever . . . rightly instituted religious performances of such a kind as the star guiding the Magi . . . and other events of the birth of Christ.' Abuses had, indeed, crept in. The same churchman denounced the desecration of the sacred edifice by an 'unfitting gathering of priests and laymen,' marked by eating and drinking, disguises, buffoonery, and the presence of 'shameless wenches.' The special object of his attack seems to have been the notorious Feast of Fools, celebrated in the Christmas holidays by lower orders of the clergy. It was, however, less of a dramatic performance than a riotous revolt against the strict discipline under which the performers lived for the rest of the year. There is, moreover, little trace of this festival, widespread on the Continent, in English churches. Better known in England was the somewhat similar festival of the Boy Bishop, another holiday extravagance, in which a choir boy, elected Bishop by his fellows, conducted a ludicrous burlesque of the sacred service. Choir boys, however, were more easily kept under control than their elders who frolicked through the Feast of Fools; there are no such denunciations of their behavior at this feast, and there is little dramatic in their simple parody.

The earliest liturgical plays were, we know, simple representations, by means of costume, action, and spoken word, of the two main events in the Christian story, the birth of Christ and the resurrection of the Crucified Redeemer. On Easter morning members of the clergy, dressed

3

to suggest the three women of the Gospel story, walked through the church to visit the sepulchre where on Good Friday the Cross had been deposited. They were met there by one costumed to represent an angel, who told them the great news of the empty tomb and the risen Lord. The dialogue was in Latin, the sacred language of the Church, and at first, certainly, it was chanted rather than spoken.[1] At Christmas a star was drawn through the nave of the church, guiding those who played the Shepherds and the Magi to the cradle of the Child at the foot of the altar. The purpose of the pious playwrights was, of course, to present these events in such a way as to persuade a devout audience that they were not happenings of a distant past, but were occurring here and now before their very eyes. In such a simple purpose there was no place for comedy. As time went on, however, more and more scenes were added to the visit to the sepulchre and the adoration at the cradle. The Resurrection play stretched backwards in time to embrace the Passion of Christ and forward to the Ascension and, at last, to the Day of Judgment. The Christmas play ran back to include figures of the prophets who had foretold the wondrous birth, and behind them to Eden and the Fall of Man. In these longer sequences, figures began to appear that lent themselves to comic characterization. Here we find the blustering Herod, foiled in his attempt to kill the Holy Child in the massacre of the Innocents; the greedy prophet Balaam, whose journey to curse God's chosen people was halted when the ass that bore him saw in the path an angel with drawn sword; and the devils of the Judgment, who, like some of Dante's demons, were as grotesquely comic as they were terrifying.

Such comic figures and the irreverent laughter they provoked may have been one of the causes that drove the drama out of the church. Quite as important was the length of time the growing play demanded for its performance. The primitive *Quem quaeritis* could easily be embodied in the liturgy at Easter or at Christmas. It was otherwise with the long sequences; they took up so much time that they began to detach themselves altogether from the regular service and so became an object of attack to the stricter clergy, who abhorred *spectacula theatricala* in the house of God. Whatever the cause, the fact remains that somewhere in the thirteenth century the longer plays began to move

[1] Elaborate directions for the performance of an Easter play, the *Quem quaeritis in sepulchro*, are given in the *Regularis Concordia* (965-75) of Ethelwold, Bishop of Winchester. His directions prescribe not only the dialogue, but also the costumes and mimetic action of the performers, being, in short, a little dramatic performance inserted into the regular service on Easter day.

out of the church into the churchyard, the market place, or the village green.

Once outside the church, the plays promptly came under the control of the craft guilds, the dominant forces in social as well as economic life in medieval English towns. When the clergy lost control of the performances, edification yielded to the more popular aim of entertainment; as has been well said, *officia*, religious rites, became *spectacula*, or shows. It must not be supposed, however, that the guild plays lost their religious character; on the contrary, they retained the old themes of the church drama and were slow in introducing new topics. The playwrights of the new drama, liberal-minded members, no doubt, of the clergy, set themselves to expand and diversify the old themes with an eye to the entertainment of a mixed and illiterate audience. This purpose could be attained in various ways: by costumes, such as a gilded robe and golden wig for God, weapons and armor for Herod and his Knights, grotesque masks for the prancing devils; and by interesting action—a whole play in the York cycle is devoted to the building of the Ark to allow the Shipwrights, who produced it, a chance to exhibit their craftsmanship. The long paraphrases of Holy Writ, which the reader today is apt to skip over impatiently, must have had a strong appeal to a pious folk who had no Bible in their homes and heard a half-intelligible Latin in the church. Little by little came the expansion of old and the introduction of new comic elements. It would be wrong to assume that the craft plays promptly became such amusing specimens of comedy as are their best-known examples, the Wakefield *Noah* or the *Secunda Pastorum*. The Chester cycle, probably the oldest, certainly the most archaic, collection of English guild plays, has more edifying exhortations and less comic matter than any of the others. No cycle, of course, was written at one time by one or more learned clerks; the cycles developed like English cathedrals, adding a topic here, splitting an old scene into several parts to gratify guilds clamoring for a share in the popular entertainment, and, what is more to our purpose, by emphasizing wherever possible the comic opportunities of the situation.

It is well worth while to examine the comic elements of these plays, remembering always that for several centuries they furnished the stock entertainment of the English people and established, so to speak, a tradition of comedy.

The simplest and most primitive form of comedy is that of action, sudden, incongruous, and laughter-moving. It has no need of words and its appeal is well-nigh universal, as is shown by the world-wide success of Charlie Chaplin in the era of the silent film. A fight is always funny, provided, of course, that no one is badly hurt. In matters of this sort the English guild plays abound; even the staid Chester cycle raises a laugh when it shows Mrs. Noah refusing to enter the Ark, boxing her husband's ears, and finally being dragged to safety by her impatient sons. In a Coventry play an old wife of Bethlehem beats one of the killers of the children over the head with a pot ladle. In the same play a stage direction reads: 'Here Herod rages in the pagend [the float on which the scene was acted] and in the street also.' When Hamlet denounced the ranting actor whose performance 'out-Herods Herod,' Shakespeare was, perhaps, recalling a scene which, as a boy, he had witnessed in Coventry, an easy walk from Stratford. The incongruous enters at times, as when in a Chester play a rough but pious shepherd presents the Holy Child with a pair of his wife's old hose.

As the dramatic interest quickens and the art of the nameless playwright ripens, we get little actions that last longer than the mere exchange of blows or the presentation of an absurd gift. We see Pilate and his wife indulging in marital endearments under the disapproving eye of a beadle. In the Wakefield *Processus Talentorum,* a satyr play annexed to the grim realism of the Crucifixion, Pilate is called from his bed to decide the quarrel of Christ's executioners over the seamless coat. The pompous Roman forgets his dignity, throws dice, 'the byched bones,' with the gamblers, and, when he loses, stoops to wangle the prize from the winner by a blend of flattery and threats. One of the liveliest of these scenes of action occurs in the *Woman Taken in Adultery* in the late Ludus Coventriae. Here a young man, surprised in the arms of his mistress by intruding accusers, rushes onto the stage with his dress in disorder—'his shoes untied and holding his breeches in his hand,' the stage direction says—threatening to put his dagger 'in the crop' of whoever dares stop him, yet confessing, as he escapes, that he is sore afraid. This young gallant is the playwright's pure invention; there is no mention of him in the simple narrative of the Gospel.

Such comic scenes as the last mentioned combine action with the spoken word. The word alone is, of course, often potent to provoke a laugh, and the old playwrights were quick to employ this means. The simplest form, perhaps, is that of dirty language. In the Ludus the Devil repeatedly takes his departure with a foul word and an obscene gesture. The speech of Cain in the Wakefield *Killing of Abel* is so gross that a modern editor deletes line after line, and the language of Caiphas in the *Buffeting* is most unbecoming to a High Priest. The ribald jests of the accusers in the Ludus *Trial of Joseph and Mary* is what might be expected when the young wife of a decrepit old man is found with child. On the whole, however, the old Miracle plays are freer from this form of fun than much of the literature of the late Middle Ages.

Closely allied with gross language is the use of profanity. It is, perhaps, questionable whether the varied oaths with which the pages of these plays are thickly sprinkled were primarily a comic device. Our medieval ancestors employed on every occasion a rich and highly ornamental form of profanity, and it may be that much of the speech serves only for the purpose of realism. Yet there are certain phrases that can hardly have been used for other than comic purposes. In the eyes of the old playwrights, all others than Christians, whether Roman, Jew, or Infidel, were worshipers of Mahomet, and the parodies of Christian oaths in the mouths of unbelievers could hardly have been designed for other purpose than to raise a laugh. Herod swears by 'St. Mahound, our God so sweet,' and elsewhere he prays to 'Sir Satan, our Sire, and Lucifer most lovely.' The Roman Pilate swears by 'Mahound's blood,' and the heathen King of Marcyll offers a besant of gold to Mahound, 'a glorious ghost.' Pharaoh in the York *Exodus* exhorts his men: 'Heave up your hearts to Mahound,' a perversion of the *Sursum Corda* of the Mass; and in the Digby *Mary Magdalene*, a heathen priest and his choir boy perform an elaborate parody of divine service in which the boy reads the lesson for the day: *Lectio Mahowndis,* a babble of unintelligible, Latin-sounding words, ending with a prayer in English that his hearers may get grace to die on the gallows. Humble Christians at times have difficulty with sacred forms; Mak's goodnight prayer in the *Secunda Pastorum* runs: *Manus tuas commendo Poncio Pilato,* and a shepherd on waking ejaculates: *Judas carnas Dominus.*

Quite apart from gross language or profane parody, another form of speech lent itself easily to comic ends. It was an established convention, which carries on into Elizabethan drama, for a leading character to announce himself at the beginning of the play, partly for the purpose of identification, partly, it is clear, to command silence on an unruly audience. The enemies of the faith, Pharaoh, Herod, Caesar Augustus, and Pilate, soon distinguish themselves by a voluble flow of boastful speech mingled with fragments of French and Latin, such as sovereigns might be expected to use. In *Magnus Herodes* the conventional introductory speech attains the height of comic absurdity. It is delivered by a Nuntius who introduces his master with a proclamation of his royal titles as King of Tuscany and Turkey, of India and Italy, of Sicily and Surrey. Even the most ignorant auditor must have realized something of the comic quality of this exaggeration.

Social and political satire is, of course, a recurrent element in medieval literature, and there are occasional flashes of satiric speech in the Miracles. These are, for the most part, late and not especially enlivening; the topics are familiar enough: the miseries of married life with special reference to shrewish wives; oppression of poor folk by the gentry; ill-treatment of servants by stingy masters; and the fantastic costumes of gallants who go gay while their children hunger. Only in the mouth of the lively little devil Tutivillus, who bobs up in the Wakefield *Judgment Day,* do we catch a note of diabolic mirth that rings the changes on a whole catalogue of human follies and vices.

A higher form of comedy appears when the playwright's art is sufficiently advanced to enable him to present amusing and laughable characters. His art, of course, is limited, since as a playwright he can only present characters by the dramatic devices of speech and action. He cannot analyze their minds or comment on their behavior, as the novelist does. Nor is it enough for the playwright to present a mere puppet who will serve as a mouthpiece for the voice of his creator. Such a character, for example, is Herod's Nuntius, already referred to. His ridiculous proclamation tells us something about the man who wrote his lines, little or nothing about the Nuntius himself. Much the same may be said of the Somnour, who rattles off a prologue in the Ludus play of the *Trial of Joseph and Mary,* though his behavior in the ensuing action shows that the playwright had at least the intention of presenting the typical insolent and greedy Somnour familiar to Englishmen from Chaucer's day to Heywood's. A more developed technique is shown in the Digby *Innocents.* It was, apparently, an established convention to have the women of Bethlehem beat the soldiers who killed the children, but the author of this play creates a character for the special purpose of being beaten. This is Watkin, Herod's messenger, who begs of his master the boon of knighthood provided he does good service in the Bethlehem campaign. He is ready to kill children, but expresses mortal fear of the women with their distaffs, and, sure enough, after the massacre four women set on him and dub him knight with their blows till he is rescued by his fellow-killers. Watkin is the first *miles gloriosus* in English drama.

A more fully developed comic character is the Cain of the Wakefield cycle, a miserly, foul-mouthed, blasphemous boor. His business of counting over his sheaves when he is reluctantly haled to the altar, and of laying aside one after another as too good for God, is rough but vital comedy. The pietistic Abel serves him as an admirable foil, and Abel's smug satisfaction over the acceptance of his offering and the rejection of Cain's is the natural, if hardly justified, cause of the first murder.

Character contrast, of course, is a simple and effective means of characterization. It is skilfully employed in the Wakefield *Buffeting*, where Caiphas, a realistic portrait of the fighting prelate of the Northern border, is paired with his fellow churchman, Annas, a representative of the clergy in the service, legal or financial, of the King. Caiphas bawls 'wolf's head and outhorn' at Jesus; he would like to pluck out his eyes and kill him with his own hands. Annas, equally determined to do away with Jesus, coolly reminds his fellow that he is a man of holy kirk, quotes law Latin at him, and sends Jesus to Pilate, 'the temporal power,' with the same assurance as a persecuting prelate would hand a Lollard over to the King's judges for death at the stake. This is a grimly comic interlude in the tragedy of the Passion. In the Weavers' play at Coventry there is a little scene of pure comedy that depends entirely upon character. Preparing to go to the Temple for her purification, Mary bids Joseph go in search of the turtle-doves required by the law. He objects that he is too old to go bird-nesting. Here is the familiar situation of marital discord, but the old playwright handles it in a new fashion. Mary is not, she could not be, the conventional shrewish wife; yet she is quietly determined to get her way, not because it is hers, but because it is God's will. After an appeal to married men in the audience to corroborate his statement that men who will not please their wives shall often suffer 'much dis-ease,' Joseph sets out on his search; he wanders up and down in vain; his feet are tired, his clothes are torn by the hedges, until he sits quietly down to await the Lord's will. His patience is rewarded, for an angel promptly appears with the required doves. He takes them home and, with no mention of the angel, greets Mary with the words: 'Lo, dame, I have done your bidding,' adding the naive and natural question: 'Am I not a good husband?' Here at least was another form of comedy than that of the blustering Herod.

There is, as has been shown, plenty of comic matter in the Miracles, but it would be almost true to say that there is not in all of them a single comedy, no one play written to entertain by comic action, speech, or character. After all, this was hardly to be expected; the old playwrights were still bound by the tradition of the church drama; they were limited in their choice of theme to the stories of the Bible, the apocryphal gospels, and the saints' legends. It was their task to present such themes in as entertaining a fashion as possible, to exploit a hint or to develop a character found in the source. At best they might insert a brief scene drawn from contemporary life, as in *The Conversion of St. Paul* where the persecutor of the saints stops at an inn on his way to Damascus to give his servant and the local hostler an opportunity for an exchange of very dirty language. Comedy in the Miracles, however broad or witty, is strictly incidental. Yet an exception must be made in the case of one playwright, the so-called Wakefield Master.

The repertoire of the playing guilds at Wakefield came apparently into the hands of a clever clerk at a time when it needed a bit of freshening, and he seized the opportunity to revise old plays and to write several new ones. All that is best in the Wakefield cycle, itself the most entertaining of those that remain, can be attributed to his hand. His, for example, is the character of Cain, introduced, indeed, in the York play of *Cain and Abel,* but here far more realistically and humorously portrayed. The *Processus Talentorum,* on the other hand, is an original play by the Master; there is nothing at all like it in any other cycle. Starting from the bare statement in the Gospel that the executioners cast lots for the coat of Christ, it develops into a little masterpiece of comic speech and absurd action. Only at the very end does the author salve his conscience by a brief sermon against the sin of gambling. But the most striking example at once of his originality and of his comic power is the *Secunda Pastorum.* Here, moreover, we are now in possession of evidence unknown to early editors and neglected by later commentators. There are two Shepherds' plays in the Wakefield cycle and both are, quite certainly, the work of the Master. Now the *Prima Pastorum* is a perfectly satisfactory play, a lively bit of realism with silly shepherds quarreling over nonexistent sheep, eating and drinking—very well, by the way, for poor shepherds—singing and sleeping, till roused by the angelic chorus, and finally adoring the Christ Child with rustic gifts. What induced the Master to write another play on the same theme, a third as long again, beginning and ending as the

Prima does in conventional fashion? There can be but one answer. He had in the meantime come upon a sheep-stealing story, possibly in a Northern ballad form, which he saw would fit exactly into the middle of a new and livelier Shepherds' play, since it would offer a comic contrast in true medieval fashion to the visit of the shepherds to the Child in the manger at Bethlehem. A ballad corresponding in many details to the Mak episode in the *Secunda* is, in fact, in existence. It appeared for the first time under the title of *Archie Armstrang's Aith* in the third edition of Scott's *Minstrelsy of the Scottish Border,* signed by Scott's friend, John Marriott. According to Scott's note to the poem, 'the exploit detailed in the ballad has been preserved . . . by tradition and is at this time still current in Eskdale.' This tradition was, no doubt, unearthed there by Scott and passed on to Marriott, for it is impossible that Scott could have known the *Secunda,* which was still in manuscript and not printed till four years after his death.

The Mak episode attains its primary purpose of adding a fresh zest to an old Nativity play, but it does more than that; it attains the stature of an independent play, a genuine little comedy. It could be detached from its setting and acted by itself with no loss of interest. Here, for once in the Miracles, comedy is not merely incidental, but independent and self-sufficing.

Long centuries of Miracle performances throughout all England established a dramatic convention that was destined to continue and to influence, though with important modifications, Elizabethan drama proper. It trained amateur actors in the art of impersonation and so prepared the way for the later professional companies. It taught audiences composed of every class of English society to enjoy and appreciate dramatic entertainment. This is especially true in the field of comedy, for there is little of genuine tragic matter in the Miracle cycles, and even what there is is modified by the insertion or addition of comic characters and scenes, like Cain's boy in the *Killing of Abel* or the play of the dice-throwers that follows hard upon the Crucifixion. It is a fair assumption that there would have been no drunken Porter in *Macbeth,* no jesting Grave-diggers in *Hamlet,* had not the English audience long been trained to expect that a tragic action would be 'mixed full of pleasant mirth.' All the protests of Renaissance humanists against such irregular confusion of dramatic types were impotent against a long-established popular convention.

The comic element in the Miracles consists, as has been seen, of action, language, and character. The action is for the most part naively realistic, a realism attained largely by a shifting of the scene from Palestine to England, from antiquity to contemporary life. We may notice the permanence of this convention in such later plays as *Ralph Roister Doister* and *The Comedy of Errors*. The physical fun of the Miracles, the buffetings and tossing in blankets, carries on into Elizabethan comedy, as witness Sir Andrew's broken head in *Twelfth Night* and the blanketing of Horace-Jonson in *Satiromastix*. There is less of this rough action in the work of Shakespeare than in that of his contemporaries, but it is present even in his plays, and persists even in the more sophisticated comedy of his successors.

The language of the Miracles, like the action, is for the most part simply realistic; it lacks, with rare exceptions, poetic inspiration—that was to come much later—and merely attempts to render in plain English the thoughts and emotions of the actors. It attains comic effects sometimes by absurd exaggeration, as in the tirades of Herod and other potentates, more often by the use of profane and gross language. The Miracles, to be sure, are freer from this abuse than many later plays, particularly those of the Morals and Interludes, but there was nothing mealy-mouthed about our medieval English ancestors, and their enjoyment of a broad joke survived in Shakespeare's audience.

Finally we may mark the recurrent appearance in the Miracles of clownish comic characters. We do not find in them the professional jester, like the Vice of the Interludes or the Court Fool of Shakespeare's comedies. That came later with the development of professional acting and the increasing dominance of the chief comedian. But shrewish Mrs. Noah, the timid Joseph of the Ludus Coventriae, and the cowardly Watkin of the Digby *Innocents* are characters created to provoke a laugh. Again and again we find in Shakespeare's plays clownish figures like Costard and Bottom intruding into the higher comedy of the main action. They are the direct descendants of the rustic shepherds of the Nativity plays, whose rough horseplay and homely speech contrast so strongly with the angel's song and the prayer and praise of Mary.

MORALS

It was while the cyclical Miracles were at their height in the third quarter of the fourteenth century that a new type of drama sprang up to rival them and to contribute in its development to genuine native English comedy. This was the Morality, better called the Moral Play, or more simply the Moral. It may be briefly defined as dramatized allegory with didactic intent.

Allegory is, of course, an old and well-established literary form. It was, however, rather late in entering the field of drama in England. Probably the popularity of the Miracle plays suggested to learned clerks, ambitious of distinction, the idea of composing another type of drama that might, like the Miracles, be performed by the civic guilds and shown on pageants in the streets. We know, at least, that in spectacle-loving York a special guild was formed to present the *Pater Noster Play* in English, and in the minster town of Beverly there was a cyclical Moral of eight pageants. It seems probable, indeed, that the earliest Morals, like the Miracles they were meant to rival, took this cyclical form, but none such have come down to us. The longest, and probably the oldest, extant Moral, *The Castle of Perseverance,* c. 1425, looks like an attempt to compress such a cycle into one long performance.

The origin of the Morals, like that of the Miracles, was within the Church, but instead of drawing material from the church services, with their Bible stories and legends of the saints, the Morals fastened upon the sermon with its ethical and didactic purpose, illustrated often, as surviving specimens testify, by entertaining anecdote and dramatic dialogue. The aim of the sermon was to strengthen the believer in his warfare against the sins that so easily beset mankind; the Beverly cycle, we know, had a pageant for each of the Seven Deadly Sins, on which, no doubt, a series of contests was waged for the soul of man. This contest, indeed, is the central dramatic idea of the older Morals and, since it invariably ended in the defeat of the powers of Evil, a certain uniformity, not to say monotony, soon began to show itself in the dramatic action. The authors of the Morals, debarred by the allegorical form of the new drama from dealing with Bible stories and saints' legends, were forced to invent new situations and create new characters, new in name at least, by means of which they might at once present in dramatic form this central idea and hold the flagging interest of the audience. As a result they found themselves forced to rely for popular approval more and more upon elements foreign to their origin.

It has been noted that entertainment, at least in the form of comedy, was only incidental in the Miracles. In the Morals, on the other hand, it comes more and more to occupy an essential, at last even a dominating, place. It is perhaps unfortunate that the popular conception of a Moral play should be based upon the only one of them at all generally known, the extremely effective *Summoning of Everyman*. But *Everyman* stands alone among English Morals; there is reason, indeed, to believe that it is not really an English play, but a translation or adaptation of the Dutch *Elckerlijk*. For the purpose of this study we may pass it by, for with all its dramatic power it has no gleam of comedy, even if modern actors have sometimes raised a laugh by a rendering of Cousin's complaint of a 'cramp in my toe.'

It is impossible to date the surviving Morals with any degree of accuracy, but a survey of certain characteristic specimens in approximately chronological order will show the increasing tendency to subordinate the original purpose of ethical edification to a frank effort to entertain the audience by an increasing emphasis upon the comic.

The archaic *Castle of Perseverance* shows only the sort of comic matter that may be found in the Miracles. There is action in the flagellation of the minor Vices by the Devil and the Flesh for their failure in allowing Humanum Genus to escape from their clutches to the refuge of the Castle, and there is a blend of the comic and the grotesque in the figure of Belial advancing to the assault on the Castle with 'gunpowder burning in pipes in his hand and in his ears and in his—(let us say)—hind-quarters.' Yet it must be noted that this is not the comic Devil of later plays, but a grim and dangerous character, the old enemy of mankind. As in the Miracles, there is the usual amount of serio-comic rant on the part of the Powers of Evil; the World, the Flesh, and the Devil all indulge in long tirades after the fashion of Herod and Pontius Pilate. There is, perhaps, in these speeches a somewhat stronger taint of foul language than is usual in the older Miracles. This is an element that was unfortunately destined to increase with the development of the Moral until we are startled at the license of language employed by polemizing bishops and zealous reformers. The characters are, with perhaps one exception, simply type figures; there is little or no attempt to present them in realistic form. The exception is the small part of Garcio, a boy with the significant name of 'I wot never who,' who appears at the deathbed of Humanum Genus as the heir of his ill-gotten wealth, and mocks his despairing master. Yet when all allowance is made for such scattered comic elements, it must be admitted that this early Moral is at once long, dull, and highly edifying in purpose.

In the fragmentary *Pride of Life,* almost contemporary with *The Castle,* there is, it would seem, a significant forecast of change. The

Prologue promises spectators 'mirth' as well as 'care,' and a character
by the name of Mirth plays the part at once of the King's Messenger
and his Jester, a role no doubt developed in the lost part of the play.
Another early play, *Wisdom which is Christ,* also known as *Mind,
Will, and Understanding, c.* 1460, has little of comedy in speech or
action. Lucifer, who perverts the intellectual powers and thus corrupts
the soul of man, is by no means a comic devil but an expert theological
disputant. A stage direction, which seems to show that toward the
close he picked up 'a shrewd boy'—perhaps from the audience—and
ran roaring off with him, is probably an interpolation by the actors
in a despairing effort to get a laugh. Yet even this intensely serious
play makes an effort to entertain by music, dancing, and costume. The
sudden appearance of the sinful Anima, 'fouler than a fiend,' with six
little devils running out from under her 'horrible robe,' must have
given the audience a mingled thrill of horror and amusement.

It is with *Mankind, c.* 1475, that we notice a decided shift from
edification to entertainment, a shift due probably to the fact that it
was presented by a little group, three men and three boys, of professional actors dependent for their livelihood upon the collection they
could wring from the audience. The action, in fact, is suspended before the entrance of the comic devil, Tutivillus, and the hat is passed
round before the spectators are allowed to behold his 'abhominable
presence.' The conventional framework of the Moral is indeed retained: the play opens and ends with long effusions of 'mellifluous
doctrine' by Mercy; and Mankind, the protagonist, is tempted, falls,
repents, and is saved. But within these limits the action becomes the
wildest sort of farce; Mercy is unmercifully chaffed by his opposite
number, Mischief, attended by three little devils, Newguise, Nowadays,
and Nought. Mankind at first beats them off with his spade, but soon
falls to Tutivillus, who induces him to join this lively company in a
tavern. There is an amusing parody of a Manorial Court, in which
fallen Mankind obediently answers orders to fornicate, rob, and kill
with 'I will, Sir.' The special characteristic of the play, however, is the
gross obscenity of the dialogue. The dirty jokes are the very sort to
raise a laugh from the boorish audience to which they were addressed;
the audience, in fact, is invited to join the young devils in a filthy song
that ends with a blasphemous parody of the sacred 'Holy, Holy, Holy.'
The unknown author stooped very low to entertain, but he had, none
the less, a quick sense of lively action and effective dialogue.

It is a very different story with *Nature, c.* 1500, the work of Henry

Medwall, chaplain to the scholarly Cardinal Morton. This long and tedious play is touched with the spirit of the New Learning. The contest for Man is between Sensuality and Reason; the goal sought is not salvation from hell, but a rational life on earth. New and noteworthy is the repeated reference to contemporary life; there are allusions to the London 'stews'; we hear that fallen Man visits a tavern, where he takes Margery—not some allegorical figure—upon his knee; and Lust tells of his visit to a house of ill-fame in a way that shows Medwall had been reading Chaucer.

The popular play, *Hickscorner,* repeatedly printed in the·early sixteenth century and still selling in 1582, shows plainly the drift toward realism. The scene is evidently laid in contemporary London; Imagination and Hickscorner have lain in Newgate jail together; Freewill's mother was a 'lady of the stews,' his father a 'knight of the halter.' There is some lively action, including a comic scuffle among these rogues, who later clap Pity into the stocks and leave him to lament the corruption of the age.

The Nature of the Four Elements, c. 1517, printed by Rastell, More's brother-in-law, continues the line struck out by Medwall. Rastell was evidently aware of the danger of taxing the patience of an audience beyond bounds, for, though he advertises the play on the title-page as 'a new interlude and a merry,' he wisely remarks to prospective performers, 'if ye list ye may leave out much of the sad—i.e. serious—matter . . . and then it will not be past three quarters of an hour in length.' The author goes a step beyond Medwall and actually brings a real character onto the stage in the person of the Taverner, who cracks coarse jokes with his visitors and mentions his girl friends—'little Nell, a proper wench and danceth well,' Jane, and bouncing Bess. The girls, to be sure, do not appear on the stage, but their mere names draw this play farther away from the zone of the allegorical Moral.

With the advance of the New Learning in English schools it became the fashion to train boys in dramatic performances, first apparently of Latin comedies, then of English, composed by a play-loving master like Udall. One of these, *Wit and Science, c.* 1530, by John Redford, Master of the choir boys at St. Paul's, was evidently written for his scholars to perform. It is one of the best constructed of all the Morals, a pleasant little comedy with a simple but credible intrigue conducted to a happy ending. The characters, to be sure, are all allegorical, but they behave like human beings. Wit, a gay and self-con-

fident young gallant, neglects his lady, is overthrown by Giant Tediousness, and seduced by Idleness, who arrays him in a Fool's costume,
'coxcomb and all.' After he has been admonished by Reason and chas-
tised by Shame, his eyes are opened to his folly; whereupon he attacks
Tediousness with a sword his lady has sent him, drives him off-stage,
and re-enters bringing 'in the head'—the ugly mask of the Giant—
'upon his sword'—perhaps the first mention of the 'property' head,
which recurs more than once in Shakespeare's plays. Finally Wit and
Lady Science are joined in marriage, with music and dancing. There
is plenty of lively action in the play, less of the long-drawn edifying
discourse than usual, little bad language, and an amusing parody of
the latest progressive method of instruction in primary schools.

About a generation later, c. 1579, a professional playwright seems
to have acquired a copy of Redford's play—it was never printed—and
set himself to adapt it for performance by a little troupe of actors—
'six can play it'—with a leading role for Idleness, the Vice. *The Marriage of Wit and Wisdom* shows how swiftly the Moral is approaching
the plane of realistic comedy. The characters for the most part still
carry their allegoric names, but Wit's parents, Severity and Indulgence,
are quite plainly an honest English couple, anxious to see their son
well settled in marriage. Idleness, in particular, is a genuine Elizabethan rogue; he steals Wit's purse and is promptly robbed, beaten,
and bound by two ruffians, Snatch and Catch, who berate him in such
foul language that the first editor deleted it—*pudoris causa*. Later in
the role of a strolling beggar, Idleness steals Dame Bee's porridge pot,
which brings down a shower of blows on her servants, Doll and Lob,
who have been 'tumbling in the hay' instead of working in the house.
In general the clean-cut, well-sustained allegory of *Wit and Science*
has been recast into a farce of horseplay and smutty dialogue to catch
the ear of the groundlings.

There were other matters more important, perhaps, than the rational life and the marriage of Wit and Wisdom that forced themselves upon inquiring minds in the troubled first part of the sixteenth
century. It was a period of profound revolutionary changes, social,
political, and religious, and a whole group of Morals exploit these
themes in dramatic form. The earliest and one of the best of these is
Skelton's *Magnificence, c.* 1516.

There seems reason to believe that this play is a veiled warning to
the young King, Henry VIII, to distrust the extravagant and daring
policy of Wolsey and to rely rather upon his old councilors. What con-

cerns us here is the comic matter with which the pill was guilded. This consists mainly in the introduction into the allegorical scheme of a pair of Vices, Fancy and Folly, apparently costumed as Court Fools. They play the parts not only of intriguers but of fun-makers, and their lively patter, spiced by satiric thrusts at fashionable vices, contributes the essential comic element to the action. Contrary to what one might expect of 'beastly Skelton,' their speech is pure in comparison with other propaganda plays of the period.

Perhaps the chief offender in this respect was John Bale, the bilious Bishop of Ossory. He boasts of having written twenty-two plays, of which, fortunately, only five are extant. His best-known play, *King John*, a curious anticipation in the Moral of the later Chronicle Play, is distinguished by the presence of a Vice, Sedition. He appears at first as a jester, declaring that he 'came hither to be merry,' but he proves to be the King's bitterest enemy, playing also the roles of Civil Order, i.e. the legal profession, and of Stephen Langton, the historical Archbishop who opposed the King. In the end he encourages Dissimulation to poison John in a wassail bowl. Throughout he is a foul-mouthed rogue, and drops out of his character as Jester by his savage satire on the Roman Church, which he is supposed to be supporting against the King. A striking instance of this is the scene where he poses as a Pardoner and, like that character in Chaucer and in Heywood, rattles off a list of his relics beginning with 'a bone of the blessed Trinity' and ending with 'a rib of St. Rabart and the hucklebone of a Jew,' but what is broad jesting in Chaucer and Heywood sinks to obscenity in Bishop Bale. Finally Sedition is condemned to be hanged and quartered at Tyburn, a sorry end for a jesting Vice.

A better play, though heavily weighted with Protestant edification, is *Lusty Juventus, c.* 1548-9, by R. Wever. Here at least we have a comic Devil, who bewails the falling away of youth from the good old days of superstition, and a really witty Vice, the Devil's own son, Hypocrisy. The hero, Juventus, makes his entrance with a pretty song, 'In youth is pleasure,' looking for a minstrel. Instead of a minstrel he meets Good Counsel and Knowledge, who belabor him with good advice and send him forth with the Bible at his girdle like a 'New Gospeller.' The poor youth, however, is not firmly grounded in the faith and it is an easy matter for Hypocrisy, introducing himself as Friendship, to persuade him to absent himself from the preaching to which he was bound, and to go with him and Fellowship to visit 'little Bess.' This damsel now appears, under the unfortunate name of 'Abomina-

ble Living,' and twits Juventus with being such a holy man that he
would not kiss a young woman for twenty pounds in gold. He is
prompt to prove her wrong and takes delight in kissing her 'pleasant
mouth.' The merry company then go off with a four-part song. When
next Juventus enters he runs into Good Counsel and offers to throw
dice with him. This brings down a sermon upon him, freighted with
fearful texts from Paul's Epistles. Overcome with remorse Juventus
gives himself up for lost, but he is rescued from despair by God's
Merciful Promises, and Wever ends the play with a pious exhortation
to the young. There is some lively patter by Hypocrisy in praise of
the additions he has made to religion such as:

> Holy crosses, holy bells,
> Holy relics, holy jewels,
>
> . . .
>
> Holy candles, holy tapers,
> Holy parchments, holy papers.

'Had you not a holy son?' he asks his Satanic father. Had Wever not
been so determined to preach, he might have written an excellent
comedy, but a sermon was probably what his audience wanted; the
play, we know, was printed more than once. It is one of the plays in
the repertoire of the little troupe of actors, four men and a boy, who
are introduced into the play of *Sir Thomas More,* and, although More
orders a performance of *Wit and Wisdom,* it is actually a fragment of
Lusty Juventus that is given, with More himself extemporizing in the
part of Good Counsel. It was not wholly forgotten in 1616, when Jonson refers to the wild behavior of 'a lusty Juventus' in Iniquity's first
speech in *The Devil is an Ass.*

After the scurrility of Bale and the prolixity of Wever it is a relief
to turn to the affable scholarship of the unknown author of *Respublica,*
1553. *Respublica* is the only extant Moral presenting the Roman side
of the case in the battle of propaganda and persecution. Interestingly,
it presents this side not from the theological but from the social-politi-
cal point of view. The author, like most honest Englishmen of that
day, before the Marian persecutions began, had recoiled in disgust
from the corruption and knavery of the plunderbund of greedy councilors who surrounded the pious and impotent young Edward VI.
In brief the action is as follows: Avarice, the Vice, introduces himself
and explains how under the name of Policy he will insinuate himself into favor with the distressed Lady Respublica. As co-workers he

gathers around him Adulation, Insolence, and Oppression, and, re-baptizing them Honesty, Authority, and Reformation—observe the hit at the Protestant party—introduces them to the Lady. One can imagine what happens; Oppression, for instance, who knows no Latin, 'chops into a deanery' and takes his livelihood away from a bishop. Apparently the only protest against this new deal comes from People, a comic character speaking a broad dialect and perpetrating one malapropism after another—he calls his respected mistress Respublica 'Rice-pudding cake.' Like a good citizen of Tudor England, People trusts the monarch, but he is quite dissatisfied with the monarch's ministers. There is an amusing scene in which People, after being berated by the precious gang and ordered home, inquires: 'Ye'll give volk leave to think?' 'No, marry will we not,' says Oppression, 'nor to look, but to wink.'

The author was evidently a student of classic drama, for the play is divided into acts and scenes in classic fashion. The denouement, too, is classic, for it is brought about by a 'Deus ex machina'—only in this case the Deus turns out to be the well-known allegorical figures, the Four Daughters of God. They arrest the wicked ministers, strip Avarice of his moneybags, and turn the others over to Nemesis for sentence, a quite satisfactory ending to a well-planned play. There is plenty of lively action, little or no horseplay, and a dialogue remarkably free from foul language, but packed with puns and malapropisms. There is, too, a not unsuccessful attempt at characterization: Avarice is not only a miser, but a clever liar; Adulation is a simple fool, Oppression a bully; while People is a capital embodiment of the long-suffering Commonality. Compared with Bale's *King John,* this is not only a real play, but a clever and comic satirical drama.

Morals continued to be written and acted well into the Elizabethan period proper, but with a distinct difference. An early Proclamation by the Queen, 1559, forbade the performance of plays touching on 'matters of religion.' It is still possible to find a play of Protestant propaganda in the early years of the Queen's reign, but as a rule the Elizabethan Moral aims to amuse rather than to edify, and shows a drift toward realistic satiric comedy. A brief review of some Elizabethan Morals may serve to make this clear.

The Trial of Treasure, 'a new and merry interlude,' 1567, contrasts the lives and fates of Just and Lust. The comic scenes deal with Lust's life in sin. He joins up with Sturdy, a bully, and Greedy Gut, a clown who patters dialect; he marries Lady Treasure and lives riotously with her till struck down by God's Visitation. All this is along the lines of the old Moral; what marks this play as Elizabethan is the part played by the Vice, Inclination. He is no longer the Devil's agent in tempting man, but a mere fun-maker. He sings, talks broken French and Dutch, is bridled by Just, freed by Lust, bridled again, and led off kicking like a horse. This stage business was long remembered; in *Sir Thomas More*, the actor who begs Sir Thomas for an opportunity to play before him takes the part of Inclination and enters with the property bridle in his hand.

The increasing importance of the Vice's part is one of the distinguishing characteristics of the later Elizabethan Morals and points to the dominance of the comic actor in the professional companies of that day. This is even more apparent in Fulwell's *Like Will to Like, Quoth the Devil to the Collier*, 1568. Here the old theme of the contest of Vice and Virtue for the soul of man has vanished. Its place is taken by a series of episodes showing the Vice, Nichol Newfangle, pairing off like characters. He begins with a comic Devil whom he unites with a black-a-vised Collier, and the three do a song and dance; 'Vice must have a gittern,' says a stage direction, 'or some other instrument (if it may be) . . . if not they must dance . . . and sing.' After coupling such mates as drunken Hance with a tipsy Fleming, Tom Tosspot with Ralph Roister, and Cuthbert Cutpurse with Pierce Pickpurse, the Vice rides off to hell on the Devil's back, the first recorded instance of a bit of stage business that seems later to have become the more or less conventional exit for the Vice.

All for Money by T. Lupton, 1578, is advertised on the title-page as a 'pitiful comedy,' whereas the author himself calls it in the Prologue 'a pleasant tragedy,' an interesting example of the Elizabethan vagueness of dramatic terminology. As a matter of fact, it is a curious farrago of scholarship, morality, satire, and crude farce, revolving about the Vice, Sin. The family tree of this character is represented in action: Money, who opens the play, is taken violently sick, and after a hard struggle vomits up Pleasure, 'by some fine contrivance,' possibly through a trap on the stage; Pleasure in turn vomits up Sin, who, not to be outdone, vomits up Damnation, 'with a terrible vizard.' Sin is shortly confronted by a comic Devil, bottle-nosed and long-tailed, an affable familiar fiend, who is outrageously mocked by the Vice, and reduced to howls before he can persuade Sin to work with him in the corruption of mankind. The chief means of this corruption is the love of money, and this is presented in a series of brief scenes that draw near to satiric comedy. To help his grandsire, Money, Sin installs a friend, All-for-Money, to act as a magistrate, a thrust, perhaps, at a later familiar figure in Elizabethan drama, the local Justice of the Peace. Before this judge and his clerk, Sin, there appears a succession of characters from real life, whose cases are decided solely on the basis of their ability to bribe the court. The Vice accompanies the proceedings with a flow of cynical, often indecent, comment and, when the session ends, retires to solace himself with a can of beer. *All for Money* represents the final dissolution of the old Moral; the pious and scholarly author in his attempt to present in dramatic form an ethical lesson stoops to attract his public by a combination of costume, stage device, and gross buffoonery.

The Three Ladies of London, 1584, is sometimes classed as a Moral. It is better described on the title-page as 'a right excellent and famous comedy'; in fact it represents the final merging of the Moral into social comedy. The Three Ladies, to be sure, bear the allegorical names of Conscience, Love, and Lucre, and they are surrounded by a group of allegoric figures, Fraud, Usury, Simony, and so on. But the story, told in effective dramatic terms, is simply what might happen to unprotected ladies in the wicked world of London. Conscience, for example, is reduced to selling brooms on the street and Love is tricked into an unfortunate marriage with Dissimulation. Lady Lucre, on the other hand, takes all sorts of rogues under her protection and flourishes apace till the end of the play, when a Judge Nemo, appearing from nowhere, calls the three ladies to the bar and hands out appropriate sentences. There is a certain allegoric structure in this; the author apparently was unable to shake himself quite free from the old convention. Yet the scene is laid in London, and there are constant references to contemporary conditions, to the unpopular aliens who seemed to be taking the bread from the mouths of English workers, to the shady tricks of lawyers, and to the graft involved in Church preferment. The chief comic character is no longer a tricky Vice, but a country lad in London, whose Simplicity—that is his characterizing name—makes him the butt of his companions.

It had been a long course from *The Castle of Perseverance* to *The Three Ladies of London*, and much had entered into it that could not have been in the minds of the clerks who composed the first pageant Morals for York and Beverly. The Moral kept, indeed, until the very end the allegorical framework and characters. Nor did it ever quite lose its ethical purpose; even in such a late play as *All for Money* the writer is striving to show how the love of money is the root of all evil. Yet from the beginning the element of entertainment, which had been incidental in the Miracles, was present as a germ that was to grow till it dominated the Morals. And there was a steady shifting of the scene of action from the imaginative world, in which the Castle of Perseverance stood, to the homely and familiar scene of contemporary England. With this shift, naturally, there comes an increase of the comic element, till the whole action of the later Morals revolves about the comic figure of the Vice. It is well to remember also that with the waning of the cyclic Miracles in the sixteenth century, it was the Morals, or their offspring, the Interludes, carried about the country by little troupes of professional actors, that afforded the main, if not the only, dramatic entertainment to the English public of that day. What, after all, was the comic element in these plays that endeared them to the public and induced an audience to listen patiently to the long ethical tirades with which the dialogue was loaded?

There was, of course, the element of action. This does not differ greatly at first from what we have already noted in the Miracles. There is plenty, an over-plus perhaps, of rough physical fun: the beating that the hero of *Mankind* inflicts on the three little rogues of that play; the mock fight of Hickscorner, Imagination, and Freewill. There is the parody of combat in *Nature,* when Gluttony appears armed for the fray with a cheese and a bottle; and there are such comic incidents as the stocking of Pity and the bridling of Inclination. Another element enters, however, of which there is hardly a trace in the Miracles, the dance, single or in company, gay, grotesque, or broadly comic. Wit dances a 'gaillard,' a brand-new dance in England, with Honest Recreation; Sensual Appetite leads a company of dancers in *The Four Elements;* and Giant Tediousness 'with a vizor over his head' performs a solo song and dance. There is little sustained comic action; *Wit and Science* comes, perhaps, closest of the Morals to a well-contrived comic plot. There is, however, an abundance of comic scenes which rely on something better than horseplay for their fun: the mock manorial Court in *Mankind,* or the series of suitors who appear before Judge All-for-Money. And it may be noted that such scenes break away from the allegorical convention and appear as parodies, with satiric intent, of situations in contemporary life.

The comic element in the spoken word is richer and more varied in the Morals than in the Miracles. There is, on the whole, less of the boisterous tirade in the manner of Herod. On the other hand, there is a startling increase of foul language. In the Miracles this occurs infrequently and then often is used as a means of characterization; in the Morals it seems to be used mainly as a means of raising a laugh. This is a phase of that humor of filth so widely prevalent in the sixteenth century in Western Europe, of which the classic example is the work of Rabelais. There is on the whole comparatively little of the reference, so frequent in later Elizabethan drama, to irregular sex relations; on the other hand there is a positive revel in human ordure and constant reference to the bodily organ that emits it. Happily there is something else in the dialogue than this humor of filth. There is plenty of 'flyting' or comic abuse, a delight in word-play, puns, malapropisms, and distortions of foreign languages, French and Dutch. There is an exploitation of rural dialect as a comic device, attaching itself naturally to stupid or clownish characters, but used with real effect at times, as in the character of People in *Respublica*. Finally we may notice the employment of song as a means of enlivening the action. There is, of course, song in the Miracles, but it is as a rule an adaptation of the music of the Church to the purpose of the play. The lyric note so constant in English sixteenth-century verse is heard again and again in the Morals. The songs do not always appear in the text; *Nature* ends with the stage direction: 'then they sing some goodly ballet'; but there are two pleasant songs in *Lusty Juventus;* Bishop Bale unbends to write a drinking song in *King John;* Lust sings a love song in *Trial of Treasure;* and the Vices of Elizabethan Morals are singing fools.

In character portrayal it can hardly be said that the Morals show much advance over the Miracle plays. In fact so long as the Moral remained true to its early pattern, anything like individualized character was all but impossible. The respective Vices and Virtues were cast in a fixed mold; Pride could not be humble, nor Mercy cruel. Minor characters, where some degree of individuality might be expected, remained, for the most part, types—Riot, Folly, and Adulation—rather than creatures of flesh and blood. As for the central character, whether called Humanum Genus, Mankind, or Youth, he was a passive rather than an active figure, doomed by the convention to play a fixed part, to succumb to temptation, to repent, and to be redeemed. Only when the convention began to break, when figures from real life, a Taverner, a Courtier, or a wanton Maid, enter the scene, does a breath of life begin to animate the action. Yet such figures are late in appearing and play as a rule very minor parts; there was little to be gained from them in the way of comic effect. The two characters that the makers of Morals relied on for entertainment were taken over from the Miracles and transformed, almost beyond recognition, from evil powers to comic characters: the Devil and the Vice. The Devil, of course, is a familiar figure in the Miracles, but he is almost without exception a grim and terrifying figure, the old enemy who fell from heaven for the sin of pride, the tempter in the Garden, the tormentor of damned souls. It is not until the last phase of the Miracles, in the hands, as might be expected, of the unconventional Wakefield Master, that we get our first view of a comic devil, and then, indeed, of a devilkin, the jesting Tutivillus of the Towneley *Judgment*. For a time, indeed, the Moral preserved the accepted convention; Belial in *The Castle of Perseverance*, like the Devil of the Miracles, is man's chief and terrible enemy. Even here, perhaps, the touch of grotesque in his appearance, as he advances to the attack in a blaze of exploding squibs, was meant to move laughter as well as fear. But in the quite early *Mankind,* a play where the old motive of edification is swamped by the author's desire to get a laugh at any cost, we meet a devil Tutivillus, about whom there can be no manner of doubt; he is indeed a wicked tempter, but he is also a figure of fun. He announces his entrance with a foolish jest instead of the roar and blustering with which the Devil of the Miracles was wont to appear. He promptly tries to borrow money from his fellow-actors, who have just taken up a collection, and failing this he turns to his proper errand, the temptation of Mankind. He slips a board under the rushes of the stage to stop Mankind's digging; he steals his seed corn and later his spade. While Mankind, weary of his fruitless labor, sleeps, Tutivillus whispers in his ear that Mercy, his guide and councilor, has been hanged on the gallows for stealing a horse. His work accomplished, he turns to the audience with a farewell:

> I have done my game
> For I have brought Mankind to mischief and to shame.

It is by a comic devil that this, the central incident of the action, is presented in a spirit of broad farce. After *Mankind,* the fearsome Devil of the Miracles disappears altogether. On the other hand we find a lugubrious Devil in *Lusty Juventus,* whose lamentation over youth's abandonment of the good old ways is certainly not to be taken seriously. His son, the Vice Hypocrisy, irreverently compares the Devil's voice to the grunting of a hog. It is in this play, in fact, that we find the subordination of the Devil to the Vice, which marks the later Elizabethan Morals. In *Like Will to Like* the Devil enters dressed like a bear, with 'Lucifer' written on his breast and back—Fulwell wanted to make sure there was no mistake about this character—but all he has to do is to dance with the Collier in the beginning and carry off the Vice at the end of the play. In *All for Money* the Devil cries and roars when Sin, the Vice, threatens to desert him.

This is the last appearance of the Devil in the true Morals, but he appears, if only for a scene, in his role of fun-maker in a late Miracle, the *Conversion of St. Paul,* and in the interlude of *The Disobedient Child.* The ludicrous description of the Prince of Hell in Heywood's *Four PP,* smiling upon the Pardoner, shaking his ears as rugged as burrs and rolling his eyes 'as round as two bushels,' shows to what comic depths this once terrifying figure had sunk. It is in this comic form that occasionally he enters the Elizabethan drama proper. Shakespeare had seen him on the stage and refers to him as the 'roaring devil i' the old play, that every one may pare his nails with a wooden dagger' (*Henry V*, IV. iv. 72-3). Jonson, too, knew him, and in his *Staple of News* expresses, through the mouth of Mistress Tattle, the old playgoer's delight in this comic character: 'My husband, Timothy Tattle, God rest his poor soul . . . was wont to say, there was no Play without a Fool and a Diuell in't; . . . The Diuell for his money, would he say, I would fain see the Diuell.' Jonson's own opinion is clearly expressed in the Dedication to *Volpone,* where he stigmatizes Fools and Devils as 'antique relics of barbarism.'

The Vice entered into drama at a later date than the Devil. In fact it is not until the Interludes of Heywood, between 1520 and 1530, that the term 'the Vice,' applied to a character in the play, appears. Yet there is no doubt that this figure had been active in drama long before the characterizing name is used. He springs from the company of the Seven Deadly Sins, which form the Devil's retinue, and in the Morals is the allegorical embodiment of one or even all of these, as may be seen from the names he bears: Avarice, Idleness, and Iniquity. His original function as a tempter is revealed in the Mystery-Moral play of *Mary Magdalene,* where one of the Seven Sins, Lechery, is deputed to seduce Mary and by means of Curiosity, disguised as a young gallant, leads her into a life of sin. In *Mankind* Mischief plays a double role; he tempts the hero to despair and suicide, but earlier in the action he had played the part of the jester. In the development of the character it is this function, that of the fun-maker, which finally triumphs. The Vice, to be sure, long retained his connection with Satan, the supreme power of evil; but the makers of Morals came more and more to realize the possibilities of a comic Vice as a means of lightening the heavy weight of the ethical tirades. Inclination in *The Trial of Treasure* shows little sign of the Vice's connection with the Devil; and Simplicity in *The Three Ladies of London* presents a Vice in whom all trace of original viciousness has vanished, to be superseded by the comic quality of guileless innocence.

As the dominant comic figure of the Morals, the Vice makes use of all possible means to provoke a laugh. He beats his fellow-actors or is beaten by them, and is never happier than when he starts a brawl between his companions. He sings, dances, and speaks directly to the audience, often with coarse or ribald jokes. The foul talk, which is so frequent in the Morals, comes as a rule from the mouth of the Vice; offensive as it is to us, it was at that time a provocative to laughter. Yet foul speech is not the only sort of talk the Vice uses to amuse the audience; he indulges in word-play of all sorts, mocks and parodies official proclamations, wilfully misunderstands orders given him, mispronounces names and titles, boasts of his prowess yet shows himself a coward, and launches a flood of satirical comment on the follies and fashions of the day. The role of the Vice gave a far greater opportunity for the actor's art than was afforded by any of the allegorical characters of the plays in which he figured. It is not surprising that the Vice became the most popular character in popular drama, and that he gradually pushed himself into other types of plays than the Morals. We find a Vice, Hardy-dardy, in the biblical play, *Queen Hester;* in the early romantic drama, *Common Conditions,* where the Vice gives his name to the play; even in tragedy, Ambidexter in *Cambyses,* a striking example of the English determination to mingle 'pleasant mirth' with serious action, and, as we shall see, into the Interlude.

The figure of the Vice is absent in later Elizabethan drama; the character had already begun to develop along lines that gave rise to two familiar Elizabethan comic figures, the professional Jester, often the Court Fool, and the stupid Clown or country bumpkin. Yet the Vice had so recently vanished from the stage that the character was well known to Elizabethan playwrights, to Shakespeare for example, and to Jonson. Falstaff compares the gaunt Justice Shallow to the Vice's dagger of lath; Richard Crookback likens his own ambiguous speech to that of 'the formal Vice, Iniquity,' and Feste links the Vice and the Devil in one of his jesting songs. In *The Devil is an Ass* Jonson introduces Iniquity as a characteristic example of the old-fashioned Vice who might have passed muster fifty years back:

> When every great man had his Vice stand by him
> In his long coat, shaking his wooden dagger.

THE INTERLUDE

About the end of the fifteenth century when the Moral was extending its scope beyond the old field of the struggle of Vice and Virtue for the soul of man, a new type of drama began to appear. For this there is, unfortunately, no generally recognized name. The term Interlude, originally suggested by Collier, has been accepted by few historians of the drama. Yet it would be hard to find a better or a briefer term for the type of play that discarded the allegorical features of the Moral, drew its characters from real life, and definitely subordinated edification to entertainment. Moreover, this new type, worked within narrower limits, offered an entertainment that could be presented by a little group of professional actors in the brief space of a pause between the dinner in a great hall and the following 'banquet,' or, indeed, in any appropriate pause in a formal entertainment. It is from this phase that the new type originally took the name of Interlude, i.e. a *ludus* or game, presented *inter,* i.e. between, two parts of a feast. The term Interlude was not new in English. It appears in the beginning of the fourteenth century as a form of entertainment opposed to, or offered as a substitute for, singing. When Interludes are lacking, we hear in *Sir Gawain and the Green Knight,* song and laughter may take their place at Christmas feasts. The term was seized on by printers at the beginning of the sixteenth century, when, for the first time, plays issued from the press. Skelton's lost *Nigramansir* seems to have been the first printed play (1504), and the publisher, Wynkyn de Worde, described it as 'a moral interlude.' The long lost and lately (1919) discovered *Fulgens and Lucres* was printed by John Rastell between 1513 and 1519 and was offered to the public as a 'Godely interlude.' From this time on it became the common term for every type of play till well into the reign of Elizabeth. Little distinction was made between varying types of drama: Bale, who was scholar enough to know better, calls one of his biblical plays 'a tragedy or enterlude'; *Jack Juggler,* an imitation of classical comedy, appears as 'a new enterlude'; as does *Queen Hester,* a biblical play, and *Lusty Juventus,* an old-fashioned Moral. It was not until much later that a proper distinction began to be observed: *Gorboduc* was published by the authors themselves as a 'Tragedie' in 1570; *Gammer Gurton's Needle* appeared in 1575 as 'a comedy.' It is clear that contemporary usage affords no guidance; we may best discern the true type of the new drama by an examination of the first extant specimen.

Fulgens and Lucres is the work of Henry Medwall, chaplain to Cardinal Morton. The household of this great clergyman served as a link between the medieval past and the dawning Renaissance in England. Like many of his forerunners Morton was statesman as well as priest; but he was also a patron of the New Learning. It was in his household that Thomas More was trained at once to serve the state and to promote the cause of the Renaissance in England. Tradition relates that More often took a part extempore in the plays performed in the Bishop's palace, and around More there gathered later a little group, connected by ties of marriage as well as by kindred tastes: John Heywood and the two Rastells, all concerned with composing and publishing the new type of drama. Erasmus, the great champion of the New Learning, was More's intimate friend, and the Interlude often voices the protest of Erasmus against the corrupt and decadent medievalism of his day. This tone rings clear in *Fulgens and Lucres:* the debate that forms the nucleus of the play represents the struggle between the old feudalism and the New Learning.

For his source Medwall turned to the recent work of an Italian humanist, the *De Vera Nobilitate* of Bonaccorso, lately translated into English and printed by Caxton. Bonaccorso tells in Ciceronian Latin how Fulgentius, a Roman Senator, had a fair and virtuous daughter, Lucretia, who was sought in marriage by the rich but idle patrician, Cornelius, and by the virtuous plebeian, Flaminius. Since the lady declared that she would marry the nobler of the two, the suitors argue their claims before the Senate. The Latin treatise breaks off without a decision rendered, but Medwall was too good a playwright to be satisfied with so impotent a conclusion. To lighten and diversify the formal debate of his source, he introduces a pair of comic servingmen, evidently professional actors brought in for the occasion. They attach themselves to the suitors and parody the formal suit of the Romans by their courtship of the lady's maid. To win her favor they engage in a contest of song, in wrestling, and in a mock tourney, apparently a sort of cockfight, for the maid ties them up and, after they upset each other, beats them both. The play, begun in a pause of the dinner, stops short so that the guests may return to the feast, and an actor bids the usher serve them with good wine.

The second part opens with an address by one of the actors, evidently speaking for the author. He reminds the hearers of the theme: Of True Nobility, but remarks:

> Divers toyes mingled in the same there was,
> To stir folk to mirth and game.

Some care only for such trifles, he says; some desire only 'matter of sadness.' The author wishes to content everyone, and so after a couple of comic scenes packed with foolish and bawdy jests and a dance of maskers, the formal debate between the suitors takes place and Lucres decides in favor of the virtuous plebeian. The play ends with a lively comment by the comic actors on the justice of the decision and a direct appeal to the women in the audience, asking if they had chosen their husbands on the ground of virtue. 'What the devil is virtue?' says one of the comedians; 'I curse my cat if I can tell.'

That this is an Interlude, in the strict sense of the word, is plain. It is hard, moreover, to praise too highly the daring originality of the play. At a time when the allegoric Moral was the popular form of entertainment, Medwall chose for his characters ancient Romans and, with a happy disregard of chronology, modern serving-men. There is no trace of allegory in *Fulgens and Lucres,* and the moral purpose is overshadowed by the antics of the comedians.

It is hard to find another play among those of the first half of the sixteenth century that exemplifies so clearly the nature of the Interlude. Many plays of this period show a blending of the Interlude and the Moral; they keep the allegorical characters, but set the scene in contemporary England and offer a brief action primarily by way of entertainment. Yet we may discover a few that dare to discard the allegory and present a picture of real life. Such, for example, is *The Nice Wanton,* printed in 1560 but written before 1553. It has, indeed, a pair of characters with allegorical names: Worldly Shame and Iniquity. Of these, however, the first appears only in one scene as a sort of Chorus; the other, the Vice of the play, is, in spite of his name, a very human character. As a matter of fact, this Interlude is a primitive form of Domestic Tragedy, the story of three children of a foolish mother. The names taken from the Bible—Barnabas, 'the son of consolation,' Ismael, and Delilah—indicate their characters. The two bad children throw away their school books and plunge into riotous living. Delilah becomes the mistress of the wild gallant, Iniquity, turns common whore, and shortly comes in dying of the pox. Her brother loses at dice what he had stolen at home, and next appears before Judge Daniel, who sentences him to be hanged in chains for 'felony and burglary, and murder.' Iniquity, who here acts as court bailiff, tries in vain to bribe Daniel, is denounced by Ismael as his accomplice, and like him is sentenced to death. Their mother, overwhelmed with shame, is about to 'stick herself with a knife,' when Barnabas stops her hand, tells her the two others had at least repented before death, and bids her also turn to God. In spite of a heavy emphasis on the old maxim, 'Spare the rod and spoil the child,' the play is a vivid picture of real life. What comedy there is appears in the character of the foolish mother, who spoils the bad children and beats her good son, and in a very lively scene between Ismael, Delilah, and Iniquity, of singing, gambling, loose talk, kisses, and blows.

The Disobedient Child (printed 1560), described in the Stationers' Register as 'an interlude for boys to play and to pass the time at Christmas,' is a good example of the school drama in Interlude form. It discards all pretense at allegory and presents the unfortunate career of a rich man's son. He deserts the school where, according to his account, boys are hung up by the heels and beaten to death, and plunges hastily into matrimony. A comic scene between Cook Longtongue and his maid, Blanche-blab-it-out, describes the extravagant preparations for the wedding dinner. So extravagant, indeed, were they that the young couple soon find themselves reduced to poverty. The wife promptly turns shrew, beats her husband, sends him out to sell wood, and beats him again because he has brought so little money home, till, according to the stage direction, 'he must lie along the ground as though he were sore beaten and wounded.' When she departs to make merry with her gossips, he decides to return to his father. An intercalary scene presents a comic Devil shouting, 'Ho, ho, ho,' and boasting that 'there comes more in one hour into hell than into heaven in a month or twain.' After this interruption the son confesses his folly to his father, who promises him a little present help but sends him back to his shrewish wife. The play ends with a long tirade by the Perorator enforcing the all too obvious moral. If the boys who acted it took it as seriously as the author did, they must have learned 'a witty lesson' on the folly of leaving school and taking a wife. Yet in spite of the heavy burden of didacticism, The Disobedient Child is a thoroughly English play, with its comic servants, comic

Devil, a Priest who bewails the behavior of his drunken clerk, and a realistic report of the riotous marriage feast.

The one real master of the Interlude is John Heywood, 1497-1578, the first example of the actor-playwright so common in Elizabethan days. We hear of him first, 1519, as 'a singing man' in the Court of Henry VIII, but there is some reason to believe that he had been a boy singer in the Chapel Royal and had later studied at Oxford. Becoming an intimate of the liberal humanist group that gathered about Sir Thomas More, he married John Rastell's daughter, and turned over four of his plays to be printed by his brother-in-law, William Rastell. He was attached to the household of the Princess Mary, for whom in 1538 his 'children,' i.e. boy actors under his control, presented an interlude. Like Chaucer and Langland before him, like More and Erasmus in his own day, Heywood was a good Catholic; and after the definitive breach with Rome under Elizabeth he fled from England and died in exile. Yet he was not blind to the need of reform in the Church and allowed free play to his satiric wit against such scandalous figures as the cheating Pardoner and the begging Friar.

Besides his plays Heywood wrote also a *Dialogue . . . of Proverbs,* several collections of epigrams, and a political allegory in verse, *The Spider and the Fly.* It is his plays alone, however, that concern us. To determine their exact chronology seems at present impossible, yet it is not difficult to see the development in matter and style. Three presumably early works may be quickly passed over. *Witty and Witless* is not really a play, rather a *Débat* in dialogue. *Gentleness,* a play ascribed to Heywood by its latest editor, is, perhaps, a little better. The *Débat* form remains, as a Merchant and a Knight dispute 'who is a verey gentleman.' They are interrupted by a Plowman, who asserts, partly by words, partly by blows of his whip, that he is a better man than either of them. The play of *Love,* on the other hand, shows a distinct advance. Four characters argue interminably about the pleasures and pains of love. Yet the fine-spun argument is interrupted from time to time by the coarse jests of the Vice, who also tells a tale, somewhat in Chaucer's style, of a trick played on him by a wanton lady. There is a bit of boisterous action toward the end, where the Vice enters 'running about the place among the audience with a tank on his head, full of squibs, crying: "water, water, fire, fire." '

In the *Play of the Weather* Heywood for the first time writes something approaching drama. Jupiter, having composed the disputes of the four gods who control the weather, descends to earth to hear, like a good Tudor sovereign, the complaints and requests of his earthly subjects. Merry-report, the Vice, offers himself as the usher of this court, and introduces, one after another, eight suitors, all clamoring for the sort of weather that will be profitable to them. Last of the suitors enters little Dick, a boy, 'the least that can play,' begging on behalf of his schoolmates plenty of snow for snowballing. Jupiter finally utters his decision: he will give the world all sorts of weather and expect each man to make the best use of it, and the Vice comments: 'Now ye shall have the weather even as it was.' The whole play marks a distinct advance over *Love*. There is considerable action in the coming and going of the suitors, the characters are no longer types but individuals, and there is genuine characterization in their portrayal. There is a far better role for the Vice, who is continually on the stage jesting and mocking, and the formal arguments of the earlier plays have been cut down to lively altercations. This gives rise to vigorous dialogue, marred to modern taste by much foul speech, but apparently considered funny by a courtly Tudor audience.

The Play Called the Four PP was apparently the most popular, as it is today the best known, of Heywood's works; it was thrice reprinted in his lifetime and it appears in the repertoire of the actors in *Sir Thomas More*. This is due, presumably, to its essentially English character. The Four PP are well-known figures in the life of Heywood's day: a Palmer, a Pardoner, a Potycary, i.e. an itinerant quack doctor, and a Pedlar, four genial rogues who magnify their callings and swap tales to show who is the greatest liar. The Palmer boasts of his many pilgrimages and of the sanctity acquired thereby; the Pardoner retorts that this was labor lost since he could save souls at a cheaper rate:

> Give me but a penny or two pence,
> And as soon as the soul departeth hence,
> In half an hour—or three quarters at most—
> The soul is in heaven with the Holy Ghost.

The Potycary brags that he has helped more souls to Heaven than either of them, for

> Whom have ye known die honestly [i.e. unhanged]
> Without help of the potycary?

The Pardoner displays his relics: the jawbone of All Hallows, the great toe of the Trinity, a slipper of one of the Seven Sleepers, and so on, to the accompaniment of obscene jests by the incredulous Potycary, a scene derived from Chaucer. In the lying match that follows, the Potycary tells of a miraculous cure; the means by which it was wrought are quite unmentionable to ears polite. The Pardoner caps it with the tale of his rescue of the soul of Margery Corson from hell, the best piece of dramatic narrative since the time of Chaucer. But the Palmer ends the contest by his quiet statement that in all his travels he had never seen a woman lose her temper. This is acclaimed as the winner, 'a plain and patent lie.' The little play ends on a serious note; the mockery has been directed only against frauds and abuses; for the rest it is better to waive private judgment and submit humbly to the Church. This is the note of More and his circle: the Pedlar who utters it is speaking, no doubt, for the author. Yet Heywood did not write *The Four PP* to teach this or any other lesson; he says quite plainly:

> To pass the time in this without offence,
> Was the cause why the maker did make it;

pastime, not edification, was his purpose.

The Four PP is in many ways a delightful piece of work; it is packed with broad humor and distinguished above Heywood's earlier work by realistic characterization. Yet it hardly attains the rank of true comedy; there is little action, no plot of any sort, and the end drags heavily after the climax of the Palmer's lie. This, apparently, was as far as Heywood could go in reliance upon and improvement of English models. In two other playlets ascribed to him by internal evidence, he turns to a foreign source, French farce, for inspiration.

The Pardoner and the Frere is an amusing skit of about a thousand lines. It draws upon a French farce, *D'un Pardoneur, d'un triacleur, et d'une tavernière,* but it alters characters and situations. For the *triacleur,* a quack vender like the Potycary of *The Four PP,* Heywood substitutes a begging Friar whom he has boldly lifted from Chaucer. These worthies meet in a parish church, each intent on getting what money he can from the congregation. They chant their appeals in antiphonal chorus, each objecting to the other's presence, till at last they fall to fisticuffs. They are interrupted by the local parson, who calls on Neighbor Prat, the constable, to arrest these defilers of the sanctuary. The rogues, however, are too strong for the honest men and get off scot-free, a conclusion as ingenious as it is amusing; it would be hard to draw a moral lesson from this farce.

John John, Tib, and Sir John, like the preceding play, depends upon a French farce, *Pernet qui va au vin,* dealing in Gallic fashion with the eternal triangle, the cuckoldy husband, the wanton wife, and her lover. Heywood retains the general outline and some of the incidents of the French play, but he has given it a thoroughly English setting; for the nameless lover of his source he substitutes the parish priest, Sir John, a bold stroke at immorality in the Church. The action of the little play—it is less than 700 lines—moves swiftly; the long speeches and tales of the earlier plays give way to brisk dialogue. It ends, as might be expected, with a three-cornered fight between the husband, the 'piled priest,' and the 'priest's whore.' Tib and Sir John run off together; the husband stands triumphant for a moment till the thought dawns on him that they are probably in the priest's chamber. He will after them, and with a bow to the audience he leaves the stage.

This is the nearest approach to realistic comedy so far in English. Yet it is, after all, a comic sketch rather than a comedy. There is nothing like a well-developed plot with a beginning, intrigue, and solution. It ends very much where it began. The lively dialogue reeks of foul language, and the bawdy jests of Sir John are something new in English drama, which so far has been dirty rather than lewd. On the other hand, even in this brief sketch there is clean-cut characterization in the figures of the boastful, suspicious, yet cowardly husband, the shrewish, domineering wife, and the licentious and hypocritical priest. Heywood did not put his name to either of these farces and his authorship has recently been challenged. Yet they were printed by his brother-in-law and belong to the dramatic circle about Thomas More.

Heywood had remarkable gifts as a comic playwright: a genial sense of humor, an insight into human nature, and a talent for brisk dialogue. He was, if not the inventor, at least the one real master of the Interlude. It seems at first sight strange that he did not go on to create English comedy. One reason, perhaps, lies in the circumstances of his time. His plays belong, so far as we can judge, to the early and happier years of Henry VIII's reign. The later years were overshadowed by social and religious revolution. Heywood himself was caught in the struggle; he saw his friend More go to the scaffold rather than admit the King's supremacy in matters of religion; he himself was at one time condemned to death on the same ground, and only saved his life by public recantation. The drama of these later years took on a tone of propaganda, savagely anti-Roman as in the work of Bale, frankly reactionary as in *Respublica*. There was no place left for the comic criticism of life in which Heywood excelled. Yet, perhaps, the cause of his failure to create true English comedy lies deeper, in the nature of the man himself. Heywood seems to have thought of comedy in the terms of the Interlude. There is little sense of atmosphere or background in his plays; they are too brief to allow the development of a well-planned intrigue. Though he was a member of a humanist group, there is no sign of classical influence in his work; a belated medievalist, he caught inspiration from Chaucer or from French farce.

Yet the influence of Heywood upon later sixteenth-century comedy is clear: he banished the allegorical characters of the Moral and substituted figures from contemporary English life—an influence seen in the increasing number of such figures in the later Morals; he cut down the length of the drama to briefly actable proportions; most of all he set himself frankly to amuse rather than to edify his audience—'to pass the time without offence.' It was in this direction alone that comedy could make progress. This was much, but it was not sufficient. English comedy needed an infusion of new blood, and this was to come in the first place from a study and imitation of classic models, later from the reawakening of the romantic spirit.

2

The Impact of the Renaissance

CLASSICAL FORM

THE impact of classical studies upon English drama in general, upon English comedy in particular, was one of the results of the wave of Humanism that swept over western Europe in the fifteenth century. The crest of this wave was late in breaking upon the shores of England. It was delayed not only by England's distance from the Italian center, but by the wars, foreign and civil, which distracted England during the greater part of that period. Not until the establishment of the Tudor peace under Henry VII was it possible for English scholars to exploit the new fields that were opening to them, and in the early years of his son's reign the cultivation of Greek and Latin classics went on apace in the newly founded and re-endowed schools and colleges. The medieval studies of logic, law, and theology were pushed aside; 'We have put Duns [Duns Scotus, representative of scholasticism] in Bocardo [the university prison],' wrote a royal commissioner sent to Oxford to reform the curriculum. As early as 1517 two Oxford colleges, Brasenose and Corpus Christi, prescribed the study of classic authors, Plautus among others, for their undergraduates.

The mention of Plautus has a peculiar significance. During the Middle Ages, when most of his plays were lost to the world, his very name was hardly known. Indeed the first English writer to mention him seems to be Skelton, some time early in the sixteenth century. With the discovery in 1427 of his twelve lost comedies a great impetus was given to their study and their stage presentation, first in Italy, later in England, where in 1520 'a goodly comedy of Plautus' was presented at Court before Henry VIII. It was not long, indeed, before Plautus came to be regarded as the master of comedy even as Seneca was of tragedy; the comment of Polonius on the repertoire of the actors at Elsinore may be taken as representing the conventional opinion of Renaissance England. It may seem strange at first sight that the work of Plautus so overshadowed that of his successor, Terence, for Terence had long been known and taught in medieval schools. But the plays of Terence were then taught not as plays, but as models of conversational Latin and as a treasury of sententious sayings. In fact the rediscovery of Plautus gave new zest to the study of Terence, whose plays now began not only to be published, but also- to be performed in the original Latin in the English grammar schools. Yet, after all, the lively action and boisterous mirth of Plautus were more in accordance with the English taste for drama than the simpler stories and more polished dialogue of Terence.

The influence of Plautus upon English comedy begins in the schools; it is long before it effects the popular drama still clinging to the old Morals and their modification in Interlude form. The earliest example of school drama under the influence of classical studies seems to be *Thersites,* 1537. This is a farce Interlude with classical characters set in an English background. The protagonist is a Miles Gloriosus, a type more fully and perfectly presented in such Elizabethan characters as Falstaff, Bobadil, and Bessus. He is armed for battle by Mulciber, but his only fight is with a snail; when threatened by 'a poor soldier from Calais,' he takes refuge behind his mother's skirts, as if 'pursued by a thousand horsemen.' The language is still that of the later Morals, lively patter, plentifully interlarded with obscenity. There is almost no trace here of the formative influence of Latin comedy, or of a well-developed plot.

A real advance appears in *Jack Juggler,* 'a new interlude for children to play,' c. 1553. Here we have an actual adaptation of a Plautine comedy, the *Amphitruo,* for the English stage. The little play resembles the 'drolls' of the Commonwealth period, in that it lifts and elaborates one episode of a comedy with complete disregard of the whole. Here the episode is the Mercury-Sosia intrigue of the original. The parts of Mercury and Sosia are taken by two English pages, Jack Juggler, the Vice, and Jenkin Careaway, the servant of Mr. Bongrace. Like Mercury, Jack takes on the semblance of his opposite, and by threats and blows forces Jenkin to disclaim his own identity. The fun is mainly physical, and the language rather gross. In spite of the fact that the author has lifted his story from Plautus, he has little conception of the Plautine intrigue; he does not even trouble to provide a solution for the incident he has used. Yet the author deserves some credit for being apparently the first of English playwrights to recognize the possibility of adapting Latin comedy to the English stage. He was to have a long line of followers, including among others the master playwright in *The Comedy of Errors.*

Another schoolmaster was far more successful in his dealing with Latin comedy. This was Nicholas Udall (1506-56), once a student at Corpus Christi, Oxford, and later Headmaster successively of Eton and of Westminster. It was for the boys of one of these schools— critics differ—that he wrote the first 'regular' English comedy, *Ralph Roister Doister*.[1] It is 'regular,' in the sense that it is carefully divided into acts and scenes according to the classical convention, but it is much more than that. Instead of translating or adapting a Latin play, Udall writes a Plautine comedy in English. He takes a typical Plautine character, the Miles Gloriosus, and weaves about him a typical Plautine intrigue. As the active agent of the intrigue he creates the character of Merrygreek, an ingenious combination of the Latin parasite and the English Vice, mischievous and fun-loving, who abets Ralph in his absurd courtship of the widow Custance. This highly respectable woman takes the place of the courtesan or dancing-girl of Latin comedy, and she, like all the minor characters—her betrothed husband, Gawin Goodluck, her neighbor Tristam Trusty, and two housefuls of servants—is English to the core. So is the setting, which might be London or, indeed, any English town. There is plenty of action with the old-fashioned fisticuffs, and one pitched battle between the men and the women, but the blows are all in fun and no one is hurt in the brawl. A complication is neatly introduced in the fourth act, by which doubt is thrown on the fidelity of Custance, and this must be cleared up before the play can end with her marriage. That it may be an altogether happy ending the disappointed suitor, Ralph, is invited to the wedding feast; Udall was too fond of his Miles Gloriosus to dismiss him baffled from the scene.

One cannot expect in so early a play anything like the rounded characterization of the great Elizabethans, but we may note the air of homely realism that Udall throws about the household of Dame Custance and the strict discipline that she maintains over a group of idle and gossipy maids. Her nurse, Madge Mumblecrust, seems like a faint foreshadowing of Juliet's guardian. The dialogue, written for the most part in rhymed couplets, is smooth and easy, with some amusing patter speeches and a rather daring parody of the Catholic requiem for the dead. What is perhaps most remarkable is the almost entire absence of foul speech; Udall, it seems, was more tender of his boys' tongues than he was of their backsides, if the report of his floggings

---

[1] The date of composition is uncertain, probably before 1552. The unique remaining copy may date from 1566.

as Headmaster at Eton is true. There are, as might be expected in a schoolboys' play, plenty of songs; it is hard for any group of characters to get together in the action without bursting into full chorus. Udall himself must have been well pleased with his work, for he is bold enough in the Prologue to dignify it with the name of Comedy. It was, indeed, an immense advance over the Interludes and Morals of the day. One thing, however, was still lacking, a touch of poetry, a breath of romance.

There is, in fact, little of either poetry or romance in Latin comedy, and this holds good as well for another English play, *Gammer Gurton's Needle*,[2] by William Stevenson, Fellow of Christ's College, Cambridge. This is not a school but a college play, and perhaps for that reason the author works with greater freedom than the Headmaster allowed himself. The influence of Latin comedy is plain not only in the conventional division into acts and scenes, but in the carefully constructed plot, which builds up an elaborate and diversified action from the trivial fact of the loss of her only needle by Gammer, i.e. goodwife, Gurton. But there is no partial re-creation of stock types of Latin comedy as in Udall's play. The intriguer, who sets the action going and keeps it alive by repeated attacks, is a thoroughly English figure, Diccon the Bedlam, discharged from Bethlem, the London lunatic asylum, to wander through the country as a licensed beggar—the character, by the way, that Edgar adopts as his disguise in *Lear*.

The scene is laid in a little English village and the characters are correspondingly rustic: two old wives, Dame Gurton and Dame Chat; Hodge, Dame Gurton's man, a stupid, cowardly boor; Dr. Rat, the parish priest; and Master Baylye, who exercises a mild police jurisdiction over the community. Diccon's lies, his charges and counter-charges set the old wives in a rage that leads to a knock-down fight. The solution is as physical as most of the action, for the needle, lodged where it was lost, in Hodge's breeches, is discovered when it is driven into his buttocks by a blow of Diccon's fist.

The language is as vigorous as the action. There is a constant give and take of rhymed dialogue, couched for the most part in the West of England dialect that served the old playwrights as a conventional form of rustic speech. It is by no means so free from dirt as that which Udall wrote for his boys, but the gross language serves mainly as a means of characterization. The scholar-playwright had thoroughly as-

2 Probably *c.* 1552-3. It was first printed in 1575.

similated the teaching of Latin comedy and built on this foundation a truly English play.

The primary contribution of Latin comedy to the developing English drama was form, that is the recognition of the value of plot construction. This implied not only a remodeling of the old amorphous Moral but also an expansion of the brief Interlude to a scale within which a plot could be developed. *Gammer Gurton's Needle*, for example, could be cut to the dimensions of the Interlude by omitting the complications of the plot and reducing the whole action to the loss and the recovery of the needle. On the other hand, the necessity of a plot to reshape the Moral in formal order may be seen in a little-known but interesting play, *Misogonus*.

This play, preserved in a badly damaged manuscript, seems to be the work of a Laurence Johnson who became Master of Arts at Cambridge in 1577. It resembles a Moral in that it treats in dramatic form the story of the Prodigal Son. What is singular about this one of many dramatic versions of the parable is its treatment of the theme in classic form. It is not only divided into acts and scenes, but it reshapes the story along Plautine lines. The leading character, Misogonus, is at once the Prodigal and the wild youth of Latin comedy. He differs from his Gospel prototype in that he does not depart to squander his substance in riotous living, but stays at home to associate with a Meretrix, lifted from Plautus, and a dissolute priest, Sir John, strikingly reminiscent of a Heywood character. Conversely, the virtuous elder brother of the parable does not stay at home to grudge the Prodigal's return, but is discovered opportunely at the crisis of the action. He was, it appears, the elder of a pair of twins, dispatched by his mother, now dead, to distant lands without the father's knowledge. Why he was so dispatched or why the secret was kept so long are matters which the author does not trouble himself to explain, but he does make clear that the returning child is recognized, as often in Latin comedy, by a birthmark. His return, of course, balks Misogonus of his expectation of the inheritance, whereupon he repents and is forgiven by a too indulgent father.

Apart from this extraordinary application of Plautine technique to a Bible story, the play is of interest for its vivid pictures of life in rural England. The father is evidently a landed gentleman with tenants and household servants, among whom his Fool, Cacurgus, plays a chief role. There is a merry song 'to the tune of Heart's Ease,' a tune which Peter calls for at a moment of general lamentation in the Capulet household. The most striking characteristic of the dialogue is its constant and often forced distortion of language: 'drumbledary' for dromedary, 'excommunication' for communication, 'symplication' for supplication, and so on. This device is not used to characterize a particular actor; more than one of them indulges in it. The author evidently employs it as a means to provoke laughter. It is one of the signs of the Elizabethan love of word-play, used, with some restraint, by Shakespeare himself.

The influence of Latin comedy, felt first in school and college plays, spread to other types of drama, and its effect may be seen in various sixteenth-century plays of older genres. An interesting example of this influence is seen in *The History of Jacob and Esau*, 'a new merry and witty comedy or interlude,' licensed in 1557-8. A dramatized version of a Bible story, in subject it may be considered a belated Miracle, but its technique is far from the simple one of the early Miracles. It opens with a Prologue by a poet who recites the argument of the play —a characteristic Plautine device; it adds a group of servants to the Bible characters, notably Ragan, Esau's attendant, who plays the part of the Fool, but who also resembles the classic parasite in his greed for food and in the blows he suffers. The play is divided into acts and scenes and is carefully plotted, with Rebecca playing the role of the intriguer, up to the climax, in which Jacob wins the blessing, and to the happy ending in which Esau renounces his purpose of revenge. The old desire for realistic presentation appears in the note prefixed to the names of the players, 'who are to be considered Hebrews and should be so apparelled with attire,' but the whole action has been recast in the classic mold and adorned in various scenes with the classic device of stichomythia.

The Moral also shows in some of its later examples the influence of Latin comedy. This is evident in *Respublica;* another striking example is seen in the late (1579) revision of Redford's *Wit and Science,* which is carefully divided into acts and scenes in the classic fashion. It would be possible, perhaps, to discover other scattered instances of the early influence of Latin comedy, but it is not until the appearance on the scene toward the end of the century of the group of poet-playwrights, all classically trained gentlemen, that the full influence of Latin comedy takes effect on the popular Elizabethan drama.

ROMANTIC SPIRIT

It is, perhaps, impossible to define the word 'romance,' or to limit exactly the meaning of 'romantic.' Yet it is by no means difficult to recognize a romance when one sees it or to trace the romantic strain in a play or poem. In English drama this is particularly easy when we pass from such classically influenced plays as those we have been discussing, to later work that comes distinctly under the romantic influence. It is not until late in Elizabeth's reign that this influence makes itself markedly felt upon English drama, more especially upon English comedy. The underlying cause was the almost complete transformation of English life in that period from a medieval to a Renaissance civilization, a civilization that turned from the former contemplation of death and its consequence in Hell or Heaven, to a frank enjoyment of the newly enriched life upon earth. Instead of longing for Jerusalem the Golden, man now turned his eyes upon the treasures of the Indies, and English adventurers fought to share them with the power of Spain. English commerce pushed into hitherto unknown seas and brought home spoils from every quarter. Along with this material enrichment went a general intellectual advance due mainly to the invention of printing; poems, histories, and romantic tales, formerly locked up in manuscripts possessed by the favored few, were published and became public property. There was an increasing tendency to express this new material, the rich, the strange, and the beautiful, in appropriate language. English poetry, indeed, underwent an almost complete transformation in the sixteenth century; new forms, the sonnet and blank verse, came in with the courtly poets under Henry VIII; new motives, especially Petrarchan love-longing, appear in English verse; and the English lyric strikes at once a lighter and an intenser note. We must not expect to find this new poetry in full flower in early Elizabethan drama; it is not until the conquest of the stage by the poet-playwrights of the 1580's that English drama attains the lovely utterance that culminates in a long series of Shakespearean comedies from *Love's Labour's Lost* to *The Tempest*. Yet the striving for appropriate poetic expression is increasingly evident in earlier work, often, indeed, in the strained diction and far-fetched metaphors of the dialogue.

One motif, of prime importance for later comedy, is directly traceable to the new impulse. This is, to use the jargon of the drama, the 'love interest,' or, to put it in somewhat more appropriate words, the theme of romantic love. In medieval drama this theme seems to have been taboo; there is no trace of it in the Miracles and Morals. In classical comedy, by reason of the social conditions from which this form sprang, there was no possibility of a romantic love affair; marriage was a matter of convenience and family arrangement; a young man's passion was not for a virtuous maiden, but for a courtesan or dancing girl. The same is true of English comedy as long as it held to classic models; the courtship of Ralph Roister Doister is ridiculous rather than romantic; Misogonus pursues a meretrix; and it is impossible to conceive of a true love strain entering into the rowdy action of *Gammer Gurton's Needle*. In the sources, however, from which the new comedy drew its material the theme of romantic love was of dominant interest. These sources were both native and foreign; the romance of chivalry, long domesticated in England, and, on the other hand, the plays, poems, and prose narratives of the Romance Languages.

A good example of this new romantic comedy is furnished by *Sir Clyomon and Sir Clamydes,* or to give it the full descriptive title of the old edition: *The History of Two Valiant Knights, Sir Clyomon Knight of the Golden Shield, Son to the King of Denmark: and Sir Clamydes, the White Knight, son to the King of Suavia.* This absurd play was published in 1599, the year when *Much Ado About Nothing* made its bow upon the boards. There is reason to believe, however, that the date of composition must be pushed back into the 1570's, the period when this type of play was repeatedly presented at Court. The late publication is an interesting testimony to the long hold of dramatized romance upon a section of London audience who, like the Citizen and his Wife in Beaumont's play, wanted to see a knightly hero do 'admirable things,' 'kill a lion with a pestle,' or conquer the ugly giant, Barbaroso. There is no lion in *Sir Clyomon,* but there is a flying serpent in the Forest of Strange Marvels, which is killed by one of the knights, as well as a wicked King of Norway, who is slain by the other.

There is no act or scene division in this play, and there is no trace of plot construction; it is simply a dramatized romance of chivalry, presenting in action the adventures of the two valiant knights. It would take far too long to recount all their adventures; suffice it to say that they wander through unknown lands like the Isle of Strange Marshes, meet at the Court of Alexander the Great, a well-known figure in medieval romance, and encounter a crafty magician, Brian Sans Foy, who, like Archimago in *The Faerie Queene,* disguises himself in the armor of one of the knights and passes himself off on a lady as her true lover. For, we may note, both these knights are lovers who in the end win their ladies; Sir Clamydes, the Princess Juliana; Sir Clyomon, the Princess Neronis, who has followed him in the disguise of a page.

All this, of course, is pure romantic stuff undigested as yet into dramatic form. By way of comic entertainment the author introduces an old-fashioned Vice in the person of Subtle Shift, a stupid cowardly rogue, who alternately serves and betrays first one knight and then the other. A touch of more or less realistic pastoral is added in the figure of the shepherd Corin, who for a time takes Neronis into his service as his boy Jack.

The source from which the author of *Sir Clyomon* drew his material is unknown, but another play of the same period, *Common Conditions,* licensed 1576, reveals on the title-page the fact that it is an attempt to present in action the story of a then well-known romance. *Common Conditions* is offered to the public as 'an excellent and pleasant comedy . . . drawn out of the famous history of Galiarbus Duke of Arabia.' Unfortunately this 'famous history' has disappeared; it must have been one of the many prose versions of chivalric romance which kindled the imagination of the English reading public in the latter half of the sixteenth century. Like *Sir Clyomon, Common Conditions* presents, to use Gosson's phrase, 'the adventures of amorous knights passing from country to country for the love of their ladies.'

There are many points of resemblance between this play and *Sir Clyomon,* but there is one marked difference, the dominance here of the Vice. He gives his name, *Common Conditions,* i.e. 'Things as they are,' to the play; he starts the action by procuring the exile of Galiarbus, and he ends it by bearing false witness against the lovers. This malicious function is properly that of the Vice in the Morals, but Common Conditions is not altogether malicious; in general he plays the part of a witty jester, able to extricate himself from any scrape into which he has fallen. Probably the predominant position of the Vice is due to the fact that this play was designed for popular performance; it may be acted, we are told, by six players, the common number of a touring troupe. *Sir Clyomon,* on the other hand, was designed for a courtly audience; it was repeatedly performed by the Queen's Company. 'The more Fool the better luck' would seem to have been the device of a popular playwright.[3]

The Rare Triumphs of Love and Fortune—'played before the Queen's most excellent Majesty'—was published in 1589, but it is almost certainly earlier, possibly the *History of Love and Fortune* presented at Court by Derby's players in 1582. It is a fully developed specimen of the combination Masque and romantic comedy so popular at Court. A highly romantic tale of true love crossed, but happily concluded, is set in a mythological framework. The whole first act deals with the rivalry between Venus and the Goddess Fortune, which has risen to such a pitch that Jupiter holds a council of the Olympian divinities to compose their strife. After various 'shows' of lovers and heroes—Troilus and Cressida, Caesar and Pompey, et cetera—who have been cast down by Love or by Fortune, Jupiter orders the rival goddesses to try their powers upon a pair of lovers. Here the action of the play proper begins.

Hermione, a gentleman of unknown birth, at the Court of King Phizantes has won the love of the Princess Fidelia. Surprised and denounced as a traitor by her brother, Hermione is banished from the Court. This is a triumph for Fortune, proclaimed by drums and trumpets, but Venus has still a card to play.

Bomelio, a nobleman long since driven from Court by false charges, now living as a hermit with magical powers, learns that Hermione is his son and promises to aid him. This is a triumph for Venus heralded by 'a noise of viols,' but Fortune's 'sport' is not begun.

Disguised as a Doctor, Bomelio visits the Court and manages to bring Fidelia back to her lover. Unfortunately, in his father's absence Hermione has discovered and burned Bomelio's magic books. The discovery of their loss drives Bomelio raving mad and he lays violent hands upon Fidelia. This triumph of Fortune is hailed by a special flourish of trumpets and drums backed by a discharge of guns.

By this time we have come to the last act, and the patience of Jupiter, if not of the audience, has been exhausted. He bids the contending goddesses lay aside their quarrel and sends Mercury to cure the mad

---

[3] In 1907 a unique and perfect copy of the first quarto of *Common Conditions* was discovered in a remote country house in Wales. It was acquired by the Yale Elizabethan Club and has been admirably edited by Professor Tucker Brooke. Up to that date all that was known of this play was based upon a study of the sadly mutilated Devonshire copy of the second quarto, now in the Huntington Library. Since this copy lacked title-page, beginning, and end, much that was earlier said of it was founded on mere conjecture.

Bomelio. Venus and Fortune intervene to save the lovers from the wrath of the King, who has surprised them at Bomelio's cave, and all quarrels end in a general reconciliation.

It would not be a true Elizabethan play without an intermixture of comedy. This is furnished by the comments of Vulcan in the council of the gods and by the characters of Penulo, the tricky parasite, and Lentulo, the foolish servant, in the main action. The Vice of popular drama is excluded from this courtly play, and attention is concentrated upon the tale of romantic love. It is interesting to note that this old play seems to have furnished Shakespeare with some hints for his transformation of an Italian *novella* into the tragi-comedy of *Cymbeline*. The progress toward the poetic Elizabethan drama is shown in the easy dialogue of this play with its admixture of rhymed couplets, stanzaic forms, and occasional bits of blank verse.

The lost two-part play, *Palamon and Arcite* by Richard Edwardes, Master of the Chapel Children, must have been another example of the drama of chivalric love. Based upon Chaucer's *Knight's Tale*, it was performed on two successive days in the Hall of Christ Church, Oxford, before Queen Elizabeth, 1566. Her majesty was delighted with it, and gave the pretty boy who played Emilia a handsome present. Were the play extant, it would probably prove an interesting example of a romantic theme presented in more or less regular dramatic form.

This seems evident from Edwardes' handling of the theme of romantic friendship in his one surviving play, *Damon and Pythias,* apparently played at Court during the Christmas festivities of 1564-5. In an interesting Prologue Edwardes insists upon 'decorum' in the dialogue of comedy as prescribed by Horace, but goes on to assert that this play, since it presents 'matter mixed with mirth and care,' is properly to be termed a 'tragical comedy,' the first appearance of this term in English. The serious scenes of the play develop the well-known story of the friendship of Damon and Pythias and bring a tragic situation to a happy end. Into this action Edwardes introduces a figure from Latin comedy, Carisophus the parasite, whose feigned friendship for the courtier, Aristippus, is contrasted with the true love that unites Damon and Pythias. The native English strain appears in the realistic figure of the hangman—cf. Abhorson in *Measure for Measure*—in the burlesque character of Grim the collier, and in two knavish pages, forerunners of characters in later comedy, who wash and shave Grim and run off with his purse. The action tends to drag and is somewhat loaded with moralizing speeches, but the developed plot works up to an effective climax. One may see the author's effort to bring dramatic order into the loosely constructed plays of early romantic comedy; the influence of classical models is making itself felt even in this type of drama.

The spark that first kindled romantic comedy in England came, strangely enough, from Spain rather than from Italy. Its source was the Spanish dramatic novel, *Calisto and Melibea,* better known by its later title, *Celestina.* This strange blend of romantic passion and drastic realism spread from its home in Spain about the end of the fifteenth century over all western Europe. A copy may have been brought to England by the Spanish humanist, Juan Luis Vives, who in 1523 was appointed reader in rhetoric at Corpus Christi College, Oxford. Vives, to be sure, had denounced *Celestina* as a *liber pestifer,* but he could hardly have avoided showing the notorious book to More, with whom he was on intimate terms. Someone in More's circle, apparently, took upon himself the task of adapting a part of it for presentation as an Interlude, and John Rastell set it up in print sometime between 1523 and 1530 with the following title: *Calisto and Melibea,* 'a new comedy in English . . . wherein is shown . . . as well the beauty and good properties of women as their vices and evil conditions with a moral conclusion.' A unique copy is preserved at the Bodleian.

The *Celestina* tells in detail, in dialogue divided into twenty-one acts, the story of Calisto's desperate passion for the lady Melibea, of the success of his suit by means of the bawd, Celestina, and of the tragic conclusion of the affair in which all three principal characters come to sudden and violent ends. This tale of hot-blooded young love is set off against a sordid background of bawds, harlots, witches, thievish and murderous servants. It is inconceivable that any intimate of More's should have wished to reproduce the whole of this scandalous work. It would, however, be possible to extract and dramatize an episode and conclude it with a moral, so changing the *liber pestifer* into an *exemplum.*

And this is exactly what happened. *Calisto and Melibea* opens with a scene in which the lady rejects Calisto's advances. He is in despair when he reflects upon her grace, her virtue, and her beauty, but on the advice of his servant determines to enlist the aid of Celestina. For a hundred gold pieces the bawd undertakes the task and after an interview with Melibea, stormy at first, she persuades the lady to surrender her girdle to cure Calisto of an alleged toothache and to promise him another interview. So far the unknown playwright has followed the novel, at times minutely; but in *Celestina* this interview is the beginning of Melibea's fall from virtue. Such an event, of course, would be altogether repugnant to the circle for which the little play was written, so here the author claps on an ending of his own. Melibea's father enters and tells her of an ominous dream: he seemed to see an ugly bitch enticing her with spaniel-like fawning to the brink of a foul stinking pit. Struck with remorse Melibea recognizes the significance of the dream: the bitch was Celestina, the pit the sin of unchastity into which she had almost fallen. She goes down on her knees, begs and obtains forgiveness, and the play closes with a discourse on the necessity of bringing up children in the paths of virtue.

This is an ingenious ending, considering the limitations under which the author worked, and he deserves none the less credit in that he lifted the device of the dream from the *Rudens* of Plautus where a father's dream leads to the rescue of his daughter from slavery. In spite of the author's firm intent to moralize his source, he was not without some sympathy for Calisto, and the Chaucerian stanzas in which the play is written more than once give expression to love-longing in lines that approach true poetry. Here, at least in choice of theme, was a real beginning of romantic comedy. But the age of More, dominated as it was by social and ethical studies and shortly overwhelmed by theological controversy, was unfruitful ground for this genre. We must wait till well into the reign of Elizabeth for another example of a play dealing with romantic love drawn from a foreign source.

The author of *Calisto and Melibea* is unknown; the writer of the next romantic comedy was a distinguished figure in early Elizabethan literature, George Gascoigne (1525?-77), scholar, soldier, poet, and playwright. While a resident at Gray's Inn in 1566 he and a fellow student, Francis Kinwelmarsh, arranged a pair of plays for the entertainment of the society, a comedy and a tragedy. The tragedy, *Jocasta*, does not concern us; the comedy, *Supposes*, in which Gascoigne worked alone, is one of the landmarks in the evolution of English drama. Not that there is anything original in it; it is simply a translation of one of the earliest, and perhaps the most famous, of Italian comedies, the *Suppositi* of Ariosto. Gascoigne's merit consists in his recognition of this type of play as fit for presentation to the learned society of the Inn and also in choosing the prose version of the Italian comedy rather than the verse. To drop the lumbering verse forms of contemporary drama in favor of a brisk and lively prose dialogue was at once original and daring.

The story of the *Suppositi,* followed step by step in *Supposes,* may be briefly told.

> A young Siciliañ student at Ferrara falls in love with the daughter of a rich citizen. To gain access to her he exchanges clothes and names with his servant and enters her father's house. Here he not only wins the lady's heart but enters into secret marital relations with her. Their love, however, is threatened by the suit of a rich lawyer for her hand. To block the lawyer's suit, the disguised servant, posing as the student, enrolls as a suitor, offering a dowry to match the lawyer's. Since this dowry, however, must come from his patrimony, he needs a father to guarantee his offer, and persuades a foolish stranger in the town to play the father's role. Unhappily just at this time the true father arrives on the scene and is startled to find the servant posing as his. son, and still more shocked when the roguish fellow disclaims all knowledge of him. He appeals to the lawyer to help him in his trouble, and the servant is about to be convicted of malicious impersonation, theft, or murder, when a report comes to them that makes things still worse. The citizen has discovered his daughter's intrigue and has locked her lover up for condign punishment. Overwhelmed by the news, the servant now confesses all; he is pardoned since, strange to say, he turns out to be the lawyer's long-lost son. The visiting father, rejoiced to find his son alive, patches up the affair with the girl's father and unites the young lovers in a proper marriage.

Students of the classics will recognize the indebtedness of the Italian play and of Gascoigne's version to Plautine comedy, particularly in the clever handling of the intrigue, the mistaken identity business, and the discovery of a lost child. Readers of Shakespeare, on the other hand, will at once note the likeness of the action to the minor plot of *The Taming of the Shrew.* It is this anticipation of greater things that gives *Supposes* a place in the history of English comedy. At a time when pale imitations of the classics were in vogue in academic circles, Gascoigne was bold enough to translate an Italian comedy that dealt with a romantic love affair. He did not shy off from the shady side of the affair nor did he feel bound like the author of *Calisto* to alter the conclusion and append a moral. And in his translation he renders in a manner quite new in English the sparkling dialogue of his original.

Supposes was, as it deserved to be, a successful play. It was reprinted more than once, and seems to have been revived for performance in an Oxford College some years after Gascoigne's death. It may, indeed, have set a fashion of translating and adapting Italian comedies for the English stage. Some time after 1566—the date is uncertain—an unknown author adapted *La Spiritata* by Grazzini, 1561, for performance by a company of boys. As this play, *The Bugbears*,[4] remained in manuscript till the end of the last century it can hardly have been generally known or exerted any special influence. We need only remark that the author did not follow Gascoigne's example of writing in prose; on the contrary he turned the prose of his original into clumsy English Alexandrines. Spenser's friend, Gabriel Harvey, by no means a kindly critic, pronounced *Supposes* 'a fine comedie,' and we know from the Harvey-Spenser correspondence of 1578-9 that Spenser himself had written nine comedies in the manner of Ariosto. These are lost, but in 1585 a comedy, *Fedele and Fortunio,* was published, 'translated out of the Italian [Pasqualigo's *Il Fedele*] . . . as it hath been presented before the Queen's most excellent Majesty.' This is probably the work of Anthony Munday, one of the earliest, as he was one of the busiest, Elizabethan playwrights. Records of payments for plays at Court now lost seem to show various other comedies of presumably Italian origin —*Ariodante and Genevora,* for example, in February 1583.

For the sake of completeness and because of its relation to Shakespeare, it may be well to mention here Whetstone's *Promos and Cassandra,* 1578, the well-known source of *Measure for Measure.* Whetstone, it seems, sent this two-part, ten-act play to the printer when he was about to sail with Sir Humphrey Gilbert. Four years later he retold the tale in prose in his *Heptameron of Civil Discourses,* remarking incidentally that his play had never been performed. We must, of course, take his word for this, but the careful stage directions for costume and 'business' seem to show that he had meant it for the stage and in the uncertainty of his return from the voyage had rushed it at once into print. What concerns us here is that *Promos and Cassandra* is a dramatization of an Italian *novella,* one of the *Hecatommiti* of Cintio, 1565. Whetstone, to be sure, does not admit this; in fact he

[4] First printed in *Archiv für das Studium Neueren Sprachen,* 1896-7.

denounces Italian comedies as 'so lascivious that honest hearers are grieved.' He deals very freely with his source, bringing in a good deal of low comedy which is lacking in the Italian; one scene, where a rustic lover is shaved and loses his purse, is directly taken over from *Damon and Pythias*. The most important change, however, is that he spares the life of the heroine's condemned brother, as Shakespeare was later to spare Claudio. All this prepares the way for the frequent drafts upon Italian narrative and drama made not only by Shakespeare but by many of his fellow playwrights. It became a convention, in fact, to set the scene of a romantic comedy in an Italian background.

It may be noted in closing that after the false dawn of *Calisto and Melibea* there is no trace of the new romantic spirit in English comedy for nearly half a century. Then examples multiply: dramatic versions of chivalric romance, and comedies dealing with the theme of love. As the study of classic models served to bring form, technique, and a sense of structure into English comedy, so the new romantic impulse at once quickened and heightened the native drama. The examples we have discussed are, it must be confessed, poor specimens of dramatic art, but they show a dawning recognition of new values. Gone, for the most part, are the scenes of horseplay, the beatings and buffetings of the old native comedy; gone too, for the most part at least, is the 'humor of filth' that defiles so many Morals. Not that this early romantic comedy is as chaste as Galahad; it indulges often enough in *double entendre*, or in broader jest, but it turns from the stench of ordure to dally with the humorous side of sex. And apart from and above this, it seeks no longer to edify, but to delight by presenting romantic adventure and romantic love.

3

The New Comedy

ELIZABETHAN drama proper, the drama of Shakespeare, his immediate predecessors, and his contemporaries, is not coterminous with the reign of Elizabeth. The period from her accession, 1558, for nearly a quarter of a century is one of transition and confusion. Old forms of drama, Miracles, Morals, and Interludes, still maintain a struggle for existence, though gradually yielding to the impact of classical conceptions of form and to the infusion of the romantic spirit. Two things were needed before a full-fledged English drama could come to life: actors to perform it and theaters where it could be performed. Toward the close of this period both these needs were supplied and the ground was prepared for the sudden flowering of Elizabethan drama in the 1580's.

The amateur performers of medieval drama had been to a large extent superseded in the late fifteenth and early sixteenth century by little groups of professional actors. These groups rarely consisted of more than six men with a boy or two, as is shown by the frequent statement on the title-pages of late Morals and Interludes: 'Six may play it easily.' For a considerable period these actors, deserters from the crafts and guilds, were regarded as masterless men, mere vagabonds, liable to arrest and punishment as vagrants. As early as the close of the fifteenth century, however, they had found a way to evade the law by enrolling themselves as the 'servants' of some nobleman. One of the earliest instances of such a connection is the company that in 1482 enjoyed the patronage of the Duke of Gloucester, later Richard III. No doubt such service was often merely nominal, and strolling companies usurped or abused the privilege. Accordingly, in 1572 an act was passed limiting the number of such companies. This had the natural and immediate effect of strengthening those companies that survived, and from this time on we may notice the growth in number of members and in importance of various groups, which, under different names as their patrons varied, became the mainstays of the new drama.

Chief among these companies were the servants of the Queen's favorite, the Earl of Leicester, of such high officials as the Lord Chamberlain and the Lord Admiral, and for a decade, 1583-93, of the Queen herself. These companies, organized somewhat in the fashion of the craft guilds, with 'masters,' i.e. full members sharing alike profit and loss, with 'journeymen,' i.e. actors hired for a term at a fixed wage, and with 'apprentices,' i.e. boys bound to the service of individual masters, were able to present Elizabethan drama in a way that would have been impossible to the small strolling groups. And this became the more possible when in the 'seventies and 'eighties these companies found themselves possessed of fixed and permanent playhouses. From then on they ceased to be 'strollers'; periods of plague that closed the theaters might drive them from time to time to touring the provinces, but it was upon a London paying audience that their existence depended.

Even before the establishment of these companies in permanent playhouses, the children's companies had contributed to the development of the drama. These were not groups of children, casually assembled to perform a play, nor the schoolboys who presented a play composed for them by a drama-loving master. They were the regularly maintained choir boys of the Royal Chapel, commonly known as the Chapel Children, the choir boys of Windsor and those of St. Paul's Cathedral. They were trained to act as well as to sing, and were special favorites at Court. Little by little their training took on a theatrical rather than a liturgical character, and by the close of the century they had become, as a well-known passage in *Hamlet* shows, the rivals of the adult companies. Shakespeare, through the mouth of the Prince of Denmark, asks whether they would 'pursue the quality,' i.e. continue acting, after their voices changed. He did not know that Nat Field, one of the Chapel Children, was to become a leading member in Shakespeare's own company in the year of the poet's death.

It was in 1576 that William Farrant, Master of the Windsor choir, who had been presenting plays with them at Court every year since 1566, leased some space in the old building that had once been the Blackfriars monastery in a fashionable part of London, avowedly for rehearsing his boys there for Court performances, actually, as he later confessed, with the idea of making money by charging admission to rehearsals and preliminary performances. The notion of a theater, even a 'private' theater, as the Blackfriars was called, in the very heart of London was most repugnant to the stricter sort of citizens, and the owner of the property, Sir William More, started a law suit against Farrant that ended in the closing of this theater. Before this, however, a successor to Farrant in the lease was able to use its stage for the production of a play, Lyly's *Campaspe,* 1583.

In the same year in which Farrant acquired a theater for his children, James Burbage, a member of Leicester's Company, conceived the happy idea of a permanent playhouse for himself and his fellow-actors. They had played at Court more than once in the early 'sixties, but they had spent much time upon the road. In 1574, however, the Queen licensed them by special patent to play in London itself in spite of the objection of the city magistrates. It may have been this special favor that encouraged Burbage to act. He was a poor man, but he enlisted the aid of his brother-in-law, a rich grocer, obtained a lease on a plot of land north of the city wall, clapped a mortgage on it, and began building the playhouse of his dream. He worked on it with his own hands, for he was a carpenter by trade, and actually had plays showing there before the building was completed, 1576-7. He called it 'The Theatre' and until his death in 1597 it was continuously occupied by his own and other companies.

It is not necessary to repeat the well-known descriptions of the Elizabethan theater. Suffice it to say that this first of them was built by an actor for his fellow-actors and was exactly suited to their needs. It proved, indeed, to be the inspiration and the model for playhouse after playhouse that sprang up in the next twenty years. The Curtain, so called from the plot of land on which it stood, was built in 1577 in the near neighborhood of The Theatre. When The Theatre was closed in 1597, Shakespeare's Company occupied the Curtain and performed *Romeo and Juliet* and other plays on its boards. After Burbage's death his sons, Richard, the famous actor, and Cuthbert, who seems to have inherited his father's business ability, found themselves unable to obtain a renewal of the lease of the land on which The Theatre stood. The landlord, a Mr. Allen, apparently planned to seize the building and take over the profits. To foil this design the Burbage brothers tore the old building down, carted the materials across the Thames, and there erected the most famous of Elizabethan playhouses, the Globe, open for performances some time in 1599.

Their choice of this situation on the Surrey side was, no doubt, due to the fact that the Bankside, on which the Globe was built, had long been a favorite playground for Londoners, lying as it did outside of the control of the city magistrates. In fact two theaters had already been erected there: the Rose, 1587-8, financed by the enterprising Henslowe and managed apparently by the great actor, Alleyn; also the Swan, 1595-6, of which an interesting sketch remains.

The Burbage invasion of the Bankside seems to have roused Henslowe and Alleyn to counteraction; in the next year, 1600, they moved north across the Thames into a northwest suburb of the city, and built there the Fortune, modeled almost exactly upon the pattern of the Globe and called by a contemporary 'the finest play-house in this town.' Both the Globe and the Fortune caught fire and burned down; both were promptly rebuilt by their owners. The example set by James Burbage had proved profitable.

All these theaters were, of course, the so-called 'public' playhouses, open to the sky except for the roofed-in galleries and a portion of the stage. Farrant's Blackfriars, on the contrary, had been constructed out of part of the old monastery and was protected by roof and walls from wind and rain. It occurred to James Burbage some time in 1596 that a playhouse of this sort would be a fine addition to his Theatre, affording a place where his company could act, and where a select audience could watch them at ease, in the vile weather of a London winter. Accordingly he rallied all his resources and for £600, a handsome sum in those days, bought a set of rooms in the old building, which he began to remodel into a sheltered 'private' theater. But the same prejudice that had ousted Farrant's successor worked now against Burbage. A petition against a playhouse in their neighborhood was sent up to the Privy Council. The petition was granted; the rebuilding stopped, and the disappointed projector laid himself down and died, leaving the unoccupied rooms to his son Richard.

In 1600 Richard rented these rooms to a certain Evans, who planned to bring the Chapel Children there. Apparently there was less objection to the Children's rehearsing, as the pretext was, for plays at Court, and Evans and his partners ran the second Blackfriars theater for some eight years. Their productions rivaled those at the Globe and they gathered a brilliant group of playwrights, Ben Jonson among them, to supply plays. By 1608, however, Evans was in deep trouble by reason of plays offensive to authority—*Eastward Ho, Biron,* and others; the Children's performances were stopped, and the Burbage brothers were able to resume the lease. By this time their company, for which Shakespeare had already written some of his best plays, had become the King's Majesty's Servants and Grooms of the Royal Chamber. Naturally no unfriendly petition objected to performances by such a company before the select audience that had become accustomed to patronize the Children's plays. Blackfriars now became the 'private,' especially the winter, theater of Shakespeare's Company, and till the closing of the theaters in 1642 it was a far better paying property than the Globe.

Enough has been said to show how the ground had been prepared, companies of actors properly organized, and theaters erected. Only playwrights were lacking and now they came with a rush. In the early 'eighties one young poet after another appeared in London, intent on winning fame and fortune by his pen. There was then no reading public able to support them, so they turned of necessity to the theater, lured by the hope of fame and by the cash paid for stage copy. We must not think of these young writers as constituting a school with a formula for creating a new drama. They were sometimes friends, sometimes strangers and even enemies; each was an individual genius with something of his own to contribute to the stage. They had, however, this in common: they were born poets, inventors, rebels against the accepted dramatic conventions of their day. They were, too, university men, scholars trained in classical studies, yet at the same time imbued with the romantic spirit, eager to express their love of novelty and beauty in prose romances, lyric verse, or drama. They were the forerunners and the masters of Shakespeare, for when he came to London, sometime probably in the late 'eighties, it was their plays that were packing the theaters. We must remember, too, that such plays as theirs were new to the youth from rural Stratford. We know that Shakespeare's father, bailiff of Stratford in 1568-9, granted permission to Worcester's company to play in the town, the first theatrical performance recorded in the Stratford annals. William, then a boy of four years or less, was too young, we might think, to see the show, but we happen to have a charming contemporary account by a boy just Shakespeare's age of a performance that same year in near-by Gloucester. 'I stood between my father's legs,' he says, 'while he sat upon one of the benches and where he saw and heard very well.' What this boy saw and heard was *The Cradle of Security*, an old Moral cut down to Interlude length, and a play like this, apart from a possible sight of the antiquated Miracle cycle at Coventry, is the only sort of performance that the boy Shakespeare probably can have seen.

In 1586-7, however, two of the best companies of the day, Leicester's and the Queen's Men, visited Stratford. Even though they brought none of the new plays with them, the tales the actors told of London, of theaters, plays, and lucky playwrights, must have burned in young Shakespeare's heart and lured him to the city.

What Shakespeare's wondering eyes saw there was to him a new drama. It is needless here to discuss Elizabethan drama as a whole, but three writers of comedy do deserve particular consideration. Of these the oldest and the most immediately successful was John Lyly. Born in 1553 or 1554 of a gentle Hampshire family, he studied at Oxford where he took the degrees of B.A. in 1573 and M.A. in 1575. Coming to London he enjoyed the friendship of Lord Delawar, to whom he dedicated his first work, *Euphues,* 1578, sometimes called the first English novel. It seems to us today a long-winded and tedious piece of moralizing, couched in an elaborately fantastic style, but it attained an instant and unparalleled success. Editions poured from the press in rapid succession for ten years, and a sequel, *Euphues and his England,* was almost as well received. Fifty years later Blount, who collected some of Lyly's plays for publication as *Six Courtly Comedies* (1632), declares: 'Our nation are in his debt for a new English which he taught them. . . All our ladies were then his scholars and that beauty in Court which could not parley Euphuism was as little regarded as she which now there speaks not French'—this at a time, be it noted, when the young French Queen, Henrietta Maria, was setting the fashion of speech at the court of Charles I.

Lyly's success attracted the attention of the brilliant Earl of Oxford, himself a poet and a playwright, and Oxford's influence secured him a lease of Farrant's theater in Blackfriars. Here his *Campaspe* was performed in 1583, followed by a presentation at Court by the combined Chapel Children and Paul's Boys on New Year's night. It was quickly followed by *Sapho and Phao* on Shrove Tuesday, i.e. 3 March 1584. Shortly thereafter the owner of Blackfriars succeeded in closing the theater, but he could not close Lyly's mouth. The unprecedented success of *Campaspe*—three editions were published within a year—led to Lyly's informal appointment as playwright in chief to Paul's Boys. For them he wrote one of his most characteristic comedies, *Gallathea,* early in 1585, also performed before the Queen, as was his masterpiece, *Endimion, c.* 1588. *Midas* was played at Court by this company in 1590; *Mother Bombie* of uncertain date did not attain a Court presentation, but it too was acted by Paul's Boys in their own theater. So was *Love's Metamorphosis,* later performed, apparently in a revised form, by the Chapel Children, *c.* 1600-1601. Lyly's last play, *The Woman in the Moon,* sometime in the early 'nineties, is the only one with which Paul's Boys were not concerned. It seems to have been written for an unknown company after the plays at Paul's had been suppressed in 1591.

This suppression seems to have been caused by Lyly's unlucky connection with the scandalous Marprelate controversy. A savage Puritan attack upon the episcopal government of the Church of England was answered by a counterattack in the form of lampoons, scurrilous pamphlets, and satirical plays, the work of various young writers who probably hated Puritans more than they loved the Church. It is not unlikely that Lyly had a hand in some of the plays; it is certain that one of them was played by Paul's Boys. But the Queen and her Council were as determined to keep plays dealing with matters of religion off the stage as they were to prosecute radical attacks upon the Church, and Paul's Boys were silenced for about nine years. This interruption seems to have put a stop to Lyly's play-making. Always something of a courtier rather than a professional man of letters, he now sought preferment in other ways. He entered Parliament and sat in four sessions of the House of Commons. He was a long and fruitless petitioner for office, and like Spenser he suffered from hope deferred. Lyly's petition to the Queen in 1598 is a veritable cry from the depths:

> Most gracious and dread Sovereign [it begins], thirteen years your Highness servant but yet nothing; twenty friends that though they say they will be sure, I find them sure too slow; a hundred promises, but yet nothing. Thus casting up an inventory of my friends, hopes, promises, and times, the sum total amounteth to just nothing . . . I bequeath my patience to my creditors, melancholy without measure to my friends, and beggary without shame to my family.

One feels that Lyly had better have stuck to the stage, and yet there are signs that his period of popularity in the theater had waned as swiftly as it had waxed. In the 'nineties other and better poets had stormed the stage, and except for one experiment in verse, *The Woman in the Moon,* Lyly was silent until his death in 1606. One would give something to hear his comment upon such masterpieces of comedy as *A Midsummer Night's Dream, Much Ado,* and *Twelfth Night,* all of which he lived to see.

Lyly wrote comedies only and, with one exception, comedies of a certain genre, adapted for presentation at Court. Yet there is less monotony and more variation of type than a hasty reading would reveal. *Campaspe* deals with historical figures: Alexander the Great, Campaspe, his fair captive, and the painter Apelles. *Sapho and Phao* treats of the legendary passion of the heroine for a lovely youth, but with a gay disregard of history and legend it changes her from a Lesbian poetess into a Princess of Syracuse. *Gallathea* is what Lyly called another of his plays, a 'Gallimaufry . . . a mingle-mangle.'

> The moving force is the wrath of Neptune demanding the yearly sacrifice of a fair virgin to a sea monster. This is an old classical motif, but here Neptune's wrath has been incurred by sacrilegious Danes who destroyed his temple in Leicestershire, of all places in the world, and the monster is none other than a local tidal wave, the Aigre. As if this were not enough, Diana's nymphs, who haunt the woods of Leicestershire, fall victims to the wiles of Cupid, who in turn is seized and punished by Diana. Venus intervenes to free her son and induces Neptune to remit the virgin tribute. Into this 'gallimaufry' of classical deities Lyly introduces characters from contemporary life: three shipwrecked boys, an alchemist, and an astrologer, who contribute nothing to the action except a few farcical scenes. Yet this summary omits the central theme of the play, the mutual passion of two pretty girls, disguised as boys to escape the virgin tribute. Their dilemma is solved by the promise of Venus to change one of them—Lyly doesn't say which and it doesn't matter—into a real boy.

In *Endimion* classic deities are absent, although the source of the poem is the lovely Greek myth of the passion of Selene, the moon-goddess, for a sleeping shepherd boy. In Lyly's transformation the moon-goddess, Cynthia, becomes an earthly queen, ruling a court where Lady Tellus, the earth, is at once her subject and her rival, and Endimion is her favored courtier. Around this trio play a group of lords, ladies, and pages, along with a foolish Sir Tophas, and a Constable and his Watch off the streets of Elizabethan London. *Midas* reintroduces the gods of Greek mythology, Bacchus to bestow on the king the fatal gift of the golden touch, Apollo to equip him with asses' ears for his folly. The inevitable pages are present, along with a group of pastoral shepherds, but the only contemporary note is the patent identification of Midas with Philip of Spain, and his enemies of the Lesbian isle with England. *Mother Bombie,* on the other hand, stands alone among Lyly's plays in discarding both classical theme and apparatus.

It dramatizes a tale of contemporary life in the English town of Rochester somewhat after the pattern of *Roister Doister,* but with a plot more complicated than the most tangled plays of Plautus. Lyly's one condescension here to the classical taste of his audience is to baptize all his characters, except the page, Halfpenny, with Latin names: Memphio, Prisius, Dromio, and so on.

In *Love's Metamorphosis* Lyly reverts again to classic myth, the curse of famine imposed by Ceres upon Erisichthon for his violation of her sacred tree. This myth, however, is a mere framework in which he sets the wooing of three coy nymphs of Ceres by three enamored shepherds, the metamorphosis of the nymphs by the angry god of love, and their restoration to human form on condition of yielding to his power. Contemporary realistic figures are wanting in this play; possibly they were cut out when it was revised; a Lylian play without his pages seems quite unusual. The heroine of his last play, *The Woman in the Moon,* is the classical Pandora, the all-gifted woman. Lyly departs, however, from the classic legend: his Pandora is created by Nature in answer to the prayers of a masculine world, and around her he constructs a masque-like play in which the heroine, dominated in turn by the seven gods who preside over the seven planets, runs through all the changes from overweening ambition to raving madness, until at last she is transported to the moon to get her out of harm's way.

It is easy to dismiss Lyly's plays as artificial. They are so, indeed, but artifice postulates an artist, and it is not too much to say that Lyly is the first conscious artist in the field of English comedy. He knew what he wished to do and proceeded to do it, expanding, elaborating, and embroidering his design as he progressed. His intention plainly was to rescue comedy from its low estate and to make it an entertainment fit for gentle folk, more especially for gentle ladies.

Lyly refined English comedy in various ways. He excised the horseplay, the scuffles and beatings that had been laugh-getters from the time of the Miracles. One exception, indeed, occurs in his last and least characteristic play, when Pandora lays about her with her hands and even strikes an amorous shepherd with a spear, but this behavior is meant to show in action the influence exercised upon the heroine by malignant planets; it has dramatic, rather than merely comic, significance. For the same purpose of refinement he dropped the popular comic characters of the Devil and the Vice, with their vulgar speech and rowdy action; he does not even permit himself the Court Fool or the Country Bumpkin. Again a possible exception occurs in his last play, where Gunophilus approaches the type of the foolish comic servant frequent in the plays of Shakespeare. Apparently in this play Lyly condescended to write a buffo part for the comic actor of some unknown company. Most important of all, Lyly refined the dialogue of comedy. His comedies might be read aloud to a church sewing-circle without raising a blush.

These are, of course, negative virtues, but there are positive values in Lyly's comedies. He had the art of telling an entertaining story in dramatic form. His themes from classic myth and legend are cleverly reshaped to catch the fancy of an Elizabethan audience. Moreover, these plays on classic themes are touched with the spirit of romance: the love motif is ever present, naturally and rightly, for they are courtly plays, and courtiers, Lyly tells us, call for comedies—'their theme is love.' Love in Lyly's plays, is, to be sure, a graceful fancy rather than a consuming passion; we look in vain in them for a Juliet or an Antony, but we are not far from the lovers of Shakespeare's early comedies. Even this fancy Lyly handles with careful restraint; an 'obligatory scene,' the confession by Apelles and Campaspe of their mutual love, was never written; we must imagine it off-stage. Other romantic notes are also heard: that of friendship rising superior to love, an old motif in medieval romance, reappears in *Endimion,* as it does later in *Two Gentlemen of Verona.* In *Endimion* we find also a magic fountain whose secret can be read only by a true lover; here, too, are the fairies and the witchcraft of folklore. Lyly's favorite poet seems to have been Ovid, the most romantic of Latin authors, and it is from Ovid that Lyly lifts the magical transformations that occur in several of his plays.

The strain of allegory, ethical and personal, that runs through some of Lyly's plays must have given them an added interest to his con-temporaries, as it does, indeed, to modern scholars. There has been, perhaps, too much scholarly industry expended in the attempt to pluck out the heart of Lyly's mystery; his allegory, like that of *The Faerie Queene,* is veiled and shifting. It is plain enough in *Midas;* in *Sapho* the heroine's conquest of her passion may, perhaps, reflect Elizabeth's final rejection of the suit of Alençon. In *Endimion* there is little doubt but that Cynthia, a name applied by other Elizabethan poets to the Queen, is at once Elizabeth and the moon-goddess of the legend; the hero may, perhaps, be Leicester, lately restored to royal favor. This identification, however, is not necessary; Endimion may quite as well represent an ideal courtier, smitten with that fantastic blend of love and adoration which was a recognized fashion in the great Queen's days. On the other hand, the play may be interpreted as a dramatic allegory of the soul of man, divided between heavenly and earthly love, cast into oblivious sleep by the charms of earth, yet restored to life by divine grace, the kiss of Cynthia. A passage of brilliant creative criticism in Thorndike's *English Comedy* reconstructs a Court performance of *Endimion,* showing spectators guessing at the half-hidden meaning. Probably Lyly meant at once to puzzle and to intrigue his hearers; after all, he had saved himself from discovery by his warning in the Prologue against 'the application of pastimes,' i.e. personal interpretations of the play, and by his frank avowal that *Endimion* was only 'a tale of the man in the moon.'

Character portrayal of the finest sort is beyond the reach of Lyly's art, yet even here he has something to contribute to the development of English comedy. His characters are more varied than those of earlier plays, which usually run along certain conventional lines. He is fond of introducing humorous eccentric figures to contrast with, sometimes to comment upon, the high-flown sentiment of the main action. Such, for example, is Sir Tophas, whose sudden passion for the witch, Dipsas, affords a comic contrast to the ideal devotion of Endimion to Cynthia. The cynic, Diogenes, utters satiric comment upon the heroic aims of Alexander. Figures from contemporary life, like the shipwrecked boys in *Gallathea,* mingle with nymphs and goddesses; Lyly's recurrent pages form a characteristic group of gay, impertinent young rogues with a special turn for mocking their masters. One may find their counterpart from time to time in various plays of Shakespeare. It is in his characterization of women, however, that Lyly excels himself. He was, it seems, peculiarly interested in feminine sentiment and psychology, and his command of a company of boys to interpret his parts enabled him to exhibit more, and more varying, female characters in one play than was at all possible for a dramatist depending upon a traveling troupe with its one or two boys for women's parts. In a single play, *Endimion,* Lyly's women run through the scale of feminine qualities from the queenly Cynthia through the passionate Tellus and the sharp-tongued Semele to the tender Floscula and the repulsive witch. In *Sapho* he shows us a group of girls jesting at love: 'We are mad wenches if men mark our words,' one of them says, 'where we cry "away," do we not presently say "go to" '—they are prototypes of the wise girls that mock their lovers in the comedies of Shakespeare. And, indeed, on the lighter side of love Lyly has something to teach the greater master.

It is in the field of language, however, in dramatic dialogue, that Lyly makes his main contribution to Elizabethan comedy. The mere fact that all his plays except the last are written in prose is in itself a new and surprising phenomenon. Gascoigne's *Supposes* had, of course, been written in prose years before Lyly's first comedy, but *Supposes* is an academic play, never, so far as is known, performed before a public audience. Lyly may, perhaps, have caught a suggestion from Gascoigne, but the author of *Euphues,* the inventor of a new and dazzling style of prose discourse, needed little suggestion to apply this style to dramatic dialogue. It is possible, indeed, to note the characteristic marks of Euphuism in Lyly's first play and to watch their slow but steady diminution as he feels more and more assured of his power of expression. Between *Supposes,* 1566, and *Campaspe,* 1583, English comedy still clung to the old verse forms. A quotation from *Damon and Pythias,* 1571, may serve as a convenient contrast to Lyly's prose.

> Thrice happy are we
> Whom true love hath joined in perfect amity;
> Which amity first sprung—without vaunting be it spoken—that
> is true—
> Of likeness of manners, took root by company, and now is con-
> served by virtue;
> Which virtue always, though worldly things do not frame,
> Yet doth she achieve to her followers immortal fame.

Compare Lyly in *Endimion* on the same topic of friendship:

> Believe me, Eumenides, Desire dies in the same moment that Beauty sickens, and Beauty fadeth in the same instant that it flourisheth. When adversities flow, then love ebbs, but friendship standeth stiffly in storms. . . O friendship! of all things the most rare, and therefore most rare because most excellent, whose comforts in misery is always sweet, and whose counsels in prosperity are ever fortunate.

Yet this is not Lyly at his best; it is part of a long set speech and in such passages he is apt to give free rein to his euphuistic impulse. Take now a bit of dialogue. Apelles and Campaspe are hesitating over a declaration of love, which he fears to make and she hesitates to evoke:

APEL.: What might men doe to be beleeved?

CAMP.: Whet their tongues on their heartes.

APEL.: So they doe, and speake as they thinke.

CAMP.: I would they did!!

APEL.: I would they did not!!

CAMP.: Why, would you have them dissemble?

APEL.: Not in love, but their love. But will you give mee leave to ask you a question without offence?

CAMP.: So that you will aunswere mee an other without excuse.

APEL.: Whom doe you love best in the world?

CAMP.: He that made me last in the world.

(That is, of course, Apelles himself who has just painted her portrait.) The interchange gocs on. . .

APEL.: That was a God.

CAMP.: I thought it had beene a man. But whom doe you honour most, Apelles?

APEL.: The thing that is likest you, Campaspe.

CAMP.: My picture?

APEL.: I dare not venture upon your person. But come, let us go in: for Alexander will thinke it long till we returne.

These two extracts mark the extremes of Lyly's prose in drama. He is fond—too fond in his early plays—of long tirades that must have taxed the wind of his boy actors. On the other hand, he is a master of swift give and take in repartee which points, as nothing else in earlier comedy does, to the wit-combats in Shakespeare's plays.

Lyly was less of a poet than most of his fellows among the young playwrights. Yet he has the art to steep his prose in poetic imagery. Here, for example, is Cupid's curse upon a hardhearted girl whom he is about to transform into a rose:

Thy face as fair as the damask rose, shall perish like the damask rose; the canker shall eat thee in the bud, and every little wind shall blow thee from the stalk.

There is a fragrance of sentiment in this which contrasts sharply with the sheer extravagance of the Astronomer's boast in *Gallathea:* 'When I list I can set a trap for the sun, catch the moon with lime-twigs, and go a batfowling for stars.'

Like the good Elizabethan that he was Lyly loved to play with words. His command of all the tricks of style, alliteration, assonance, and repetition was pushed to excess in his *Euphues,* but in his plays he checked his tendency to extravagance and imparted to his prose dialogue a free and flowing rhythm not even approached in earlier drama. Here is an example from *Gallathea* where a boy is bidding farewell to the Alchemist, his master.

> ALCHEMIST: Why, thou has not yet seene the ende of my arte.
> RAFFE: I would I had not known the beginning. Did not you promise me, of my silver thimble to make a whole cupboard of plate, and that of a Spanish needle you would build a silver steeple?

There is nothing new in Lyly's decoration of his dialogue with songs; that had been an established practice for a century or so. The authorship of the songs in Lyly's plays has been questioned upon what seem insufficient grounds; they were certainly thought to be his by Blount, the first editor of his plays. And if they are Lyly's, they show him in command of a true lyric gift, unmatched in earlier comedy. Apelles' song, 'Cupid and my Campaspe,' has found its way into many anthologies; Shakespeare himself did not scorn to lift a phrase from Lyly's bird-song, where the lark claps her wings 'at heaven's gate'; and the Fairies in the *Merry Wives* echo the notes of their forerunners in *Endimion.*

Conscious artist that he was, Lyly had a very definite conception of his aim in comedy. 'Our intent was at this time,' he says in the Prologue to *Sapho and Phao,* 'to move inward delight, not outward lightness, and to breed (if it might be) soft smiling, not loud laughter.' This is not far from Meredith's test of true comedy, the awakening of 'thoughtful laughter.' The audience to which Lyly appealed resembled in more ways than one Meredith's requirement for the audience of the comic poet: 'a society of cultivated men and women.' The courtly circle that Lyly addressed was cultivated enough to appreciate his choice of classic themes, his quotations from classic poets, and his frequent scraps of Latin prose. Meredith demands also a society in which women have attained a certain social equality with men, and that was surely the case in the courtly circle dominated by a cultured, proud, and pleasure-loving Queen. To this society Lyly offered a comedy of entertaining plots, shaped with classic art, and imbued with the romantic spirit. Yet even in his own day Lyly's career after a brief and brilliant success ended in comparative failure. The reason is not far to seek: Lyly's comedy lacked for the most part the native strain of realism; it was out of touch with the broad stream of national life. His 'dreams,' his 'tales of a man in the moon,' are insubstantial pageants which fade and leave not a mark behind.

The contribution of George Peele, 1557-96, to English comedy is, perhaps, less important than that of Lyly, but it is closer to the national and natural line of development. He was the son of a Londoner, a clerk in Christ's Hospital, from whom he seems to have inherited a love of the stage, for the elder Peele was known as a maker of civic pageants. Like Lyly, Peele studied at Oxford, taking the degrees of B.A. in 1577 and M.A. in 1579. An order by the Governors of the Hospital, 1579, directing the elder Peele to eject his son from his lodging there, shows the presence of the young graduate in London and probably suggests already the riotous life for which he later became notorious. He had not, however, lost credit at Oxford, where he was already known as a poet and play-maker; we find him there in 1583 directing two Latin plays to be performed before an illustrious Polish visitor. It was, perhaps, the success of these performances that gave Peele his chance in London. In 1583-4 he was associated with Lyly in writing for the Chapel Children at Blackfriars, and his first play, *The Arraignment of Paris*, was performed by that company at Court in the spring of 1584. This is, to be sure, less a regular play than a lyric-dramatic pageant, culminating in an outburst of flattery of the Queen, extreme even by Elizabethan standards. One might have thought that such a performance would have won him Court favor, but the Chapel Children were silenced in that very year, and Peele turned to the adult companies and the public stage.

It is not easy to determine the chronology of Peele's plays; it is, in fact, impossible even to establish an exact canon of his work. His hand is shrewdly suspected in various anonymous plays, two of which, *The Troublesome Reign of King John* and *The Tragical History of King Leir*, served as sources for Shakespeare. He seems certainly to have led a busy life as poet and playwright. He composed the Lord Mayor's Pageant in 1585 and another in 1591; he wrote a *Farewell* to Drake and Norris on their departure for the Portugal expedition in 1589, and a gratulatory poem to the popular favorite, Essex, on his return from that voyage. His *Polyhymnia*, 1590, commemorating the retirement of old Sir Henry Lee, the Queen's Champion, contains the lovely song, 'His golden locks Time hath to silver turned,' which Thackeray applied so gracefully to the old age of Colonel Newcome. In the field of drama we can be sure of only four plays after *The Arraignment: The Battle of Alcazar, c.* 1589, a hasty dramatization of the famous Battle of Three Kings in Africa; *Edward I,* a chronicle play; *David and Bethsabe,* an interesting attempt to present a Bible story in terms of Elizabethan drama; and his masterpiece, *The Old Wives' Tale.* Two of his plays are certainly lost, *The Hunting of Cupid,* which Drummond of Hawthornden read and copied bits from, and *Mahomet and Hiren,* from which Shakespeare's Pistol spouts a phrase.

As early as 1589 Nashe had praised Peele as the 'Atlas of Poetry' and 'primus verborum artifex,' but the be-praised poet seems to have gone swiftly to the bad in the wild life of London playhouses and taverns. A book of scandalous tales, *The Jests of George Peele,* 1605, can hardly be taken as true biography; many of the jests are old stuff, going back to Villon and still further. Yet it is not without significance that they were retold of Peele. Not even an Elizabethan scandalmonger would have hung tales of such cheap and shabby roguery on the courtly Lyly or the passionate Marlowe. In 1596 Peele sent a pitiful begging letter, 'after long illness,' to Lord Burghley; he was buried in November of that year—'died by the pox,' wrote Meres two years later, but perhaps Meres was as wrong about Peele's death as he was about Marlowe's.

There is much of Peele's work that does not concern the student of English comedy, but there are three plays: a pastoral pageant, a chronicle, and a dramatized blend of folklore and romance, that reveal his special contribution to the genre and illustrate what Nashe so aptly called his 'manifold variety of invention.'

The first of these, *The Arraignment of Paris,* resembles the work of Lyly in that it places a classic theme in a romantic setting. But the tone and temper of the play is poles away from that of Lyly's comedies. It is wholly in verse; instead of Lyly's artful prose Peele uses verse of 'manifold variety'; stately blank verse, written at a time when Marlowe was still in college, lilting old-fashioned 'fourteeners,' and smooth pentameter couplets, interspersed with dainty lyrics. Peele, 'verborum artifex,' was from the beginning a true singer. His songs, moreover, are not detachable from the action like Lyly's but form an essential part of it. Take, for example, the duet of Paris and Oenone before the golden apple came to disturb their loves. 'They sing,' runs the old stage direction, 'and while Oenone singeth he pipeth.'

OEN.:
> Fair and fair and twice so fair,
>   As fair as any may be;
> The fairest shepherd on our green,
>   A love for any lady.

PAR.:
> Fair and fair and twice so fair,
>   As fair as any may be;
> Thy love is fair for thee alone,
>   And for no other lady.

OEN.:
> My love is fair, my love is gay,
>   As fresh as bin the flowers in May,
> And of my love my roundelay,
>   My merry merry roundelay,
> Concludes with Cupid's curse,—
> They that do change old love for new,
>   Pray gods they change for worse!

AMBO SIMUL.:
> They that do change, *et cetera.*

One can almost hear two boys of the Chapel Choir caroling this roundelay before the music-loving Queen and her Court

With a true Elizabethan disregard for decorum Peele introduces among the classic deities on Mount Ida a lovelorn shepherd, Colin, who, it seems, is no other than 'divine Master Spenser'—Nashe's phrase —surrounded by other 'Groomes' from the *Shepheardes Calendar.* Peele goes on to predict in verse the fate that threatens Thestylis— Spenser's Rosalind—when after her lover's death she squanders her affection on a 'foul crooked churl.' The Colin-Thestylis matter is a topical episode; the main theme of the play deals with Paris's award of the apple to Venus. He is arraigned for partiality before the full session of the gods; his decision is reversed, and the award of the apple is entrusted to Diana, who presents it to 'the nymph Eliza, a figure of the Queen.'

> In state Queen Juno's peer, for power in arms
> And virtues of the mind Minerva's mate,
> As fair and lovely as the Queen of Love,
> As chaste as Dian.

There is little chance for comic action in such a plot, though an occasional laugh may have been raised by Vulcan's limping pursuit of a nymph who blows a horn in his ear and runs away, or by the shambling Cyclops who comes with Mercury to arrest Paris. There is some light jesting about the amours of Venus, but no gross speech; the dialogue, though less pointed than Lyly's, is quite as clean and even more instinct with poetic sentiment as, for example, in Flora's words, preparing Mount Ida for the reception of the three goddesses:

> And round about the valley as ye pass,
> Ye may ne see for peeping flowers the grass.

Here is the true Elizabethan poetic utterance, heard for the first time in English drama.

Edward I (printed 1593) represents Peele's bid for popular applause as *The Arraignment* was for Court favor. This chronicle play was apparently printed from the author's manuscript—or a copy thereof—for it is signed at the end: 'By George Peele, Master of Arts at Oxenford.' But the manuscript seems to have been a playbook that had passed from hand to hand and had been revised and altered till it was left in a state of inextricable confusion. It is hard to believe that Peele, who constructed so neat a plot in his first play, was guilty of such careless work. That the play was popular and passed from company to company seems clear from the fact that Henslowe records a performance of *Longshanks*—Edward's nickname—fourteen times by the Admiral's Men in 1595-6 in a form marked in his diary *ne,* i.e. new or, at least, revised.

It is impossible to apply strict tests to a play that has come down to us in such a state; yet it is worth consideration as the sort of play that held the boards during Shakespeare's first years in London. It presents in action the career of a great English king from his triumphant return from a Crusade to his final defeat of the Welsh and Scottish rebels. It is imbued with the spirit of exultant nationalism that was rampant in England after the defeat of the Armada. To such a pitch, indeed, does this spirit carry Peele that he presents Edward's *chere reine,* Elinor of Castile, as a cruel and adulterous Spaniard, on no better evidence, apparently, than that of a contemporary ballad. The greater part of the play is written in bombastic blank verse; Peele, the juggler with words, seems to be trying to outdo the resonant verse of Marlowe. In marked contrast to this inflated style the comic scenes of the play are written alternately in rhyming doggrel and in lively prose, and it is in these scenes that the play contributes to Elizabethan comedy.

The central figure is a Friar, not the begging hypocrite of Heywood's Interlude, but a character straight out of English balladry, Friar Tuck of the Robin Hood cycle. Peele's hero is better equipped for comedy than Friar Tuck, for he has not only his quarterstaff, but also his wench, Guenthian, and his novice, Jack. The three are a musical trio and are always ready to break into song; Guenthian in fact favors the audience with a Welsh song, thus anticipating by some years Lady Mortimer's 'turn' in *King Henry IV*. Three Welsh princes, who meet this merry company, declare that it would be a deed of charity 'to remove this stumbling-block, a fair wench, a shrewd temptation to a friar's conscience.' But Friar David is a stout defender of his wench and he cudgels good lessons into the princes' jackets. Then just as Robin took Friar Tuck into his band after their bout at quarterstaff, Lluellen of Wales now makes Friar David his chaplain. The Robin theme continues, for ere long the Welshmen, beaten in the field by Edward, retire into the mountains, where they resolve to live the life of Robin and his men; Lluellen will be Robin, his lady Elinor, Maid Marian, his cousin Rice, Little John, 'and here's Friar David as fit as a die for Friar Tuck.' To make the company complete, Mortimer, the English lover of Elinor, joins them disguised as a potter, another figure in the Robin Hood cycle. Finally Edward himself appears in disguise, lays down half his money as the customary tribute to Robin, and offers to fight him for the whole. This, perhaps, is the first appearance in English drama of the disguised king in a humorous role; it lingers on, as we recall Prince Hal in Dame Quickly's tavern and King Henry on the night before Agincourt, to attain its final glorification in the meeting of the Black Knight with the Clerk of Copmanhurst in *Ivanhoe*.

This jolly fellowship is broken up by the conquering English; Lluellen is slain in battle and his brother David taken prisoner. Thereupon the Friar hangs up his quarterstaff with a farewell song and goes down on his knees to beg a pardon of Mortimer. Along with his boy and Welsh harper he attends David as he is drawn on a hurdle to the gallows.

The important thing about these thoroughly English scenes is that they are not mere comic interludes, but an integral part of the serious action, like the Falstaff scenes in *King Henry IV*. There is, to be sure, a liberal allowance of scuffles and blows, but the humor is not merely physical; the Friar, with his love of a wench, his zest for song, and his readiness to turn his coat at need, is a true comic character evidently designed for performance by the chief comedian of an adult company.

There is some reason to believe that the *Troublesome Reign of King John*, 'as it was sundry times publicly acted by the Queen's Majesty's Players,' is in part, if not altogether, the work of Peele. This two-part chronicle play printed in 1591 was apparently composed to take advantage of the extraordinary success of Marlowe's *Tamburlaine* in 1587. So much is clear from the address to the Gentlemen Readers prefixed to the first edition:

> You that with friendly grace of smoothed brow
> Have entertained the Scythian Tamburlaine,
> And given applause unto an Infidel,
> Vouchsafe to welcome with like courtesy
> A warlike Christian and your countryman.

Peele's chauvinism, so marked in *Edward I*, appears here in his portrayal of King John as the champion of England against Rome. Shakespeare, who toned down this fierce anti-papal note, nevertheless thought well enough of the old play to preserve its scenario almost intact while writing a complete new text for his *King John*.

One exception, however, is a scene of some value for the student of English comedy. Philip, the Bastard Falconbridge, has been dispatched from France to plunder the abbeys and churches for the King's treasury. He appears leading in a friar and 'charging him to show where the Abbot's gold lay.' The friar's plea for mercy,

> Gentle gentility,
> Grieve not the clergy,

is answered by the Bastard's threat,

> Grey-gown'd good-face, conjure ye? Ne'er trust me for a groat,
> If this waist-girdle hang thee not, that girdeth in thy coat.

Another friar intervenes, promising if his brother's life is spared to lead Philip to the Prior's treasure chest. The chest is broken open and the Friar exclaims:

> Oh, I am undone!
> Fair Alice, the nun,
> Hath took up her rest
> In the abbot's chest.
> Sancte benedicite!
> Pardon my simplicity.

In her turn the nun intercedes:

> Oh, spare the Friar Anthony, a better never was
> To sing a Dirige solemnly, or read a morning mass.

To ransom him she promises to reveal the secret hoard of an old nun. This chest, too, is opened and what appears there?

> Friar Laurence, my lord, now holy water help us,
> Some witch or some devil is sent to delude us:
> Haud credo, Laurentius,
> That thou should'st be pen'd thus,
> In the press of a nun.

But Laurence has a ready excuse:

> *Amor vincit omnia,* so *Cato* affirmeth;
> And therefore a friar, whose fancy soon burneth,
> Because he is mortal and made of mould,
> He omits what he ought, and does more than he should.

Various German and Victorian critics have lifted scornful eyebrows at what they call the 'low ribaldry' of this scene, but a hardier taste cannot but admit its comic vigor. One must try to visualize it on the Elizabethan stage: the two chests placed at opposite sides, the swaggering Bastard and the cringing Friar in the center; the successive opening of the chests with the appearance first of a nun in the abbot's chest, then of a friar in the nun's, with all the action punctuated by the rattling doggrel lines. One can imagine the roar of laughter from the groundlings in the pit. It is, of course, to Shakespeare's credit that he sacrificed these easy laughs, partly, perhaps, because he disliked the gross attack upon the old Church, his mother's faith, partly because the broad farce clashed with his conception of Falconbridge, whom he had promoted to the role of the hero, the true representative of England in her war with foreign foes. Perhaps it was for a like reason that he canceled the serio-comic colloquy between the murderous monk and the timorous Abbot, which immediately precedes the poisoning of John. It might detract, he feared, from the tragic agony of the King's death scene. In both these scenes Peele, if he be the author, and the rhymes in the first of them remind one irresistibly of the doggrel lines in *Edward I*, shows his love of weaving comic stuff into a serious action, and this, of course, is in the native tradition of 'tragedy mixed full of pleasant mirth.'

The Old Wives' Tale, 'a pleasant conceited comedy played by the Queen's Majesties players. Written by G.P. 1595,' occupies a unique position in the work of Peele, as indeed it does in English comedy. It is the only one of Peele's surviving plays that is straight comedy from beginning to end. It is also comedy of a peculiar type, a blend of folklore and romance, flavored with a dash of literary satire, and set in a framework of homely realism. It is probably Peele's last play, written some time after 1591 and turned over to the printer by the Queen's Men, 'when they broke and went into the country to play' in the plague year of 1594. The long sickness to which Peele's letter of January 1596 alludes would have disabled him for any work for the theater after the resumption of acting in London.

As its name implies, *The Old Wives' Tale* is the dramatization of such a story as an old woman might tell to pass the time upon a winter night. The 'tale' is preceded by an Induction and briefly rounded out by a sort of Epilogue, which brings us back to earth again.

> The Induction opens with three serving-men lost in a wood; their young master has abandoned them to visit his fair lady, and they are at their wits' end. They are rescued by Clunch the Smith, who leads them to his house, where they are hospitably received by his old wife, Madge. After supper and a song, Clunch goes to bed with one of the guests while the other two sit by Madge to listen to her tale of a King whose daughter was stolen by a conjurer. She begins with the old formula: 'Once upon a time,' but loses the thread, repeats herself, and exclaims: 'O Lord, I quite forgot,' when suddenly two figures appear upon the stage. 'Soft, gammer,' says one of her hearers, 'here some come to tell your tale for you.' From here on the tale is acted out upon the stage.
>
> Even as acted, it is a tangled web, a little difficult for the

reader to follow with its shifts and interruptions. In the main the action revolves about Sacripant, the conjurer, and the stolen Princess. Her rescue is attempted first by her two brothers—it was here that Milton caught a hint for *Comus*—but they are easily overcome by Sacripant. A second rescue party consists of the foolish Knight, Huanebango, in whom, no doubt, the initiated of the audience recognized the lineaments of the pedant, Gabriel Harvey, along with his squire, the clown Corebus, whose chatter parodies his master's brags. They, too, fall easy victims to Sacripant, who strikes them deaf and blind. Last of all comes the lady's true lover, Eumenides. He too would have failed but for the aid of an attendant spirit—compare *Comus*—the 'grateful ghost' of Jack, whose burial fees Eumenides had paid. Jack kills the conjurer, dispels his charms, and unites the Princess with her brothers and her lover.

All this is in the style of old romances, already dramatized in *Common Conditions* and *Sir Clyomon,* but Peele is mocking them and reducing them to absurdity by pulling them down to the level of an old wife's tale and by blending them with bits of English folklore. Such bits, for example, are the Well of Life, where two girls go to draw water and get them husbands, also the White Bear of England's wood, a bear by night and an old man by day, whose riddling speeches direct the characters in the romantic action. In strong contrast to this fantastic stuff is the homely realism of such scenes as the quarrel between the girls and the row in the graveyard between Jack's friends and the parochial authorities, Elizabethan forerunners of Bumbledom. When the tale is ended by the rescue of the Princess, we return to the Smith's cottage; Madge, roused from the sleep into which she has fallen, takes her hearers in for a cup of ale with bread and cheese for breakfast, and the play is over.

This amusing melange of incongruous elements is presented in diction as varied as its matter: vigorous prose; regular blank verse:

> The day is clear, the welkin bright and gay,
> The lark is merry and records her notes;

jigging rhymed couplets:

> Bestow thy alms, give more than all,
> Till dead men's bones come at thy call;

and a parody of contemporary neo-classic meter:

> Safe in my arms will I keep thee, threat Mars or thunder
> Olympus.

Interspersed at frequent intervals are lyrics in the purest Elizabethan style. What one best remembers, perhaps, after rereading the play is the song of the amorous harvesters:

> All ye that lovely lovers be,
>   Pray you for me:
> Lo here we come a sowing, a sowing,
>   And sow sweet fruits of love;

or the call of the enchanted head as it rises from the Well of Life:

> Gently dip, but not too deep,
> For fear thou make the golden beard to weep.
> Fair maid, white and red,
> Comb me smooth and stroke my head,
> And every hair a sheaf shall be,
> And every sheaf a golden tree.

A laughing humorist with a voice that carols like a lark, Peele must have thoroughly enjoyed writing this merry play. He turns here from the courtly flattery of *The Arraignment* and the rant of his chronicle plays to mock the extravagancies of romance and dally with the superstitions of the English countryside. Scholar and poet though he was, Peele shows here, as in the Robin Hood scenes of *Edward I,* a genuine sympathy with common people that foreshadows some of the best of Shakespeare's comic scenes. It is his delight in the common things of life:

> Strawberries swimming in the cream,
> And school-boys playing in the stream;

and his gift of fresh spontaneous song that constitute Peele's real contribution to English comedy.

Robert Greene, 1558-92, was primarily a man of letters—a writer of romances, a pamphleteer, and a poet—rather than a playwright. Yet his contribution to English comedy, although not so large as Lyly's or so varied as Peele's, is not without real value. A student at St. John's, Cambridge, 'that most famous and fortunate nurse of all learning,' he took his B.A. in 1578, and after travel on the Continent, during which he practiced, if we may believe his words, 'such villainy as is abominable to mention,' he returned to take his M.A. in 1583. Five years later he received the same degree from Oxford, after which he proudly signed himself upon the title-pages of his pamphlets *academiae utriusque magister in artibus.* He belonged to a little, closely knit group of university wits who in the 'eighties and early 'nineties dominated the literary life of London, and it was his scholar's jealousy that prompted his dying outburst of spite against the unscholarly 'Shakescene,' who dared to challenge their supremacy upon the stage. Yet Greene's life was no credit to his academic training. Married early after his return from the Continent, he deserted his wife in the country and plunged into the lowest depths of London life. He was on intimate terms with a notorious cut-purse, Ball, later hanged at Tyburn, and Ball's sister became his mistress and bore him a son, baptized with bitter irony Fortunatus Greene. He supported himself by a series of love stories, setting forth 'the axioms of amorous philosophy,' by a group of 'cony-catching' pamphlets exposing the tricks of London thieves and swindlers, with which he was, unhappily, only too familiar, and, last of all, by writing for the stage. Yet in spite of his prolific fluency—'he could yark up a pamphlet,' says his friend Nashe, 'in a day and a night'—and the apparent success of his plays, he sank into bitter poverty and died after a lingering illness brought on by a debauch on pickled herrings and Rhine wine, in September 1592.

There was until the last something of the mockingbird in Greene. He began his career as a writer of love stories in the highly euphuistic style of Lyly, adorned with charming but rather conventional poems. Only one of these tales, *Pandosto, the Triumph of Time,* is still read, and that because it gave Shakespeare the story and characters of *The Winter's Tale.* Even his cony-catching pamphlets drew heavily upon earlier works, and his penitential tracts repeat each other. It is in his dramatic work, however, that it is possible to trace both this imitative note and his own peculiar talent, slowly developed till it found full expression.

Greene came rather late to the drama. He had been writing prose and verse for years before he attemptd a play. It seems to have been the immense success of *Tamburlaine,* 1587, that fired him with the ambition to rival it upon the stage. His first play, *The Comical History of Alphonsus, King of Arragon, c.* 1588, is a patent imitation of

Marlowe's tragedy. It is, in fact, a ridiculous imitation: the only funny thing in it is Greene's attempt to swagger in the heroic garb of Marlowe.

Greene had better luck with his next play: *A Looking Glass for London and England, c.* 1590, written in collaboration with Lodge. It seems to have been repeatedly performed by various companies and was a marked success with the reading public, for it was reprinted again and again, the last quarto appearing in 1617, a year after Shakespeare's death. This success was due, no doubt, to its theme and its moral, for it is an attempt to dramatize the story of Jonah and to apply the lesson to contemporary London, which, the play intimates, is a no less sinful city than Nineveh. To see, or even to read, a play packed with sensational action and enlivened with boisterous clownage, which, none the less, conveyed a moral lesson, must have been a rare treat to pious but pleasure-loving Londoners.

It is not easy to divide *A Looking Glass* scene by scene into the respective Greene and Lodge portions. Yet there can be little doubt that the scenes in which Adam, the clown, romps through the streets of Nineveh are by wild Robin Greene rather than by his graver partner. This clown is an Elizabethan version of the Vice of the old Morals, a swaggering rioter with a voluble flow of realistic speech. Apprenticed to a smith, he seduces his mistress and beats his master for the heinous sin of jealousy. Perhaps the best scene in the play, certainly the one likest to the comic scenes of the later Morals, is that in which a Ninevite, 'clad in divel's attire,' tries to put the fear of God into the clown by threatening to carry him off to Hell. But Adam discovers that this devil 'hath never a cloven foot,' whereupon he conjures him with his cudgel till the impostor runs off roaring for mercy. Adam is not a little proud of this feat, for it may, after all, have been a real devil, and he brags: 'Now who dare deal with me in the parish? or which wench in Ninivie will not love me when they say "There goes he that beat the divel"?' His final exit is quite in the old convention of the Vice: a fast of forty days has been proclaimed in repentant Nineveh, but Adam prefers the gallows to fasting and is led off to be hanged. There is nothing markedly original or witty in these scenes, but they have a rough comic vigor and are a refreshing change from the bombast of *Alphonsus*. Greene was probably writing with an eye upon the stage, perhaps upon a particular actor, for the role of Adam is a capital part for such a comedian as Kempe, who doubtless played it when Strange's men took over this play.

The History of Orlando Furioso, 1591, 'as it was played before the Queen's Majesty' may have been suggested by the appearance in 1591 of Harrington's translation of Ariosto's poem. Not that Greene needed a translation, for he read Italian and actually quotes sometimes from the original. Greene's return to the drama may also have been prompted by the recent success on the London stage of two plays: *The Spanish Tragedy* and the old *Hamlet,* in each of which the hero plays the part of a madman. Greene seems to have resolved, perhaps with his tongue in his cheek, to write a play in which his hero, the mad Orlando, should out-Herod Herod. The rant of this play is so absurdly exaggerated that it is easier to believe that a clever rogue like Greene wrote it as a parody than that he took it seriously. Yet if Greene did not take it seriously, it seems clear that the actors and the audience did. The play was performed at Court, probably by the Queen's Men; later, when they went on tour, Greene resold the play-book to the Admiral's company—a breach of professional ethics according to the standards of the day—and a manuscript of about a thousand lines still exists from which Alleyn studied his role as Orlando for the Admiral's production. We may be sure that this creator of the roles of Tamburlaine and Barabas gave full value to the mad Orlando's ravings.

In addition to this veiled dramatic satire, *Orlando* includes a good deal of old-fashioned comedy of the horseplay kind. There is neither Fool nor Vice in the play; the comic part is played by the crazy hero. He tears a shepherd limb from limb—off stage, of course—and swaggers about with a property leg which he uses as a 'massie club' to beat an army of soldiers. He equips his own army with spits and dripping pans and marches before them beating a drum; he mistakes his lady-love, Angelica, for a squire who has done well in battle, and rewards her with the accolade of knighthood. Dressed as a poet—one wonders what the costume was—Orlando snatches a fiddle from a strolling minstrel, who has been singing 'any odd toy' to him, and breaks it over the singer's head. All this is further proof, if any were needed, of the Elizabethan way of looking at madness as something funny.

If Greene's work for the stage had stopped with *Orlando,* he would have held at best a very minor rank among Elizabethan playwrights. But in the short time that was left him he wrote two plays, each of which plants something new and fragrant in the pleasant garden of Elizabethan comedy. The first of these is: '*The Honorable History of*

Friar Bacon as it was played by Her Majesty's Servants. Made by Robert Greene, Maister of Arts, 1594.' It is impossible to fix an exact date to this play, but it was certainly written after Marlowe's *Faustus,* 1588-9. Presumably a date in 1591, sometime after *Orlando,* is not far out of the way.

Once more Greene seems to have been inspired by the success of a Marlowe play, but this time, instead of trying to rival it, he hit on the happy idea of treating the theme of magic with a lighter touch and presenting it in the form of a comedy. As a source for his plot he drew upon an English prose tale, *The Famous History of Friar Bacon,* in which the great philosopher of the thirteenth century is presented as a wonder-working magician, who in the end burned his books and died in the odor of sanctity. Greene's play, so far as it deals with Bacon, is little more than a clever dramatization of incidents in the prose tale. What is new and important in this play, however, is the story of Margaret of Fressingfield and her love for Lord Lacy.

For this theme we need not seek a source. Robert Greene, 'love's philosopher,' as he called himself, had only to turn back to his own long series of love stories to find some such theme as this. There is nothing, to be sure, in his earlier prose work that quite matches the story of Margaret; this strain in the play breathes the air rather of English balladry than of Greene's amorous pamphlets. What Greene has in effect done here is to introduce into English comedy a human love story with a simplicity of expression and with real characters that make the lovers of Lyly's plays look like pale phantoms. He uses this theme, moreover, to give a certain unity to a rather loosely knit action.

The play opens with Prince Edward's avowal of his passion for the lovely girl he has seen playing the milkmaid in her father's dairy. To win her love on cheaper terms than marriage, he posts to Oxford to enlist the aid of the 'brave Nigromancer,' Friar Bacon, sending at the same time his friend Lacy to court Margaret for him. Naturally Lacy and Margaret fall in love with each other, and their marriage by Friar Bungay is only prevented by Bacon. He shows Edward the scene of the wedding in his magic glass, strikes Bungay dumb to stop the ceremony, and sends a devil to carry him away. Then follows the scene in which the angry Prince threatens Lacy with death, but is slowly won by the entreaties of Margaret to forgive him and to join the hands of the lovers. Here Greene might have ended his play as Lyly did when Alexander handed Campaspe over to Apelles, but

Greene has another bolt in his quiver, and he has still to link the story of Margaret more closely with that of Friar Bacon.

During Lacy's absence at Court, Margaret is sought in marriage by two neighboring gentlemen, who as a result of her indecisive answers kill each other in a duel. Margaret has barely dismissed her suitors when she receives a letter from Lacy, couched in pure Euphuism, which informs her that he is to wed a Spanish lady, one of the train of Edward's Spanish bride. There is not the slightest motivation for this letter; it must have been a surprise to Greene's audience as it is to the reader today, but it provides suspense and leads up to the best scene in the play. The love-test, for such the letter turns out to be, was a familiar motif in English ballads. Margaret in despair resolves to become a nun, but just as she is about to take the vows she is caught, 'in nun's apparel,' on the steps of the convent by Lacy and his friends, who have hurried down to bring her to be married at Court along with Edward and Elinor of Castile. There is a brief debate, Margaret holds off a little, but when the alternative is proposed,

> God or Lord Lacie; which contents you best?

her answer is quick and decisive:

> The flesh is frail; my Lord doth know it well
> That when he comes with his enchanting face,
> What so ere betide I cannot say him nay.
> Off goes the habit of a maiden's heart.
>
> . . .
>
> Lacie for me, if he will be my lord.

There has been no such scene of living breathing human characters in earlier English comedy and there will be nothing like it till we come to Shakespeare.

This is the proper end of the play, but for good measure Greene gives us two more scenes. In one of them we see Miles, the Vice, carried off to Hell on the back of a comic devil—'Exeunt roaring' is the stage direction; in the other we get a spectacular wedding procession in which Margaret attends Princess Elinor and Bacon foretells the glories of England under Elizabeth.

There is plenty of amusing action in the play, not all of it of the old physical type. There is a good comic touch in an early scene when Bacon's devil brings a hostess from Henley to shame an Oxford Master who had mocked at Bacon's art. There is comic use of spectacle in the scene where Vandermast conquers Bungay and is conquered in turn by Bacon. Greene must have strained the resources of the stage machinery of the early theater with his demand for the 'Hesperian tree' and the 'Dragon spouting fire.' In two scenes Greene exploits the balcony, or upperstage, in a way that seems new in English drama. In one the Oxford boys in Bacon's study—front stage—see in his glass—rear stage—their fathers fighting; but the actors who play their fathers' parts are actually at swords' points in the balcony. In the same way Edward sees in the glass the faithless Lacy kissing Margaret, while Lacy, Margaret, and Bungay are in the balcony. The outburst of anger that sends the Prince dashing sword in hand at the glass gives a genuine comic touch to the scene.

One of the interesting features of *Friar Bacon* is Greene's renunciation of the high-flown rant of his earlier plays. The blank verse is for the most part keyed down, at times to an almost conversational pitch. There is still, to be sure, a plethora of classical allusion; in Margaret's mouth this tends, to us at least, to diminish the realism with which Greene presents her. Yet, after all, this was the sort of ornament that the audience expected from a playwright who was *Magister Artium*. A good part of the dialogue, especially in the scenes with Miles, is in prose, a simple easy prose without any of Lyly's mannerisms. Miles, a scholar, though 'the greatest blockhead in all Oxford,' patters at times a doggrel rhyming Latin: 'Salvete omnes reges, that govern your greges,' or 'Ecce asinum mundi, figura rotundi,' which, no doubt, raised a laugh, but there is little true wit in his talk. Greene relies rather on action and character for his comic effects.

It is especially in his treatment of character in this play that Greene rises above his predecessors in English comedy. He has cleverly split the conventional role of the Vice into two parts: Miles, the foolish Bumpkin, and Ralph, the professional Fool, thus allotting two comic parts to members of the Queen's Company. Ralph, it must be owned, is a rather dull Fool, but the part is no easy one to write; it took a Shakespeare to create a Touchstone and a Feste. Friar Bacon plays his part with a genial alternation of gravity and good humor, and Edward is a satisfactory Prince, passionate, yet magnanimous. Margaret, however, is a new creation, the first girl, loving and beloved, in English comedy who is clearly perceived and realistically presented. There is nothing either sentimental or fantastic about her; she is a genuine English girl who picks her lover, takes him captive, and marries him. She can face an angry Prince with firm resolution:

Why, thinks King Henry's son that Margaret's love
Hangs in the uncertain balance of proud Time?

and she is prompt to exchange 'all the show of holy nuns' for the embrace of an earthly husband. Greene puts into the mouth of one of Lacy's companions his own humorous comment on her case: 'To see the nature of women, that be they never so near God, yet they love to die in a man's arms!' It is Margaret's character quite as much as her story that makes this play the first true romantic comedy in English.

As such it met with well-deserved success.[1] It was first played by the Queen's Men, later by Lord Strange's. Henslowe loaned the playbook for a joint performance by the Queen's and Sussex's companies. The Admiral's Men presented it at Court in 1602; many years later the Palsgrave's Company, successor to the Admiral's, revived it, and on their dissolution, gave their copy to the printer to be published, 1630, with a crude woodcut of Miles and the Brazen Head.

James IV, probably the latest in date of Greene's plays, has sometimes been listed as a chronicle play. This error apparently springs from the title-page of the first edition, 1598, which reads: '*The Scottish History of James the Fourth slain at Flodden. . .* Written by *Robert Greene, Maister of Arts.*' But this title-page, printed six years after Greene's death, is the advertisement of a publisher, more enterprising than honest, who wished to pass the play off as one of the chronicles so popular at that date. There is no reason to believe that Greene meant to identify the Scottish King of this play with the James who fell at Flodden; on the contrary, in the Induction he speaks of his protagonist as a Scottish king who reigned in 1520, seven years after the death of James IV. So far from being a chronicle play the misnamed *James IV* is an early example of romantic tragicomedy.

It is possible to date this play fairly accurately, since in it Greene quotes a passage from Peele's lost play, *The Hunting of Cupid*, which was entered in the Stationers' Register on 26 July 1591. Greene seems to have broken with the players sometime before his death in Septem-

---

[1] This success may have tempted Greene to write a second part. An anonymous play, *John of Bordeaux*, first printed 1936 by the Malone Society from manuscript, carries on the roles of Friar Bacon and his clownish servant in a play of romantic adventure. The manuscript, apparently a cut version of a longer play, is too imperfect to permit a critical appreciation, but Greene seems more likely than any other contemporary playwright to have been the original author.

ber 1592, so that *James IV* must be dated between late 1591 and early 1592. Somewhere in that period Greene came upon a romantic story in Cintio's *Hecatommiti* and decided to recast it in dramatic form. Cintio's story tells of an Irish king's lawless passion for Ida, a lady of his Court, of his attempt to kill his wife, of her escape in male dress, her subsequent adventures, and final reconciliation with her husband.

In the main Greene follows his source rather closely, but he modifies and enlarges it for dramatic effect. He shifts the scene, making the protagonist a King of Scotland, his wife the King of England's daughter. He may have done this to give a historical background to the play, for, as a matter of fact, Margaret Tudor, daughter of Henry VII, was married to James IV of Scotland. He invents a villain, Ateukin, a sycophantic courtier, to prompt the hesitating King to the murder. He arranges to have the letter commanding the deed put into the Queen's hands, who, with full knowledge of her husband's guilt, yet begs the Scottish lords to stand by him while she flies to her father. He creates an English suitor for Ida so as to contrast an innocent love with a guilty passion, and finally he stresses the victorious progress on the King of England in order to heighten the effect of the forgiving Queen's intervention between her father and her husband.

But Greene did more than alter some details of his source. He set his borrowed plot into an ingeniously devised framework, so that it is in a sense a play within a play, except that here, unlike Kyd's device in *The Spanish Tragedy*, the inserted play is the main action. The Induction opens with a dialogue between Oberon, the fairy king, and Bohan, a misanthropic Scot. Bohan tells Oberon that he has found 'the Court ill, the Country worse, and the City worst of all'; and he promises to show Oberon 'by demonstration' why he hates the world. They withdraw into 'the gallery,' i.e. the upper stage, and the play proper begins. Bohan's two sons, Slipper, the clown, and Nano, the dwarf, take part in this play; Slipper becomes the merry servant of Ateukin and Nano the devoted page of the Queen. Slipper and Andrew, a roguish serving-man, furnish the low comedy in contrast to the romantic action, which, again, is broken by dumb-shows, songs, and dances between the acts. At the end of the play one expects a return to and, perhaps, some comment by the characters of the Induction, but Bohan and Oberon simply disappear from the scene, like Christopher Sly in *The Taming of the Shrew*. Possibly this expected conclusion has been lost.

The text of *James IV* is in a sorry state; at times it is almost unintelligible. The last act contains a long debate between a Lawyer, a Merchant, and a Divine, which has no bearing on the action and is so unlike Greene's style as to suggest that it may have been inserted by some moralizing reviser of the script. The reconciliation scene of the denouement, a most important scene, has been cut down to a few lines, and the action closes with Nano in the role of the ever-hungry Clown, inviting the assembled company to dinner.

James IV has been called Greene's masterpiece. It might have been that, if Greene had been bold enough to carry out what seems to have been his first plan, the dramatization of Cintio's tale. But he perhaps feared that a simple dramatic version of his source would not hold his audience, and consequently he devised the Induction with the contrasted figures of Bohan and Oberon, and interrupted the flow of the main action with intercalated shows and dances. As a result the action is at times curtailed, at times confused, until its significance is lost; this is especially true in the episode of Lady Anderson's passion for the disguised Queen. Yet even so, credit must be given Greene for his early perception of the value of the Italian *novella* as a source for Elizabethan comedy.

There is much less of the old rough comedy in *James IV* than in the earlier work of Greene. Its place is largely taken by the antics of Slipper, his jesting with the old Countess, and his attempt to pose as a gentleman. It would seem that Greene relied in the main upon the romantic action, particularly upon the devotion of Queen Dorothea to her unworthy husband and upon the chaste innocence of Ida. He handles this action in such a fashion as to present the first romantic tragi-comedy in Elizabethan drama. A serious theme involving adulterous passion and intended murder is brought to a happy conclusion; the King repents of his guilt, even before the return of his wife; even the villain Ateukin repents and is allowed to escape punishment, a precedent that was to become an established convention in later tragic-comedy. Slipper, condemned to the gallows, is rescued by the intervention of Oberon; in short, all's well that ends well—something of a triumph for Greene when such bloody dramas as *The Jew of Malta* and *The Spanish Tragedy* dominated the London stage.

About a quarter of the play is in prose. In the comic scenes Greene uses a long-established convention, dialect or broken English, Scottish speech, or what served on the stage for such, in the mouth of Bohan, the French-English jargon of the Captain. The blank verse is simpler

and freer from rant than in Greene's earlier plays; in particular it
avoids almost entirely the heavy apparatus of classic mythology, which
still encumbers *Friar Bacon*. An interesting feature of the verse is
the frequent use of rhyme, not merely in tag-ends or sententious passages, but wherever it strikes a note of sentiment. These rhymed lines
may even take stanzaic form, as in the disguised Queen's speech to
her attendant page:

> Oh, Nano, I am weary of these weeds,
>   Weary to wield the weapon that I bear,
> Weary of love from whom my woe proceeds,
>   Weary of toil since I have lost my dear.
>   O weary life where wanteth no distress,
>   But every thought is paid with heaviness!

or more simply in rhymed couplets, as in Greene's pretty theft from
Peele:

> And weele I wot, I heard a shepherd sing,
> That, like a bee, Love hath a little sting.

Rhymed lines like these may occur at any moment in passages of formal blank verse, a device that appears repeatedly in the early comedies of Shakespeare. It is Greene's way of lightening the heavy tread
of blank verse and bringing it nearer to the music of romantic comedy.

In characterization, Greene seems to have reached his highest point
in this play. Slipper, for example, is less of an arrant fool than Miles,
more of a jesting merrymaker; his brother, Nano, is a rather pathetic
comic figure, but not without a witty word at times. The King has
been distinctly elevated above Cintio's lustful, brutal tyrant, a character Greene evidently thought out of place in comedy. It seems plain
from his prose tales that Greene was especially interested in the characters of women and, despite his wild life, he always reverenced their
beauty and goodness. This is particularly true of the women in *James
IV*. The old Countess is only a sketch, but one clearly and firmly
drawn; and while Greene seems to have bungled the character of Lady
Anderson, his Ida is a true and charming portrait of the Elizabethan
girl. Her replies to Ateukin soliciting her love for the King are as
courteous as they are firm; she does not fly into a passion because a
man, even a king, is in love with her, but, like Margaret, she is quite
sure that there is no true love that does not end in marriage. The
character of the Queen, however, is Greene's supreme achievement. It

is hardly by chance that he changed her name from the stately Arrenobia of his source to that of the wife he had loved and deserted; 'Doll, I charge thee by the love of our youth,' he wrote her from his deathbed. There is something of the Amazon in Cintio's heroine, 'trained under her father's roof to bear arms,' who presents herself to the King in the last scene in full armor with her visor down. Greene's Dorothea, on the other hand, is all woman, an obedient daughter and a patient wife, more than ready to overlook a husband's fault:

> The King is young, and if he step awry,
> He may amend, and I will love him still.

Greene invents the scene—there is nothing like it in his source—in which these lines occur, so as to show Dorothea pleading with the Scotch lords to remain true to the King and firmly rejecting the prudent advice that she should seek her father's aid against him. Indeed it is her father's fierce attack upon him that brings Dorothea back to her husband, and she stops his effusive outburst of repentance with the quiet words:

> Shame me not, Prince, companion in my bed.
>
> . . .
>
> 'Tis kingly to amend what is amiss.

One cannot but regret that Greene's life was cut so short; had he but lived a few years longer, and created more such figures as Margaret of Fressingfield and Queen Dorothea, he would in the field of comedy have stood a little nearer than he does to Shakespeare.

Various anonymous plays and parts of plays have been at one time or another ascribed to Greene. Yet when we consider his brief career as a playwright and the profusion with which during this time he poured out his prose pamphlets, it seems unlikely that he wrote many more than his signed plays. One, however, *George-a-Greene, the Pinner of Wakefield,* is so close in subject matter and treatment to *Friar Bacon* as to suggest the possibility of Greene's authorship. This play, dealing with one of the characters of the Robin Hood cycle, is founded, like *Friar Bacon,* on a popular prose romance, and like that play breathes a genuine atmosphere of the English countryside. Yet Greene's characteristic style, especially in verse, is so markedly absent as to suggest that he may at most have plotted the play for another to compose. His latest editor, T. H. Dickinson, includes it only with hesitation among his plays.

Greene's sudden leap from the horseplay of *Orlando* to the comedy of *Friar Bacon* and the romance of *James IV* is without a parallel in the history of English comedy. It resembles those sudden changes in the biological world that have received the name of mutation rather than evolution. It is by these last two plays alone that Greene's contribution to English comedy should be judged, and this contribution can be stated with sufficient certainty. He brought back romance from the Forest of Strange Marvels and anchored it firmly on ·English ground, thus giving romance a familiar background of realism. The realism of the scene at Harlston Fair in *Friar Bacon* is a forerunner of the sheep-shearing feast in *The Winter's Tale,* and the play of fairies about the affairs of mortals in *James IV* looks forward to the activities of Oberon and Puck in *A Midsummer Night's Dream.*

4

The Young Shakespeare

Now that the background, dramatic and theatrical, for Shakespeare's work in Elizabethan comedy has been set, it may be well to pause and consider what manner of man this Shakespeare was who came to London to play so distinguished a part there. Regret is sometimes expressed that we know so little of Shakespeare the man; as a matter of fact we know more of him than of most of his contemporaries in the field of literature, and when facts fail us we may rely with some confidence on legitimate inference.

What do we know of the young Shakespeare and what may we infer? The old conception of Shakespeare's coming up as an ignorant boy from an insignificant village to conquer fame and fortune has in the main given way before the research of scholars. Yet it still lingers and is presumably responsible for various heresies which, affirming that such an ignoramus could not possibly have written the plays and poems that bear his name, endeavor to shift their authorship to some learned or courtly contemporary, to Bacon (though the Baconians, *Deo gratias*, are almost extinct today), to the Earl of Derby, Sir Edward Dyer, or the Earl of Oxford. If the fallacy of the premise on which these heresies are founded, that Shakespeare of Stratford was, in Carlyle's words, 'a poor Warwickshire peasant,' was once fully realized, there might come a happy end to these follies, for it is not unfair to say that those who deny Shakespeare's authorship of Shakespeare's plays and poems are really incapable of weighing and judging the value of evidence.

The William Shakespeare who was born and buried at Stratford was no Warwickshire peasant, but the citizen of a thriving little town with a long history behind it, a town which in past years had given an Archbishop of Canterbury and a Lord Mayor of London to England, and which in Shakespeare's youth was the trading center of a prosperous farmland. Under a charter granted by Edward VI, Stratford enjoyed almost complete self-government, and in the management of its municipal affairs William's father played an important part.

John Shakespeare was a farmer's son who left the plow at an early age and came to Stratford to seek his fortune. He does not seem to have made a very good start, for the first news we have of him records a fine imposed for a pile of manure before his door. That was before his marriage; he seems to have done better thereafter. John made a good marriage, for his bride, Mary Arden, the daughter of his father's landlord, was in a small way an heiress. We find him enrolled in one of the trade guilds of the town, the Glovers, Whittawers, i.e. skin-dressers, and Collar-Makers, but he turned his hand to other things than skins and gloves: he traded in timber and barley, probably also in wool, and bought and sold houses in Stratford. Before long he was recognized as one of the up-and-coming citizens and was elected by his fellows to one office after another, beginning with that of 'ale-taster,' the official chosen to supervise the quality and price, both strictly regulated, of beer and bread. He rose to be one of the constables in charge of the town watch, one of the chamberlains in control of municipal finance, and finally, 1568, High Bailiff, or Mayor. In this capacity, he granted licenses to the first touring companies ever to show in Stratford. In the next year he and his friend, Quiney, then High Bailiff, entertained Sir Thomas Lucy, the magnate of the neighborhood, at an official dinner in Stratford. As a town official John used to sign documents with his mark, from which it has been inferred that he was illiterate, but we know that well-educated citizens of Stratford did the same. Sometime in the late 'seventies he actually applied to the Heralds' Office, for the grant of a coat-of-arms, which, if obtained, would qualify him to write himself Gentleman, as his son was to do later. But a coat-of-arms was an expensive luxury; the fee of £30 would be equivalent to something well over $1,000 today, and the project was dropped till twenty years later. Just at this time, in fact, something began to go wrong with John's affairs. He was involved in vexatious law suits, mortgaged and lost his wife's bit of farmland, and in 1586 was heavily fined, £40, by the Queen's Court at Westminster, possibly because of his stubborn Puritan principles.[1] So bad were matters, in fact, that he ceased to attend meetings of the Town Council, and in 1586 was dropped from the office of alderman,

[1] While he was Chamberlain the images in the Guildhall were defaced and a table was placed where the altar had stood. Some years later as Deputy Bailiff he and Quiney sold the Romish vestments of the chapel.

which he had held for some fifteen years. He lived, one is glad to know, long enough to see William retrieve the family fortune, buy New Place, the largest house in town, and secure the coveted coat-of-arms. Tradition records a visit to the shop of John Shakespeare, 'a merry-cheeked old man,' who said: 'Will was a good honest fellow, but he durst have cracked a jest with him at any time.' From his father it would seem that Shakespeare inherited his enterprise, his ambition for worldly success, his sense of humor and, strange as it may seem, his taste for law suits.

Of Shakespeare's mother there is less to say. She belonged to a fine old Warwickshire family, the Ardens, that traced its descent back to and before the Conquest and was distinguished in Elizabeth's day for its firm adherence to the old faith. Her father, 'a gentleman of worship,' died a professing Catholic, and it is probable that Mary, though the wife of a stout Protestant, never quite renounced her family's creed. This would account, at least, for the respect with which Shakespeare, in contrast to most of the playwrights of his day, always treated the Roman Church. To William, her first-born son, she bequeathed, we may be sure, his instinctive sympathy with courtesy and refinement, and the charm of manner that won for him the stock epithet of 'gentle' Shakespeare.

Of William himself in his youth, to be frank, we know very little; there is not a single fact that can be proved by documentary evidence between the record of his baptism on 26 April 1564 and the bond securing the license for his marriage on 28 November 1582. A word must be said later on the vexed topic of his marriage, but there is a period of eighteen years between these dates that needs to be examined.

Along with heredity the most important influence in a man's life, probably, is his education. Fortunately we know a good deal about the opportunity for education in Shakespeare's Stratford and what sort of an education was offered there in his day. The old Guild School had been transformed in 1553 into the King's New School of Stratford-on-Avon; it was a grammar school of the fixed Elizabethan fashion, and a very good school of its kind. We know the masters who presided over it in William's day, and note that they were all good scholars with Bachelor's and Master's degrees from Oxford. The salary was fixed at £20 and a lodging, excellent pay for that time, even though the master had to pay for the services of an under-master. The curriculum was established by law. First of all, Lyly's *Latin*

Grammar, which the boys had to learn by heart, and exercises in Latin conversation, since Latin was still a living language. Then came reading in Latin prose and verse: Cicero, especially, and Ovid. Passages were memorized, translated into English, and put back again into Latin to be compared with the original. The boys were even obliged to compose Latin verses on set themes, as Tom Brown and Harry East were to do centuries later at Rugby. Along with this went a careful drill in the principles of rhetoric. Little else was taught except a year or two of Greek, mainly the New Testament, in the top forms, and, of course, Holy Writ in the standard Bishops' Bible version. As school hours lasted with brief intermissions from 6 or 7 A.M. till late in the afternoon, it seems likely that any boy except a hopeless dullard would acquire a mastery of Latin that would amaze most graduates of an American college.

The most interesting fact, however, in connection with Shakespeare is that this education was absolutely free to all sons of Stratford citizens. We do not *know* that Shakespeare attended this school; we do not *know* that any Stratford boy of his time did; the school rolls have long been lost. It is quite unthinkable, however, that the oldest son of so important and ambitious a citizen as John Shakespeare should not have enjoyed this privilege. We may assume that William did, and that the intimate knowledge of certain standard Latin classics and the thorough grasp on the Latin element in English which appears in Shakespeare's work are the result of his years of study at the King's School at Stratford.

How many years, we may ask? Again the answer is that we do not know, but we may infer with some degree of certainty. Before a boy was allowed to enter a grammar school he was expected to pass through the Petty, we should say, the primary school. Here he was taught to read and write, to do simple exercises in arithmetic, and to get the Lord's Prayer, the Creed, and the Catechism by heart. About two years of this training, from the age of five to seven, qualified the little scholar to enter the grammar school. William, then, presumably completed this course about 1571 and entered the King's School in that year. Seven years, as a rule, would carry a boy through the prescribed curriculum there, which brings us to about 1578. Rowe, Shakespeare's first biographer, declared that John Shakespeare 'bred' William in a 'Free-School . . . but the narrowness of his circumstances and the want of his assistance at home forced his father to withdraw him from thence.' This statement has often been repeated, but there is reason to believe it quite incorrect. It is not until 1577 that John Shakespeare's financial difficulties begin to appear, by which time William would all but have finished his course in school, and it is hard to see how a boy of fourteen would have been of much assistance to his father at home. Professor Baldwin, whose vast knowledge of Elizabethan schools entitles him to speak with authority, asserts that we have good reason to believe that William completed the grammar school curriculum. It would, in fact, be hard to see where Shakespeare could have acquired the Greek, which Jonson's dictum—'small Latin and less Greek'—allows him, had he not spent a year or more in the upper forms of the King's School. The master, by the way, who presided over this school for the greater part of William's time there, 1575-9, was Thomas Jenkins, a Fellow of St. John's, Oxford. He was a Welshman and it seems likely that some of his eccentricities of speech reappear in the Welsh schoolmaster, Sir Hugh, in *The Merry Wives of Windsor.*

Shakespeare, of course, was not a scholar in the sense that his fellow playwrights, Ben Jonson and Chapman, were. He apparently performed his prescribed tasks, assimilated what he could appropriate, and let the rest slide gently out of mind and memory. His favorite poet was the romantic story-teller Ovid, of whom he must have read hundreds of lines in school. On the other hand, there is no trace in the brisk prose of his comedies of the Ciceronian style so diligently taught in Elizabethan schools. We should not picture young Shakespeare as a bookish boy; there seems, on the contrary, evidence in his work that he took part in the usual schoolboy games: blindman's buff, prisoner's base, and football, and that he fished and swam in the Avon. In particular all his work shows a familiarity with and delight in field sports, hawking, and hunting. D. H. Madden's delightful *Diary of Master William Silence,* the final authority on this matter, shows that Shakespeare possessed a knowledge of these sports, of the training of hawk and hound involved in them, and in the nature and behavior of the horse, such as could only have been acquired by long hours of following on foot the chase of stag and hare, and the falconry along the Avon, and by more hours spent in the mews, stables, and kennels of such a country house as Charlecote in long talks with falconers, grooms, and huntsmen. Such knowledge as Shakespeare shows could not have been picked up from books, or acquired in his busy years in London; it derives from happy hours of truancy from school and shop.

Had John Shakespeare's finances been in better shape when William left school about 1578, he might well have sent his son to a university. We have no great reason to regret, however, Shakespeare's lack of a university education. In his day Oxford and Cambridge were essentially training schools for the learned professions and it is hard to picture Shakespeare preaching in the pulpit, pleading a case in court, or practising the ignorant medicine and brutal surgery of his day. What we now recognize as a training in the humanities was in Shakespeare's time the business of the grammar schools, and, as we have seen, the King's School gave him every opportunity to profit by it. In default of a university career and a consequent profession, the natural thing for William was to be apprenticed to a trade, his father's or another. Perhaps John Shakespeare expected his son to take over his business and retrieve his falling fortune. If so, he was sadly disappointed, for within a few years after leaving school William took a step that must have added to his father's burden. Not yet eighteen, he married and brought home a fatherless girl without a dowry, whom he had got with child.

There has been so much dispute about the nature and the consequences of this marriage that it seems best to state the known facts and let the reader draw his own conclusions.

William's bride was Anne, daughter of Richard Hathaway, a farmer at Shottery, a hamlet near Stratford, who had died in the summer of 1582. She was eight years or so older than William and, apparently, quite uneducated. On 28 November of that year two friends of the late Richard appeared before the Bishop of Worcester, in whose diocese Stratford lay, and secured a license for the marriage of Anne and William without the delay involved in the customary triple asking of the banns in church. Such a delay would have carried the young couple into the Advent season and by Church law marriage was prohibited from the first Sunday in Advent till mid January. That there was need for a speedy marriage appears from the birth of William's first child, Susanna, in May of the following year. John Shakespeare took no part in securing the license, possibly because in 1582 he was not considered good security for the £40 bond posted by Anne's friends. He must, however, have given his consent, for without it the marriage of his son, still a minor, would have been illegal, and the then Bishop of Worcester was a stickler for discipline. Possibly William, like Laertes, had wrung from his father a 'slow leave by laboursome petition.'

Apologists for Shakespeare have insisted that a formal, but secret, betrothal must have preceded the application for the license. Such a betrothal was generally recognized as giving the bridegroom full marital privileges. Marriage and baptism records in and around Stratford at this time go far to show that the bridegroom often availed himself of this right. What Shakespeare himself thought of it in later years may, perhaps, be inferred from Olivia's insistence on her betrothal's taking place before a priest and from Prospero's stern warning against cohabitation before marriage in spite of Ferdinand's formal betrothal to Miranda.

There has been much idle discussion about the happiness or unhappiness of Shakespeare's married life. The shrewish Adriana in *The Comedy of Errors,* for example, has been held up as a portrait of Anne Shakespeare; but one would be loath to attribute such discourtesy to the poet. All that we know is that in February 1585 she bore him two more children, the twins Hamnet and Judith, named after William's friends, Hamnet and Judith Sadler; that he left her in Stratford when he went to London—there is no evidence that she ever joined him there—and little Hamnet was buried in Stratford in 1596; that he later installed her and his daughters in New Place, came back finally to live with them there, and died in New Place, leaving her a widow to survive him for seven years, sleeping, we may presume, in the second-best bed left her in his will. This does not exactly suggest a marriage of true minds.

Various traditions have clustered about Shakespeare's youth in Stratford. The curious in such matters may find them assembled under the head of the 'Shakespeare-Mythos' in Sir Edmund Chambers' *William Shakespeare.* None of them are recorded till half a century and more after Shakespeare's death. One of the oldest of them, that Shakespeare 'exercised his father's trade,' that of a butcher, is demonstrably false; John Shakespeare was not, and could not by contemporary Stratford regulations have been, a butcher. The most familiar of them, that William stole deer from Sir Thomas Lucy's park at Charlecote, that he was prosecuted—'oft whipt and sometimes imprisoned,' the earliest account says—by that gentleman, and in consequence forced to fly from Stratford, has been generally discarded by scholars. Certainly the details of the story are inaccurate: Lucy had no 'park' at Charlecote, and the law of the land would not have allowed him to whip or imprison Shakespeare. Yet we may note that Lucy had deer, if not a formal 'park,' at Charlecote, that poaching was regarded by high-spirited youth of that day as an adventure rather than a crime—something like raiding a watermelon patch today—and that Shakespeare himself makes a jest of it in an early play:

> What, hast thou not full often struck a doe,
> And borne her cleanly by the keeper's nose?

says Demetrius in *Titus Andronicus*. Such tales as this, and that of Shakespeare's defeat in a drinking match with the 'Sippers' of 'Drunken Bidford,' and his night's sleep under a crabtree on his way home, are not told of poets who left behind them the memory of a grave and studious youth; no such tales are told, for example, of young John Milton.

One report, however, the earliest and most credible, has received curiously little attention until a comparatively recent date. The antiquary Aubrey, gathering material, *c.* 1681, for his notes on Shakespeare, was directed by the actor Lacy to consult the actor William Beeston, 'who knows most of him.' Now this Beeston was the son of Christopher Beeston, an actor in the Chamberlain's Company, who played beside Shakespeare in Jonson's *Every Man in his Humour*. Christopher, presumably, knew Shakespeare well and what he transmitted to his son may be received as authentic. What Beeston told Aubrey among other things was that 'Shakespeare understood Latin pretty well, for he had been in his younger years a schoolmaster in the country.' Poets and romantic novelists may prefer Shakespeare the deer-stealer to Shakespeare the schoolmaster, but this seems to be the truth and we had best stick to it, even if the mind recoils from the thought of young Shakespeare, rod in hand, beating Latin into the posteriors of country boys. The question naturally arises in what country school did Shakespeare teach. The natural answer would be, in his home town; but we know that Master Aspinwall presided over the King's School from 1581, a year before Shakespeare's marriage, to 1624, eight years after his death, and Aspinwall, we know, had an usher to help him with the younger boys. Had that usher been Shakespeare surely some memory of it would have lingered in Stratford. It seems possible, at least, that Shakespeare secured a post as undermaster in some little town in the neighboring county of Gloucester. The names of Shakespeare and of Hathaway occur repeatedly in Elizabethan records of that county, so that William may have had relatives and connections there who would help him to a post that his training in the King's School qualified him to fill. In *King Henry IV*

Part II Shakespeare shows a knowledge of family names and local customs in the Cotswold district of Gloucestershire that points to a period of residence there. And such a period fits neatly in between his marriage and his departure to London. He would have been hard pressed at that time to provide bread and butter for a wife and three children, and a schoolmaster's pay, however small, would be a better support for his family than an occasional raid on Lucy's deer.

We do not know exactly when Shakespeare came to London. He was presumably in Stratford in 1585; certainly his wife was when the twins were baptized there in February of that year. Leicester's Company visited Stratford in the summer of 1587 and it may have been talk with the actors at that time that tipped the scales and started Shakespeare on his way to London. There seems some reason to believe that he was connected with this company, later Lord Strange's Men, as early as 1588. The story accepted by Dr. Johnson, that he used to hold horses outside the Theatre, organized a company of 'Shakespeare's boys' to help him, and gradually worked his way into the company of actors, may be dismissed as a late and incredible fiction. A much earlier report that he was 'received into the playhouse as a serviture'—Rowe says 'in a very mean rank'—may mean that he was at first connected with the company as an apprentice to one of the members; it was unusual, but not unheard of, for a man of Shakespeare's age in 1588 to become an apprentice. Or he may have been taken on as a hired man to play minor parts. He must, at any rate, have begun before long to attract attention not only as an actor but as a playwright, for the first definite allusion to him in London points to his activity in both these roles.

In the late summer of 1592 Robert Greene, then on his deathbed, wrote a tract, *A Groatsworth of Wit,* which he hoped to sell for enough to pay his debts. He died before it was printed, but his friend Chettle saw it through the press as a last service for him. In it Greene appealed to his fellow authors, Marlowe, Peele, and 'young Juneval,' probably Nashe, to stop writing plays, 'for there is an upstart crow beautified with our feathers, that with his tiger's heart wrapt in a player's hide supposes he is as well able to bumbast out a blank verse as the best of you: and being an absolute *Johannes factotum,* is in his own conceit the only Shake-scene in a country.' The pun on Shakespeare's name makes it quite clear who the 'upstart crow' was, and Greene's parody of a line from *King Henry VI Part III,*

O tiger's heart wrapp'd in a woman's hide,

connects Shakespeare in some fashion with that play. The whole point of Greene's outburst is a warning to his friends no longer to trust the players, who will probably abandon them as, Greene declares, they have forsaken him. Why should the actors pay Marlowe and Peele for plays when one of their own crew can do so well?

Greene's tract seems to have aroused considerable excitement, so much indeed that Chettle felt called on to explain and apologize. In his *Kind-Heart's Dream,* registered for publication in December 1592, he remarks that two of the playmakers spoken of in the tract had taken grave offense and, since they could not get at the dead Greene, had attacked him. 'With neither of them,' he says, 'was I acquainted, and with one of them I care not if I ever be'—that one, of course, is Marlowe, of ill-repute and angry temper. 'The other,' he continues, 'whom at that time'—i.e. when he was preparing Greene's manuscript for publication—'I did not so much spare as I since wish I had . . . I am as sorry as if the original fault had been my own fault, because myself have seen his demeanor no less civil than he excellent in the quality he professes. Besides divers of worship have reported his uprightness in dealing which argues his honesty, and his facetious grace in writing that approves his art.'

Chettle's Elizabethan English calls for a bit of explanation. He had apparently met Shakespeare for the first time after the outcry over Greene's attack, and had been struck by his 'civil demeanor,' i.e. well-bred behavior, which matched his excellence as an actor; 'quality' is the stock Elizabethan word for the actor's profession. Moreover, says Chettle, certain gentlemen of rank and station had testified to Shakespeare's 'uprightness in dealing'—he was too honest to plunder another man's work as Greene had insinuated—and to the graceful humor of his verse. Shakespeare comes rather well out of the affair; he was already prominent enough in the theatrical world for the envious Greene to hurl insults at him, and yet well-liked enough to force the man responsible for Greene's attack to make a sincere and hearty apology, due in part, it would appear, to the interference of some highborn friends, or patrons, of the young playwright-actor.

What Shakespeare had done for the theater to attain such prominence in 1592 we do not know. There is no record of any play of his before *Titus Andronicus,* in 1594; but four years later Meres, a scholar interested in poetry and the drama, credits Shakespeare with twelve plays besides his poems, and it is hard to believe that he wrote all these in less than four years. He may have contributed some scenes to a chronicle play, 'Harey the VI,' i.e. *King Henry VI,* which was produced by Strange's Company, March 1592, with immense applause. If this was Shakespeare's first success in the theater his triumph was short-lived. Three months later a scandalous riot of London apprentices provoked an edict by the Privy Council closing all theaters for three months, and before that time had elapsed the plague broke out in London with such violence that the theaters remained closed, except for a few brief intervals till the summer of 1594.

In May 1593 Strange's Company went on tour; a special license gives us the names of the chief members of the company, but Shakespeare's is not among them. Presumably he stayed in or near London at work on his poems; *Venus and Adonis* had been licensed for publication in April and appeared later in the year with a respectful dedication to the Earl of Southampton, one of the 'divers of worship,' perhaps, who had spoken up for Shakespeare in 1592. In the dedication Shakespeare calls this poem, 'the first heir of my invention,' which does not mean, as has sometimes been said, that it was his first work, but only that it was the first thing he was willing to claim. Shakespeare, it seems, always regarded his plays as things to be acted rather than read, and was indifferent, not to say careless, about their publication. The startling success of *Venus and Adonis*—eight editions appeared in Shakespeare's lifetime—led him to employ his 'idle hours' while his fellows were on tour in the composition of another long poem, *Lucrece,* which came out in 1594. It, too, was dedicated to Southampton, in an epistle that seems to show that their acquaintance had now ripened into a warm friendship: 'the love I dedicate your Lordship is without end,' Shakespeare wrote. *Lucrece* never attained the popularity of *Venus and Adonis,* but the scholar, Gabriel Harvey, noted that *Lucrece* and *Hamlet* have it in them to please the 'wiser sort,' who were, or pretended to be, scandalized by the erotic strain of the earlier poem. The success of the two poems and the knowledge that Shakespeare enjoyed the patronage of Southampton no doubt contributed to his admission into his company, now known as the Lord Chamberlain's Men, as a full-fledged member. A payment to this company for two plays at Court in the Christmas season of 1594 joins Shakespeare's name with those of Kempe and Burbage.

Here we may leave him. By 1594 he had won his spurs as actor, playwright, and poet, and was to go on from triumph to triumph till he returned to spend his last years at home, wealthy and respected.

5

Apprentice Work

THE COMEDY OF ERRORS

IT IS right and proper to begin our study of the work of Shakespeare with his earliest comedies and among these, by the common consent of scholars, we find *The Comedy of Errors*. It is certainly the first comedy from his pen of which we have a definite record, for it was performed at Gray's Inn on 28 December 1594, during the Christmas revels of that society. There is no reason to believe that the *Errors* was written for the occasion; on the contrary it seems likely that it was specially commanded by the directors of the revels as a lively farce-comedy, particularly suited to an evening of high jinks by a learned body. References in the play to the Spanish Armada and to the Civil War in France carry the composition of the play back to some date between 1589 and 1591, as does the borrowing of a name, Menaphon, from Marlowe's *Tamburlaine*, 1587, and another, Dromio, possibly from Lyly's *Mother Bombie*, on the stage between 1587 and 1590.

If we combine the conjectures of two Shakespearean scholars and draw what seems a fair conclusion from them, we may shift the composition of the play back for some years. Professor Adams [1] suggests that the poet came to London from the school where he was teaching —this rests, of course, upon the Beeston statement that Shakespeare had been a schoolmaster—with a draft of the play in his pocket. Professor Baldwin [2] feels sure that this first draft was much closer to its source, the *Menaechmi* of Plautus, than the present text—which, of course, would be only natural in a schoolmaster's play. But this draft, however much its gaiety may have recommended it to the players on a first reading, would have seemed to them in many ways old-fashioned. It must have been written in the rhyme doggrel, varied by rhymed couplets, conventional in early Elizabethan comedy, for Shakespeare

[1] *William Shakespeare*, Houghton Mifflin, 1923, p. 96.
[2] *The Comedy of Errors*, Heath, 1928, pp. 123 ff.

could not have heard, much less written, Marlovian blank verse before he came to London. The players may, perhaps, have told Shakespeare that such an imitation in so old-fashioned a style might do for a school play, but would hardly pass muster on the public stage. Where, they might ask, was the love interest that Lyly and Greene had taught the public to anticipate, where the note of romantic adventure? Let the young writer visit the London theaters, study the popular successes, and return when he had reshaped his interesting but unsatisfactory draft. Shakespeare, we may suppose, did so, and the result is *The Comedy of Errors* as it stands in the Folio text. About half the present text is in resonant blank verse. Shakespeare's ear soon caught the tune of Marlowe's music and he promptly proceeded to imitate it. The archaic doggrel has been dropped except for scenes of broad comedy, and rhymed couplets are retained only for moralizing and sentimental passages and for tag-ends of scenes and speeches. There is, moreover, a strain of sentiment and romance in the play as we have it, which could hardly have been present in a close imitation of the *Menaechmi,* along with an interest in travel and adventure particularly appealing to an Elizabethan audience. All this, of course, is mere conjecture, but it is pleasant conjecture, not without a ground of credibility, and it goes far to explain the varied strands and varying metres of the play.

The *Menaechmi* of Plautus has always been considered one of the best of the Plautine plays; it was a very natural play for a schoolmaster, aspiring for success on the popular stage, to try to transform into an Elizabethan comedy.

The story of the *Menaechmi* is so well known and so easily accessible, in the original and in translations, that it is needless to rehearse it. Suffice it to say that it deals with the adventures of identical twins, brothers separated in youth, but meeting years later in a foreign town, where one is constantly mistaken for the other with absurdly amusing consequences. Mistaken identity is, of course, an old and often repeated comic motif, and this particular variant, the mistaken identity of twin brothers, seems to have exercised a perennial attraction on playwrights. The play of Plautus is said to be founded on a lost Greek comedy, the *Didumoi,* i.e. the *Twins,* of Posidippus. With the revival of interest in Plautus during the Renaissance a host of imitations of his play appeared in Italian, French, and German. Long after Shakespeare a French farce, *Les Jumeaux de Brighton,* 1908, by Tristan Bernard, exploited the motif with typical Gallic humor, and in our own time a Broadway musical comedy, *The Boys from Syracuse,* re-clothed it in up-to-date American slang and rollicking music.

There is, of course, much matter in *The Comedy of Errors* that is not in the *Menaechmi.* Even if Shakespeare did not put it in during the revision of his first draft, as we have allowed ourselves to conjecture, there it is, and he found it somewhere. It is amusing and, perhaps, instructive to examine these differences and to trace their sources, for they throw some light on Shakespeare's reading and on the things that interested him.

The first thing we notice in a comparison of the two plays is that there is but one pair of twins in Plautus while in Shakespeare there are two, a pair of masters and a pair of men-servants. There can be little doubt that Shakespeare got this idea from another play of Plautus, the *Amphitruo.* Like the *Menaechmi* this play has been admired and imitated in many ages and in many languages from the crude English interlude, *Jack Juggler,* to the brilliant French adaptation, Giraudoux's *Amphitryon 38,* in which the acting of Lunt and Fontanne once took our country by storm. In this Plautine play we have two pairs of indistinguishables: Jupiter in the form of Amphitruo, and Mercury in the form of Amphitruo's servant, Sosia. It was this latter doublet, probably, that gave Shakespeare the idea of the twin servants in his play. This doubling of the twins gives an opportunity for doubling and redoubling the instances of mistaken identity—there are many more in the *Errors* than in the *Menaechmi*—and the fun grows fast and furious as master mistakes man and man his master, to say nothing of the cases when the citizens and the wife mistake the stranger for their neighbor and her husband. But this is not all that Shakespeare has borrowed from the *Amphitruo.* The central scene of that play shows the husband denied admission to his house and insulted as an impostor by Mercury-Sosia on the ground that Amphitruo is already within, as indeed he is in the form of Jupiter-Amphitruo. There is nothing in the least like this in the *Menaechmi;* Shakespeare has cleverly lifted a scene from one Plautine play and put it into his adaptation of another with capital comic effect. It is, indeed, a situation provocative of lusty laughter, as those who saw *The Boys from Syracuse* will remember. This combining two Latin comedies into one English one—'contamination' is the technical term—was to become the regular practice of the Elizabethans, even of such scholarly playwrights as Jonson in *The Case is Altered* and Chapman in *All Fools.* They must have felt that the comparatively simple plots of

Plautus and Terence would not suffice to meet the demands of the Elizabethan audience for livelier and more varied action. Shakespeare seems here to have shown his contemporaries the way.

There is yet another and quite an important difference between the *Menaechmi* and *The Comedy of Errors*. Shakespeare's play begins with the father of the twins arrested and in danger of death in the hostile city of Ephesus; it closes with the reunion there of the whole family: the brothers, the father, and his long-lost wife. This is the so-called 'enveloping action' in which, as in a framework, the play proper is set. In Plautus, on the other hand, the father dies before the play begins and the mother never appears at all. This action was apparently suggested to Shakespeare by the famous medieval tale of Apollonius of Tyre, retold in Elizabethan prose by Laurence Twine in 1579. Here we have the separation of a family in a storm at sea, the father's long search for his wife and child, and their final reunion in the town of Ephesus. Readers of Shakespeare will recognize this as the central theme of one of his latest plays, *Pericles, Prince of Tyre*. It is, of course, an essentially romantic theme, possibly, as has been suggested, Shakespeare's later addition to his draft for the purpose of giving it something of the romantic flavor so dear to Elizabethans. Finally one more element in the *Errors* must be mentioned, this time clearly one of Shakespeare's own invention. This is the introduction into the action of Luciana, the gentle sister of the jealous wife. She not only furnishes character contrast, but brings in, however mildly, the required love interest, since she is courted by the wandering twin, whom, of course, she mistakes for her sister's husband. Such a character was impossible in Latin comedy, which reflected a society where unmarried girls were kept, so to speak, under lock and key, but her introduction gave Shakespeare the chance to end his play with the prospect of a wedding, a conventional close of Elizabethan comedy.

From what has been said so far it might seem as if Shakespeare's sole merit in this play consisted in getting the proper materials and neatly joining them together. This, however, is far from being the case. *The Comedy of Errors* is rather an admirable texture than a mechanical adjustment. Given a working pattern in the Plautine play, Shakespeare proceeds to weave his strands together into a new design. Of all the many adaptations of the *Menaechmi*, *The Comedy of Errors* is by far the freest and the most original. Shakespeare has transformed the sordid atmosphere of his source into a setting that breathes an air of travel, adventure, and romance. He shifted the scene of action from the little-known town of Epidamnum to Ephesus, a city famous for the cult of Diana, who in her other form of Hecate was the goddess of witches. Shakespeare, moreover, had learned from his school reading in the Bible (Acts XIX. 12-19) that Ephesus was a town notorious for evil spirits, exorcists like Dr. Pinch, and books of magic. Strange things might happen in such a town, and both the traveling twin and his servant suspect enchantment in their surroundings.

> They say this town is full of cozenage;
> As, nimble jugglers that deceive the eye,
> Dark-working sorcerers that change the mind,
> Soul-killing witches that deform the body,

says Antipholus of Syracuse. 'This is the fairy land,' cries his man, Dromio, 'we talk with goblins, owls, and sprites.' Yet, strange as it may seem, this haunted Ephesus is a very English town, a sea-port like London, with its harbor and mart, its inns and houses distinguished by painted signs: the Centaur, the Phoenix, and the Porpentine. Apart from the 'errors,' men behave there much as they would in Shakespeare's London; merchants transact business in the open street and debtors are arrested by an officer clad in a suit of buff. In all this, of course, Shakespeare was but following a native convention that went back past Udall to the makers of the Miracles, who shifted the scene of the Nativity from Bethlehem in Jewry to a stable on the Yorkshire moors, and sent Joseph bird-nesting in the hedgerows of East Anglia.

While shifting the scene Shakespeare at the same time bettered the manners, not to say the morals, of the original characters. The twins of Plautus are really a sorry pair of rogues; the citizen slips out of his house with his wife's cloak, a present stolen for the courtesan whom, he says, he loves far better; the traveler emerges from this gay lady's abode, chuckling over the food, drink, and embraces he has enjoyed there while mistaken for her lover. He goes off with a cloak given him to be altered, and a bracelet—a chain in Shakespeare, as more conspicuous on the stage—to be enlarged, with the firm purpose of keeping as his own these unexpected gifts from the gods. The prominent role of the courtesan in Plautus is cut down to a minimum by Shakespeare; it is worth noting that the citizen visits her only when he is locked out from his own house where his wife, he thinks, is feasting a party of friends. This Shakespearean twin has been a soldier and saved his lord's life in battle; his brother, the traveler, offers like an honest man to pay for the chain thrust upon him by the goldsmith, flies from the courtesan as from the devil, and makes honorable love to a decent girl. It is a very different world, this of Shakespeare's.

The dominant comic element in *The Comedy of Errors* is that of action. After a rather tedious first scene which serves as a prologue, the fun begins with the first case of mistaken identity and runs on unbroken with increasing speed to the final solution. It is the best plotted of Shakespeare's early comedies, due, no doubt, to the fact that he had the play of Plautus as a model and preserved the Plautine unities. The whole action takes place in a single day and in one place, a street in Ephesus, for we should disregard as the work of modern editors such scene-headings as 'a hall in the Duke's palace' and 'the house of Antipholus.' There is a certain, though limited, amount of the old physical comedy, the repeated beatings of the unfortunate servants, and there is an amusing report of the revenge taken off-stage by Antipholus of Ephesus upon the exorcist. In the main, however, the comedy is that of situation, the ridiculous results of repeated instances of mistaken identity, culminating in the central scene before the citizen's house, and only ending when for the first time the twins are brought face to face and are recognized by their parents, who at the same time regain each other after years of separation. For this final recognition scene Shakespeare assembles the full strength of the company upon the stage, whereas in the corresponding Plautine scene only the twins and a servant are present, and, far from any reconciliation, the citizen declares he would sell his wife, if anyone would buy her. Beginner as he was Shakespeare had already a keen sense of theatrical effect; he uses here a device that he was to employ again and again in later and better plays. The whole series of complications is absurdly incredible, but it develops logically from the primary hypothesis of indistinguishable twins, and the very absurdity contributes to the comic effect.

There is little in the spoken dialogue of this play either to amuse or to delight. The text, composed of blank verse, rhyme, and prose, shows evident marks of revision. The prose scenes, packed with word-play and puns after the manner of Lyly and, indeed, that of the older Interludes and Morals, need elaborate annotation to be understood today, but so do the plays of Aristophanes, the first great master of comedy. Jokes that are current in one age lose their point in the passage of time. Dromio's geographical description of the kitchen wench seems to show that Shakespeare was already reading Rabelais, as we know he did later from the borrowed name Holofernes in *Love's Labour's Lost*, and from an allusion to Gargantua's mouth in *As You Like It*. There is some lively patter of speech and reply in the talk between the masters and their servants, and one flash of genuine dramatic utterance when the courtesan, deciding to go to Adriana in the hope of regaining her ring, exclaims: 'Forty ducats is too much to lose.'

There is surprisingly little in this play of the poetic expression we might expect from the author of *Venus and Adonis*. It would seem, indeed, as if the young playwright had sternly curbed his poetic vein in his determination to construct an effective stage-play in the manner of Plautus. Only in the appeal of Antipholus of Syracuse to Luciana is there a gleam of the fanciful poetic conceit so common in the other early plays:

> O, train me not, sweet mermaid, with thy note,
> To drown me in thy sister flood of tears:
> Sing, siren, for thyself, and I will dote:
> Spread o'er the silver waves thy golden hairs,
> And as a bed I'll take them and there lie.

It would be idle to expect in so early a play any distinct foreshadowing of Shakespeare's later mastery of characterization. Yet there is, perhaps, more skill in character portrayal in this play than has usually been noticed. Antipholus of Ephesus is a moody, hot-tempered man, the *homo iracundus* of Plautus; his brother is a gentler, mildly melancholic soul, with a vein of sentiment and superstition. There is a distinct and purposed difference between the servants; Dromio of Syracuse is a jolly wisecracker who lightens his master's humor with his many jests, a role that must have been written for the leading comedian of the company, presumably Will Kempe. The other Dromio, on the contrary, is a mere household drudge, the target of blows from his master, his mistress, and the traveling twin.

There is, however, one character in the play firmly conceived and realistically developed, the passionate and jealous Adriana. Shakespeare had two models on which to fashion her: the querulous *mulier* of Plautus and the conventional shrew of the native drama, such as Mrs. Noah. He chose neither, but created on his own a character quite new in English comedy. Adriana appears first merely as the jealous wife, vexed by her husband's indifference at home and suspicious of his affairs abroad. It becomes more and more apparent, however, that her jealousy springs from her love; when she hears he is arrested for debt she is prompt to bail him out; when it seems that he has run mad she is profoundly distressed and takes the only known means to cure him. In her wrangle with the Abbess she betrays her master passion:

> I will attend my husband, be his nurse,
> Diet his sickness, for it is my office,
> And will have no attorney but myself.

The key to her character seems to be given in her words to the Duke:

> Antipholus, my husband,
> Whom I made lord of me and all I had,
> At your important letters.

She was, it seems, an heiress, a ward, as Shakespeare's audience would understand, of the Duke, who had bestowed her in marriage on a soldier of fortune—for Antipholus was a stranger, brought to Ephesus by 'that most famous warrior, Duke Menaphon.' No doubt she loved her husband; he was hers, bought with all she had, but it is not surprising that Antipholus was at times restless in the arms of a rich and domineering wife, who, he says, 'is shrewish when I keep not hours.' Adriana is the possessive woman, a type not unfamiliar today, revealed with tragic intensity in *The Silver Cord*. To the Elizabethans, it seems, there was something amusing in this type; Elizabethan women, it appears from *The Taming of the Shrew*, were more easily brought to heel than their descendants today. Yet one wonders if to Shakespeare Adriana was altogether comic.

The Comedy of Errors is in many ways an interesting play, but it would be foolish to call it a masterpiece. It is, on the contrary, a clever specimen of prentice work, following a given pattern with original additions and embroideries. Some of these have already been pointed out and little remains to be said in conclusion. Yet we may recall that here as in many later plays, notably in *The Merchant of Venice*, Shakespeare allows a cloud of danger, even of threatened death, to overshadow the comic action. There is here, also, a real, if far from profound, interest in human affairs: in the troubled relations of man and wife, in the promised happiness of young lovers. It is a good example, one of the best in English, of farce comedy. On the other hand it is a play of curiously little promise. Had Shakespeare died at as early an age as Greene and left but this play behind him, it

108 APPRENTICE WORK

would have been impossible to foretell his future greatness as a poet, a humorous observer of human follies, and as the supreme creator in dramatic form of living breathing men and women.

THE TWO GENTLEMEN OF VERONA

If *The Comedy of Errors* is a piece of prentice work following a set pattern, *The Two Gentlemen of Verona* may be regarded as an example of work by the same apprentice given a free hand to compose without a model. The result is a pleasant little play, full of promise, but quite as full of faults, particularly in the matter of plot construction. This, it seems, the apprentice had not yet mastered. Faulty construction, vagueness of characterization, except for a few figures, and uncertainty of metrical expression all mark *The Two Gentlemen* as an early play, possibly *c.* 1592. It has never been a popular stage-play, a fact which, after all, is not surprising; the prentice was still far from becoming a master of his craft.

What the young playwright planned seems clear enough; it was to be a comedy of romantic love and friendship, something in the manner of Lyly, but one that dealt with real men and women instead of the mythological figures of that courtly dramatist—this, because Shakespeare was writing for the public stage. It is clear, from internal evidence, that he had been reading Brooke's poem, *Romeus and Juliet*. This might suggest Verona as the scene of the play, but Brooke's tragic tale furnished no material for a comic plot. Where, we may ask, did Shakespeare get the material out of which he built up the action of *The Two Gentlemen?* It has been usual to point to an episode in Montemayor's Spanish romance, *Diana Enamorada*, 1562, possibly transmitted through the medium of a lost play, *Felix and Philiomena*.[1] The correspondence between some scenes of *The Two Gentlemen* and the *Diana* is so close that it is certain that Shakespeare must have known this romance, in one form or another. There is no reason to believe that he read Spanish; an English translation by Bartholomew Yonge, 1598, is too late for our play, so unless he read this translation in manuscript, which seems unlikely, we are thrown back upon French

[1] This lost play was performed by the Queen's Company in January 1585 and, as this company was still active till past the date, 1590-91, generally assigned to Shakespeare's play, there is no reason to believe that Shakespeare could get possession of their play-book.

versions of *Diana* in 1578 and 1587. Shakespeare could, no doubt, pick his way through a French story.

The essential features of the episode in the *Diana* may be briefly rehearsed.

> The lady, Felismena, tells her story to a group of Diana's nymphs. A noble cavalier, Don Felix, she says, fell in love with her and sent her a love letter by her maid. Felismena's account of her refusal in feigned anger to receive the letter notwithstanding her eagerness to see it, the maid's trick to get it into her hands, and her final perusal of it are very close to the action in the play. All that is new in Shakespeare is Julia's tearing of the letter, a palpable bit of stage business. A correspondence then sprang up between the lady and Don Felix, which led at last to her confession of love for him. His father, however, eager for the advancement of his son, despatched him to the Court and Felix left his lady without a word of farewell. Felismena now disguised herself as a man and followed Felix to the Court. Here the master of the house where she lodged invited her to step to her window and hear a serenade. Next day Felismena learned of her false lover's courtship of the lady Celia, and shortly after she entered his service as the page, Valerio. In this role she became, like Julia in the play, a bearer of love letters to her rival, but unlike Julia, she pleads her master's cause. Celia, however, distrusts Don Felix, since she knows he has been false to a former mistress, and she herself falls in love with his messenger. When her avowal of love is rejected by the disguised Felismena, Celia flees, and, apparently, kills herself. At this news Felix leaves the Court for parts unknown and is again followed by Felismena in a new disguise, that of a shepherdess. Later on she sees three men attacking a single knight; she kills two of them with her arrows and the knight accounts for the third. He now reveals himself as Felix, whereupon Felismena discloses her identity and reproaches him for inconstancy in love. He swoons away, but, revived by a magic elixir, is forgiven by Felismena and promptly married to her.

Two things are plain at a glance. First, Shakespeare has completely recast the end of the original episode; Celia's death would be out of place in a comedy and the wandering of Felix with Felismena's pursuit and rescue of him would be hard to present on the stage. A new denouement would have to be devised. Furthermore the episode furnished material only for the sub-plot of the play, the story of Proteus and Julia; it contains a false lover, who is not, however, a false friend. Now the rivalry between love and friendship was, as the *Sonnets* show, very much in Shakespeare's mind in the early 'nineties. Another character, missing in the source, was called for, the true lover and perfect friend, both for the sake of character contrast and to enhance the dramatic action. Accordingly Shakespeare invents this character and calls him Valentine, a name of more significance then than now. With this we get our two gentlemen. The faithless lover of the source, rebaptized Proteus, another significant name, can now function also as the false friend, while the true lover, Valentine, can show himself the perfect friend by renouncing his love for friendship's sake, as Lyly's Eumenides does in *Endimion*. The Celia of the source may serve as Valentine's mistress, Silvia, and the set of four main figures is complete. All that is further necessary is to devise an action in which to exhibit them in their characteristic behavior. Let us examine the plot that Shakespeare constructed for this end, always remembering that the source was far from setting him a pattern.

The play opens with a dialogue between the two gentlemen: Valentine, heart-free and scoffing at love, is leaving home for the Court; Proteus in love with Julia remains behind. The second scene between Julia and her maid develops the incident of his love letter and shows Julia's love for him; in the third, the course of their love is interrupted by his father's decision to send Proteus to join his friend at Court. In both these scenes we see the influence of the source. The second act shows Valentine at Court in love with Silvia, the Duke's daughter, and made aware of her love for him by a pretty device on the lady's part. Proteus now joins him, learns of his love and of his plan to elope with Silvia, but promptly falls in love with her himself and decides to betray his friend. The act closes with Julia's decision to follow Proteus disguised as a page, a scene charmingly developed from a mere hint in the source.

In the first scene of the third act Proteus betrays his friend to the Duke, and the Duke banishes Valentine on pain of death. Valentine departs, comforted by the promise of his false friend to carry letters from him to Silvia. After his departure, Proteus deceives the Duke by promising to estrange Silvia from Valentine and by forwarding her marriage to the rich and foolish Thurio; he also arranges a serenade at which he may have the chance to plead his own cause.

With the fourth act the scene shifts. The banished Valentine is captured in a wood by a band of outlaws. Charmed by his good looks and supposed command of languages, they offer to make him their captain. He accepts, but only on condition that they refrain from outrage 'on silly women and poor passengers.' The scene is one of the poorest in Shakespeare's plays, so tame and flat, indeed, that one is tempted to suspect a reviser's hand here. There is but one line in the scene that has the true Shakespearean ring, an outlaw's oath: 'By the bald scalp of Robin Hood's fat friar.' Here, perhaps, is the clue to the scene. Shakespeare needed Valentine as captain of an outlaw band for the denouement he was planning, and when he thought of outlaws he instinctively thought of Robin and his band, as he was to do later when he wrote of a banished Duke 'and a many merry men with him,' living in Arden 'like the old Robin Hood of England.' But it is a sudden shift from Italy to Sherwood, and the device of putting Valentine at the head of an outlaw band is a curious example of Shakespeare's occasional carelessness, or, perhaps, poverty of invention, when confronted with some pressing problem of dramatic construction. It belongs in the same category as the pirate ship in *Hamlet* or the bear that devours Antigonus in *The Winter's Tale*.

The scene shifts back again to the court, where Proteus and Thurio are serenading Silvia. They are overheard by the disguised Julia and the Host of her inn, and a little later Julia hears Proteus paying court to Silvia at her window. Silvia rejects his suit and reproaches him as a traitor, both to love, for she has somehow heard of Julia, and to friendship. Julia's running commentary on the protestations of Proteus and the replies of Silvia is in the true vein of comedy, but hardly equals in simple humor the remark of the Host at the end of the long scene: 'By my halidom I was fast asleep.' Wearied by the importunity of Proteus, Silvia enlists a hitherto unknown Sir Eglamour to escort her in her flight to Valentine, but before she escapes she has to undergo an interview with the disguised Julia, now the page and messenger of Proteus. The dialogue between the ladies is in Shakespeare's best early manner; he is here working on and improving his source, and that he was already competent to do.

The last act opens briskly with a group of short scenes. Silvia and Sir Eglamour fly together; the Duke discovers her escape and sets out in pursuit accompanied by Proteus and Thurio. Silvia next appears in the hands of the outlaws, Eglamour having run off, never to appear again. It seems rather too bad of Shakespeare to treat a gentleman so, but he had to get rid of Eglamour, and the convention of comedy forbade him to let the outlaws kill the knight. This brings us to the last scene, always a stone of offense to realistically minded critics. It opens with a soliloquy by Valentine invoking the memory of Silvia, but hardly has he spoken her name when she appears attended by Proteus, who has rescued her from the outlaws, and the disguised Julia. Proteus presses his suit upon the defiant Silvia, but when at last he lays violent hands upon her, Valentine rushes out on him. Here is a situation fitter, perhaps, for melodrama than for comedy, but it is comedy that Shakespeare is writing and it must have a happy ending. Accordingly Proteus repents, Valentine forgives him, and to show the full extent of his forgiveness utters the, to us, amazing words: 'All that was mine in Silvia I give thee.' This is too much for Julia; she swoons, and on recovering reveals herself by means of the ring Proteus gave her at parting. The inconstant Proteus promptly returns to his first love, and Valentine joins their hands. The outlaws now bring in the captured Duke and Thurio; Valentine sets them free, the Duke hands Silvia, who has been silent all this time, over to Valentine and pardons the outlaws. And with this the party leaves the stage for a double wedding, a most lame and impotent conclusion.

So unhappy, in fact, is this conclusion that two recent editors of the play are quite certain that Shakespeare was not guilty of it. One of them, the lamented Quiller-Couch, ventures the strange suggestion that 'Shakespeare invented a solution which at the first performance was found to be ineffective; that the final scene was rewritten—not by Shakespeare—and given its crude and conventional *coup-de-théâtre*.' It would be hard, if not impossible, to imagine a scene from Shakespeare's pen less effective than the present text, yet such a scene is implied in this suggestion. The truth is that Quiller-Couch was no fit judge here; he so resented Valentine's speech that he was, he admits, tempted to exclaim: 'By this time there are *no* gentlemen in Verona.' But what did Shakespeare, who was proud to sign himself 'gentleman,' think of such a renunciation as Valentine's? The answer may be found in his *Sonnets;* in Sonnet xxxiv he shows himself so moved by the repentance of the friend who had robbed him of his mistress that he declares the friend's tears 'ransom all ill deeds'—compare Valentine's words to Proteus:

Who by repentance is not satisfied
Is not of heaven nor earth.

Shakespeare goes even further, for in Sonnet XL he cries to his repentant friend: 'Take all my loves,' as complete a renunciation certainly as that of Valentine's. Clearly this renunciation which shocks us so seemed to Shakespeare—and to his Elizabethan audience—a heroic example of romantic friendship.

Yet after all is said in its defense, the business of the renunciation is anything but satisfactory. The main fault, perhaps, is the haste with which it is handled. Within the compass of about twenty lines Proteus tries to force Silvia; Valentine rescues her and denounces him as a 'ruffian'; Proteus begs forgiveness; Valentine is satisfied and renounces his lady in favor of his friend. This is more than racing speed, especially when compared with the leisurely dialogue between Valentine and the Duke which follows. Perhaps a modified form of Quiller-Couch's suggestion might be tentatively put forward. Shakespeare's first draft of the scene ran, let us suppose, along the lines of the present text, but was far longer and included a debate between the two gentlemen packed with the conceits and metaphors so frequent in the *Sonnets* that deal with the theme of love and friendship. The actors, however, impatient to bring the play to an end and well aware that figures of speech permissible in sonnets were impossible on the stage, may have insisted on heavy cuts. The young playwright, not yet established as a master, would be forced to turn over his script to some playhouse hack. This scribbler then not only cut it to bits, but patched up the holes with jigging rhymes: 'most accurst'—'Be the worst'; 'plain and free'—'I give thee'; 'I may spy'—'constant eye'—rhymes that grate upon the ear. If this hypothesis is too fanciful and the present text must stand as Shakespeare wrote it, we can only suppose that the young playwright invented a situation that he was incapable of handling. There is no such situation in the source which furnished a pattern for earlier scenes, and without such a pattern the prentice playwright made a bad mess of his denouement.

The foregoing summary of this seldom read play does, perhaps, more than justice to the plot construction. There is a constant shifting of place, and the topography of the play is most confusing. Valentine leaves Verona for the Court at Milan, but later the Duke of Milan says he loves 'a lady in Verona here,' and Valentine tells Thurio, a courtier at Milan, 'Verona shall not hold thee.' Valentine is supposed to live in exile at Mantua, but he turns up in a wood near Milan, and Speed welcomes Launce to Padua, where neither of them has any business to be. Where, after all, is the action taking place? Unless this confusion is due to revision without the author's knowledge, we must find Shakespeare guilty of inexcusable carelessness. The main action, also, is repeatedly interrupted by long stretches of witty word-play and by scenes in which a clown plays up to the audience. Perhaps Shakespeare felt that the plot he had devised was too slight to hold the interest of his hearers, and so proceeded to pad it out with whatever came handy. It is not for the story that we read *The Two Gentlemen* today.

Yet to the student of Shakespeare's development there is much of interest in the story, particularly in its anticipation of later and better work. Julia's discussion of her suitors with her maid is a forerunner of the dialogue between Portia and Nerissa on the same theme, and her embassy on her master's behalf to Silvia looks forward to Viola's mission to Olivia. Valentine's rope ladder and Silvia's pretext of confession at a friar's cell reappear in *Romeo and Juliet,* and Valentine's lament over his banishment anticipates the frantic outburst of Romeo. There is even a likeness between the reported interview of Silvia with her 'uncompassionate sire' and the scene on the stage between Juliet and her irate father. In such things, as in much else, this early play is full of promise.

Shakespeare's use of language in *The Two Gentlemen* looks at once forward and back. The backward glance is reminiscent of the dialogue in Lyly's plays. The opening scene, for example, presents two of Lyly's gentlemen in debate and runs on into a dialogue between a lover and a page that reads almost like a transcript from one of Lyly's comedies. Valentine and Proteus mock the foolish Thurio in the very style of Lyly's witty gentlemen, and Lylian antithesis, quips, puns, and word-play besprinkle the dialogue throughout. The considerable amount of prose, between a third and a fourth of the whole play, is itself a testimony to Lyly's influence, although the best prose scenes, Launce's soliloquies, are marked by a homely realism that Lyly never knew.

On the other hand we have the forward-looking aspect in the lyric-poetic diction of this play. The vein of poetry that was checked in *The Comedy of Errors* breaks out here in musical flow. And this is right and proper; the *Errors* is a play of action and situation; this is a comedy of sentiment and emotion. The horseplay of beatings, of the rope's end and the crowbar, has vanished along with most of the clownish doggrel, the poet of *Venus and Adonis* and the *Sonnets* gives himself free hand here. He has not yet attained the height of supreme dramatic utterance, but there are already hopeful signs as in Julia's cry when she retrieves her lover's name from the letter she has torn in feigned anger:

> Poor wounded name! My bosom, as a bed
> Shall lodge thee till thy wound be throughly heal'd.

For the most part the verse is graceful and easy, rather fanciful than forceful. Such an imperfect quatrain as this might come from a lost sonnet:

> O, how this spring of love resembleth
>   The uncertain glory of an April day,
> Which now shows all the beauty of the sun,
>   And by and by a cloud takes all away!

As might be expected from young Shakespeare, there is a goodly portion of Elizabethan conceits:

> Except I be by Silvia in the night,
> There is no music in the nightingale;
> Unless I look on Silvia in the day,
> There is no day for me to look upon.

Finally we hear the pure lyric note in the song, 'Who is Silvia?' familiar today in Schubert's musical setting to hundreds who have never read the play. It is, perhaps, the first of the enchanting songs with which Shakespeare adorns his comedies.

In the field of characterization *The Two Gentlemen* at once surpasses the *Errors* and gives promise of better things to come. In the *Errors* the tangled plot depends upon the simultaneous presence in Ephesus of two pairs of identical twins. This is an external fact in no way dependent upon the characters of the actors. In *The Two Gentlemen*, on the contrary, all that happens to the four chief characters happens because they are what they are: Valentine a true lover and a trustful friend; Proteus inconstant both in love and friendship; Silvia a modest, but faithfully loving lady; Julia a reckless and passionate girl. It might be objected, perhaps, that the gentlemen are types rather than fully rounded characters. They have been created to carry out a preconceived action and the action at times is so hurried as to throw a shadow of unreality upon them. This is particularly noticeable in the final scene, but it appears elsewhere as well. It is hard to believe, for instance, that Proteus at the first sight of Silvia should forget, to use his own words, 'the remembrance of my former love.' Romeo, to be sure, does much the same, but his behavior is at least excused by the hardheartedness of Rosaline and the instant response of a Juliet ready to return 'grace for grace, and love for love.' There is no such excuse for Proteus, and it may be that Shakespeare realized this, for in a scene that almost immediately follows this change of affection he puts into the mouth of Proteus a long soliloquy attempting to justify his behavior by a string of sophistical arguments, culminating in the pure egotism of 'I to myself am dearer than a friend.' Silvia is rather a charming sketch than a full-length portrait, but there is something delightfully feminine in her first advances, always within the bounds of courtly etiquette, to a shyly hesitating lover. Julia, on the other hand, the first of Shakespeare's loving girls, has been completely transformed from the conventional heroine of romance in the source. Her struggle between desire and shame before she dons a page's suit to follow her lover, her firm confidence in the welcome she will meet, her disillusion falteringly revealed by her comments on the serenade that betrays the inconstancy of Proteus, the soliloquy in which she compares Silvia's picture with her own forsaken charms, all are original with Shakespeare, and all go to build up the image of a woman, 'not too good for human nature's daily food.' There is, indeed, something almost feline in her instinctive impulse to scratch out the eyes of her rival's portrait. And, if we may trust the text as it stands, it is her quick wit and instant interference at the moment of supreme complication that brings about the happy ending.

The two comic servants play a very small part in the action; yet *The Two Gentlemen* would be a duller play without them. They are called in 'the names of all the actors' affixed to the Folio text, 'Speed, a clownish servant to Valentine' and 'Launce, the like to Proteus.' Modern editors religiously follow this designation, but to group Speed and Launce together as Clowns is to ignore Shakespeare's plain intention. There is nothing of the Clown in Speed, unless the term is stretched to cover every type of merrymaker. We hear of Speed early in the play as 'Sir Valentine's page,' and a sensitive reader will recognize him on his appearance in the first scene of the play as a typical Lylian page, saucy, critical both of his master and of his master's friend, and very wide-awake to what is going on about him. It is he who picks up the glove Silvia has dropped for a love-token, unnoticed by her dreamy lover, and it is he who interprets to his master the significance of the letter that Silvia first bade him write and then returned to him. That a modern editor should call Speed 'a poor stick without character' betrays a strange misapprehension of the role he plays.

Launce, on the other hand, is a true Clown, the first and one of the best of the noble company of Costard, Bottom, and Dogberry. He and his fellows derive from a late development of the Vice, the boorish, stupid butt of the mischief-makers. Shakespeare raised them above this rather clumsy type by giving them a good conceit of themselves, and a homely, hardly self-conscious, gift of humor. Launce, for example, is not aware of the fun in the funny things he says. The actor who plays this role must keep a straight face even when he cracks such a joke as 'when didst thou see me heave up my leg.' We may be sure that the first actor to play this part was Will Kempe, and the part, no doubt, was written with an eye on him, since a play for Shakespeare's Company without a good part for the chief comedian would be quite unthinkable. Launce has even less to do with the plot than Speed; he does not appear till the action is well in progress and he drops out before the last act. But it is a capital role for Kempe, famous as early as 1590 as 'that most comical jest-monger.' In his two best scenes Launce has the stage to himself and can talk, as doubtless Kempe did, directly to the audience. In two other scenes he plays over against Speed, and in both his rustic mother-wit gets the better of the smart young page. We can almost hear the chuckle with which he sends the boy off to the whipping he has earned by his delay in prying into Launce's love affair. It is impossible, of course, to think of Launce without thinking of his dog, Crab, and one of Launce's most sympathetic traits is his affection for this ill-mannered cur. We may easily imagine the play that Kempe made on the stage with Crab. Perhaps his play was a bit too far on the side of buffoonery for Shakespeare's taste; certainly Shakespeare wrote other parts for Kempe, but Crab never appears on Shakespeare's stage again.

With all its faults *The Two Gentlemen* is a landmark in the development of Shakespeare's art. It heralds his entrance into the field where he was to win some of his greatest triumphs, that of romantic comedy. It develops the theme of love, checked and crossed by misadventure, but winning at last to its happy goal. To prevent this theme from sinking into sentimentality Shakespeare balances it with scenes of wit and humor. The young poet joins hands with the prentice play-wright to throw a gleam of April sunshine on the love story; the humorist allows himself to laugh at times at its extravagance. Most important of all, Shakespeare here creates for the first time characters who control the action by the inner necessity of their being, and two at least of these characters, Launce and Julia, are lasting contributions to Shakespeare's gallery of living men and women.

LOVE'S LABOUR'S LOST

Love's Labour's Lost is the most puzzling of the comedies of Shakespeare's youth, and this for the reason that it is not a homogeneous piece of work. The revision suspected in the plays already discussed is made certain here by the evidence of the title-page of the first edition. This, the quarto of 1598, advertises the play as:

> A PLEASANT CONCEITED COMEDIE . . . AS IT
> WAS PRESENTED BEFORE HER HIGHNESS THIS
> LAST CHRISTMAS. NEWLY CORRECTED AND
> AUGMENTED BY W. SHAKESPEARE.

It is the general belief of scholars that this edition was published to supersede an earlier quarto, now lost, which, like the first editions of *Romeo and Juliet* and *Hamlet*, was a 'stolen and surreptitious' copy. This unsatisfactory publication was, it appears, 'corrected' by the author, but Shakespeare did more than 'correct'; he 'augmented' it, no doubt for the Christmas festivities of 1597 when it was to be presented before her Highness. We have besides the quarto the Folio text, printed from a copy of the quarto, but further 'corrected' by another hand than Shakespeare's. The result is a text in three stages: as it was first composed, as it was revised, and as it appears in the Folio, all three of which are blended in modern editions.

The date of the first composition is uncertain; guesses vary from 1588 to 1596, but there is a fairly general agreement that it is a work of Shakespeare's youth—1592-3 is probably an approximately correct date—whereas the revision is the work of the successful author of *Romeo and Juliet, The Merchant of Venice,* and *King Henry IV.* In other words *Love's Labour's Lost* contains work by the prentice hand along with that by the master of his craft. Some of this work is casually juxtaposed, some new matter has taken the place of old; and in two instances—IV. iii. 296-317, and V. ii. 827-32—old lines that Shakespeare meant, but failed, to cancel appear just before a later and better version, Apparently the 'copy' sent to the printer was Shakespeare's first draft, 'corrected and augmented' in such a way as to bewilder the poor compositor, as it has puzzled editors ever since. It is another instance of Shakespeare's indifference to the printed version of his plays; so long as the performance went off well, Shakespeare was careless what readers might think of a work designed primarily for the stage rather than the study.

It is not too much to say that neither the quarto nor the Folio gives us an intelligible reading version. Both abound in mistakes and contradictions, and it is sometimes impossible to tell who is speaking to whom. It has taken the editorial labor of scholars for a couple of centuries to produce a readable text and even yet scholars are not always agreed. Into the bitter controversies of editors it is, happily, unnecessary for us to enter. The main drift and meaning of the play is plain enough and it is that which we may now consider.

There is no known source of *Love's Labour's Lost*. Shakespeare had here no pattern to work from as with *The Comedy of Errors,* nor even such hints as Montemayor furnished him for certain scenes in *The Two Gentlemen of Verona.* He could, however, dispense with such aid, since what he was planning was less a regular drama involving interesting action than a gay evening's entertainment for a select audience. What we may call the framework of the play, the visit of a French princess to the King of Navarre, seems to have been suggested to him by an actual embassy of Marguerite de Valois to the Court of Henry of Navarre in 1578, to settle questions involving the sovereignty of Aquitaine and an alleged debt of 100,000 crowns on the part of Henry. Marguerite and Henry were husband and wife, but that does not seem to have troubled either of them, and while diplomats and secretaries were at work on the business of the embassy, the court became a center of amorous intrigue. Shakespeare may have heard of this embassy from some of the English gentlemen who flocked to the Huguenot Court of Navarre. It is probably more than a coincidence that the unconventional ending of this comedy without a marriage, so that the whole action is in a sense 'love's labour's lost,' corresponds to the final departure of Marguerite from her husband's court.

Furthermore, Professor Campbell has shown that the action of *Love's Labour's Lost* is so planned as to resemble the entertainment offered to Queen Elizabeth by one of the noblemen whom she visited in her stately progresses. The action all takes place out of doors in the royal park; the amusement offered the Princess in the play—shooting at the deer, dancing on the green, the Masque of Russians, the rustic pageant of the Nine Worthies, and the final country song—corresponds quite closely to what we know of the progresses of the English Queen. This explains the absence of a coherent plot in the play and in particular the disproportionate length of the last act in which the entertainment of the Princess concludes.[1]

What has been said so far concerns only the text and the form of the play. What of its content and meaning? The main action deals with the fortunes of the King of Navarre and his three Lords. In order to pursue their studies and turn the court into 'a little academe,' they have forsworn the society of women, but the embassy of the Princess forces them to break their vow. The King and his lords promptly fall in love with the Princess and her ladies, who, instead of accepting their suit, mock them with merry jests until this courtship is broken off by the news of the death of the King of France. The Princess and her ladies depart with half promises of a return of love at the expiration of a year of trial. As Berowne remarks:

> Our wooing doth not end like an old play;
> Jack hath not Jill.

This brief analysis takes no account of the subordinate comic characters or of the general purport of the play. This may, perhaps, be best described as topical satire compounded of incidental thrusts at contemporary follies, and of a central theme as valid today as it was in Shakespeare's time. *Love's Labour's Lost* is the first opening of the satiric vein which flows with greater force than has been generally recognized through more than one of Shakespeare's plays. Many of the contemporary allusions, such as that to the dancing horse and to the Harvey-Nashe controversy, require annotation today. These we may pass by. It is another matter, however, with the personal satire passing into caricature which has been suspected in this play. Holofernes has been identified with the Italian scholar, Florio; Moth is supposed to stand for Nashe, because among other reasons, his name spelled backward, *Htom*, resembles Shakespeare's spelling of Nashe's Christian name, Thom; a reflection of the great philosopher, Gior-

---

[1] We should remember, however, that in its first printed form this play was not divided into acts, but ran unbroken in a continuous performance. The present division was made by the editors of the Folio.

dano Bruno, has been found in the first lord because the old spelling of his name, Berowne, rhymes in the play with 'moon.' Here, indeed, be proofs of Shakespeare's ingenuity of malice.

Several recent editors and critics have conceived the whole play as a thinly veiled attack upon the group of scholars and studious gentlemen that gathered about Sir Walter Raleigh, upon which group they have hung the label of 'The School of Night.' It is, however, unfortunate that this label is taken from a line in the play (iv. iii. 255) where the important word, *school*, has long been suspected as a misprint and has been emended in all possible ways: *scowl, stole, scroll,* et cetera. There is no reason to believe that Raleigh's coterie was ever known to his contemporaries as 'the school of night.' The charge most frequently brought against them was that of atheism, and to atheism there is not the most remote allusion in the play. As a matter of fact, there is not the slightest possible resemblance between the mathematicians, geographers, and misogynists of Raleigh's group and the 'well-accomplished,' merry, and amorous King of Navarre and his lords.

What Shakespeare aimed at in *Love's Labour's Lost* was something deeper and more permanent than a contemporary 'school of night'; it was the whole body of pedantry, affectation, and formal control of life, which flew in the face of nature. This tendency was, perhaps, especially dangerous in Shakespeare's day when enthusiasm for the newly discovered classics was degenerating into blind pedantry and the new delight in the exploitation of language was blossoming into fantastic affectation. Yet it is not unknown in our time, when academic formalism insists upon a doctor's degree as a *sine qua non* for a post in a college faculty. In our day, too, the passion for novelty of expression is, no doubt, one of the reasons why modern poets indulge in a preciosity of speech unintelligible to the common reader.

Shakespeare's sound sense revolted against this tendency away from nature, and *Love's Labour's Lost* is in essence a laughing philippic against both pedantry and affectation. It is a merry, but none the less vigorous, plea for simplicity and natural behavior. The unnatural vow of the King and his lords to follow learning at the expense of youth, pleasure, and beauty is broken by the natural passion of love. The pedantic Masque of the Worthies is driven from the stage by a quick fire of quips, puns, and broad jests such as rose naturally to the lips of laughter-loving Elizabethans. The pompous Spaniard falls a victim to the charms of a country wench and is 'infamonized among potentates' by a country clown. Berowne himself, too sensible to yield wholly to fashionable affectation, too courtly to escape them alto-gether, is beaten from his point device wooing, 'taffeta phrases, silken terms precise,' to 'russet yeas and honest kersey noes.' Everywhere sim-plicity and common sense triumph over pedantry and affectation; 'Young blood doth not obey an old decree.' Nature conquers art, and the play closes fitly with a nature lyric rising from the heart of the young poet lately come from rustic Stratford. Amid the follies and fancies and witty affectations of the town, Shakespeare has not for-gotten the Warwickshire meadows with 'daisies pied and violets blue,' or the homely sights and sounds about the cottages 'when icicles hang by the wall.' This is the conclusion of the whole matter, and 'the words of Mercury are harsh after the songs of Apollo.'

There is comparatively little comic action in *Love's Labour's Lost*. A play designed for a courtly audience could dispense with the rough fun the groundlings clamored for. The threatened fight between Ar-mado and Costard is averted by the news of the King of France's death. The central scene of the play (iv. iii) has a capital bit of action when three perjured lovers are in turn discovered and denounced: Dumaine by Longaville, Longaville by the King, and the King by Berowne, who himself is betrayed by Costard's arrival with his love letter to Rosaline. The fun of mistaken identity in the last scene, when the lovers court the wrong ladies, is a matter of words rather than of action, a statement which, in the main, holds good for the play as a whole.

The language of *Love's Labour's Lost* runs the gamut from prose and doggrel verse to rhyme in couplets, quatrains, and sonnet forms, and blank verse of varying excellence. Shakespeare has by now mas-tered the use of prose as a vehicle of comic comment. Take, for ex-ample, Costard's characterization of the Curate: 'a foolish mild man; an honest man, look you! and soon dash'd. He is a marvellous good neighbour, faith, and a very good bowler; but for Alisander—alas! you see how 'tis—a little o'erparted.' This is one of Shakespeare's magic touches which make a minor character, like the husband of Juliet's nurse, come suddenly alive before us. Sometimes, though rarely, the prose has almost the cadence of verse, as in Armado's pro-test against the wanton mockery of his presentation of Hector: 'The sweet war-man is dead and rotten. Sweet chucks, beat not the bones of the buried: when he breathed, he was a man.' The word-play of puns, quips, and retorts coruscates with a more than Lylian brilliancy. Many of the jests dealing with grammar-school studies sound very tame today, but they passed current with an audience in which every educated man had worked through the same curriculum. The best of the blank verse, probably the work of Shakespeare's revision, like Berowne's apology for love rises into lyric beauty:

> For valour, is not Love a Hercules,
> Still climbing trees in the Hesperides?
> Subtle as Sphinx; as sweet and musical
> As bright Apollo's lute, strung with his hair;
> And when Love speaks, the voice of all the gods
> Make heaven drowsy with the harmony.

It is especially in the field of characterization that *Love's Labour's Lost* surpasses both in variety and distinction the other comedies of the prentice period. This is due, no doubt, to the revision which gave Shakespeare a chance to heighten the telling touches of his portraits. It seems clear that in his first draft he paired off his characters in something like a Lylian balance; the King and three lords are opposed to the Princess and three ladies; a country lad is paired with a country lass; and a page is attendant upon his master. In the revision Shakespeare seems to have paid attention to only a few of the main figures. Little was done to heighten the character of the King, and it is impossible to distinguish Dumaine from Longaville. The character of Berowne, on the other hand, has been so elevated as to demand a separate and later treatment. Much the same may be said of the Princess and her ladies, except that the Princess is marked by a certain noble courtesy that seems to make her a royal cousin of Theseus in *A Midsummer Night's Dream*. The portrait of Rosaline, too, has been retouched till her wit-combats with Berowne foreshadow the clashes between Benedick and Beatrice in one of Shakespeare's supreme comedies. Moth [2] is a typical Lylian page in his precocious impudence; his association with a master whom he ridicules is exactly that of Epiton with Sir Tophas in *Endimion*. Costard is another Kempe role, with less of clownish action and more stress on speech than that of Launce. Some of his lines suggest Kempe's impromptus written in during rehearsal.

It has been suggested that Armado and Holofernes, the Braggart and the Pedant—titles which appear from time to time in the original speech headings—are figures borrowed from the Italian *commedia dell'*

[2] His name, pronounced *Mote,* indicates not only his diminutive figure, but also his teasing character, like the mote that annoys the eye.

arte, well known and popular in England at that time. This may be true, but Shakespeare has made them thoroughly individual figures. Armado, though labeled the Braggart, retains none of the distinguishing marks of the Miles Gloriosus, as his forerunner, Sir Tophas, does. He serves as the mouthpiece of Shakespeare's satire on Elizabethan extravagant abuse of language. Armado is a man 'of fire-new words' with 'a mint of phrases in his brain,' but, as the Princess shrewdly comments: 'He speaks not like a man of God's making.'

Holofernes is not merely the Pedant of Italian comedy; he is a vividly realistic portrait of the English schoolmaster of Shakespeare's day. Shakespeare's dislike of the teacher's profession is evident in several of his plays, but never so strongly expressed as here; by the time he came to draw the portrait of Sir Hugh in *The Merry Wives,* he was evidently in a more charitable humor. Possibly if Shakespeare had lately escaped from the bondage of schoolteaching, the iron was still rankling in his soul. The very name that he gives this character marks his satiric intent, for it is that of the stupidly pedantic tutor of Gargantua, Master Tubal Holofernes. It is hard for us today to appreciate the keenness of Shakespeare's satiric characterization of Holofernes, but it would be instantly perceived by his cultured audience, for the speech of the Pedant is crammed with fragments of the school drill, bits of Latin conversation, quotations—and misquotations—of familiar verse, and strings of synonyms, such as teachers were wont to hand out to their pupils. In addition, Holofernes is inordinately vain of his 'gifts'; he extemporises an 'epitaph' on the death of a deer marked by an excess of the alliteration which was being rapidly discarded by Elizabethan poets, and he devises a masque for the entertainment of the Princess which is ludicrously inappropriate for a courtly show. His self-complacency is heightened by the flattery of the ignorant curate, who is lost in admiration of the Pedant's 'rare talent' and praises God for the presence in his parish of such a master. Holofernes is a portrait drawn once for all of the perennial Pedant. The fashion of his speech has changed, but the spirit remains the same, that of the plodder, blind to life around him and content to win 'base authority from other's books.'

There is, finally, a special reason for the attraction *Love's Labour's Lost* exerts upon all lovers of Shakespeare. It is that here, for the first time, he seems to draw aside the veil that conceals his inmost self and to present, as he was later to do in the *Sonnets, Hamlet,* and *The Tempest,* something that might be likened to a painter's self-portrait.

There is, of course, a difference. The painter studies his face in a mirror and consciously reproduces on canvas the lineaments that he sees there. Shakespeare was not trying to draw a portrait of himself in the costume of Berowne. On the contrary this character seems to express what Shakespeare wished to be. When in moments of depression he wrote of himself as

> Wishing me like to one more rich in hope,
> Featur'd like him, like him with friends possess'd,
> Desiring this man's art, and that man's scope,

he must have longed to exchange places with one of the hopeful, well-bred, and witty favorites of the Court, an Oxford or a Southampton. Rosaline's description of her lover voices Shakespeare's secret longing:

> but a merrier man,
> Within the limit of becoming mirth,
> I never spent an hour's talk withal.
> His eye begets occasion for his wit;
> For every object that the one doth catch
> The other turns to a mirth-moving jest,
> Which his fair tongue, conceit's expositor,
> Delivers in such apt and gracious words,
> That aged ears play truant at his tales,
> And younger hearings are quite ravished;

And a man's aspiration often reveals a true portrait of his inner self. And that is the special characteristic of *Love's Labour's Lost;* it reveals, as no other early play does, the promise and to some extent the personality of William Shakespeare.

A MIDSUMMER NIGHT'S DREAM

With *A Midsummer Night's Dream* Shakespeare graduates from the rank of a prentice to that of a master playwright. This lovely comedy might well be compared to the *Preis Lied* with which Walter von Stolzing won his post among the Meistersinger of Nürnberg. In its mastery of dramatic technique and its power of characterization this play far surpasses the other comedies of the prentice period. Its peculiar charm, however, is the union with these skills of a lyric grace and beauty that make it, like the poet's love, 'half-angel and half-bird.'

Scholars are fairly well agreed that the *Dream* was written late in 1594 or early in the following year. The date helps to explain the apparently sudden advance shown in this play over earlier work. For long periods of time from 1592 to 1594 the plague raged in London. Theaters were closed and opened briefly only to be closed again. Shakespeare's Company seems to have spent part of this time traveling in the provinces, but he himself did not accompany them. Staying in or near London, he devoted himself to the composition of his poems, *Venus and Adonis*, 1593, and *Lucrece*, 1594. Both were enthusiastically received, and such acclaim must have encouraged the young poet to stronger efforts. Shakespeare now, in fact, has his foot firmly planted on the ladder and begins to climb with bold assurance. In *A Midsummer Night's Dream* we have, to use Max Beerbohm's words, 'The Master confident in his art, at ease with it, as a man in his dressing-gown.'

There seems reason to believe that this play was first performed during the festivities attending some noble wedding, possibly that of William Stanley, Earl of Derby, 25 January 1595. Stanley's brother, Ferdinand Lord Strange, had been the patron of Shakespeare's Company until his death in April 1594, and it seems likely that his former company would be asked to contribute to the celebration of his brother's wedding. The fairy song at the end of the play is a true epithalamium and makes a perfect close to a play that deals with love in its varied phases, from the stately union of Theseus with his Amazon bride to the infatuation of Titania for the clownish Bottom. Yet if the play was first performed in private, it was later revised for the public theater; Puck's epilogue with its appeal for applause is plainly addressed to a general audience. The first edition, the Quarto of 1600, like all later texts, preserves both endings.

There is no single source for the *Dream*, no play, poem, or novel that gives singly or in combination all the elements of its plot. When Shakespeare at the request of his fellows sat down to write a play for a noble wedding, he naturally thought first of all of an appropriate theme. Nothing could be more suitable than a tale of young love crossed by circumstance, but winning through at last to happy marriage. Montemayor's *Diana*, which had furnished material for the *Two Gentlemen*, once more served him as a starting point, this time not for isolated scenes, but for the main plot of the play he was planning. The episode in this pastoral romance that gave Shakespeare the germ from which the *Dream* evolved runs as follows.

The shepherdess Silvania relates to a pair of disconsolate lovers the tale of her unhappy passion. She had loved and been loved by the shepherd Alano, but he deserted her to court Ismenia. Ismenia, however, would have none of him, but loved and was loved by the shepherd Montano. This is clearly the situation at the beginning of our play, where Demetrius, the former lover of Helena, has deserted her to press an unwelcome suit on Hermia, who loves and is loved by Lysander. In the romance as in the play the situation changes. Montano for some unknown reason deserts Ismenia to court Silvania. She turns a deaf ear to him and pursues the faithless Alano, while the newly deserted Ismenia follows Montano. There results in consequence a perfect 'love chain': Silvania loves Alano who loves Ismenia who loves Montano who loves Silvania. Once more we find an exact parallel to the situation in the play after the first application of the 'love juice,' when Helena loves Demetrius who loves Hermia who loves Lysander who now, as a result of Puck's mistake, loves Helena. Further than this the parallel does not hold. Montemayor furnishes no solution for his tangled plot; Silvania's narrative stops here and the episode of the love chain merges in the main current of the romance. Elsewhere, however, in *Diana* and in Gil Polo's continuation, 1574—translated like Montemayor's work into French and English—Shakespeare found various incidents which he used first to complicate and then to resolve his own plot. The first of these is a love philter which changes the object of a lover's passion. This corresponds to the juice of the 'little western flower,' the misuse of which by Puck shifts Lysander's love from Hermia to Helena. The second is a charm composed of 'the magic of herbs,' with which a priestess of Diana restores a faithless lover to his first mistress. This in turn corresponds to the 'Dian's bud' of the play by which Lysander is restored to Hermia and the love chain is dissolved into two happy couples.

From the point of view of dramatic construction and, indeed, of action on the stage, the plot of the four lovers in *A Midsummer Night's Dream* is the very heart of the play. Take this away, or diminish its importance, and the whole structure collapses. This is what happened in Reinhardt's transformation of the *Dream* from the stage to the cinema. He overloaded it with unessential, though fascinating, details from fairyland, and cut down the story of the lovers to the dimensions of a squabble between undergraduates in a co-educational college. In the play, on the other hand, everything else serves some function in the main plot. The Theseus-Hippolyta theme is not even a minor plot; it is a mere background or enveloping action, like the Aegeon story in *The Comedy of Errors.* The fairies furnish what might be called the machinery. It is Oberon's intervention in the affairs of the lovers that first starts the complication and then untangles it. This is Shakespeare's alteration and improvement of the motiveless changes of affection in the romance, and he has further provided Oberon with the means for this intervention, the 'love juice' with which he plans to punish his rebellious queen, and also the antidote in 'Dian's bud.' Finally the 'base mechanicals,' Bottom and his crew, furnish a realistic strain which keeps this fantastic play from flying off into a never-never land like one of Lyly's comedies. This group has, to be sure, less connection with the main plot than the fairies, but it is closely united with the Theseus background, with the fairies through Bottom's transformation, and finally with the reunited lovers before whom they perform their interlude. Shakespeare has blended the various elements of the play into a harmonious whole.

Shakespeare drew upon his reading, upon folklore familiar to him from childhood, and upon direct observation for these various elements. The wedding of Duke Theseus with the Amazon Hippolyta comes to him from Chaucer's *Knight's Tale,* as does the name, Philostrate, the Duke's Master of the Revels. Various references to the exploits of Theseus in love and war Shakespeare drew from Plutarch's *Life* of that hero, and Plutarch furnished him also the classical names: Lysander, Demetrius, and Helena.[1] Oberon, the fairy king, comes ultimately from the old French romance, *Huon of Bordeaux,* but Shakespeare found him nearer to hand in *The Faerie Queene* and in Greene's *James IV.* Titania, Shakespeare's strange name for the fairy queen, he found in his favorite poet, Ovid, who gives it as one of the names of Diana, goddess of the nymphs, whom the Elizabethans identified with the more familiar fairies. It may be suggested that Shakespeare chose this classical name instead of the English Mab, of *Romeo and Juliet,* in order to connect fairy royalty more closely with the antique world in which he placed his main action; both Oberon and

[1] The name Hermia, classical as it sounds, is only a common Elizabethan misrendering of the Greek masculine name Hermias.

Titania have come from farthest India to attend the wedding feast of Theseus. Puck, of course, is not so much a proper name as an appelation; he is *the Puck*, i.e. a sprite or goblin, the Robin Goodfellow of folklore, 'famosed,' an Elizabethan tells us, 'in every old wive's chronicle for his mad merry pranks.' In sharp contrast to the royal pair, Oberon and Titania, with their atmosphere of magic and romance, Robin represents the homely English conception of the fairies as 'the good folk,' fond of fun and ready for mischief, but never malevolent, and always ready to lend a hand in household tasks and bring good luck to the well-deserving. As the *Puck* of the play, Robin's function is that of the Vice in the Morals; he is the mischief-maker who by accident and design starts and complicates the main intrigue, and claps the ass's head on Bully Bottom. The names of Titania's attendant elves—Peaseblossom, Cobweb, Moth, and Mustardseed—are redolent of an English garden.

It is from his own shrewd observation of life in a country town like Stratford that Shakespeare drew the names and the behavior of Bottom and his fellows. Their names are, with one exception, trade names indicative of their crafts: the weaver gets his name from the 'bottom,' or core of a skein of yarn; Snout means nozzle or spout, a fit name for a tinker; the tailor is Starveling, for, as is well known, 'it takes nine tailors to make a man.' Characteristic of Elizabethan England, too, is their purpose to present a play at the wedding of their sovereign. Shakespeare's England from the Queen's Court to the remotest hamlet was drama-mad, and enough of the old tradition of community playing still lingered to embolden a group of villagers anywhere to put on a show before visiting royalty.

In spite of the absence of a source or pattern to work from, Shakespeare produced in *A Midsummer Night's Dream* what his two immediately preceding comedies had lacked, a coherent and interesting action. The contrast with the almost plotless *Love's Labour's Lost* is remarkable, and the neat solution of the intrigue, first induced and then resolved by magic, is an immense improvement on the hurried and unsatisfactory denouement of *The Two Gentlemen*. The action starts promptly in the first scene and runs its course unbroken to the close of the fourth act. The last act, devoted almost entirely to the Pyramus and Thisbe interlude, serves in a measure to bring us back to earth again after a night in the fairies' enchanted wood. That the main action is in the highest degree improbable does not make it the less entertaining. Like Lyly's *Woman in the Moon* 'all is but a poet's dream,' as, in fact, the very title tells us; yet the characters that move through this dream are more substantial flesh and blood than any of Lyly's shadowy figures.

It would be absurd to equate Shakespeare's power of characterization in this play with that shown at the height of his career. Yet one has only to compare the Duke of the *Dream* with Duke Solinus of *The Comedy of Errors* to see Shakespeare's advance in this phase of his art. Both belong to the enveloping action; neither has an essential part in the main plot; but here the likeness ends. Solinus is a mere puppet, wholly lacking individuality; Theseus, on the contrary, is a firmly realized figure, a soldier, a sportsman, breeding hounds 'of the Spartan kind,' like an English squire, and a lover, whose sane and sensible affection contrasts, as Shakespeare meant it to do, with the fickle fancy of the lovers. A man of action rather than of sentiment, Theseus is a little contemptuous of the fine frenzy of the poet, but like a courteous Tudor prince he is ready to accept whatever entertainment his subjects offer him, whether the 'premeditated welcomes' of great clerks which broke down half-spoken, or the homely shows of rustics; for, says he,

> Never anything can be amiss,
> When simpleness and duty tender it.

Shakespeare refrained from characterizing sharply the two gentlemen of the main plot; to have done so would have defeated his purpose in showing them the helpless victims of the fairy charm. Of the ladies an anonymous critic, quoted by Cunningham in his edition of this play, remarks that Helena and Hermia differ only in height. They do, indeed, so differ. Evidently Shakespeare found in his company two boys for these roles, one tall and slender, one short and plump, and he cleverly exploited these physical differences. But only wilfully blinded criticism can fail to distinguish between the warm-hearted, quick-tempered, little Hermia and her tall, sentimental, spaniel-like friend. The ladies, we may note, never come under the love spell, and accordingly it was possible for Shakespeare to endow them with more individual and distinguishing characteristics than he could allow their lovers. There is a delightfully feminine touch in Helena's appeal to the men for protection against the physical violence threatened by her former playmate, who 'was a vixen when she went to school.'

Shakespeare's supreme piece of character portrayal in the *Dream* is the figure of Bully Bottom. This is, of course, a clown's role for Kempe and by far the best that Shakespeare had yet composed for him. For Bottom, while he retains many of the Clown's old tricks, develops into something much more than a mere clown. He is one of the eternally comic figures of literature, not a country bumpkin like his predecessor Costard, but the perennial 'life-of-the-party' in a small town, cheery, loquacious, conceited, and unabashed. Although a prominent figure in a romantic comedy, there is not a trace of romantic sentiment in Bottom. Modern psychology would, perhaps, classify him as a pragmatist, for he meets each situation as it arises with complete self-confidence. Cast for the part of a lover he promptly offers to play the lady's part, or the lion's, though his chief humor is for a tyrant, a part to 'tear a cat in,' 'a lover is more condoling.' Abandoned by his comrades and alone in the haunted wood at night, he sings and jests to show that he is not afraid. Courted by the Queen of Fairyland he has no sense of the glamor and the danger of his situation—for that we must turn to the old ballad of *Thomas the Rymer*. Bottom accepts the kisses of his fairy mistress with the utmost complacency and calls for a 'bottle of hay' and the music of tongs and bones. Incongruity is one of the essentials of the comic and there is no more incongruous situation in literature than that of Bottom with his 'fair large ears' asleep in the arms of the dainty Titania. Romance and realism are here contrasted and combined.

A Midsummer Night's Dream has never enjoyed great success upon the stage, but it is one of the most delightful of Shakespeare's plays for the closet. The diction of this play, less marred by fanciful conceits than that of earlier comedies, less obscured by involved passages where thought seems to wrestle with expression as in later and greater plays, offers a constant source of enjoyment to the reader. Through the simple medium of language without the charm of theatrical illusion, Shakespeare tells an interesting story of human lovers and opens to the imaginative reader the magic gates of fairyland. It is in his use of language, as in so much else in this play, that Shakespeare shows himself the master. There is a fair proportion of prose, strictly reserved for the realistic talk of Bottom and his fellows. Bottom's lines, in particular, have been most carefully written; Shakespeare seems determined to prevent his clown in this play from speaking more than was set down for him. Kempe had no chance in the *Dream* to address the audience directly as he had done in the role of Launce, or to work impromptus into the dialogue, as he seems to have done during the rehearsals of *Love's Labour's Lost.* Modern readers can enjoy Bottom's chatter without trying to visualize Kempe's jigs.

Over half the verse lines of the *Dream* are in rhyme. The 'jigging vein' of the Pyramus play is Shakespeare's mockery of the 'mother wits' who wrote plays before the new group of playwrights, Peele, Marlowe, and Greene, established blank verse and rhymed iambic couplets on the stage. The lovers, for the most part, speak in rhyme, which is as it should be, but Shakespeare restrains here the exuberance that had flourished so freely in *Love's Labour's Lost;* there are no sonnets embodied in the dialogue of the *Dream.* The extravagant language of Lysander and Demetrius, awaking after their eyes had been touched by the love juice, is purposely designed to show the power of that spell; they do not rant in this vein either before or after.

The blank verse of the *Dream* is distinguished at once by ease and beauty; there is little or no rhetorical declamation in this play. Shakespeare has gained full control over the meter he had learned to use from Marlowe, and has put something new into it, a lyric quality of tone. The fairy scenes seem to have been written to music: Shakespeare, it is clear, was able to command for the first performance a group of singing boys whose fresh voices ring out in solo, recitative, and chorus. Their songs, naturally and rightly, are in rhyme, but even in the regular blank verse speeches of Oberon and Titania the lyric note is heard. Take, for example, two passages of many that might be culled from this fair garden, Oberon's words to Puck:

> But I might see young Cupid's fiery shaft
> Quench'd in the chaste beams of the wat'ry moon,
> And the imperial votaress passed on,
> In maiden meditation, fancy-free.
> Yet mark'd I where the bolt of Cupid fell:
> It fell upon a little western flower,
> Before milk-white, now purple with love's wound,
> And maidens call it, Love-in-idleness

or Titania's order to her attendant elves:

> Come, now a roundel and a fairy song;
> Then, for the third part of a minute, hence;
> Some to kill cankers in the musk-rose buds,

Some war with rere-mice for their leathern wings
To make my small elves coats, and some keep back
The clamorous owl, that nightly hoots, and wonders
At our quaint spirits. . .

The distinguishing characteristic of the *Dream,* in fact, is that it
attains what *The Two Gentlemen* had aimed at and failed to achieve:
lyric romantic comedy. Shakespeare was to do still better work than
this; he had not yet mastered all the stops of his organ, but there
is a gay and youthful freshness in the music of this play that makes
it a joy forever. It was surely of the *Dream* that Milton was thinking
when he spoke of Shakespeare warbling 'his native wood-notes wild.'

There is something more, of course, in *A Midsummer Night's
Dream* than Shakespeare's wood-notes. The central action is concerned
with that phase of human love which the Elizabethans called 'fancy':
the irrational emotional impulse that draws man to maid and maid
to man. Love as 'fancy,' 'love-in-idleness,' is a conception of love
proper to comedy, and this early comedy plays with it and exhibits
its most fantastic form in Titania's infatuation. Shakespeare's mastery
of his art permits him here to sport with his theme in easy good
humor. Like Puck he is vastly entertained by human follies. 'What
fools these mortals be' might serve as a second title for the play, but
there is nothing satirical or malicious in the playwright's laughter.
The shadow of death or danger that hangs over his earlier comedies,
and was to reappear in still darker shades hereafter, has vanished in
the enchanted moonlight that floods the wood near Athens. Nowhere
in all Shakespeare's work do we hear him singing in so carefree a
strain as in *A Midsummer Night's Dream.*

6

The Master Craftsman

IF *A Midsummer Night's Dream* is the play in which Shakespeare achieves full mastery of his art, *The Merchant of Venice* is the first comedy composed after he entered the ranks of the masters. Yet it is not pure comedy like the plays of the first period; rather it approaches the hybrid form of tragi-comedy, already established on the Elizabethan stage in such a play as *Damon and Pythias*. The *Dream* is a lyric romantic comedy, sporting with the theme of love; the *Merchant* on the contrary, is a rather serious dramatic treatment of some important phases of human life, of love and marriage, of the use and abuse of wealth, and of racial hatred and intolerance. Shakespeare was, of course, growing older and more serious in his outlook on life, but a special reason for the change of tone and temper in the *Merchant* may, perhaps, be found in certain events in the political and theatrical world which startled London in 1594.

In that year Dr. Lopez, a converted Portuguese Jew, physician to Queen Elizabeth, was found guilty of complicity in a Spanish plot to poison the Queen. He was accordingly hanged, drawn, and quartered at Tyburn amid the yells of an angry mob. There was grave doubt about his guilt, but Essex, the Queen's favorite, who presided at the trial, was determined to secure a conviction, and Shakespeare's friend, Southampton, the intimate associate of Essex, could have informed the poet of all the details of the trial. Shakespeare, a good Elizabethan, must have been shocked at the crime charged against Lopez, but he may well have been too humane and reasonable to be fully convinced of the Jew's guilt. Whether Lopez was guilty or innocent, however, his trial and execution fanned the embers of anti-Semitism in London into a blazing flame, and the Admiral's Company, Shakespeare's rivals in the theatrical world, took advantage of this outburst to revive Marlowe's *Jew of Malta,* which had been for some time withdrawn from the stage. Alleyn, their leading actor, took the part of the monstrous caricature of humanity, Barabas the Jew, the chief figure in that play;

he must have made a great hit in the role, for in the year 1594 *The Jew of Malta* was played again and again to crowded houses. It seems reasonable to suppose that Shakespeare's fellow-actors urged him to write them a wicked Jew play that might compete with Marlowe's melodrama. If so, it is a striking tribute to Shakespeare's humane temper that his Jew, wicked as he is—and the title-page of the first edition advertises his 'extreme cruelty'—none the less remains a credible and human character, far above the demoniac figure of Marlowe's protagonist.

To construct a play in which a wicked Jew should play a leading part Shakespeare looked about him for a source to furnish the framework of the action. He found a fit one in *Il Pecorone*, a fourteenth-century collection of Italian tales. Few of them have any real merit, but one, at least, the story of the pound-of-flesh bond, is fairly familiar to English students because of its relation to Shakespeare's play. No translation of *Il Pecorone* in Shakespeare's time is known; the poet may have read it in the original Italian, no impossible task for a man with Shakespeare's mastery of Latin, or he may have come across it in one of those 'fond books of late translated out of Italian into English, sold,' says Roger Ascham, 'in every shop in London.' The *Pecorone* story has been so often retold in popular editions of *The Merchant of Venice* that the barest summary may here suffice.

> Giannetto, a young gentleman of Venice, is fitted out by his godfather, Ansaldo, a rich merchant, for a trading voyage. On his way he puts in at Belmont, where he learns that the lady of the land has made a law that whoever enters the port must woo her. If he can obtain possession of her person, she will marry him and make him lord of the land, but if he fails he must forfeit all his goods. Giannetto makes the trial and fails because the lady has given him a cup of drugged wine as he was entering her bedchamber. He returns to Venice where Ansaldo equips him for a second trial in which again he fails. For a third attempt Ansaldo borrows ten thousand ducats from a Jew, pledging a pound of his flesh to be cut off by his creditor if the money is not repaid at a certain date. This time Giannetto wins the lady, for a friendly serving-maid whispers to him the secret of the drugged wine. He marries the lady and lives happily with her till he suddenly remembers that on this very day the bond has fallen due. His wife

sends him to Venice with money enough to pay the debt ten times over; but the Jew refuses to receive it, saying that he would sooner kill the greatest Christian merchant than get all the gold in Venice. In the meantime the lady, disguised as a lawyer, comes to Venice and is asked to act as judge in the case. She first urges the Jew to take the money offered, but when he refuses she bids him take the pound of flesh, but avoid spilling a drop of blood or taking either more or less than an exact pound on pain of death. Thereupon the Jew declares that he will take the money, but is told that he must have his bond or nothing. At this he tears up the bond and departs, having lost even the sum he had loaned Ansaldo. Giannetto offers the disguised lady the money he had brought to free his friend, but she will accept nothing but a ring from his finger. He gives it reluctantly since it was a gift from his wife as a pledge of her love. When he returns to Belmont the lady, who was there before him, receives him coldly and asks what he has done with the ring. On his reply that he has given it to the lawyer she swears he has given it to a woman and bids him return to Venice. At this Giannetto bursts into tears, but the lady laughs, kisses him, and gives him back the ring, telling him the whole story of her disguise. They live happy ever after.

It will be remarked at once that the method of winning the lady in the play differs entirely from that in the *Pecorone* tale. For the physical possession of the lady's person Shakespeare substitutes the business of the caskets, the choice of which by a suitor will determine his failure or success. The source of this alternate method, which Shakespeare develops into a subplot, is probably the *Gesta Romanorum,* a Latin collection of legends and moral tales, translated into English in 1577 and very popular in Shakespeare's day. Briefly this story runs as follows:

To test the fitness of a princess sent to Rome to marry the Emperor's son, the Emperor bade her make a choice of three caskets. The first, of gold, was full of dead men's bones and bore the inscription: 'Who chooseth me shall find what he deserveth.' The second, of silver, full of earth and worms, bore the inscription: 'Who chooseth me shall find what his nature desireth.' The third, of lead, was full of precious stones, with the inscription: 'Who chooseth me shall find what God hath disposed to him.' The princess chose the leaden casket because she knew that what God disposed was always good. And so she won her husband.

The likeness between this tale and the casket scenes in the play, especially as regards the material of the three caskets and their inscriptions, is too close to be a mere coincidence. Shakespeare has expanded the simple story to show the failure of two unworthy suitors before the correct choice is made by the predestined lover of the lady. More than that, by the substitution of the caskets he has moralized and rationalized the Italian tale. The lady of Belmont is no longer lost or won by an unworthy trick on her part or by the avoidance of the trick by her suitor, but by a test of the suitor's character. And this test has been devised, we are told, by her 'ever-virtuous' father, and 'holy men at their death have good inspirations.' As a matter of fact, the test with its conditions preserves Portia from a group of unworthy suitors who are unwilling to run the risk, from the braggart Morocco and the conceited Arragon, and delivers her to Bassanio, whom she already loves. And it is Bassanio alone who is wise enough to read the riddle of the inscriptions. Dramatically as well as morally Shakespeare's alteration is a vast improvement on the Italian tale.

In their eagerness to deprive Shakespeare of the credit of such an improvement and to attribute it to the unknown author of a lost play he is thought to have recast into *The Merchant of Venice,* certain critics, including some of the latest editors, have cited a reference by Gosson in his *School of Abuse,* 1579, to the play of *The Jew,* 'shown at the Bull . . . representing the greediness of worldly choosers and the bloody minds of usurers.' This title and brief description of a lost play tell us, to be sure, that the chief character was a Jew, presumably a bloody-minded usurer, but to interpret the phrase 'the greediness of worldly choosers' as implying a scene or scenes in *The Jew* equivalent to the casket scenes in Shakespeare's play is to stretch the phrase beyond what it can reasonably bear. Neither Morocco nor Arragon is really guilty of greediness in his choice; in a worldly sense each is a suitable match for Portia. There is, however, a stronger argument than this. Gosson's *Jew* must have been written some time, even if a short time, before 1579. Now this is the age of the drama in transition when the old Morals and Interludes contended on the stage with such essentially undramatic romances as *Sir Clyomon* and such inept imitations of the classics as *Jack Juggler*. It is hard, if not impossible, for anyone familiar with the drama of that period to believe that any playwright before 1579 was capable of an alteration of his source at once so rational and so dramatically effective as that which appears in *The Merchant*, or that any playwright of that early day had the technical skill to weave the two themes together with the art that Shakespeare displays. Let us give the master the credit he seems to deserve.

Another slight variation between the tale and the play may reasonably be ascribed to Shakespeare. In the tale it is only the lady who gets the ring from her husband as a reward for saving his friend. Shakespeare has doubled the rings here as he did the twins in *The Comedy of Errors*. The lady's maid also wheedles a ring from her husband, and it is the maid's demand of the ring in the final episode that prompts Portia to ask hers from Bassanio. It may be noted further that Bassanio does not burst into tears like Giannetto, but makes a sober and sensible defense of his gift of the ring, and that the mock quarrel is ended when Portia restores it to him by the hand of Antonio. However modern sensibility may cavil at the mockery of marriage implied in this episode—a mockery converted to laughter by the arch humor with which Ellen Terry played the scene—there can be no doubt that Shakespeare's change adds greatly to the stage effect of the whole episode.

A minor plot in *The Merchant* deals with Jessica, the Jew's daughter, and her elopement with a Christian lover. There is no such character in the Italian tale. She may have been suggested to Shakespeare by the presence in Marlowe's play of Abigail, the Jew's daughter who, like Jessica, has a Christian lover. But Shakespeare avoids the sensational action of Marlowe's play in which the Jew poisons Abigail and the whole convent in which she has taken refuge. He uses Jessica for other dramatic ends: partly to contrast her romantic passion for Lorenzo with the deep-rooted love of Portia and Bassanio; more importantly, perhaps, to motivate her father's desire for revenge, if not upon the daughter who has escaped his grasp, then upon the chief figure of the group of Christians who have injured and insulted him. The Jew of *Il Pecorone* is a quite incredible character; he has no motive for revenge upon Ansaldo, only a desire to kill the greatest Christian merchant in Venice. Shylock, on the other hand, bears an ancient grudge against Antonio, compounded of personal, economic, and racial motives, for Antonio has spit upon his Jewish gabardine, hindered him of half a million, and scorned his sacred nation. Shakespeare makes it clear at the first interview of the two rivals in business that Shylock proposes the 'merry bond' with the firm intention of catching Antonio upon the hip. Whether the Jew would have proceeded to the extremity of his revenge without further motive is a question that may be left unanswered, for Shakespeare supplies a sufficient additional motive in the elopement of his daughter with a Christian along with his gold and jewels.

There is yet another difference between the tale and the play which has been too little regarded by critics. In both, the disguised lady saves the endangered merchant by insisting that in the exaction of his bond the Jew must not shed one drop of blood nor cut more or less than a pound 'by one poor scruple.' These, of course, are mere legal quibbles, retained by Shakespeare as part of the story, and, no doubt, amusing to his audience. He himself must have been dissatisfied with them, for he has added a third and quite new point, the old Venetian law that condemns to death and confiscation of goods the alien who plots against the life of a citizen of Venice. This is no quibble, but a fundamental principle of justice, embodying the right and duty of the state to protect its citizens against alien plots. Shylock's case plainly falls under this law and in Portia's decision we see the triumph of the spirit over the letter, of equity over legalism. Here as in his treatment of the wooing of the lady Shakespeare is using all his art to rationalize and render credible what is essentially an impossible romantic tale. In the *Dream* he made no such attempt, but by introducing into the action the fairies and their magic he frankly asked his hearers to accept the incredible as part of the fun of the play. In this, as in so much else in *The Merchant*, we may mark the increasing seriousness of Shakespeare's temper.

How much of comedy is there, after all, in this play, overshadowed as it is till near the end by the threat of shameful death to the character who gives the play its name? Enough at least to make this blend of grave and gay one of the most popular of Shakespeare's plays upon the stage. Certainly in action the gay that is comedy outweighs the grave. It far outweighed the grave in Granville's alteration, *The Jew of Venice*, 1701, in which Doggett, a leading comedian, took the part of Shylock and at Bassanio's banquet rose to drink a health to his mistress, Money. On the other hand since Macklin restored to the stage in 1741 'the Jew that Shakespeare drew,' there has been a tendency to stress, perhaps to overstress, the tragic element in Shylock.

Heine records a performance at Drury Lane at which his neighbor, 'a fair, pale Briton,' burst into tears at the end of the fourth act, exclaiming passionately: 'The poor man is wronged.' Edwin Booth in early performances went so far as to end the play at the close of the trial scene, though on more mature consideration he allowed the last act to be played. This, certainly, was a return to Shakespeare's intention; he would never have written that act, with its blend of poetry, music, and mirth, had he wished to dismiss his audience with the figure of the Jew, 'wronged,' or even justly thwarted, in their minds. Apart from the business of the rings there is but little action at the end of the play. The whole purpose of this act is to make us forget the near tragedy of the trial scene in the happiness of the married lovers. A performance at the Old Vic. in 1932 was directed in such a way as to present the play as something like a fairy tale, through which the figure of Shylock moved like that of the big bad wolf in the Disney film. This, no doubt, minimized the common humanity of Shylock, but it seemed closer to Shakespeare's intention than a performance like Henry Irving's, which presented the Jew as a noble representative of a martyred race.

It is in keeping with Shakespeare's growing seriousness that he discards entirely in *The Merchant* the old rough comedy of physical violence; there are no scuffles and beatings here; even the clown escapes them, though Launcelot surely deserves a blow or two for his impudence. The comedy of action is limited to the scenes in which he appears, to those in which Morocco and Arragon fail in their choice of the caskets, and to the business of the rings. It is in characterization and in diction that we find the true comedy of this play. Yet the main figures of *The Merchant* are far from comic characters. Shylock certainly is not. A potentially comic scene in which his howls of lamentation for his ducats and his daughter are mocked by the street boys of Venice is carefully kept off-stage, reported, not presented. In this comedy Shylock is simply the incarnate form of that shadow of death and danger which appeared less vividly and less dramatically in earlier plays. His counterpart, Antonio, is even less a character of comedy. His pensive melancholy, his devotion to Bassanio, and his resignation in the face of death mark him rather as a figure in a play of sentiment. Bassanio, also, is only so far a figure in comedy as he is the successful suitor in a play of love and marriage. The charges hurled at him by certain critics as a mere spendthrift and a fortune-hunter—Q. calls him 'a predatory young gentleman'—reveal a complete misunderstanding of Shakespeare's conception of the character. Bassanio, we are distinctly told, is a soldier and a scholar; if he has no opportunity to show his martial prowess, he shares that fate with Hamlet. His affection for Portia is sensible and rational; he desires to win a noble, rich, and lovely lady who has already given him evidence of her good will. His choice of the caskets is dictated by a strong good sense that at once distrusts appearances and is ready to give and hazard all in the lottery of marriage. It has been suggested that the song that precedes his choice gives him a clue to the proper casket; even so, and the case seems very doubtful, it would be his quick intelligence that caught the clue.

In the character of Portia the grave and gay of this comedy mingle happily and graciously. She first appears mocking the disreputable suitors that clutter up her court at Belmont; yet along with the mockery goes the half-suppressed sigh over the curb laid on her by her father's will, so that she may neither choose whom she would— her choice has already been hinted at—nor refuse whom she dislikes. She winds up the action in the last scene with the jest of the rings, but she quickly stops the mouth of Gratiano when the jesting grows too broad. In between, she is the great lady, markedly so in her dealing with Morocco and Arragon, most perfectly revealed in her speech of sweet and dignified self-surrender. Yet this great lady of the Renaissance is, after all, little more than the girl she once calls herself; her youth is specially dwelt upon in the trial scene. Shakespeare, of course, had it always in mind while penning the lines of this noble role that it was to be played by a boy, the most gifted boy, naturally, of the well-trained lads of his company. A less talented boy was assigned what we might call the soubrette's role of Nerissa.

Little need be said of the minor characters of *The Merchant:* most of them—the Duke, the walking gentlemen, the Messengers, and so on—are mere stock figures. Lorenzo becomes a mouthpiece for some lovely poetry, and the coarse-grained Gratiano serves as a foil to the finer texture of Bassanio. Launcelot Gobbo plays the clown, a distinct throwback to Launce in *The Two Gentlemen.* Like Launce he plays on words, utters malapropisms, and addresses himself on his first appearance directly to the audience. Shakespeare writes one scene (III. v) for him apparently to give the boys who played Portia and Nerissa time to change from their hoop skirts and ruffs into the robes of a doctor-of-law and his clerk. He brings Launcelot holloing on the stage in the last scene to prolong the time needed for them to change back again into the costumes of the lady and her maid. Launcelot's part is hardly as good as Launce's, or so good a part by half as that of Bottom. Shakespeare was thinking of other things here than the broad humor of the clown.

The Merchant of Venice is, of course, a better stage-play than *A Midsummer Night's Dream,* which was designed primarily rather for entertainment at a noble wedding than for the theater. And this superiority reveals itself as well in the diction as in the action and the characterization. It is less lyrical and more dramatic. Shakespeare attains here a command of lucid and direct dramatic dialogue that he was seldom to better. The fantastic conceits of the early plays are almost entirely elided from the simple and fluent run of the discourse. The lyric music of the *Dream* often gives way to set rhetorical speeches. The most famous of these, of course, is Portia's plea for mercy, and, staled as it is by constant repetition, its simplicity and beauty are unmatched outside the work of Shakespeare.

There is a fair proportion of prose in *The Merchant,* more evenly distributed among the speakers than in the *Dream,* where it is reserved for the speech of the mechanicals. The clown, of course, speaks prose; that was the convention of his role. But Shakespeare uses prose also for the strong realism of Shylock's outburst affirming the essential humanity of the Jew and for his dialogue with Tubal with its alternating currents of bitter grief and fierce revenge. Most remarkable of all, Shakespeare puts prose into the mouth of Portia on her first appearance. This is a scene of pure comedy, and Portia is the first of Shakespeare's witty heroines to talk in prose. She anticipates such mistresses of the art as Beatrice and Rosalind. Shakespeare was beginning to realize that prose rather than verse was the proper vehicle for comic dialogue.

On the other hand, there is comparatively little rhyme in this play. Shakespeare uses it mainly for tags at the end of scenes and speeches, occasionally for emotional outbursts such as Portia's cry of joy when Bassanio chooses the right casket. There is less of the lyric note in *The Merchant* than in *A Midsummer Night's Dream,* but when Shakespeare touches the lyric stop, it answers in the loveliest of blank verse. The antiphonal dialogue of the lovers at the beginning of the last act is pure lyric, drenched in the natural magic that Arnold thought peculiar to English poetry:

> In such a night
> Stood Dido with a willow in her hand

Upon the wild sea-banks, and waft her love
To come again to Carthage.

And from such a lyric strain the transition is easy to a passage of meditative beauty:

. . . Look, how the floor of heaven
Is thick inlaid with patines of bright gold:
There's not the smallest orb which thou behold'st
But in his motion like an angel sings,
Still quiring to the young-eyed cherubins;
Such harmony is in immortal souls.

It is hard to praise too highly the art with which Shakespeare has handled the crude material of his source and converted an amusingly improbable tale into a drama peopled with flesh-and-blood characters. Even more than his art, however, it becomes us to notice the tone and temper that informs this play. At a period of fierce anti-Semitism, Shakespeare put into the mouth of the hated Jew the strongest plea yet uttered for racial tolerance. The stipulation that Shylock change his faith, a demand that sticks in our throats today, seemed to Shakespeare's hearers an act of mercy, for that was a time when the water of baptism on the brow of a dying child or on a captive burning at the stake was believed to secure instant entrance into Paradise. The lady of Belmont, in the story a siren who tempts and plunders wandering mariners, becomes in Shakespeare's hands the noble Portia. Shakespeare, it seems clear, felt that there was a crying incongruity between the siren's first role and the part she plays as the deliverer of her husband's friend. His lady of the trial scene must be something other and better than the siren of the story. Hence the business of the caskets with its stress on character and its result in securing for Portia the man she loves. In the character of Portia, moreover, Shakespeare embodies his conception of the real value of worldly wealth. To Shylock money is merely a means to breed more money; if in the process human beings suffer, that is a mere incident in the business; Antonio remarks that he has often delivered unfortunates from the clutches of the moneylender. To Portia, on the other hand, money is simply a means to promote the good life, to keep open house with music and entertainment for her guests, to spend without hesitation or calculation in order to rescue 'noble amity' from threatening danger. It would be absurd to suppose that Shakespeare wrote *The Mer-*

chant to demonstrate these ideas; he was first and last a playwright, not a moralist or a philosopher. Yet it is but a narrow-minded criticism that shuts its eyes to the revelation in this play of a humane, generous, and mercy-loving personality behind the artist, a personality transfused into this product of his art. Seldom in the evolution of Shakespeare as a playwright is there a stronger contrast than that between the carefree singer of *A Midsummer Night's Dream* and the thoughtful dramatist of *The Merchant of Venice*.

THE TAMING OF THE SHREW

Striking as is the contrast between *A Midsummer Night's Dream* and *The Merchant of Venice*, it is even less remarkable than that which exists between *The Merchant* and the comedy that seems to follow it in order of composition, *The Taming of the Shrew*. It has been necessary previously to refute the statement that this or that earlier comedy by Shakespeare was derived from an older lost play. Here, however, there can be little doubt that Shakespeare's play derives immediately from an older comedy, which, fortunately, has been preserved for us. This is *The Taming of a Shrew*, printed in quarto form in 1594. It is, of course, impossible to say what led Shakespeare to undertake the rather commonplace job of rewriting this old play. Possibly he was called on while busily engaged in his long series of Histories, 1594-99, to dash off a comedy by way of varying the program his company was offering the public. If so, the material lay ready to his hand, for the play-book of *A Shrew* belonged to his company; they had, in fact, performed it in June 1594 at the suburban theater of Newington Butts.

The Taming of a Shrew is an interesting example of pre-Shakespearean comedy. It seems to have been written early in the 1590's by an enthusiastic admirer [1] of the 'university wits,' especially of Marlowe, whose early plays, *Tamburlaine* and *Faustus*, he pillaged unblushingly and whose mighty line he made a feeble effort to imitate. It consists of three strands: an enveloping action—Prologue and Epilogue—of a major plot, the 'taming' scenes, and of a minor, the courtship of the Shrew's sisters.

[1] In an article published in *Elizabethan Studies* (*University of Colorado Studies,* 1945) I suggested that *A Shrew* might be the composite work of an academic amateur and a professional playwright, possibly S. Rowley. This hypothesis would at least account for the striking discrepancy in diction and dramatic technique between its major and the minor plots.

The enveloping action opens with the ejection of the drunken Sly from a country alehouse. He falls asleep before the door and is there discovered by a Lord returning from the hunt. By way of a frolic the Lord has Sly carried asleep to his castle, there to be richly dressed and greeted on awakening as a lord who for years has been out of his mind. Before Sly wakes, the Lord's company of players appears and is ordered to perform before the drunkard. Sly is brought in asleep in a chair, wakened, and persuaded that he is really a lord. With a page in woman's clothes who pretends to be his wife, he sits to see the play, telling Sim—the name assumed by the Lord—that they will 'flout the players out of their coats.' The play proper then begins, punctuated from time to time by Sly's comments. Like a groundling in the Elizabethan theater, Sly is specially delighted with the Fool, i.e. the roguish servant of the Shrew's suitor, and like the Citizen and his Wife in *The Knight of the Burning Pestle*, he mistakes stage action for reality, and utters a vehement protest against the threatened jailing of a pair of the actors: 'I tell thee, Sim, we'll have no sending to prison; that's flat.' He calls repeatedly for drink and finally, at a point corresponding to the end of the first scene of the last act of Shakespeare's play, he falls asleep. Thereupon the Lord has him carried out to be dressed in his old clothes and deposited where he was first discovered. The play proper proceeds and at its close, we find a stage direction: 'Enter two bearing Sly . . . and leaves him where they found him.' He is wakened there by the Tapster who had thrown him out, and declares that he has had 'the bravest dream that ever thou heardest.' On the Tapster's remark that his wife will rail at him for staying out all night Sly declares that he now knows how to tame a shrew: 'I dreamt upon it all this night till now.' The two then depart to the drunkard's home.

The essential likeness of the Sly scenes in this and in Shakespeare's play needs no comment. There is an even closer likeness between *A Shrew* and *The Shrew* in the main action. In both, the shrew's father forbids all courtship of his younger daughter, or daughters— there are two of them in *A Shrew*—until Katherine is safely married off. In both this difficulty is overcome by the appearance of a man—

Ferando in *A Shrew*—ready and willing to wed her. The rough and ready courtship, the appearance of the bridegroom at the wedding 'basely attired,' his prompt departure with Kate thereafter, his outrageous behavior at his house with all the business of the burnt meat, the haberdasher, and the tailor, the feigned mistaking of an old man for a 'fair lovely maid,' with the return of Kate and her husband to her father's house, all are in both plays. There is a close parallel, too, in the closing scenes with the business of the wager won by the husband of the now well-trained shrew and with her oration to less pliant wives on marital obedience. In this plot Shakespeare has followed his scenario so closely as to provoke the charge of plagiarism. This is, of course, absurd, since the old play was now the property of Shakespeare's company and he was at perfect liberty to remodel it at will.

The underplot is a clumsy adaptation of Gascoigne's *Supposes* to the popular stage. The unknown author shifted the scene from Italy to Athens, complicated the intrigue, and was ill-advised enough to turn the crisp prose of Gascoigne's dialogue into bombastic blank verse. In strong contrast to the frank rough humor of the main action this underplot is a very wooden thing.

It is interesting to notice Shakespeare's treatment of his source. He must have been specially attracted by the Prologue, for he rewrote it completely, almost doubling its length. Near the beginning he struck out a ranting speech of the Lord, lifted bodily from *Faustus*, and substituted for it a brief dialogue between the Lord and the Huntsman, every line of which reveals Shakespeare's delight in field sports. He pounced on the character of Sly and gave the drunkard a local habitation, a family, and a group of friends. Shakespeare's Sly boasts that his ancestors came in with 'Richard Conqueror'; he is old Sly's son of Burton Heath; he knows Marian Hacket, the fat alewife of Wincot, and old John Naps of Greece, i.e. Greete. The place names are those of hamlets not far from Stratford; Sly, it would seem, is a Warwickshire man, 'by birth a pedlar, by education a card-maker, by transmutation a bear-herd, and now by present profession a tinker'—none of them highly esteemed trades. In *A Shrew* Sly is quickly persuaded that he is a lord; in *The Shrew* he fights against the imposition: 'I am Christopher Sly; call me not "honour, nor lordship" . . . Ne'er ask me what raiment I'll wear; for I have no more doublets than backs, no more stockings than legs, nor more shoes than feet.' His embarrassment on meeting the boy introduced to him as his wife is an original touch by Shakespeare: 'What must I call her?—Al'ce madam, or Joan madam?,' ending with a compromise on 'Madam wife.'

With the opening of the play proper, Shakespeare practically drops Sly out of the action. An elaborate stage direction before the second scene of the Prologue—'Enter aloft the Drunkard with attendants . . . and Lord'—shows that Shakespeare meant this scene to be played on the balcony, leaving the main stage free for *The Taming of the Shrew*. Only once at the end of the long first scene is Sly roused from his drunken slumber to comment on the action, and his words are eminently characteristic: ' 'Tis a very excellent piece of work, madam lady. Would 'twere done.' Here, possibly, a stage direction, not preserved in our text, directed the drawing of the balcony curtain to let Sly and his attendants slip down to the tiring room. At any rate, it seems fairly certain that Shakespeare, for whom the play was the thing, decided to drop Sly and omit the Epilogue of *A Shrew*. As a matter of fact, stage versions of *The Shrew* have usually followed Shakespeare's line. An attempted revival in Elizabethan fashion in continuous performance, 1844, kept Sly on the stage throughout and had him carried off drunk at the end. Augustin Daly did better with his production in New York, 1887; he kept Sly through the first act only, and let him go off while the curtain was down. This, probably, corresponds closely enough to Shakespeare's design. Of modern productions only the Lunt-Fontanne performance seems to have kept Sly on to the end.

It has already been noted that in the taming scenes Shakespeare followed his scenario closely, but only a close comparison will reveal how completely he has transformed his source. As might be expected, this transformation is especially marked in the matter of characterization. The Ferando of *A Shrew* is a stupid, mercenary lout. As a citizen of Athens, he knows Katherine's reputation as a shrew, but since her father has promised him 6,000 crowns to wed her, he means to do so. Petruchio, a stranger, is told of Kate's bad qualities, but laughs at them; he has heard lions roar and cannons thunder, and is not to be daunted with a woman's tongue

> That gives not half so great a blow to hear
> As will a chestnut in a farmer's fire.

After the wedding Ferando persuades Kate to depart with him on the promise of a speedy return. Shakespeare converts this tame business into the delightful scene where Petruchio, pretending that the wedding company would detain them by force, carries Kate off in his arms, vowing to buckler her against a million. In a scene at his house Ferando presents Kate with a piece of meat upon his dagger's point: an absurd theft from Peele's tragedy, *Alcazar*. In the corresponding scene in *The Shrew*, Petruchio brings in a dish of meat which, in loving kindness, he himself has dressed for his sweet Kate. This is characteristic of all Petruchio's behavior to his bride; no matter how outrageous it is, all is done, she herself confesses, 'under the name of perfect love.' Shakespeare's 'tamer' is a humorist; his mad behavior is part of a game in which, at last, his wife joins, since she sees it is hopeless to oppose his humor.

There is a similar development in the character of Katherine. In *A Shrew* she is reported as such a vixen that the devil himself dare scarce venture to woo her, but little evidence of this shrewishness is presented. Shakespeare, on the other hand, shows from the very first her angry temper and her bitter tongue, and in the courtship scene he shows her repugnance slowly breaking down under the impact of Petruchio's fixed resolve and imperturbable good humor. There is no explanation in *A Shrew* of Kate's sudden submission. In Shakespeare it is possible to trace the transformation of her temper step by step until she is ready to agree with any or all of his preposterous assertions:

> And it be moon, or sun, or what you please.
> And if you choose to call it a rush-candle,
> Henceforth I vow it shall be so for me.

Finally we have the delightful little scene in the street where Kate grants the demanded kiss with the words: 'Now pray thee, love, stay.' This leads up, as nothing in *A Shrew* does, to her final oration. Here, too, we may note an interesting difference between the two versions. In *A Shrew* Kate preaches a sermon on the medieval theme of woman bound to obey her man since she had brought sin and woe into the world; Shakespeare puts into her mouth a discourse on order and obedience. He wrote this speech, of course, to show Kate's complete and sincere conversion.

Shakespeare's treatment of the subplot differs entirely from his handling of the main action. He seems to have recognized its likeness to the *Supposes* and, drawing on that play, he constructed a new plot. He transferred the scene from Athens to Italy and modified the action at the beginning and the end. In true Elizabethan fashion Shakespeare opens the intrigue with Lucentio's first sight of his lady and his determination to obtain access to her in disguise. For the two younger sisters of Katherine in the old play Shakespeare has but one, Bianca, and for Bianca's hand he introduces three suitors, Hortensio, the old citizen Gremio, and Tranio, who has assumed the role of his master, Lucentio. This gives occasion for the lively comic scene in which Tranio and Gremio bid and outbid each other for the lady. Finally Shakespeare discards the conventional classic solution. There was no need, he felt, for the improbable device of the recovery of a long-lost son, as in the *Supposes* and *A Shrew;* he contents himself with inventing a widow to pair off with one of Bianca's suitors while Gremio has to satisfy himself with a share of the marriage dinner. All in all this is a clever reshaping of Gascoigne's play along later Elizabethan lines.

Along with this rebuilding of the plot goes, naturally, a complete rewriting of the dialogue. It is in the subplot that the author of *A Shrew* gives free rein to his admiration for Marlowe. This is the sort of stuff, for instance, that he puts into the mouths of the two young lovers:

POLIDOR:

    Fair Emilia, summer's sun-bright queen,
    Brighter of hue than is the burning clime
    When Phoebus in his bright equator sits,
    Creating gold and precious minerals,
    What would Emilia do, if I were forc'd
    To leave fair Athens and to range the world?

EMILIA:

    Should Polidor, as great Achilles did,
    Only employ himself to follow arms,
    Like to the warlike Amazonian queen,
    Penthesilea, Hector's paramour,
    Who foiled the bloody Pyrrhus, murderous Greek,
    I'll thrust myself among the thickest throngs
    And with my utmost force assist my love.

We need only compare such a passage with the antiphonal dialogue of Lorenzo and Jessica in the last act of *The Merchant of Venice* to realize how Shakespeare must have disliked such rant.

On the other hand, when we examine the diction of Shakespeare's subplot, we find it for the most part, so tame and flat that it is hard to believe it the product of the poet-playwright of *The Merchant*. The poetic poverty of the subplot has given rise to two interesting explanations. On the one hand it has been suggested that the subplot is the work of another author, a clever plotter but no poet, collaborating with Shakespeare. Such collaboration is possible, but it seems unlikely. Why should Shakespeare, now in the prime of his activity, call in a partner to assist him in the job of remaking *A Shrew?* We cannot trace any collaboration in Shakespeare's work until a much later period. Nor do we know of any playwright working for Shakespeare's company at this time with whom he might have joined. The collaboration theory seems a desperate attempt to absolve Shakespeare from the guilt of having written much poor blank verse in *The Shrew*. Even if we assume a collaborator, Shakespeare must be given credit for the control of the action and a final revision of the dialogue. The two plots are so deftly interwoven as to forbid the idea of separate composition by two authors, and undoubted Shakespearean lines and phrases often appear in scenes that the separationists assign to his unknown partner.

The second explanation advances the hypothesis of a lost play antecedent to both *A Shrew* and *The Shrew,* on which both these plays were based and from which Shakespeare is thought to have taken over the subplot substantially unchanged. This explanation may be briefly dismissed. There is no trace of such a play in Elizabethan annals of the stage. Its proponents argue in part from discrepant chronology in both extant plays, as though Elizabethan playwrights worked by a timetable as exact as those of Ibsen; or they argue from contradictions and impossible statements in the extant plays supposedly due to careless changes from the lost common source. But such errors are detected only by the sharp eye of the closet critic; they are unnoticed by the spectator. This theory seems advanced to explain or excuse certain flaws in Shakespeare's work; its proponents do not seem to realize that Shakespeare, like Homer, may sometimes nod. And in Shakespeare's busy life as actor, playwright, and possibly at times stage manager, there was ample excuse for an occasional drowsy fit. Perhaps, after all, the simplest explanation is that Shakespeare, while rewriting the old play, was interested only in the Sly and the Petruchio-Katherine scenes, and for the rest he dashed off, more or less mechanically, lines good enough to carry on the action in this to him uninteresting background.

When we attempt to estimate the comic values of *The Shrew*, values which have given it life on the stage from early performances in the Globe and Blackfriars to the film play of Pickford and Fairbanks and the Lunt-Fontanne tour, we may begin by disregarding the poetical element, for *The Shrew* is one of the least poetical of Shakespeare's comedies. Poetry goes hand in hand with romance in Elizabethan drama, and there is little of romance either in the taming scenes or in the somewhat colorless courtship of Bianca. Perhaps as good a specimen as any of Shakespeare's verse in *The Shrew* may be found in Petruchio's soliloquy after he has left Kate, frightened, hungry, and sleepless, alone in the bridal chamber:

> My falcon now is sharp and passing empty,
> And till she stoop she must not be full-gorg'd,
> For then she never looks upon her lure.
> Another way I have to man my haggard,
> To make her come and know her keeper's call;
> That is, to watch her, as we watch those kites
> That bate and beat and will not be obedient.
>   . . .
> Ay, and amid this hurly I intend
> That all is done in reverend care of her.[2]

It seems needless to dwell at any length upon the characterization in *The Shrew*. The figures in the subplot are the conventional characters of classic comedy: The lover, the artful servant, a pair of old fathers, and the girl who is the cause of all the trouble. In the main plot Grumio plays a clown's role akin to that of Sander in *A Shrew*, but we may note that Shakespeare carefully cut down this part: his Grumio is the subordinate comic servant, not the semi-independent Clown of older comedy.

The transformation that Shakespeare worked upon the hero and heroine of the main plot has already been noted, and it is just this transformation combined with lively action that has given *The Shrew* its extraordinary vitality on the stage. Petruchio and Katherine are

---

[2] The words of an old writer on falconry (Bert: *Treatise on Hawks and Hawking,* 1619) show how lovers of that sport in Shakespeare's audience would have approved of Petruchio's method and anticipated his success: 'I say and so conclude that your haggard [the wild hawk taken from the nest] is very loving and kind to her keeper, after he hath brought her by his sweet and kind familiarity to understand him.'

capital acting parts, but they are something more. They are representative figures in the eternal duel of the sexes, each endowed with personality and strength enough to carry a vigorous contest to a happy conclusion.

It is in this combat, this clash of wills, that the true dramatic value of *The Shrew* consists. In the hands of a modern dramatist it might easily have reached a tragic conclusion. But Shakespeare was no Ibsen; it was probably a psychical impossibility for him to conceive a Kate turning her back on her husband and slamming the door after her as she goes out into the world. For him to have entertained such a conception would have been to break with a medieval convention of long standing. We have already seen how Noah and his sons use physical force to get his recalcitrant wife into the Ark; and Tom Tyler calls in a friend to beat his shrewish wife into temporary submission. In a rude ballad, 'A Merry Jest of a Shrewd and Curst Wife,' extant in Shakespeare's youth, the shrew is not only well beaten, but finally wrapped in the salted hide of an old horse. It is to the credit of the author of *A Shrew* that he disdains this sort of 'merry jest'; Ferando never lays a hand on Kate; no more does Petruchio, though once he threatens jestingly to return the blow she gives him with a counterbuff. Shakespeare, who knew all about hawks, knew better than to make Petruchio try to tame his haggard by the use of force; his explosions of violence are wordy rather than physical, directed at others rather than at Kate, and they are, in effect, comic exaggerations of her own fierce insistence upon her will. Kate is keen-sighted enough to see the absurdity of her husband's behavior and, when at last she comes to recognize it as a fantastic distortion of her own, she is ready to renounce the role of a virago and assume that of an obedient and loving wife.[3] To lament, as some modern critics do, the ruin of a strong character under the impact of brute force is to turn Shakespeare's merry play into a psychological tragedy. The psychology of *The Shrew,* such as it is, is Elizabethan, not Freudian. Kate's shrewishness is an Elizabethan 'humor' and, as one of the servants, like a kind of Chorus, aptly remarks, Petruchio 'kills her in her own humor.' *The Taming of the Shrew* is an Elizabethan comedy, but it retains

[3] Margaret Webster makes the interesting suggestion that perhaps Kate and Petruchio 'fell headlong in love at their very first encounter.' This, perhaps, goes a bit too far. Yet we may well imagine a strong natural attraction existing from the beginning, so that their duel, to quote Miss Webster's words, is 'increasingly informed with love and finally overwhelmed in laughter.'

its comic value even today. It still is not well for the wife to wear the breeches, and the triumphant tour of Lunt and Fontanne in this play reveals an American audience readier to understand Shakespeare than some of his critics.

MUCH ADO ABOUT NOTHING

Toward the end of the century, Shakespeare saw himself approaching the close of his long self-imposed task of dramatizing English history. From about 1595 he had been almost exclusively engaged in this work; no tragedies occur in this period, and of comedies we find only two: *The Merchant of Venice* and *The Taming of the Shrew,* neither of which represents the pure type of romantic comedy. Now, however, he felt free to return to the form that was his first favorite. Already his *Midsummer Night's Dream* had raised him to the rank of a master, and now within the brief space of some three years he created his three great examples of romantic comedy: *Much Ado about Nothing, As You Like It,* and *Twelfth Night.*

These three stars in the heaven of Shakespearean comedy differ from each other in glory; each has its own peculiar excellence, as each has its own devoted worshipers. *Much Ado* has been pronounced 'Shakespeare's most perfect comic masterpiece.' That is a judgment not likely to meet with general acceptance. Yet there is little doubt that of the three, *Much Ado,* while the least poetic, is from the point of view of dramatic power and theatrical effect the first, as it is the first chronologically. It may be dated almost certainly late in 1598 or early in 1599.

To appreciate Shakespeare's skill as a dramatic artist and his mastery of his material in this comedy, it is perhaps more necessary than ever to know something of his source and to compare his treatment of the story with what other poets and playwrights had made of it. Fortunately, the source is well known; it is one of Bandello's tales of Italian life, the twentieth in his collection of *Novelle,* first printed 1554. A full translation is given in the Variorum edition of *Much Ado;* a briefer summary will serve here.

Don Timbreo, a young nobleman who had distinguished himself in the wars of King Pedro of Arragon, fell in love with Fenicia, daughter of Lionato, a poor but noble gentleman. Unable to win her by passionate letters or gifts, he decided to

marry her, and sent a friend to beg her in marriage of her
father. Lionato consented; but another nobleman, Girondo,
a brother-in-arms of Timbreo, had long loved Fenicia and
now planned to break the match in the hope of winning the
girl himself. Accordingly, he sent a friend, 'to whom evil was
more pleasing than good,' to tell Timbreo that Fenicia had a
lover whom she often received at a window of her father's
house. He offered to give Timbreo ocular proof of her guilt
if he would come that evening and watch the house. Timbreo
consented and, unseen himself, heard a man speak of his 'lady
Fenicia' and saw him enter at the window. Convinced of her
guilt Timbreo sent word to Lionato that he would not marry
her and that she had better wed the lover she had chosen for
herself. Overcome by this accusation Fenicia swooned and was
given up for dead; only when her body was being prepared
for the grave did she return to life. Thereupon Lionato sent
her secretly to his brother's house in the country, buried an
empty coffin in the church, and inscribed an epitaph on the
tomb telling how she had been killed by a slanderous report.
Girondo was now overcome with remorse and confessed his
villainy to his friend. Timbreo forgave him, but, that the
girl's good name might be restored, took him to her father's
house. There Girondo repeated his confession, and Timbreo
declared himself ready to do whatever the old man might
require by way of atonement. Lionato replied that he would
be content if Timbreo would thereafter marry only a wife of
his choosing, and Timbreo at once consented. Meanwhile at
her uncle's house Fenicia not only regained her health, but
grew so much more beautiful that no one would have recognized her. When a year had passed Lionato claimed his promise of Timbreo and introduced him to a lovely girl, Lucilla,
whom he desired Timbreo to marry. At the wedding feast
Lucilla was made known as none other than Fenicia, and so
the lovers, parted by slander, were happily united. To make
the joy complete her sister, Belfiore, was wedded to Girondo.

   This outline gives all the important facts of the story, and a glance
will show how much of it was retained by Shakespeare. It is impossible, however, in a summary to give any idea of the sentiment of the
Novella. It is drenched with the tears that flow freely from all the

main characters; it stresses the friendship that existed between Timbreo and Girondo, and it ends with a royal procession in honor of the double marriage of the hero and the villain.

Bandello declared that all his stories were founded on actual events in Renaissance Italy. This statement is probably as fictitious as are his tales; as a matter of fact, the source of this particular tale may be found in a Spanish romance, *Tirant Lo Blanch,* one of the few spared by the curate at the purge of Don Quixote's library, since he promised himself to find in it 'a treasure of delight and a mine of recreation.' This romance was well known in Italy in the early sixteenth century and Ariosto fastened upon it, probably before Bandello, and retold it as one of the episodes of his *Orlando Furioso,* the story of Ariodante and the Scottish Princess Genevra. He takes over from the Spanish a character wanting in Bandello, the lady's waiting maid, Shakespeare's Margaret, whom he makes at once the mistress of the slanderer and the innocent agent of the deceit practiced on the lover. She dons Genevra's dress and receives the slanderer at a window of the palace—cf. *Much Ado,* v. i. 231-2. Ariodante, the true lover, sees this interview, and believes that Genevra is unchaste. The conclusion of the episode, however, differs alike from the Spanish tale and from Shakespeare's play; it is a romantic chivalric version of a tale that Bandello turned into a sentimental story of domestic life in Italy.

Edmund Spenser, on the other hand, who drew his material from Ariosto, turns the story into a moral tragedy. In *The Faerie Queene,* ii. iv, Sir Guyon, the Knight of Temperance, meets a young squire beaten and abused by Furor, a maniac, and Occasion, an old hag. Guyon rescues him and hears his story, essentially that of Ariosto, except that the lover kills both his lady and her slanderer. The Palmer, Guyon's ghostly counselor, preaches a sermon on the power of the passions, wrath, grief, jealousy, and love, and the episode ends.

It is not surprising then that Shakespeare decided to dramatize the tale. He probably read it in the original Italian prose, but he also knew the Ariosto version, for like Ariosto, and later Spenser, he makes the heroine's maid the unwitting accomplice of the trick. Unlike Spenser, however, Shakespeare declined to take the story seriously. After all, this tale of a credulous lover deceived by a false friend, the business of the disguise at the chamber window, and the final exposure of the trick is, to say the least, highly improbable. To Shakespeare it evidently was what he called it, *Much Ado about Nothing;*

yet he saw dramatic possibilities in the story. If, however, his play was to be a romantic comedy of the type to which he was turning, the tale called for considerable recasting. Let us consider some of the changes he made.

In the first place in all the versions after the original Spanish, the slanderer of the lady is the bosom friend of the lover. This involves, of course, a contest between love and friendship, a conflict strongly emphasized in Bandello. For Shakespeare to preserve this feature would be to write *The Two Gentlemen of Verona* over again, and Shakespeare had proceeded far enough in his career to recognize the poor job he had done in that early play. For the false friend, as the mover of the intrigue, he substitutes a villain, catching a hint, perhaps from Bandello's courtier, 'to whom evil was more pleasing than good,' and to fill this role he creates the character of Don John the Bastard. John's base birth, his unsuccessful revolt against his brother, his grudge against Claudio, who had the glory of his overthrow, all combine to make him a malcontent, ready for any mischief; 'if I had my mouth I would bite,' he says. Unlike Bandello's slanderer, he has nothing to gain by breaking the match, but the mere spiting of his brother's favorite will be to him 'medicinable.'

This change in the agent involved a further alteration of the action. A villain like Don John could hardly be expected to confess his guilt like the remorseful Girondo. Both Ariosto and Spenser make the lady's maid the mouthpiece of the confession. Shakespeare, too, might have done so, but he had another string to his bow: the discovery of the trick was to be the work of foolish and blundering petty officers. This would add, of course, to the comedy and would still further demonstrate how small, how 'nothing' indeed, was the matter about which this ado had been made. Before the discovery, however, which clears the lady's character, there must come the accusation of her guilt. It is interesting to see how various authors have handled this important situation. Bandello's lover behaves more or less like a gentleman; he sends a messenger to the lady's father to say the match is off, since the lady had chosen her own lover; there is no open scandal. Shakespeare, of course, could make nothing of this; it is as undramatic as possible. Nor could he do better with Ariosto's hero, who departs in silence, leaving the accusation to be brought by his brother. Spenser's squire was even more impossible in a comedy, since, instead of accusing the lady, he simply kills her at first sight. Shakespeare accordingly invents the scene at the altar where Claudio interrupts the marriage ceremony with his denunciation of Hero as unchaste. This is the most effective dramatic scene in the play and it leads, as we shall see, to important consequences. Yet the reader is apt to concur in the outcry of Beatrice: 'Is he not approved in the height a villain . . . What? bear her in hand until they come to take hands, and then with public accusation. . .'

That this alteration degrades the nominal hero of the play below the lover of the story is undeniable. Presumably, however, Shakespeare found little of interest in the character of the credulous and lacrimose Timbreo, and was not reluctant to lower him in order to attain an effective scene. The truth is that Shakespeare's Claudio is anything but a true lover in the Elizabethan mode. He does not dare to court his lady for himself; he entrusts his wooing to his princely master, yet he is ready at a whispered word to suspect the Prince of playing him false. He is equally quick to suspect his bride of disloyalty, and since the match has been promoted by his master, he feels it incumbent on him to wipe off the supposed stain on his honor by a public denunciation of the lady in the presence of the Prince. It is, perhaps, too hard to call Claudio, as Swinburne does, 'a pitiful fellow,' but only in romantic comedy could such a character be at last rewarded with the hand of the lady he had so publicly slandered.

Shakespeare invented this scene to the great benefit of the acting drama, but at the same time he canceled a scene that is constant in all other versions, that at the chamber window. Perhaps he felt that it would be impossible on the stage. If the maid's disguise was too realistic, the audience as well as the Prince would be deceived; if the disguise were apparent, the audience would take Claudio and his master for greater fools than they really are. Shakespeare pushes this scene off stage and relates it by the mouth of the chief actor in it; and this actor relates it at such a time and in such a way that he is overheard and arrested, whereby the audience is made aware in advance that the trick will be detected. We need not feel too sorry for Hero, who is, after all, a rather colorless character, since we know that her innocence will soon be vindicated.

The most important alteration in Shakespeare's handling of his material is the manner in which he brings about the detection. The account of the deceit practiced on Claudio is narrated by the servant who had played the part of Hero's lover, Borachio—the name means drunkard—flushed with success and wine. His report is overheard by the night watchmen, standing butts of ridicule in Elizabethan comedy, like policemen in twentieth-century films. The honest watchmen are not very certain of what they have heard, but they are very sure of their duty to arrest such a talker. As in duty bound, they report to the Chief Constable, the egregious Dogberry, and he and his running-mate, old Verges, carry the matter up to Leonato, on the morning of the wedding, for further examination. Had it not been for the tedious garrulity of Dogberry and Leonato's impatience to get his daughter off to church, the whole story would have come out then, and Claudio's plan for denouncing Hero at the altar would have come to naught. But Shakespeare had no notion of losing the effective church scene he had planned, and so the full disclosure is deferred. A later examination of the prisoner conducted by a sexton who has some idea of criminal procedure and Borachio's full confession end this business of the revelation. It would, perhaps, appear unduly prolonged but for its illumination by the brilliant flashes of nonsense proceeding from the mouth of Dogberry. Shakespeare has his reasons for giving this character full play.

By this time we are well on in the fifth act, and Shakespeare hurries to a conclusion. He now keeps fairly close to his source: the lady is mourned as dead; Claudio offers to undergo any penance her father may lay upon him, and Leonato bids him marry a lady of his choosing. Only one slight alteration does Shakespeare allow himself: he discards the fanciful idea that the lady had so changed in the course of a year that her lover did not know her. Moreover, Shakespeare could not wait for a year to elapse between two scenes of his last act; accordingly he marries Claudio off the next day to a masked lady who then unmasks to disclose herself as Hero.

Enough has been said to demonstrate Shakespeare's mastery in transforming his material into a romantic comedy. No mention, however, has yet been made of the two characters who put the salt of life into the improbable and sentimental main action: Beatrice and Benedick. Yet to write of *Much Ado* without mentioning them would be to stage *Hamlet* without the Prince of Denmark, for these two really make the play. It was twice performed at Court in 1612, once under its proper title, once simply as 'Benedicte and Betteris'; King Charles wrote their names in his copy of the Second Folio alongside the title, and verses prefixed to *Shakespeare's Poems*, 1640, contrast the drawing power of 'Beatrice and Benedicke' with the waning popularity of Ben Jonson's comedies. D'Avenant audaciously lifted them out of their setting and transferred them into *The Law Against Lovers* in order to add a dash of comedy to that travesty of *Measure for Measure*. Ever since Garrick's revival of *Much Ado* these two roles have been the darling parts of great actors; a long succession of productions culminated in that at the Lyceum, 1882, when Irving played Benedick to the Beatrice of Ellen Terry, 'the most enchanting,' we are told, 'of all her performances.' But it is not enough to say that Benedick and Beatrice contribute parts for star actors to this play; they do more, they lift a play combining Italian romance and realistic English clownage into the sphere of High Comedy. There is no fitter theme for the Comic Muse than the dilemma of a pair of lovers, each at once too fearful and too proud to confess, trapped at last into an avowal of their affection. There can, assuredly, be little doubt that Benedick and Beatrice are in love with each other from the beginning. Her first word is an inquiry about his safe return from the war; almost his first is to address her as 'my dear Lady Disdain.' The battle of wits that breaks out whenever they meet is a mere device employed by each to shield a heart each is afraid to betray. The trick by which each is led to believe in the other's love is, of course, a palpable stage device, but Shakespeare is not satisfied with a mere trick. He reserves their mutual confession to the church scene, where these true hearts are revealed to each other as they really are, not mocking jesters, but generous champions of injured innocence. The demand of Beatrice that Benedick play a man's part and avenge her cousin's cause precipitates the characteristic Renaissance conflict between love and friendship, but the Shakespeare of *Much Ado* had advanced far beyond the playwright who allowed Valentine to surrender his mistress to his friend. It needs only the positive assertion of Beatrice that Hero has been wronged to elicit Benedick's reply: 'Enough! I am engaged, I will challenge him.' Challenge him he does at their next meeting and, in the interest of comedy, a bloody encounter is averted only by Borachio's confession and Claudio's remorse. It is well to remember, moreover, that these two sterling characters are creatures of Shakespeare's pure invention; there is no trace of them in other versions of the story. One might find an anticipation of them in a pair of jesting lovers in *Love's Labour's Lost*, but Benedick and Beatrice are far more fully realized than Berowne and Rosaline.

Of the two, Benedick seems the more realistically drawn. It is interesting to compare him with earlier lovers in Shakespeare's plays, with the sentimental Valentine, for example, or the passionate Romeo. There is no trace in him of the Petrarchan sonneteer. He is not insensible, indeed, to the beauty of Beatrice, who, he thinks, exceeds Hero as 'the first of May doth the last of December,' but he professes himself impenetrable by the shafts of love. Even when he is led to believe that Beatrice loves him, there is no outbreak of emotion on his part: 'Love me?' he says, 'why, it must be requited.' One might almost imagine that the revelation flattered his masculine vanity as much as it touched his heart. His final confession to his mistress is couched in the simplest, one might almost say the baldest, possible terms: 'I do love nothing in the world so well as you: is not that strange?' Even when, an accepted and happy lover, he attempts to comply with fashion and show his love in verse, he is incapable of poetizing: 'I can find out no rime to "lady" but "baby," an innocent rime: for "scorn," "horn," a hard rime; for "school," "fool," a babbling rime . . . no, I was not born under a riming planet.' Yet if he is deficient in sensibility, he is not lacking in shrewd common sense; it is he who first detects the source and origin of the plot against Hero; 'The practice of it,' he says, 'lives in John the Bastard.'

Beatrice, on the contrary, no sooner learns that she is loved by Benedick than she breaks into spontaneous verse:

> What fire is in my ears? Can this be true?
> Stand I condemn'd for pride and scorn so much?
> Contempt, farewell! and maiden pride, adieu!
> No glory lives behind the back of such.
> And, Benedick, love on; I will requite thee,
> Taming my wild heart to thy loving hand.

It is of these lines that Ellen Terry says: 'I have played Beatrice hundreds of times and never done this speech as I feel it should be done.' Some of Miss Terry's passing comments on the character she played so often and so well are worth pages of critical analysis: 'her brilliant mind has a strong deep heart for its consort'; her 'repartee in her encounters with Benedick can easily be made to sound vulgar and malicious. It should be spoken as the lightest raillery with mirth in voice and a charm in manner'—a perfect answer to the stupid sneer of Campbell (the poet, not the Shakespearean scholar) that her good heart was over-weighted by her bad temper. The mocking laughter of Beatrice is like the reflection of light upon the sea; she was born, she confesses, under a dancing star, but beneath its sparkling waves the sea is deep, and the Beatrice who cries to her lover: 'Kill Claudio!' has something of the depth and passion of the sea.

In strong contrast to the high comedy of Benedick and Beatrice, the watchmen with their Head Constable and Verges bring into the play the characteristic element of English realism. A tradition going back almost to Shakespeare's day records that he drew 'the humor of the Constable' from a rural officer he encountered on the road from London to Stratford. Be that as it may, Dogberry and his Watch spring rather from the English lanes than from the streets of Messina. Dogberry, in particular, is as representative of the small town official as Bottom is of the village wit. There is, indeed, a family likeness between them; one might almost imagine Dogberry a Bottom grown old in office, so old, in fact, that he had changed for the worse. Bottom's imperturbable complacency has become in Dogberry a querulous self-assertion of his worth as a man of means and as 'the poor Duke's officer'; Bottom's simple and forthright manner of speech has changed with Dogberry into a sort of official lingo which murders the Queen's English with every utterance. The malapropisms flowing from his lips are, of course, part of the conventional manner of the Clown, but it is safe to say that no earlier or later Clown perpetrates quite so many as Dogberry. And yet in spite of his self-assertion and bustling officialdom, he is an altogether delightful character; it is impossible not to rejoice in a respectable official who in and out of season persists in being written down an ass; the mask that Puck clapped on Bottom's head would fit quite naturally on Dogberry's. Both these characters reveal Shakespeare's unfailing delight in the absurdities of his beloved countryfolk; with the rogues of the city he was never, one feels, quite so much at home.

There is another tie that connects Bottom and Dogberry. Both parts were written for Shakespeare's fellow-actor, Will Kempe; in fact it seems not impossible that at some reading of the unfinished play Kempe himself suggested some of Dogberry's absurdities which Shakespeare gladly wrote into the text. Yet it may be noted that Kempe's part is strictly confined to the lines written for him; he has no chance here to play tricks on a fellow-actor as Launcelot Gobbo did with his 'high-gravel blind' father. It seems quite certain, too, that this is the last part that Shakespeare ever wrote for Kempe. Within a year of the staging of *Much Ado* this popular comedian deserted Shakespeare's Company, the only one of the closely knit group that ever broke away. It is possible that Kempe, who had no small conceit of himself, grew a little weary of Shakespeare's insistence that the Clown speak no more than is set down for him.

It is these characters—Benedick and Beatrice on the one hand, Dogberry and his fellows on the other—that turn Shakespeare's dramatization of an Italian *novella* into an Elizabethan comedy. And what a
comedy! It seems not too much to assert that in *Much Ado* Shakespeare rose to heights in romantic comedy that he had never touched
before. Less poetical than the *Dream* it is far better drama; less serious than *The Merchant* it is a gayer comedy; the threat of disaster
that hangs over the earlier play till near the end is only a passing
cloud, soon dispelled, in *Much Ado*. The main plot, one, as we have
seen, of peculiar interest to his age, Shakespeare has handled in such
a way as to make it little more than a background for a theme of his
own invention, a battle of the sexes between two such lively duelists
as Benedick and Beatrice. The interwoven action of the two plots is
always interesting, and, it may be noted, the action springs in every
instance from the character of the actors. Shakespeare has finally discarded the archaic horseplay; there is not a blow struck in this gay
comedy. He now relies on his audience to follow with attention and
delight a well-motivated intrigue. The plot against Hero starts from
the malcontentism of Don John; Claudio's ready belief in the accusation springs from his own suspicious temper; the trick played alternately upon Benedick and Beatrice comes from the natural desire
of their friends to see these mockers at Love entangled in his nets;
their final union is based upon their mutual sympathy at a moment
of almost tragic stress. The very delay that makes the church scene
and this union possible is due to the fact that Dogberry is what he
is, self-important and tediously loquacious at an inopportune moment. There is no fairy magic in this play, no strange will of a dead
father to determine a maiden's destiny; all that happens finds its cause
in the characters of normal and recognizable human beings.

    Much Ado is a play of action springing from character, but it is
also a play of vivacious and amusing dialogue. In fact a great part of
the fun of this play comes from the spoken word; often, indeed, the
action halts while we listen to a rippling stream of speech. The text
falls easily into verse and prose; easily but not equally, for about
three-fourths of the whole is in prose, a new phenomenon in Shakespearean comedy. Shakespeare's rustics and clownish servants, indeed,
had talked in prose; a merry gentleman like Mercutio might step from
verse into prose and back again. Here for the first time, however, the
dialogue of gentlefolk, male and female, is for the most part couched

in prose. It seems as if Shakespeare is now convinced that for comedy of the lighter, less romantic type, prose is the proper vehicle. The conviction may have grown on him while he was creating Falstaff, his greatest comic figure, who seldom speaks a line of verse. The conjecture seems to be confirmed by the fact that King Henry's wooing of his French bride, perhaps the least romantic courtship in English drama, is all in prose. This scene is plainly meant to round off a drum-and-trumpet play with a concluding strain of comedy, and *King Henry V* was written in the same year as *Much Ado*.

Little need be said of the verse of this play. There are good lines here and there, but there is an absence alike of the lyric music of the *Dream* and the grave eloquence of *The Merchant*. The workman-like verse is confined, almost without exception, to what is structurally the main, which is also the derived, plot, another proof, no doubt, of Shakespeare's slight regard for this action compared with his delight in the new theme and the two characters that he was adding to it. It is the prose and not the poetry of this play that lingers in the memory: the comic blunders of Dogberry, the wit-combats of the still defiant lovers, the scoffing comments of Benedick on love and marriage, the light-hearted jesting of Beatrice, and, best of all, the confession of their mutual love in simple unadorned prose. It was from Lyly, no doubt, that Shakespeare learned the use of prose in comedy, but he had by this time happily purged his style of the characteristic marks of Lylian Euphuism. Let us take a few examples, chosen at random.

Dogberry in the trial scene.

> Dost thou not suspect my place? Dost thou not suspect my years? O that he were here to write me down an ass! . . . Thou villain, thou art full of piety, as shall be prov'd upon thee by good witness. I am a wise fellow; and, which is more, an officer; and, which is more, a householder; and, which is more, as pretty a piece of flesh as any in Messina; and one that knows the law, go to; and a rich fellow enough, go to; and a fellow that hath had losses; and one that hath two gowns, and everything handsome about him. Bring him away. O that I had been writ down an ass!

Benedick, who has been scoffing at Claudio's behavior since he has fallen in love, continues:

May I be so converted, and see with these eyes? I cannot tell; I think not: I will not be sworn but love may transform me to an oyster; but I'll take my oath on it, till he have made an oyster of me, he shall never make me such a fool. One woman is fair, yet I am well; another is wise, yet I am well; another virtuous, yet I am well; but till all graces be in one woman, one woman shall not come in my grace.

or Beatrice pretending to lament that she'll never get a husband:

I will even take sixpence in earnest of the bear-ward, and lead his apes into hell.

'Well then, go you into hell?' her uncle asks her, and she replies:

No, but to the gate; and there will the devil meet me, like an old cuckold, with horns on his head, and say, 'Get you to heaven, Beatrice, get you to heaven; here's no place for you maids': so deliver I up my apes, and away to Saint Peter for the heavens; he shows me where the bachelors sit, and there live we as merry as the day is long.

In strong contrast note the quick speech and answer between Beatrice and Benedick when raillery has given place to sober truth:

BENE. I protest I love thee.
BEAT. Why, then, God forgive me!
BENE. What offence, sweet Beatrice?
BEAT. You have stayed me in a happy hour: I was about to protest I loved you.
BENE. And do it with all thy heart.
BEAT. I love you with so much of my heart that none is left to protest.

Lyly, nor any of the other Elizabethans, ever wrote prose like this; it is pure and undiluted Shakespeare.

AS YOU LIKE IT

As You Like It follows hard upon *Much Ado* in the great trio of romantic comedies that bridge the close of the sixteenth century. Both plays were entered in the Stationers' Register 4 August 1600, but *As You Like It* remained unprinted in the actors' hands until it appeared in the Folio of 1623. Yet in spite of their close connection in time, the two plays are very different. In *Much Ado* we have seen Shakespeare hard at work recasting an Italian tale to suit his own dramatic ends, and in the process altering his source at will. In *As You Like It,* on the contrary, he is simply dramatizing a popular English romance, keeping so close to his source that it is not unfair to say that there is little or nothing in the action of the play that is not in the romance, though he omits and abbreviates to compress a long-winded narrative into the limits of a two-hour play. Nothing, perhaps, could illustrate more aptly the range and versatility of Shakespeare's now fully developed art than the difference between the carefully planned construction of the one and the easy carelessness, due, probably, to haste, of the other of two plays belonging to the same dramatic genre.

There is a reason for most things, and there was good reason for haste on Shakespeare's part when his fellows called on him late in 1599 to write a new comedy for their new theater, the Globe. The year 1599-1600 must have been one of the busiest of Shakespeare's life. As shareholder of the Globe, actor, and playwright, his hands were very full. These years saw the last of his long roll of Histories, *King Henry V,* and the first of his great succession of tragedies, *Julius Caesar,* and, quite probably, the beginning of his struggle to transform the old melodrama of *Hamlet* into his own masterpiece. Accordingly, when a hurry call came to this busy man for a new comedy, he turned to a well-known romance that had recently, 1598, been reprinted, and swiftly whipped it into dramatic form. It is worth while to look for a moment at this romance to see just what Shakespeare did with it.

It has long been known that the source of *As You Like It* is Lodge's *Rosalynde.* Now Lodge was one of the little band of scholarly poets, playwrights, and romancers who invaded London in the early 1580's. Like Lyly and Peele he was an Oxford student, taking his B.A. there in 1577. He was admitted to Lincoln's Inn in 1578, but turned his attention to letters rather than to law. He championed the new drama against Puritan attack in a *Defence of Stage Plays,* 1580, and was known as a 'play-maker' as early as 1582. Only two of his plays survive: *The Wounds of Civil War, c.* 1588, and *A Looking Glass for London,* in collaboration with Greene, *c.* 1590. Lodge seems to have been a rather versatile man of letters, for, besides plays, he wrote narrative poems, satires, and pamphlets of various sorts. He was, perhaps, most successful as a writer of prose tales in which he exploited the Euphuism of Lyly to decorate romantic love stories like those of Greene. The most interesting of these tales, because of its connection with Shakespeare, is his *Rosalynde,* written to beguile the long hours of an expedition to the Canaries. He calls it 'the work of a soldier and scholar, hatched in the storms of the ocean and feathered in the surges of many perilous seas.'

Rosalynde is a curious amalgam of English balladry, pastoral romance, and moral maxims. It begins with a series of adventures drawn from the old *Tale of Gamelyn,* falsely ascribed to Chaucer.

> Gamelyn in the *Tale* is a hero of the Robin Hood type. The youngest son of Sir John de Boundys, he is cheated of his inheritance by his elder brother and lured into a wrestling match with a champion who, his brother hopes, will break his neck. But Gamelyn beats the champion, escapes later plots against his life, and flies to the greenwood with a faithful retainer, Adam the Spencer. Here he becomes the leader of a band of outlaws and later returns to hang his brother, now the King's sheriff—a genuine Robin Hood touch—and with him the judge and the jury that sat to indict him as a 'wolf's head.' For this good deed the King of England made him Chief Justice of all his free forest.

This is rather rough stuff, more to the taste of a medieval audience than to the sophisticated Elizabethans for whom Lodge was writing. Lady Olivia, we may be sure, would have called Gamelyn a 'rudesby.'

Accordingly Lodge transforms the old tale into a pastoral romance. He shifts the scene to France, and from the time his hero, now baptised Rosader, reaches the forest of Arden, i.e. the Ardennes, the narrative deals mainly with his love for Rosalynde, the daughter of a banished King of France, also living in Arden.

> Rosalynde and Rosader had met and exchanged eyes and hearts at the wrestling match, but later Rosalynde and her cousin, Alinda, were banished by the usurping king, another wicked brother. Disguised as a page and assuming the name of Ganymede, Rosalynde, along with Alinda, who takes the name of Aliena, escapes to Arden. There she meets Rosader, now in the service of the banished king, and under the safety of her disguise makes sport of his passion. She suggests that

she should play the part of Rosalynde and let him woo her; she even goes through the form of a mock marriage with him. To make the pastoral complete Lodge introduces an amorous shepherd, Montanus, and a hard-hearted shepherdess, Phoebe, who at once falls in love with Ganymede, but is persuaded to marry Montanus, if Ganymede will not wed her. To join this company comes Saladyne, Rosader's wicked brother, who has also been banished by the usurper. Rosader finds him asleep in the forest, saves him from a lion, and introduces him to Ganymede and Aliena. Saladyne, now a thoroughly reformed character, falls in love with Aliena, saves her and Ganymede from a band of robbers, and wins her love. At their wedding Ganymede reveals herself to her father as his daughter, Rosalynde, and is betrothed by him to Rosader, in consequence of which Phoebe marries Montanus. The festivities are interrupted by the news that the twelve Peers of France have risen against the usurper. Rosader and Saladyne join them; the usurper is defeated and slain, and Rosader is proclaimed heir to the kingdom.

Here, plainly, is the scenario on which Shakespeare worked. In the main he followed his source very closely; it takes a comparative study of the romance and the play to show how many minor incidents Shakespeare took over from Lodge. But it is still more interesting to note the changes he made. In the first place he cuts down the introductory matter; the long narrative of Rosader's strife with his brother is reduced to a brief physical encounter and to the mere mention of a plot against Orlando's life. Shakespeare wanted to get his characters to Arden as soon as possible. In the same way he shortens Lodge's conclusion; the detailed account of the loves of Saladyne and Aliena is cut down to Rosalind's mocking report of their sudden infatuation. The marriage of Oliver and Celia—Saladyne and Alinda in Lodge— has been called 'the one unlucky slip of the brush' in Shakespeare's play, but it was given him by his source and was, in fact, demanded by the convention of Elizabethan comedy that all eligible maidens should be married off in the last act. The Masque of Hymen, which winds up the play, is perhaps a less happy ending than Rosalynde's pretty revelation of herself in woman's dress to her father. There is, however, some reason to believe that this episode was not part of Shakespeare's original plan, but was inserted later to give a bit of spectacle with music when the play was performed at some noble wedding.

Yet it would be wrong to suppose that Shakespeare merely threw Lodge's narrative into dramatic form. He did much more; he transformed the tone of the romance as thoroughly as Lodge had done that of the tale of Gamelyn. Shakespeare called his play *As You Like It,* perhaps with a smiling admission that a pastoral romance of this sort was the dear delight of his Elizabethan audience; he himself, certainly, was too much of a realist to accept its absurdities.

By way of corrective he introduces into his play various characters whose sole business it is to comment on, often indeed to expose, the fantastic figment of the pastoral. One of these characters, the shepherd Corin, comes over from Lodge's Corydon, but while in the romance he is a singing shepherd like one of Spenser's, in the play he is a simple representative of the shepherd's life as it really is, the hired servant of a churlish master, his hands hard and greasy with handling his ewes, a 'natural philosopher.' To Corin Shakespeare added the country wench, Audrey, and her rustic lover, William. All three give a background of realism to the pastoral scene.

Jaques, another of Shakespeare's inventions, is a more important character. He takes no part in the action, yet *As You Like It* would be the poorer without him. Jaques is first of all a 'humor' character such as Jonson had lately introduced on Shakespeare's stage. His 'humor' is that of a somewhat cynical melancholy; in the phrase of that day he is a 'malcontent.' Yet he is more than a type figure; Shakespeare has taken some pains to individualize him. He is the traveler returned from the Continent where, presumably he has, like Greene, practiced 'such a villainy as is abominable to mention'—the Duke calls him 'a libertine as sensual as the brutish sting itself'—and he has come home to sneer at all things English. Rosalind's gibe hits him off exactly: 'Farewell, Monsieur Traveller: look you lisp, and wear strange suits, disable all the benefits of your own country, be out of love with your nativity, and almost chide God for making you that countenance you are; or I will scarce think you have swam in a gondola.' A professed satirist he demands the liberty of caustic criticism of society, of all human life in fact; his famous 'All the world's a stage' oration is the cynic's picture of man's life in all its periods. There is no fear that we shall take the pastoral seriously while Jaques is there to comment on it. One instance of his mocking comment has been ignored or misunderstood by most editors. In Act II. v Amiens warbles a song in praise of the open-air, carefree life in Arden. Jaques at once hands him 'a verse to this note,' i.e. tune, which he wrote yesterday, and Amiens sings it. This is the parody:

> If it do come to pass
> That any man turn ass . . .

which contains the mysterious word: *Ducdame,* thrice repeated. This word has been shown to be a corruption of the Romany *dukra mi,* i.e. 'I will foretell,' a phrase Jaques must have picked up on his travels. When Amiens asks the meaning of 'Ducdame,' Jaques replies: ''Tis a Greek [roguish] invocation to call fools into a circle,' as the gypsy fortunetellers were wont to do. He continues: 'I'll go sleep if I can; if I cannot, I'll rail against all the first-born of Egypt,' i.e. these aristocratic amateur gypsies in the Duke's band.

Like Jaques, Touchstone is a character created by Shakespeare and he is in some ways the more interesting of the two. His is the first role that Shakespeare wrote for Armin, Kempe's successor as chief comedian of the company, and the role represents a shift in Shakespeare's characterization of the principal fun-maker of a play. Heretofore this character had been a stupid servant like Launce, a rustic like Costard, or a small-town comic figure like Bottom or Dogberry. There is no trace in Shakespeare's earlier comedies of that other development of the old Vice, the professional Fool. From this time on, however, this role appears again and again, as in Feste, Lavache in *All's Well,* Trinculo in *The Tempest,* and notably the Fool in *Lear,* all, presumably, parts for Armin. There was a reason for this. Armin was evidently a very different type of comedian from Kempe. According to report he had been trained to act by the famous clown, Tarleton, but he was a man of some education, a writer of small pamphlets, one of which describes various fools and jesters. He even wrote a play, *Two Maids of Moreclacke,* where what seems to be his portrait appears on the title-page. He had been an actor of comic parts in a minor company, Lord Chandos' Men, but joined Shakespeare's company not long after they began playing in the Globe. Shakespeare soon learned to appreciate his new comrade. After *As You Like It* he went on to write the role of Feste for him in *Twelfth Night* and in that play he pays a striking tribute to him. Viola, speaking of Feste, i.e. Armin, says:

> This fellow's wise enough to play the fool,
> And to do that well craves a kind of wit:
> . . . This is a practice
> As full of labour as a wise man's art.

Touchstone's role is that of the Court Jester, the 'all-licensed fool.' It is as such that he first appears at Duke Frederick's court, using the Fool's license to mock at the Knight who swore by his honor that the pancakes were good, and indulging himself at the same time with a side thrust at the Duke, who loves this honorless Knight. He is threatened, to be sure, with a whipping, the customary penalty for the Fool who overstepped his bounds—cf. Lear's warning to his Jester —but he is clever enough to sidestep the danger at Court, and once he is in Arden all danger blows away in the forest air. Here he is free to practice, unchecked, his vocation, the exposure of folly. That, presumably, is the significance of his name; he is the touchstone that distinguishes pure from base metal. He contributes to the action of the play as little as Jaques, but he is an even more amusing commentator. He comments mainly by exaggeration and by parody. We have examples of his art in his reminiscence of his early love for Jane Smile, a wild caricature of the fantastic passion of Silvius for Phebe, and in his impromptu parody of Orlando's 'false gallop of verses.' He is even able to win a laugh from the cynic Jaques by ranting on Lady Fortune 'in good set terms,' really a mockery, though Jaques does not recognize it, of that railer's own habitual practice. His story of a quarrel with a courtier, which ran through all the degrees from the Retort Courteous to the Countercheck Quarrelsome, is a satiric parody of the behavior of gentlemen who wrangled, as they dressed, 'by the book,' the book, that is, of an Elizabethan Emily Post. This speech, by the way, looks like an afterthought on Shakespeare's part, written in, perhaps, at a rehearsal, to let Armin amuse the audience while the costumes and the music for the coming Masque were being made ready off-stage. Touchstone's one contribution to the action of the play is his wooing of Audrey. This, of course, is Shakespeare's invention; there was no place for such a courtship in Lodge's pastoral. Yet this very wooing is Touchstone's comment on the whole business of lovemaking in Arden. Silvius and Phebe are fantastic lovers in the pastoral convention; the sudden mutual passion of Oliver and Celia is quite incredible; Rosalind and Orlando are romantic lovers *par excellence*. Touchstone and his girl, on the other hand, present this relation of the sexes in its simplest realistic form: 'man hath his desires; and as pigeons bill, so wedlock would be nibbling.' Touchstone's courtship is not only comment, but parody.

Apart from characters already mentioned, the figures of any importance in the play—the two Dukes, the brothers, Orlando and Oliver, the cousins, Rosalind and Celia, along with Phebe and her lover—have all stepped out of Lodge's romance onto Shakespeare's stage. One of these characters, however, has been so transformed by Shakespeare's magic as to have become a new creation. This, of course, is Rosalind. It was long ago remarked that *As You Like It* was successful on the stage only when an actress of very superior skill performed this part. Many famous actresses, from Peg Woffington to Ada Rehan, including, strange to say, the great Mrs. Siddons, have distinguished themselves in this role. It is a striking proof of the well-trained skill of the boys in Shakespeare's company that there was among them one to whom he could entrust the part, knowing, as he did, that it was on this boy that the success or failure of his comedy depended.

For Rosalind plays a far more important part in *As You Like It* than her namesake does in the source, where the heroine divides the interest with Saladyne and Alinda, with Montanus and Phoebe. As a matter of fact, once Shakespeare gets his characters to Arden the whole action of the play revolves about Rosalind in her disguise as Ganymede. Not only that, but she has become quite a different person from Lodge's lady. Rosalynde is the conventional heroine of romance, 'the paragon of all earthly perfection.' Lodge introduces her with a veritable flourish of trumpets: 'the blush that gloried Luna when she kissed the shepherd on the hills of Latmos was not tainted with such a pleasant dye as the vermilion flourished on the silver hue of Rosalynde's countenance.' She can 'parley Euphuism' quite as well as the ladies in Lyly's plays, and like the women in Greene's love stories she is given to interminable stretches of self-analysis, debating the pros and cons of her emotional estate. She joins Rosader at one time in an antiphonal 'wooing-eclogue,' packed with the conceits of pastoral love-making, and she can, at a pinch, quote Horace in the original.

Shakespeare's Rosalind, on the contrary, is a creature of a natural and almost divine simplicity. She first appears saddened for her banished father, a striking contrast to the resplendent Rosalynde at the usurper's court. Her dawning passion for Orlando is motivated, in part at least, by the fact that he is the son of her father's old friend, a matter passed over in silence by Lodge. Rosalynde, Lodge tells us, 'to make Rosader know she affected him took from her neck a jewel and sent it by a page to the young gentleman.' This formal act of courtesy falls far short of the simplicity and grace of Rosalind's behavior:

> Gentleman,
> Wear this for me, one out of suits with fortune,
> That could give more, but that her hand lacks means.

She turns to go, but pretending to catch a word from Orlando, who really stands in dumb-struck silence, she turns back to say:

> My pride fell with my fortunes;
> I'll ask him what he would. Did you call, sir?
> Sir, you have wrestled well, and overthrown
> More than your enemies.

In the source Ganymede and Celia are together when they meet Rosader in Arden, and together they chaff him about his passion and listen to his verses in praise of Rosalynde. In the play it is Celia who first sees Orlando and brings the news of his presence to Rosalind, and this news provokes a characteristic outburst:

> Alas the day! What shall I do with my doublet and hose? What did he when thou sawest him? What said he? How looked he? Wherein went he? What makes he here? Did he ask for me? Where remains he? How parted he with thee, and when shalt thou see him again? Answer me in one word.

When Rosalind in her page's disguise first meets Orlando, she pretends not to know that he is the man who 'abuses our young plants with carving "Rosalind" on their barks.' On his confession that it is indeed he who is so 'love-shaked,' she refuses to believe him, for he shows none of the well-known signs of a lover. Yet if he is really in love, she professes her ability and willingness to cure him, provided he will call her Rosalind and come every day to her cote and woo her. Shakespeare has borrowed this business of the simulated wooing from Lodge, but he has greatly enlarged and quite transfigured it. His heroine, happy in the knowledge that she is loved, is ready to play with and torment her lover; at one moment to declare that she will love him 'and twenty such'; at another to break out in lamentation when he must leave her for two hours:

> Ay, go your ways, go your ways; I knew what you would prove, my friends told me as much, and I thought no less: that flattering tongue of yours won me: 'Tis but one cast away, and so, come, death!

Yet beneath her mockery there burns a true passion, as she confesses to Celia:

> O coz, coz, coz, my pretty little coz, that thou didst know how many fathom deep I am in love! But it cannot be sounded: my affection hath an unknown bottom, like the Bay of Portugal.

The image recalls the avowal of Juliet in Shakespeare's tragedy of love:

> My bounty is as boundless as the sea,
> My love as deep.

But Rosalind can laugh at her plight where Juliet sighs:

> I have no joy of this contract to-night:
> It is too rash, too unadvis'd, too sudden.

This is the difference between comedy and tragedy, yet there is here, perhaps, something more individual and characteristic than that. Of all the heroines of Shakespearean comedy, Rosalind in Arden is the gayest, because she is the happiest, and the happiest because she knows her lover loves her, while yet she need not confess her own passion. There is no trace of this light-hearted gaiety in Lodge's Rosalynde, any more than there is that trace of feminine weakness which Rosalind shows when she faints at the sight of her lover's blood.

This atmosphere of happiness breathes through all the scenes in Arden. The threat of danger or of death which hangs over various characters in earlier comedies is soon dispelled in this play. Duke Senior, Orlando, and Rosalind all have to fly for their lives, but they are all happier in exile than ever they were at home. The Duke strikes the keynote in his address to his 'co-mates and brothers in exile':

Are not these woods
More free from peril than the envious court?

and the lovely songs with which the play abounds: 'Under the greenwood tree'; 'Blow, blow, thou bitter wind'; 'It was a lover and his
lass'; all re-echo this note. They are happy replacements of Lodge's
formalized songs and sonnets of pastoral love. Closely as Shakespeare
has followed the action of his source, he has contrived to set it in quite
another key.

Enough has been said of the characters who contribute to, who constitute in fact, the comic element in this delightful play. It may, however, be noted that their contribution is less a matter of action than
of speech. Jaques and Touchstone reveal themselves as figures of
comedy less by what they do than by what they say, and while Rosalind's action follows in the main the pattern laid down by the source,
it is, after all, her speech that matters. It is in his free and, as it were,
almost careless mastery of language in *As You Like It* that Shakespeare surpasses most of his earlier works in comedy. There is a more
even balance of prose and verse in this play than in *Much Ado*. That
was a comedy of character revealed in action, and for that purpose
Shakespeare used mainly prose. Here, however, where action in itself
is less important, verse regains some of the lost ground. About two-
fifths of *As You Like It* is in verse—apart from the songs almost entirely in blank verse. The rhymed couplet, so frequent in the early
comedies, has disappeared except in isolated cases like Phebe's quotation from Marlowe, Orlando's imperfect sonnet, and tag-ends of scenes
and speeches. What is of more importance, the blank verse recovers
not only in extent, but in poetic quality. It is not easy to find in
Much Ado a memorable passage of more than a few lines of verse;
As You Like It is 'thick inlaid' with stars. The best-known passage,
the Seven ages of man, is a set speech, written, perhaps, to let Jaques
hold the stage while Orlando goes off to bring in old Adam. It is
rhetorical rather than lyric, which is appropriate to the speaker. In
general, the lyric strain of *A Midsummer Night's Dream* is, except
for the songs, seldom heard in this play. Its music is graver and more
equable, nearer, perhaps, to that of *The Merchant*. Listen, for example, to Adam's offer of his gold:

Take that; and He that doth the ravens feed,
Yea, providently caters for the sparrow,
Be comfort to my age!

and to Orlando's reply:

> O good old man! how well in thee appears
> The constant service of the antique world;

or to the profession of the enamoured Silvius:

> So holy and so perfect is my love,
> And I in such a poverty of grace,
> That I shall think it a most plenteous crop
> To glean the broken ears after the man
> That the main harvest reaps: loose now and then
> A scatter'd smile, and that I'll live upon.

But this verse can rise at times to sharp dramatic emphasis, as in Rosalind's rebuke of Phebe:

> But, mistress, know yourself: down on your knees,
> And thank heaven, fasting, for a good man's love.

It is not far wrong to say that when sentiment predominates, verse prevails in *As You Like It*. When the stress lies on character, character contrast, satiric comment, or the play of the comic spirit, Shakespeare reverts to prose. Touchstone regularly speaks prose; that is the proper dialect of the Jester. Rosalind swings back and forth from verse to prose—and what a prose! Shakespeare had before him as he wrote her part the highly euphuised speech of Lodge's lady, in such a strain, for example, as this:

> Infortunate Rosalynde whose misfortunes are more than thy years and whose passions are greater than thy patience! The blossoms of thy youth are mixed with the frosts of envy, and the hope of thy ensuing fruits perish in the bud.

This lament Shakespeare swiftly transmutes into Rosalind's exclamation:

> O, how full of briers is this working-day world!

Rosalind's flow of speech is most vivacious and sparkling when, disguised as a page, she amuses herself by tormenting her lover. Does he say he will die for love? She is quick to reply:

> The poor world is almost six thousand years old, and in all this time there was not any man died in his own person,

> videlicet, in a love-cause. . . Men have died from time to
> time, and worms have eaten them, but not for love.

Listen to her when, after the mock marriage, she plays the part of the
wife that is to be:

> I will be more jealous of thee than a Barbary cock-pigeon
> over his hen; more clamorous than a parrot against rain;
> more new-fangled than an ape; more giddy in my desires than
> a monkey. I will weep for nothing, like Diana in the fountain,
> and I will do that when you are disposed to be merry; I will
> laugh like a hyen, and that when thou art inclined to sleep.

This is patterned prose, to be sure, but it is a pattern of Shakespeare's
own devising, poles away from that of Lodge, or Lodge's master, Lyly.
Here is another specimen in quite a different key, but like Rosalind's
speech eminently characteristic of the speaker. Touchstone introduces
Audrey to the Duke:

> A poor virgin, sir, an ill-favoured thing, sir, but mine own: a
> poor humour of mine, sir, to take that that no man else will.

The poet-playwright of the early comedies has now become a master
of Elizabethan—really, the very best—English prose.

It is not easy to pass final judgment on a play at once so delightful
and so provoking. It is the work of a playwright fully master of his
art, yet contemptuous of probability and recklessly careless of construction. It has always been a favorite with lovers of the romantic.
During the heyday of romanticism in France Gautier, who called it
a drama written for fairies to be played by moonlight, used it in his
'golden book of spirit and sense' as the magic charm that brought the
ideal mistress to the arms of an impassioned lover, and George Sand
strove in vain to adapt it to the conventions of the Parisian stage. In
England Hazlitt, most romantic of critics, has been its most enthusiastic admirer. A realist like Shaw, on the contrary, sees in its very title
the author's contempt of a public he stooped to entertain. This, to
be sure, seems as wilfully perverse as much of Shaw's comment on
Shakespeare, for it is hardly possible to read *As You Like It* without
feeling that Shakespeare thoroughly enjoyed writing it. Perhaps the
question to be asked and answered is how it happened that Shakespeare turned at the height of his power to such an almost trivial task

as the dramatization of Lodge's romance. What drew him to a pastoral whose fantastic follies no one recognized more clearly?

The answer may be found, perhaps, in the first pages of *Rosalynde,* those that retell the tale of Gamelyn. Here is no pastoral, but a story of merry England in the time of Robin Hood; and Shakespeare, like a true Englishman, loved the tale of Robin. As early as *The Two Gentlemen of Verona* he brought upon his stage a band of outlaws, quite out of place, it must be owned, in the Italian scene, who choose a gently born hero as their chief, and swear obedience to rules such as Robin might have laid down. Shakespeare lost no time in striking this note in *As You Like It;* in the very first scene he tells us through the mouth of Charles, the wrestler—a strange person, by the way, to speak for Shakespeare, but Shakespeare was in haste—that the banished Duke is in 'the forest of Arden, and a many merry men with him; and there they live like the old Robin Hood of England.' Lodge's tale soon becomes, it is true, a conventional pastoral, but Shakespeare felt himself quite capable of dealing with the pastoral and transforming it into a wildwood comedy where outlaws, lovers, shepherds, and jesters may 'fleet the time carelessly as they did in the golden world.'

Lodge's forest is the Ardennes of France; but Shakespeare took it for Arden, the forest of his homeland, for in spite of olive trees and a lurking lioness which have somehow got into the play from the tale, the background of *As You Like It* is unmistakably that of the English countryside. Shakespeare hurries through the first act to get his characters into this beloved country. Once they are there he need not trouble greatly about them; anything may, much does, happen under the greenwood tree. Shakespeare like his characters is happy and at home in Arden.

In no play of Shakespeare's do we feel so plainly this sense of happy and carefree ease. It cost him little intellectual effort to transform *Rosalynde* into a stage-play; there were few dramatic problems to be met and mastered. The core of Lodge's romance was a pleasant story of young love; it was an easy matter to strip off its conventional absurdities and to substitute for its stock figures creatures of real flesh and blood. Even these creatures may mean less in the play than the atmosphere of Arden. Once he sat down to write this play Shakespeare left the noisy crowded town with all the demands it made on him, to forget the world for a while in the shade of this legendary wood. *As You Like It* is of all Shakespeare's plays most visibly a comedy of escape. As he shakes off the briers of this working-day world, his pen runs swiftly without pause or check through scene after scene. Here, if ever, we may believe what his fellows were to tell us after his death, that 'his mind and his hand went together'; here, if ever, we may believe that the script he handed over to the company was without a blot. Properly to appreciate *As You Like It* we must forget for a time all matters of dramatic technique, all conceptions of a 'well-made' play, and be content, like the inhabitants of Arden to 'fleet the time carelessly.'

TWELFTH NIGHT

Twelfth Night, the latest of the great trio of romantic comedies, is in some ways the most delightful. In its blend of romance and realism, sentiment and fun, its well-knit construction, vigorous characterization, and happy balance of lovely verse and lively prose, it is certainly the most finished of Shakespeare's comedies. And it is characteristic of Shakespeare's development and of his method of work that he never thereafter wrote a comedy like this. It has been called 'Shakespeare's farewell to mirth.' This is hardly accurate; there are comic characters, merry scenes, and hearty laughs in his latest plays, *The Winter's Tale* and *The Tempest;* yet there is never again a comedy which in all-round perfection can compare with *Twelfth Night.*

Contemporary readers of Shakespeare's plays had to wait for the first Folio to enjoy this play at home, but it had been on the stage for years before that date. In fact, an entry, 2 February 1601,[1] in the diary of John Manningham, a barrister of the Middle Temple, fixes a performance of this play in the great hall of that law school in 1602. 'At our feast,' he writes, 'we had a play called Twelve Night, or What You Will, much like the Comedy of Errors or Menechmi in Plautus, but most like and near to that in Italian called *Inganni.* A good practice in it to make the steward believe his Lady widow was in love with him by counterfeyting a letter as from his lady.'

There is no reason to believe, however, that this was the first performance of *Twelfth Night.* On the contrary it was presumably ordered by the managers of the Temple feast because of its success on the public stage, as *The Comedy of Errors* had been commanded for performance in Gray's Inn in 1594. How much earlier it was written we cannot tell exactly, but since it is not mentioned in the Meres' list of Shakespeare's plays in 1598, it must date after that year. The part of Feste, like that of Touchstone, was evidently written for Armin,

---

1 The date in the diary is old style; the year by our reckoning was 1602.

and since he joined Shakespeare's Company in 1599, and *As You Like It* was, apparently, written in 1600, we are fairly safe in dating *Twelfth Night* some time in 1601.

This date, however, applies only to the play in its present form, for it is almost certain that *Twelfth Night,* as we have it, is a revision of an earlier comedy of Shakespeare's. Viola's words (I. ii. 54-7)

> I'll serve this duke,
> Thou shall present me as a eunuch to him:
> . . . For I can sing
> And speak to him in many sorts of music,

seem to show that a singing part in *Twelfth Night* was originally intended for the boy who played Viola, presumably the boy who as the mad Ophelia sang to the lute—see a stage direction in the first quarto of *Hamlet*. Later (II. iv) Orsino actually calls on his page Cesario, i.e. Viola, for a song, and a rather awkward interpolation in the present text shows how this call was answered by Feste. What has happened seems fairly clear; sometime after Armin's success as Touchstone Shakespeare discovered that his new comedian could sing as well as play the Clown. Accordingly he revised the play, enlarged the role of Feste, gave him the boy's song, 'Come away, death,' and wrote one or two new songs for him. It is impossible to think of Viola in a page's costume joining in the midnight revel where Feste sings 'O Mistress mine,' and Feste's mocking song, 'I am gone, Sir,' as he leaves Malvolio pent up in 'hideous darkness,' must have been written for the Clown. The boy Viola may have originally sung or spoken an Epilogue, as Rosalind does in *As You Like It,* but the song that now closes *Twelfth Night* was meant for the Clown; in fact, it may be in part Armin's own composition.

It is impossible to fix an exact date for the original form; the frequency of rhymed couplets in *Twelfth Night* compared with *Much Ado* and *As You Like It* suggests an earlier date than either of these plays. Presumably the revision was made not long after Armin joined Shakespeare's company, and it is at least likely that the high perfection of this comedy is due, as is the case with *Hamlet,* to a careful revision by the author.

No single source for *Twelfth Night* has yet been found, no play or story so directly the source as Bandello's tale is of *Much Ado* or Lodge's *Rosalynde* of *As You Like It*. The truth is that *Twelfth Night* is a mosaic of materials drawn from various sources and skilfully combined in a harmonious pattern. The theme of identical twins and the errors occasioned by their likeness goes back to Plautus, and behind him to the New Comedy of Greece. In classic comedy the twins are of a like sex, both male, like the brothers of the *Menaechmi*. In Italian comedy and fiction of the Renaissance, a further zest was added to this theme by making the twins brother and sister, and by garbing the girl, as occasion offered, in male dress and the boy in woman's costume. Perhaps the earliest of such comedies is *Gl' Ingannati (The Deceived)*, a play performed by a literary society at Siena in 1531 and printed in 1538. A fairly complete translation appears in the Variorum *Twelfth Night*.

> In this play a pair of twins, brother and sister, were separated at the sack of Rome. The girl dons a page's dress to follow the man she loves, who had once made love to her but has deserted her for a new mistress. As his page she acts as his ambassador of love to this lady, who promptly falls in love with her. Later the girl's brother is mistaken for the page and shut up in this lady's chamber, whereupon she at once surrenders herself to him. A final recognition scene clears things up; the girl's lover returns to her, and the lady is content to take the brother as her husband.

This lively comedy of intrigue begat a numerous progeny. Two later Italian plays, an *Inganni*, printed 1562, and another of the same name, 1592, retell the story with certain minor changes. It spread beyond Italy to Spain and France, where *Les Abusés* appeared in 1542. This French version in turn served as a source for the Latin play, *Laelia*, acted at Cambridge, probably in 1595. Italian novelists also fastened upon it. Bandello, 1554, retold it, and Cintio included it in his *Hecatommiti*—Belleforest translated Bandello, and finally an English author, drawing upon both of them and, apparently, upon Cintio also, produced quite a new version of the story. This is *Apolonius and Silla*, one of the eight tales in Barnaby Riche's *Farewell to the Military Profession*, 1581. This tale is also reprinted in the Variorum *Twelfth Night*, and is the direct source of Shakespeare's comedy.

> Silla, daughter of the Duke of Cyprus, fell in love with Duke Apolonius. He, however, ignored her passion and departed to Constantinople. Determined to follow him, Silla took passage on a ship for that city. The sole survivor of a storm

which wrecked the ship, she assumed male garb for protection, and made her way to Constantinople. Here, taking the name of her twin brother, Silvio, she entered the service of Apolonius and became his favorite page. Apolonius was courting Julina, a rich and noble widow, and Silla, as his page, served as his messenger to carry letters and gifts to her. Julina fell in love with the page and declared her passion, but, naturally, without success. In the meantime Silla's brother, Silvio, pursuing his runaway sister, arrived in Constantinople. Here Julina met him on the street and, mistaking him for Silla— brother and sister here, as in all versions, are identical twins— invited him to visit her. He spent a night with her, and departed, leaving her with child. Believing that the page was the father of her unborn child, Julina came to claim him from the Duke as her husband. She reproached the page for cowardice when he, i.e. Silla, denied all knowledge of the matter. Greatly angered, the Duke threatened to kill the page unless he would satisfy Julina's claim. Thereupon Silla revealed her sex and confessed how long she had loved and served the Duke. Apolonius was so touched by the devotion of Silla that he promptly married her. Silvio, the brother, returning to Constantinople, learned from Apolonius that Silla had been accused of seducing Julina. Thereupon he confessed his guilt, and was married by Apolonius to Julina.

Riche's tales were, no doubt, known to Shakespeare, and the poet's attention may have been called, or recalled, to *Apolonius and Silla* by hearing of the performance of *Laelia* at Cambridge. In this tale Shakespeare found material fit to be fashioned into a romantic comedy: a girl shipwrecked in a strange land, assuming male dress for protection, serving as a page to the man she loves, and acting as his messenger to a lady who falls in love with her. In addition there is the appearance on the scene of the twin brother who is mistaken for the page by the lady, resulting in an immediate union of these two; the claiming of the page as her husband by the lady; the first anger of the heroine's master, the confrontation of the twins, a new feature in Riche, and the Duke's shift of affection to her from the lady, along with the final marriage of the lady and the brother.

Shakespeare took in hand the rude, unpolished narrative of Riche, and reshaped it into a delicate and charming comedy. Let us see how his alterations transform the tone of the action. His heroine does not run after the man she loves; shipwrecked in a strange land, Viola's first thought is to seek the protection of the Lady Olivia; only when that is declared impossible does she don disguise to enter the service of Orsino. There is no sign that she had seen, much less loved, him before her voyage; 'I have heard my father name him' is all she says. In the same way Shakespeare has elevated the character of the other lady of the tale. In Riche she is a widow, courted by many noble men. It seems less likely that such a lady should fall in love with the page than that the virgin Olivia, shut up in a fantastic mourning, should at once succumb; and it is impossible to think of the 'virtuous maid,' Olivia, surrendering herself to the brother on some vague promise of marriage. In the play Olivia first sees the brother when he is apparently in danger of his life at the hands of Sir Toby. It is her fright, as well as her love, that prompts her to urge an immediate betrothal in the presence of a priest. In this connection, too, the character of the brother has been changed for the better. Riche's Silvio thinks he would be a fool to neglect the *bonne fortune* offered him, and departs after his night with Julina 'for fear of further evils.' Shakespeare could not allow Viola's brother to behave so basely, nor as a playwright could he defer his return till after his sister's marriage; dramatic convention and the need for a strong final scene compel Sebastian's reappearance at the very moment his betrothed is claiming Cesario as her husband. Finally Shakespeare's Duke is quite another man than Riche's, somewhat of a sentimentalist rather than a warrior. Apolonius, on the mere report that Julina loves his page, threatens Silla with instant death. Shakespeare, it seems, picked up this motif and used it in Orsino's vague threat of 'mischief,' but Orsino's last word to his page before the final recognition is to bid him take Olivia and depart. It is, probably, this difference in tone, and especially in characterization, that has led some scholars to decry the importance of Riche's tale as a source of *Twelfth Night*. But the data of the play are combined in Riche as in no other version, and the ethical and esthetic improvements are eminently characteristic of Shakespeare's handling of a source.

What has been said so far about sources applies, of course, only to the main plot, the poetic romantic strain of the play. To offset this, Shakespeare weaves into the action a comic realistic underplot, revolving about the trick played on Malvolio. The main plot, to speak frankly, needed some such balance; its charming sentiment verges rather closely upon sentimentality. If Shakespeare's audience was to take it as a picture of real life it needed a recognizable background. And that Shakespeare cleverly provided, for the household of Olivia, which serves this purpose, would be recognized by Elizabethans as a noble English country house in the hands of a young unmarried heiress. It seems to be a picture of one of the great estates which in Shakespeare's day were passing over from medieval to modern conditions. Its doors were thrown open to a generous hospitality that at times passed into revelry exceeding the bounds of decorum, bounds vainly attempted to be enforced by a somewhat puritanical major-domo. The heiress is sought in marriage by suitors ranging in the social scale from a noble duke and a foolish knight to her presumptuous steward. Around her gather as members of the household such figures of the minor gentry as Fabian, a gentleman of sporting tastes —notice his fondness for bear-baiting—and Maria, not a serving-maid, but a girl of good family sent to be trained, and probably married off, in a better environment than was hers at home. Sir Toby is a blood relation, perhaps a younger brother of one of Olivia's parents; he may have seen service, but in these piping days of peace he has retired to a country house where there is an unlimited supply of sack and pickled herring. Below these in rank are the hired retainers, the steward, a priest, probably the domestic chaplain, and the jester, along with various unnamed attendants. No source need be sought for this background; it is Shakespeare's invention, a dramatic device similar to his introduction of the 'mechanicals' into the enchanted world of *A Midsummer Night's Dream,* still nearer, perhaps, in its effect upon the main action, to the solution of the romantic plot of *Much Ado* by such contemporary and realistic English figures as Dogberry and Verges.

A minor thread is woven into the pattern of *Twelfth Night* in the character of Sebastian. As the heroine's twin brother he is, of course, a constant in the tale, but Shakespeare makes something more of him than do the earlier versions, which concentrate upon the heroine. We first hear of Sebastian escaping from the wreck by his strength as a swimmer, then of his rescue from the sea by Antonio, an old sea-captain, a true Elizabethan sea-dog, a trader and fighter. On Sebastian Antonio lavishes a love 'without retention or restraint'; he risks his own life to follow him into an enemy's country, and puts his purse into his young friend's hands to defray his casual expenses. The charge of ingratitude that Antonio brings against him when he mistakes

Viola for her brother is an error, owing to this mistake, as is shown by Sebastian's outcry when they meet again:

Antonio! O my dear Antonio!
How have the hours rack'd and tortur'd me
Since I have lost thee!

Sebastian, in fact, repays his friend's devotion with something of the hero-worship youth owes an old soldier; it is Antonio's counsel that he longs for when he finds himself caught up in the affair with Olivia. There is a boyish innocence in his wonder at this unknown lady's passion for him, as there is a boyish burst of anger when assaulted by Sir Andrew, a purposed contrast to his sister's feminine shrinking from a fray. We may well believe Sebastian when he tells Olivia that she is betrothed to a man who is still a maid. These little touches, all original with Shakespeare, build up a character endowed with the amiable qualities of his sister, and so make him a fitter mate for Olivia than the featureless brother of the Italian versions or the reckless adventurer of Riche's tale.

In comparison with the carelessly dramatized narrative of *As You Like It,* the construction of *Twelfth Night* is a masterpiece of craftsmanship. The two plots, romantic and comic, are not adjusted, but interwoven; action in the one determines events in the other. The play opens with a scene that strikes the note of sentiment pervading the romantic action. After a brief exposition in which we meet the main characters of the two plots, the action begins with the dispatch of Viola as the Duke's page to Olivia. Viola has already fallen in love with her master, and when Olivia falls in love with her, she finds herself caught in the love chain familiar to readers of Elizabethan romance and already exploited by Shakespeare in *A Midsummer Night's Dream,* for now Viola loves the Duke who loves Olivia who, in turn, loves Viola. It is too hard a knot for the poor page to untie.

The plot is further complicated at the beginning of the second act by the introduction of Viola's brother, saved from the wreck and bound for Orsino's court. And now, lest we be sated with romance, Shakespeare gives us a scene of midnight revelry, one of the gayest he ever wrote. The resentment of the revelers at the interference of the steward starts the plot of comical revenge on that over-weening official, and before the act ends he is neatly entrapped.

Romance and comedy begin to blend more closely in the third act, when Sir Andrew, Olivia's foolish suitor, is persuaded to show his valor by an attack upon the page now marked as the recipient of the lady's favors. From the threatened duel that follows, Viola is saved by the appearance of Antonio, who mistakes her for Sebastian, and takes her quarrel on himself. Before he can strike a blow, however, he is arrested by the Duke's officers, but his appeal to Viola as Sebastian gives her the first gleam of hope that her lost brother may still survive. In the meantime the comic plot has culminated in the overthrow of Malvolio's aspirations and his confinement as a madman.

The short fourth act brings matters to a head. Sebastian, now mistaken for the page, is attacked by Sir Andrew and Sir Toby, but is delivered and led off by Olivia, who falls into the same error. Naturally readier to respond to her advances than his sister was, Sebastian consents to a secret betrothal, while in an intercalated scene Malvolio contrives to send a letter to his mistress to explain his apparent madness.

In one long scene extending over the last act Shakespeare assembles most of his characters for the denouement. Orsino, attended by his page, comes to make a final appeal to Olivia. The captive Antonio, led before him, denounces the page as an ingrate and Olivia claims him as her husband. The tension is at the highest when a sudden irruption of the comic characters, Sir Andrew and Sir Toby, brings about the solution. They have again attacked the supposed page, i.e. Sebastian, and have been roughly handled by him. When he appears to justify his behavior, the twins, brother and sister, are for the first time together on the stage, and a mutual recognition and *éclaircissement* follow. Olivia is content with the young husband she has won by mistake; and Orsino rewards the devotion of his page with the promise of his hand; the trick on Malvolio is dismissed as a bit of 'sportful malice'; and the Clown dismisses the company with a song.

The action in *Twelfth Night* is lively and varied enough to hold the attention even of a reluctant audience. In the main plot there is always the interest aroused by a well-knit intrigue, growing more complicated till the deft solution at the very end. It differs in this from *Much Ado*, in which, after the effective church scene, the interest begins to flag, since it has already been made clear that Hero will be saved. It is incomparably better in this respect than *As You Like It*, in which, strictly speaking, there is no intrigue at all. Long before that play was over, the end must have been evident to any intelligent auditor. There is, to be sure, little of broad comedy in the closing scenes of *Twelfth Night*. An exception might, perhaps, be made for the scene of the duel, in which Viola is reluctantly involved. Properly acted, however, this scene should not be allowed to sink into farce. Viola's reluctance is characteristic of her femininity, but she does actually draw her sword and prepare for combat rather than disclose the secret of her sex. She would not reveal it to the man she loves, still less to the bullies who have thrust a quarrel on her. Her rescue at the critical moment by Antonio is an ingenious stroke of Shakespeare's art; he found nothing like it in any of the versions he may have glanced at; in fact the whole scene is Shakespeare's invention. In the main what we have of comedy in the romantic action is the comedy of sentiment and situation: the disguised heroine acting as a messenger for her beloved to the lady he loves and her own involvement in the lady's sudden passion for her. This is the motif already employed in *The Two Gentlemen,* but it is far more fully and sensitively developed here.

It is a different matter with the underplot. Here there is plenty of comic action, from Sir Andrew's capers in his first scene to the midnight revel and the mockery of the imprisoned Malvolio. Yet anything like the old horseplay is avoided in this refined comedy. After a brief exchange of buffets the threatened fight between Sebastian and Sir Toby is stopped by Olivia's appearance and her rebuke of her ungracious uncle. A scene in which Sebastian breaks the heads of the two knights is reported, but carefully kept off-stage. The comedy of the underplot is mainly a matter of situation, as in the repeated instances of mistaken identity and in Malvolio's interpretation of the forged letter accompanied by the mocking comments of his unseen hearers. Sometimes it is simply a matter of words, as in Feste's catechism of his mistress and Malvolio's daydream before he finds the letter.

Such scenes as these are, of course, in prose—by this time Shakespeare's regular vehicle for comedy. In fact about two-thirds of *Twelfth Night* is in prose, a considerably larger proportion than in *As You Like It.* Yet though the verse of *Twelfth Night* falls below the prose in quantity, it surely surpasses it in quality. Apart from occasional phrases—'sick of self-love,' 'cakes and ale,' 'ginger hot in the mouth'—the comic dialogue, excellent as it is on the stage, escapes the memory. There are no such verbal fireworks as in *Much Ado,* no such cascades of gaiety as in *As You Like It.* What we remember best, perhaps, in *Twelfth Night* are bits of verse:

If music be the food of love, play on. . .

She never told her love,
But let concealment, like a worm i' the bud,
Feed on her damask cheek. . .

Let still the woman take
An elder than herself, so wears she to him,
So sways she level in her husband's heart.

In contrast with the lyrical flow of *A Midsummer Night's Dream* or the graceful eloquence of *The Merchant of Venice,* the poetry of *Twelfth Night* has an almost elegiac quality. Orsino's description of a song he calls for may serve to characterize it:

Mark it, Cesario; it is old and plain;

. . .

And dallies with the innocence of love,
Like the old age.

It is the innocence of love that Shakespeare plays with in this comedy, not the fickle fancy of the *Dream* nor the burning passion of *Romeo and Juliet.* This is especially marked in the character and action of Viola, and it is not too much, perhaps, to say that it is Viola who imparts to the air of *Twelfth Night* a fragrance all its own.

Something has already been said of Shakespeare's transformation of the characters in his sources. The change he wrought upon the heroine is one of his supreme triumphs in characterization. In the Italian plays and Bandello's story she is a clever, bold, and roguish little intriguer. In Riche she is a more romantic figure, but the Silla who pours out a flood of invective on Julina is a very different character from the Viola who pities Olivia. There is a strain of gentleness, of sweetness, even of humility, in Viola that distinguishes her from such lively characters as Beatrice and Rosalind. She does not pretend to be master of her fate; she would die a thousand deaths to give her master peace of mind; she is frank to confess that she 'had rather go with sir priest than sir knight'; altogether she is the most modest, the most wistful, perhaps the most lovable of Shakespeare's ladies.

The other principals in *Twelfth Night* are no less distinctly characterized. It is not too much to say that this play surpasses its immediate predecessor in number and variety of sharply drawn characters as it does in well-knit construction. Sir Toby and Sir Andrew come down from the plays that revolve about the comic sun of Falstaff. Sir Toby is, in fact, a minor Falstaff, less witty, more drunken, and prompter to exchange words for blows. The Falstaff type has been deliberately toned down; in Olivia's household the fat Knight would have been too much the dominant; he would have destroyed the delicate balance in this play between romance and realism. Sir Andrew, too, comes from the Falstaff circle, a blood relation of Slender in *The Merry Wives*. Like Slender he is a born simpleton, but while Shakespeare has toned down Falstaff, he apparently keyed up Slender, for Sir Andrew is the most complete and perfect fool in all the works of Shakespeare, aware apparently of his lack of brains—'many do call me fool,' he says—yet placidly content to remain a butt and laughing-stock. Lamb, in his delightful essay on old actors, draws a memorable picture of Dodd as Sir Andrew, with his 'vacant face of folly,' where 'a glimmer of understanding would appear in a corner of his eye and for lack of fuel go out again.'

Feste, too, is reminiscent of an earlier character, that of Touchstone. There is, of course, a difference. Touchstone, like the other exiles, is free and happy in Arden; Feste is still bound by the chains of professional duty; it is his business to divert the anger of his mistress by a jest, to gratify Orsino's caprice by a song, and to entertain a drunken company by talk of Pigrogromitus and of 'the Vapians passing the equinoctial of Queubus.' He can hardly have been happy in Olivia's house of professed mourning; he seems to have been left there by her father, who, we hear, 'took much delight in him.' He chafes under the contempt of her steward and takes frequent opportunity to escape to the gayer circle of Orsino's court, where, among other things, he is sure of a more liberal reward than the sixpences doled out to him by Sir Toby and Sir Andrew. For Feste differs from Touchstone in this as in other aspects by being an unabashed beggar. He knows himself superior in mind to his surroundings and is quite determined to make them pay for the entertainment he furnishes. Bradley's charming, but perhaps too subjective, study of this character in *The Book of Homage* imaginatively identifies Feste with Shakespeare himself, servant and jester of the London public, willing to play the fool for them, but always with a hand outstretched for their cash till he has gathered enough to let him say, 'Our play is done,' and retire to live like a gentleman at Stratford.

The character of Malvolio is probably the most discussed and the least understood of any in *Twelfth Night*. From tender-hearted

Lamb, who confessed that he never saw Bensley in the part 'without a kind of tragic interest,' down to Maurice Hewlett (Luce's *Twelfth Night,* p. xi), there has been a tendency to take the character too seriously and to represent his downfall as one of the shadows that Shakespeare was wont to throw across the sunshine of his comedy. This, no doubt, is a symptom of the modern humanitarian spirit which objects to pain and punishment, even when inflicted on a deserving object; but it is neither Elizabethan nor, in the absolute sense, correct and true. Malvolio was described by a contemporary spectator of the play as a 'gull,' a term defined by an Elizabethan satirist as meaning one 'who seems and is not wise.' Malvolio's first passage at arms with Feste reveals him as one who, at least to himself, seems wise, and Olivia's comment on his behavior, 'You are sick of self-love, Malvolio,' is Shakespeare's way of telling us how to regard him. He is, in fact, a 'humor' character like Jaques, but Malvolio's humor is a swollen self-conceit, a presumption that beguiles him into believing himself a possible match for his mistress, and it is precisely this presumption that renders him an easy prey to his tormentors. There is, too, a touch of the puritan spirit in his dislike of fun, whether it take the form of bear-baiting or a party of cakes and ale and song. Yet Malvolio is neither a puritan nor Shakespeare's caricature of one. Shakespeare disdained the cheap laugh his contemporaries won by their ridicule of puritans as much as he scorned applause provoked by attacks on the Roman Church. That Shakespeare disliked Malvolio there can be no doubt; he usually loves his comic characters; but Malvolio is presented with a dash of satiric comment, and the satire is directed against an upstart who fancies himself better than his fellows and equal to his betters. This was smartly brought out in Miss Webster's production of *Twelfth Night,* where Maurice Evans, her Malvolio, spoke with a slight cockney accent designed to mark him, to a New York audience at least, as the sort of superior and self-complacent butler that might be found in the establishment of a rich American lady.

In Elizabethan England the twelfth night after Christmas, 6 January, marked the end of the holidays. It was a night of revels on which often a play was commanded for performance at Court, and it has been suggested that our comedy received its name because of a first performance on that date. Be that as it may, the name of our play has, it would seem, a certain symbolic significance. It is a festival play, in action, dialogue, and character. The very name of a principal actor, Feste, connects it with the Latin *festus* and the English *feast*. And it is a fit play to mark the close of Shakespeare's festive season of romantic comedies. Gay, musical, and poetic, with a gentle undertone of sadness, it sums up all his early work in a field where he stands supreme among the playwrights of the world. Standing here we may in turn look back to the happy past, and forward to the period of tragedy and satiric comedy, and to the tragi-comedies of his sunset years.

7

The Early Tragedies

IT SEEMS probable that comedy was Shakespeare's first love. We have seen him begin his career as a playwright in that field and have traced his progress from *The Comedy of Errors,* adapted from Plautus, to *Twelfth Night,* in which, working with perfect freedom, he achieved a masterpiece of romantic comedy. It would be possible to continue along chronological lines and discuss the so-called bitter comedies that follow, the comic matter in the great tragedies, and the final romantic tragi-comedies. Yet to do so would be to neglect the comic element in earlier plays, in his first tragedies, and in the great cycle of his histories. Such neglect would be the less pardonable since there emerges in this cycle Shakespeare's supreme character in the field of comedy, the immortal Falstaff. Forgetting the chronology, then, we may turn back here to consider these plays, to notice Shakespeare's temporary submission to the dominance of Marlowe, and to mark his triumph as he swings back joyously into the native tradition of mingled sad and mirthful matter.

Few plays by Shakespeare have caused so long and bitter a controversy as *Titus Andronicus.* Ravenscroft, a Restoration dramatist, apparently started the fight by remarking in an address to the reader prefixed to his adaptation of the play, 1687: 'I have been told by some anciently conversant with the stage that it was not originally his [Shakespeare's] but brought by a private author to be acted, and he only gave some master-touches to one or two of the principal parts or characters; this I am apt to believe.' The wrangle over Shakespeare's authorship has lasted ever since. That it is not yet settled may appear from the fact that a poet and critic like T. S. Eliot calls it 'a play in which it is incredible that Shakespeare had any hand at all,' while Tillyard, a specialist in Elizabethan literature, pronounces it 'precisely the kind of writing that common sense would expect from the young Shakespeare.' Between these extremes some conservative scholars incline to consider it a revision, more or less thoroughly carried out by Shakespeare, of an old tragedy of blood of the school of Kyd and Marlowe. Into the details of this controversy there is, fortunately, no need for us to enter; it should suffice to state what is definitely known about *Titus*, and then to examine it with the purpose of discovering what evidence, if any, of Shakespeare's native genius for comedy shines through the murky clouds of this repulsive play.

On 24 January 1594, Henslowe entered in his *Diary* the receipts of a performance of *titus and ondronicus* by the Sussex Company at the Rose. Henslowe marked the play 'ne,' his symbol for a new play, or at least for a thorough revision. This performance took place during a brief winter season—December to February—when the theaters, closed because of the plague, were allowed to reopen as the number of deaths in London dropped to what seemed the safety mark. A fresh outbreak in February, however, closed them again, and Henslowe, despairing apparently of further profits from the stage production of this popular play, sold the copy to a London printer, John Danter. Danter entered it in the Stationers' Register on 6 February 1594, and published it in the same year.

The title-page of this edition announces it as '*The most Lamentable Romaine Tragedie of Titus Andronicus:* As it was Plaide by the Right Honorable the Earle of Darbie, Earle of Pembrooke and Earle of Sussex their Servants.' The title-page of an Elizabethan book, it seems, served like the modern dust jacket to catch the eye and promote the sale of the volume. The fact that three different companies had performed this lamentable tragedy must have been a good selling point, for of all the copies printed a single specimen now remains, one of the treasures of the Folger Library. The omission of Shakespeare's name from the title-page need not trouble us; it was not until 1598 that his fame as the author of the best-selling poem, *Venus and Adonis*, and of the great stage success, *Richard III*, gave his name a sale's value.

Something of the early history of the play may be inferred from this title-page. It seems originally to have belonged to Pembroke's Company, presumably sold by them on their break-up in 1593 to Alleyn, who played it during his tour with Derby's, i.e. Strange's,[1] Company in 1593-4. Another copy went to Alleyn's partner, Henslowe, who, it seems, arranged for a revision, presumably by the young poet, William Shakespeare, and for a performance by the Sussex Company.

[1] Lord Strange, the patron of Shakespeare's company, became the Earl of Derby on the death of his father, 25 September 1593, and the company took his new title. Shakespeare was not with the company on this tour.

Late in the spring of 1594 the theaters were again allowed to open, and the enterprising Henslowe arranged for a joint occupation by two leading companies, the Admiral's and Derby's, now under the patronage of the Lord Chamberlain, at the suburban theater of Newington Butts. Here on 5 June he recorded a performance of *Andronicus*, no doubt the same play as his *titus and ondronicus* of February. This performance netted him the small sum of twelve shillings, but this does not mean that the play had lost its drawing power. The Newington theater was small and not easily accessible; Henslowe's receipts there fell far below his average takings at the Rose. Shakespeare's company, at any rate, thought *Titus* good enough to take with them when they left Henslowe and began to play at the Theatre, and from this time on the play belonged to Shakespeare's company. In 1598 Meres included it in his list of Shakespeare's plays; he must have learned this from someone who knew the facts, for he did not find it on the title-page of the printed copy. In 1600 Roberts, the regular printer for Shakespeare's company, printed a second edition, as played by the Chamberlain's Company, with a few slight changes in the first and last scenes. This quarto was reprinted in 1611 'as it hath sundry times beene plaide by the Kings Maiesties Servants,' showing that it was still in their repertoire. It seems strange that Shakespeare's name does not appear on the title-page of either of these editions; Roberts, at least, must have known that Shakespeare wrote it. Perhaps Shakespeare himself, the author in 1600 of *Julius Caesar* and of *Hamlet,* was a little ashamed of this old tragedy of blood. His fellows were not, for after his death they included it in the Folio among his tragedies with a new scene, III. ii, probably added for some revival, which bears unmistakable signs of Shakespeare's hand.

In the face of these facts, particularly the testimony of Meres and of the editors of the Folio, it is simply impossible to deny Shakespeare's connection with *Titus*. On the other hand, that he wrote it in the sense that he wrote *Othello* is at least doubtful. It is hard to believe that the poet of *Venus and Adonis* was guilty of the long expanses of ranting, uninspired verse that stretch through scene after scene of this play.

Whoever devised the action of *Titus,* whether Shakespeare or an unknown playwright, planned it to capitalize on the stage success of two famous tragedies of the day, *The Spanish Tragedy* of Kyd and Marlowe's *Jew of Malta.* It has the well-planned revenge intrigue of the one and the villain hero of the other. Some legendary account of the wars of Andronicus, a Byzantine emperor, seems to have been transferred with true Elizabethan contempt of historic accuracy to the time of pagan Rome, and the Greek Emperor becomes a Roman soldier, Titus Andronicus, victorious over the Goths. Among the captives he brings back are Tamora, a Gothic queen, her three sons, and her lover, Aaron the Moor. The action opens with the human sacrifice of one of Tamora's sons to appease the shades of the sons of Titus slain in the war. The Roman Emperor weds Tamora, and she and Aaron plot a revenge on Titus that involves the rape and mutilation [2] of his daughter, Lavinia, the execution of two of his sons, the banishment of the sole survivor, and the madness of Titus. The insanity of Titus, like that of Hieronimo in Kyd's play, is dominated by the thought of revenge. This he achieves by trapping and killing Tamora's sons and baking their bodies in a pie, which he sets before their mother at a feast of feigned reconciliation. At this feast Titus kills first his daughter and then Tamora; the Emperor kills him and is in turn killed by the surviving son of Titus, who then becomes Emperor of Rome. A spectator at the Rose must have gone home feeling that he had supped full with horrors. Yet as late as 1614 Ben Jonson remarked that old-fashioned playgoers would swear that *Hieronimo* and *Andronicus* were 'the best plays yet.'

After all, however, Shakespeare, a true Elizabethan, was made of sterner stuff than a modern humanitarian; he had, in fact, just been at work on a poem which recounted in great detail the rape and suicide of Lucretia. We seem to find him lightening the ugly matter of the plot with poetic and sentimental touches. Lavinia's hands, brutally lopped off by Tamora's sons, become

> . . . those sweet ornaments,
> Whose circling shadows kings have sought to sleep in.

Where her tongue has been torn out

> . . . a crimson river of warm blood,
> Like to a bubbling fountain stirr'd with wind,
> Doth rise and fall between thy rosed lips.

Her uncle says he found her

[2] The rape and mutilation come from Ovid's tale of Philomela and Progne; the feeding of a parent with children's flesh from Seneca's *Thyestes*.

. . . straying in the park,
Seeking to hide herself, as doth the deer,
That hath receiv'd some unrecuring wound,

and her father answers with a characteristic play on words,

It was my dear, and he that wounded her
Hath hurt me more than had he kill'd me dead.

Here and there we find Shakespearean sentiments:

Wilt thou draw near the nature of the gods?
Draw near them then in being merciful;
Sweet mercy is nobility's true badge,

and striking Shakespearean imagery:

The eagle suffers little birds to sing,
And is not careful what they mean thereby,
Knowing that with the shadow of his wings
He can at pleasure stint their melody.

At times, if rarely, we come upon anticipations of later more perfect passages; Titus says to Lavinia:

I'll to thy closet; and go read with thee
Sad stories chanced in the times of old.

Compare with this the cry of Richard to his friend:

For God's sake let us sit upon the ground
And tell sad stories of the death of kings!

The gloomy texture of the old play is interwoven with gleams of poetry that surely come direct from Shakespeare.

Poetry there is in *Titus,* but what of comedy? Certainly we must not expect to find much in a tragedy of blood of the school of Kyd and Marlowe. Neither of these dramatists was dowered with any considerable share of the comic spirit, yet for success on the public stage a certain amount of comedy was demanded by established convention. We know, for example, that early performances of Marlowe's *Tamburlaine* included 'some fond and frivolous gestures—greatly gaped at, what times they were showed upon the stage,' which were judiciously omitted by the printer of the play. The great success of *Dr. Faustus* was due, probably, as much to the horseplay of the clowns and the fireworks of the devils as to its lofty poetry and tragic theme. There is less of this in Kyd, but the madness of Hieronimo had, no doubt, certain comic aspects; the Elizabethans as a rule regarded insanity as a matter for laughter. And there is a strain of grim humor in some of Kyd's scenes, notably in the hanging of Pedringano. Something of this sort of comedy should, accordingly, appear in our play.

The madness of Titus, for example, which culminates in the arrow-shooting scene, iv. iii, is patterned on that of Hieronimo; both of them rant of a descent into hell to find the justice that has fled from earth. The same scene includes the stock Elizabethan jest on horns and the cuckold husband. Only the most hardened believer in Shakespeare's authorship of the whole play is likely to ascribe this wretched stuff to him, but there are, it would seem, traces of his hand elsewhere. The villain hero, Aaron the Moor, is a direct descendant of Marlowe's wicked Jew; the speech in which he recounts the evils he has done, v. i. 124-44, is only too reminiscent of the brag of Barabas— *Jew of Malta*, ii. iii. 175-99. Alleyn, we know, created the role of Barabas, and this speech was probably written to give him a like chance to rant as Aaron. One would be sorry to think that Shakespeare wrote these lines, but he may have done so under strong compulsion, and no doubt Shakespeare could write imitation Marlowe better than any other man then alive. There is, however, one scene where we seem to find Shakespeare in his prenticeship showing a trace of that power to distinguish 'some soul of goodness in things evil' which marks his master years. This is the scene, iv. ii, where Aaron rescues the bastard babe that Tamora has borne him from her sons who would murder it. He snatches the child from the nurse's arms and defies them to touch it. It is interesting to observe the sudden change of style in the speech that follows; it begins with Marlovian rant:

> I tell you, younglings, not Enceladus,
> With all his threatening band of Typhon's brood,
> Nor great Alcides, nor the god of war,
> Shall seize this prey out of his father's hands.

Then suddenly the voice of Shakespeare rings clear, as Aaron gloats over the color that betrays the paternity of the child:

> Coal-black is better than another hue,
> In that it scorns to bear another hue;

For all the water in the ocean
Can never turn the swan's black legs to white,
Although she lave them hourly in the flood.

Look, he cries:

Look how the black slave smiles upon the father,
As who should say, 'Old lad, I am thine own.'

Here is a father's pride in his first-born son mingled with a grim
humor that Shakespeare may have caught from Kyd, but which betters
anything that playwright ever wrote. It humanizes the character as
nothing else in the play does. Shakespeare may have had a sneaking
kindness for this villain into whose human heart he looked for a
moment; at least he saved him from the death by fire which, if we
may trust a Dutch adaptation of *Titus*, was his in the original form,
like the fate of Barabas in the fiery cauldron.

If, to quote Ravenscroft, Shakespeare 'only gave some master
touches' to Aaron, there is another character in *Titus*, a very minor
one, to be sure, whom we may well believe he created out of whole
cloth. This is the unlucky Clown who enters to Titus in the arrow-
shooting scene 'with a basket and two pigeons in it,' like Old Gobbo
in *The Merchant of Venice* with his basket and dish of doves. He is
the first of Shakespeare's rustics to win a laugh from the audience by
his malapropisms and blunders. But he is something more than a
blunderer in speech; he is one of the simple souls whom Shakespeare
loves, and loves to contrast with the heroic figures of his tragedies,
like the Clown who brings the asp to Cleopatra and wishes her 'joy
o' th' worm.' The mad Titus asks if he came from heaven and the
Clown replies: 'God forbid I should be so bold as to press to heaven
in my young days.' Here is a creature of real flesh and blood, an unmistakable English peasant. His brief scene follows hard upon the
rant of Titus; it is as if Shakespeare wanted to let a breath of fresh
English air blow in on the heated atmosphere of this tragedy. One is
rather sorry for the Clown when in the next scene he is condemned
to the gallows, but he accepts his fate with a peasant's stoicism:
'Hanged? By'r Lady, then I have brought up a neck to a fair end.'

This is all, and little enough, of comedy in action, speech, and character that can be gleaned from *Titus*, but it is enough to show that
even in this repellent Senecan play, young Shakespeare was true to
the English tradition of mixing tragedy with 'pleasant mirth.'

ROMEO AND JULIET

If Shakespeare wrote or revised *Titus Andronicus*, in 1594, there is a fairly close connection in time between that play and the only other tragedy of his apprentice years, *Romeo and Juliet*, which a consensus of opinion dates about 1595. This temporal connection, however, is the only link between the two plays; in all else they are as unlike as two tragedies by the same author could well be. In *Titus* Shakespeare followed a definitely prescribed pattern, that of the Senecan tragedy of revenge; in *Romeo and Juliet* the young playwright, now a full member of a first-rate company of actors, felt himself free to write for them a drama in which his own ideas of construction, his conception of characters, and power of dramatic expression could have full play. *Romeo and Juliet* is, in one sense of the word, a truly original play. It is, perhaps, not generally recognized that here for the first time an English playwright dared to ignore the medieval taboo on the theme of love in tragedy, as Lyly, a little earlier, had evaded it in comedy.

This claim for originality does not mean, of course, that Shakespeare invented the story of the star-crossed lovers. That was not his customary method; he usually fastened upon some more or less familiar story and recast it in dramatic form. In the case of *Romeo and Juliet* we know his source and can watch, and wonder at, the art with which he transformed it into a play that for centuries has won the applause of spectators and touched the hearts of all readers who love poetry and thrill to passion. This source was Arthur Brooke's somewhat prolix narrative poem, *Romeus and Juliet*, 1562. Brooke was a talented young author, soldier and poet like so many Elizabethans, whose career was cut short by shipwreck, 1563.

The story of *Romeo and Juliet*, however, was no more original with Brooke than with Shakespeare. An Italian legend that seems to have blended incidents and characters of several well-known medieval tales took definite shape in Da Porto's *History of two noble Lovers*, printed at Venice in 1535. Here for the first time the scene is laid in Verona and the lovers take the names they have borne ever since. Da Porto's *History* attained, if not immediate, at least widespread success. Bandello included it in his *Novelle*, 1554, and Boaistuau translated it into French with some important changes in the first volume of his *Histoires tragiques*, 1559. Long before Shakespeare, poets and playwrights took up the tale. An Italian poem by 'Clitia,' probably an assumed name, appeared in 1553, and an Italian play, *La Hadriana,* in 1578. Two Spanish playwrights, Lope de Vega and De Rogas, dramatized it, and there is record of the performance of a French play of *Romeo and Juliet* in 1581.

Brooke, we know, based his poem upon the Boaistuau version, in which, as in Shakespeare, Juliet awakes from her drugged sleep after Romeo's death. In the Italian tales, as later in Garrick's stage version and in Gounod's opera, she rouses in time to hear of the poison he has drunk and to join in his lament. In Boaistuau and Brooke she kills herself with Romeo's dagger, whereas in the Italian tales she dies of a broken heart. A passage in Brooke's address to the reader stating that he 'saw the same argument [i.e. plot] lately set forth on stage' has sent scholars in a vain search for an English play on the story antedating Brooke's poem and even Shakespeare's birth. No trace of such a play has ever been found and if it were discovered, it would be hard to explain how Shakespeare could have known it or what use he could have made of a play so crude as one written before 1562 must have been.[1] Brooke's poem seems to have been Shakespeare's sole source; a later prose translation of Boaistuau in Painter's *Palace of Pleasure,* 1567, a book which Shakespeare knew and occasionally used, may have called his attention to Brooke's poem, but there is nothing in the play to show that Shakespeare turned from Brooke to borrow from Painter.

Much has been written to demonstrate the superiority of Shakespeare's play to Brooke's poem. This seems needless, for any comparison between the work of a young poet at a time when the English Muse had just begun to lisp in numbers and a play by Shakespeare, now approaching the full mastery of his powers, is, of course, absurd. 'Little Brooke,' as a contemporary called him in relating the circumstances of his death, must be given full credit for his development of the action along lines that Shakespeare followed rather closely. Shakespeare, to be sure, speeded up the action from some months, as it was in the poem, to the brief space of five crowded days. He introduced new incidents: the wrath of Tybalt at Romeo's presence in the house of Capulet with its fatal consequences, and the duel with Paris before Romeo's entrance into the tomb. He developed the character of Mercutio, 'courteous of his speech and pleasant of device' in

[1] It is perhaps possible that what Brooke, who knew French well, saw was the French play at some earlier performance than that recorded in 1581. Its author, Chasteauvieux, is known to have presented plays before Charles IX, 1560-74.

Brooke, and he practically created the character of the Nurse. His supreme achievement, however, was his transformation of Brooke's somewhat shamefaced attitude toward the story, a blend of sympathy and disapproval, into a dramatic lyric hymn in praise of young and passionate love. Shakespeare's choice of this romantic tale was made in a happy hour, for it was just at this time that he began to flood his plays with the music of his poems. *Romeo and Juliet, A Midsummer Night's Dream,* and *Richard II,* three plays of quite different genres, all belong to this period of 1595-6 and all are marked by the abundant presence of the lyric note.

What concerns us most, however, is not the poetry of *Romeo and Juliet,* but rather the evidence in this play of Shakespeare's genius for comedy. It is interesting in this connection that Shakespeare alone of the Italian and English writers who had told and retold the story before him saw in it certain comic possibilities. We have seen glimpses of his instinct for comedy even in such a bloody play as *Titus Andronicus.* Here, where Shakespeare is working more freely, we may expect to find more and clearer evidence, and it may be worth while to examine *Romeo and Juliet* to see what in the action itself would have been likely to provoke the laughter of Shakespeare's audience.

There can be little doubt that the very opening scene of the play would have amused the Elizabethans. The wisecracks of Gregory at the expense of his butt, Sampson, have lost their salt today, but a pun was still a source of mirth in Shakespeare's time, as, to judge from the pages of *Punch,* it is today to many English readers. Gregory is a direct descendant of the old quibbling, mischief-making Vice. The street fight which follows has itself a certain comic quality. Shakespeare, who had no conception of the fury of an Italian vendetta like that which raged through Florence after the murder of Buondelmonte, presents the battle of the Montagues and Capulets after the fashion of a sword-and-buckler fray in the streets of London, much noise and little harm done. Capulet in his gown, calling for his old-fashioned long-sword, while his wife insists a crutch would be a fitter weapon, is a comic figure, and he is paired off against old Montague breathing insults while Lady Montague clings to his arm. It is all very well for the Prince to denounce their bloody hands; no one seems to have been hurt, and three or four Citizens armed with the clubs of London apprentices were enough, so the Folio stage direction tells us, to part the combatants.

Immediately before the first meeting of Romeo with Juliet there is a scene of lively activity in Capulet's house, servants bustling about, clamoring for aid, and arranging for the admission of their girl friends to the ball, just as ladies of higher rank were at times smuggled into Court masques. Old Capulet's noisy hospitality with his jesting references to corns on the toes of ladies who declined to dance is a purposed contrast to the shy, serious, and poetic exchange of greetings between the lovers which follows. Shakespeare is fond of such contrasts and makes, perhaps, more use of them in this play than in any other of his tragedies. There is another such contrast at the beginning of the second act, where Mercutio's bawdy conjuration rehearsing the charms of Rosaline, Romeo's supposed mistress, gains force from the fact that it is overheard by a Romeo, deeply and honorably in love with another lady; it serves, too, as a prelude to the beauty and purity of the balcony scene. There is comedy in action a little later when the Nurse sails onto the stage, attended by Peter and calling for her fan while she tries to get Juliet's message across in the face of a fire of bold jests by that 'saucy merchant,' Mercutio, 'so full of his ropery.' After the deaths of Mercutio and Tybalt, such comic contrasts are less frequent as the tragedy thickens. There is, however, a counterpart to the scene at Capulet's ball in the preparations for the wedding just before the discovery of Juliet's apparently lifeless body. The action here rises to a climax in the nurse's attempt to wake her mistress, beginning, as it does, with pet names and sly jokes and ending with a shriek for aqua-vitae. It is, perhaps, an open question whether the scene of choral lamentation which follows— heavily cut in modern performances—was meant to have a comic slant, but the deliberate parody of a lament in the old-fashioned *Spanish Tragedy:*

> O eyes! no eyes, but fountains fraught with tears;
> O life! no life, but lively form of death

must have tickled the sophisticated in the audience, and the Nurse's howl,

> O woe! O woeful, woeful, woeful day!

breaking on the stylized chants of the others was certainly worth a laugh. There can be no question whatever in regard to the passage between Peter and the musicians which ends this scene. That is pure farce, written, no doubt, to give Kempe, who, as we know from a Folio

202 THE EARLY TRAGEDIES

stage direction, played Peter, a better chance than he had so far had to show his gifts as a Clown.

There are three characters who contribute especially to the strain of comedy in *Romeo and Juliet*. These are, of course, Mercutio, the Nurse, and Peter. Mercutio is one of the merry gentlemen who appear so often in Shakespeare's early comedies. He is, in fact, their best representative, chief figure in a 'college of wit-crackers.' Mercutio has none of this quality in Brooke's poem, where he appears for a moment at Capulet's ball only to drop out of the action thereafter. Shakespeare's Mercutio is a free-spoken and somewhat cynical realist. His famous Queen Mab speech is a tissue of realistic images: 'a tithe-pig's tail,' 'a parson's nose'; it lacks entirely the poetic magic with which Shakespeare clothed the fairy queen in the *Dream*. He is happiest when he is mocking sentiment in Romeo or affectation in the up-to-date duelist Tybalt. His language drops at times below the level of decency, yet always with a witty turn, and almost his last word is a pun; mortally wounded he exclaims: 'Ask for me to-morrow and you shall find me a grave man.' It is, no doubt, this incessant flow of witty and often caustic comment that led Dryden to remark that if Shakespeare had not killed Mercutio, Mercutio would have killed him. With all his merits Dryden was neither a humorist nor a great playwright; he failed to see that Shakespeare killed Mercutio at the very moment that his death was necessary to the action. Foully slain by Tybalt while championing Romeo's cause, his death steels the gentle nature of Romeo into a resolution for revenge, and so motivates the death of Tybalt, the banishment of Romeo, and all the consequent tragedy. One cannot imagine Mercutio surviving to crack his jests among the mourners in the final reconciliation scene. Unless the action were to have a happy ending, as in Lope de Vega's tragi-comedy and in Howard's Restoration version of Shakespeare's play, there was an imperative dramatic necessity that this brilliant comic character should drop out before the action began to slope downward to the catastrophe.

The character of the Nurse is drawn in sharp contrast to that of Mercutio. He is the conscious wit; she the unconscious humorist. And since Shakespeare was by nature more the humorist than the wit, we may well believe that he knew the Nurse better and was able to reveal her more fully in speech and action. She is, perhaps, his first complete and fully rounded character in the realm of comedy. Her only possible rival is Bully Bottom and it is a question whether even

Bottom measures quite up to the Nurse. Shakespeare loses no time in introducing the Nurse; he reveals her in all her glory on her first appearance. Lady Capulet is discussing a marriage for her daughter and the Nurse is called into council on this weighty matter, but before it can even be broached, she is off, on the excuse of fixing Juliet's exact age, into a long story of her foster-child's infancy with a triple repetition of her late husband's off-color joke on the baby's fall. It takes all the authority of mother and daughter combined to stop the flood of her garrulity. The comic quality of her speech does not depend on the conventional device of puns and malapropisms, but on the direct disclosure of a gross and sensual, but affectionate and essentially human nature. Her passing reference to her dead daughter— 'Susan is with God; she was too good for me'—is as characteristic as her final injunction to Juliet: 'Go, girl, seek happy nights.' She loves her foster-child, 'the prettiest babe that e'er I nursed,' but her love sees no other goal for the girl than marriage. In this scene she is enthusiastic over the proposed match with Paris; a little later she acts as Juliet's messenger to Romeo, and though honestly concerned lest this stranger lead her lady into a fool's paradise, she is easily reassured by Romeo's 'protest,' which she takes for 'a gentlemanlike offer.' She makes the arrangement for the marriage of the lovers and is the unseen witness to their bridal night, but she does not hesitate on the morning after to comfort Juliet in extreme distress by urging an immediate marriage with Paris, a better match after all than that with Romeo, and even if it were not, what's the use of an absent husband? In the words of Burns, though with a somewhat different sense, 'A man's a man for a' that,' and a man is what her nurseling needs. Juliet marks the end of their old, happy, and confidential relation with the curse,

Ancient damnation! O most wicked fiend,

but we have still to see the Nurse in the preparation for the wedding with Paris, checking her testy master, old Capulet, in a fashion that shows her established position in his household, and we hear her bearing her part in the choral lamentation. That, however, is the end of her. Shakespeare, it would seem, was too fond of her to dismiss her from the scene with Juliet's curse, but he was too good an artist to keep her on much longer and to bring her on in the final scene. There she would have been as out of place as Mercutio; her outcries, like his jests, would have marred the harmony with which this tragedy of young love closes.

Peter is a character of far less importance than either Mercutio or the Nurse, yet his role deserves consideration since it was played by the chief comedian of Shakespeare's company. It seems somewhat strange that so famous a clown as Kempe should have been content with so insignificant a part. Peter's one scene of any importance, that with the musicians, is often omitted in modern performances, where his appearance is limited to his accompanying the Nurse as a sort of booby foot-boy. Two explanations seem possible. We know for one thing that Kempe could put on a good show out of little material in the script. A play published some time before *Romeo and Juliet*, *A Knack to Know a Knave*, 1594, advertises on the title-page 'Kemp's applauded merriments of the men of Goteham.' When we turn to this play to discover the nature of these merriments, we are disappointed to find only a brief scene of a dialogue between three foolish villagers preparing to receive their king. The comedy, so far as the text goes, consists entirely of conventional malapropisms. If Kempe played one of these parts, he must have enlarged it by improvisation and one of the jigs for which he was famous. Or it may be that the whole scene, which has all the marks of an interpolation, was composed and directed by Kempe. We know that he was familiar with the clowns of the Italian *commedia dell' arte* and was quite capable of staging a show in their fashion. The question arises whether he amused early audiences of *Romeo and Juliet* by tricks of this kind. This seems more than doubtful in the scene where Peter first appears: any clownery on the stage at this time would ruin the effect of the important interview between Nurse and Romeo. In his one scene of any comic value, Kempe as Peter could no doubt add considerably to the text by coming in blubbering over the death of Juliet, and leaving with a jig-step and a snatch of song after quarreling and quibbling with the musicians. Another possibility, never yet suggested, is that Kempe may have played more roles than one in *Romeo and Juliet*. The play abounds in comic servants: Gregory of the first scene, for instance; the bearer of Capulet's letter with his parody of Lyly's style; the vociferous First Servant of i. v, and the Second Servant of iv. ii, who dares to jest with his master. None of these is on the stage along with Peter, so that it would be possible for Kempe to double in one or all of these roles. With the number of characters required in this play and the limited membership of Shakespeare's company, some such doubling seems necessary, and the repeated appearance of Kempe, making his well-known grimaces, in one role after another, would, of course, contribute largely to the amusement of the audience. We may be sure, at least, that in *Romeo and Juliet* Kempe played the comic servant, as he did in *The Two Gentlemen* and in *The Merchant,* and that in one way or another he added more to the comedy of the play than appears in the present text.

In a sense this is the upshot of what has here been written on *Romeo and Juliet.* The play is, of course, a tragedy, the tragedy of young love doomed to frustration in a hostile world. It is an emotional and poetic play; the modern spectator is apt to fasten upon the emotional crises; the reader to lay stress on the poetry; the comic strain, except for a scene or two with Mercutio and the Nurse, is likely to elude both spectator and reader. But *Romeo and Juliet* is an Elizabethan, not a modern tragedy, and Shakespeare, a true Elizabethan, accepts in this early play the Elizabethan convention and mingles laughter with tears. That, probably, was the way he saw life.

8

The Early Histories

THE ten plays that the editors of the Folio grouped together under the heading 'Histories' represent Shakespeare's contribution to that great body of Elizabethan literature in prose and verse, in narrative poetry and in drama, which testifies to his country's lively interest in the past history and the present glory of England. They belong to that genre of drama commonly known as chronicle plays. An early anticipation of this type has already been noted in Bale's *King John*, but its popularity coincides with the fierce outburst of patriotism in the years that immediately precede and follow the defeat of the Spanish Armada, 1588. The decade, 1590-1600, is packed with chronicle plays, and it is exactly into this decade that Shakespeare's contribution falls; one apparent exception, *King Henry VIII*, may be left out of account; it is not a true chronicle play, and it is only in part by Shakespeare.

The chronicle play was especially beloved by the theater-going public; few plays of this kind were ever shown at Court. We may expect therefore to find this genre following the native tradition and mingling mirth with serious matter. In fact in the earliest extant Elizabethan chronicle play, *The Famous Victories of Henry V*, on the stage before 1588, the comic matter, which served as a vehicle for the famous clown, Tarlton, quite overshadows the serious action. Early in this decade, however, Marlowe rendered an immense service to Elizabethan drama by transforming the clown-ridden chronicle into historic tragedy in his *Edward II*, 1591-2. Shakespeare, we know, cherished a deep and proper admiration for Marlowe—the 'dead shepherd' of *As You Like It*—his master in the art of writing blank verse, and Shakespeare's earliest histories show him working along Marlovian lines, not only in verse, but in the tragic pattern of the play. There is little of comedy to be found in Shakespeare's histories until he has definitely won free from Marlowe's influence.

It will be convenient, therefore, to divide Shakespeare's histories into two groups, without paying attention to their chronological order, that we may the better trace his early adherence to and his gradual emancipation from this influence, and mark with this emancipation his return to the native tradition and the reappearance in his work of the comic strain, running through and blending with the serious matter of the play.

KING HENRY VI PART I

We may begin with a play, The First Part of *King Henry VI,* which appeared for the first time in the Folio, but certainly dates back in its early form to the very beginning of Shakespeare's work for the theater. Fortunately we need not linger over this poor play. It is a thing of shreds and patches, and only a few of the patches can be recognized as sewn on by Shakespeare's hand. The central theme of the play is the English war in France after the death of the hero-king, Henry V. The leader of the English is the noble warrior Talbot, opposed in France by the witch, Joan of Arc, for so she was still regarded in England in Shakespeare's days, and betrayed at home by the strife of English factions. It was probably of this play that Nashe in his *Pierce Penniless,* 1592, wrote: 'How would it have joyed brave Talbot (the terror of the French) [1] to thinke that after he had lyen two hundred yeares in his tombe, hee should triumphe againe on the stage, and have his bones newe embalmed with the teares of ten thousand spectators.' It seems reasonable, moreover, to identify the play to which Nashe refers with a *Harey the VI,* produced by Strange's Company at the Rose, 3 March 1592. This was a most successful play, outrunning for a time even such a public favorite as *The Jew of Malta,* and from Nashe's remark it seems likely that its success was mainly owing to its presentation of the heroic death of Talbot in battle against overwhelming odds. Now there is a group of scenes in *King Henry VI Part I* that deal precisely with this situation. They stand out brilliantly against the dull fabric of the greater part of the play, and are marked by certain recognizable features of the style of Shakespeare's prentice years. One of these is his use of stichomathy as in a dialogue between Talbot and his son:

TALBOT:
Shall all thy mother's hopes lie in one tomb?

JOHN:
Ay, rather than I'll shame my mother's womb.

[1] Nashe's very phrase, 'the terror of the French,' appears in our play, I. iv. 42.

TALBOT:
Upon my blessing I command thee go.

JOHN:
To fight I will, but not to fly the foe.

(IV. V. 34-7)

Another is the abundance of rhymed couplets with their artful balance
of word and phrase:

JOHN:
Stay, go, do what you will, the like do I:
For live I will not if my father die.

TALBOT:
Then here I take my leave of thee, fair son,
Born to eclipse thy life this afternoon.

These scenes reveal that 'facetious grace in writing' which evoked the
praise of 'divers of worship,' and we may take it as fairly certain that
they came from Shakespeare's pen. They are probably his contribution to an old play revived in revised form in 1592, since Henslowe's
mark, 'ne' against it in his *Diary* may mean 'revised' as well as 'new.'

There are in addition two other scenes (II. iv and v), one of which is
certainly, the other most probably, the work of Shakespeare. The first
of these, the Temple Garden scene, with the plucking of the roses red
and white as party badges, has no bearing on the central theme of the
play, Talbot in France, but looks forward to the Civil Wars of Lancaster and York, that is to the Second and Third Parts of *King Henry
VI* which treat of these wars. The masterly blank verse of this scene
and, in particular, the brief but vivid characterization of an English
sporting gentleman in Warwick's speech,

Between two hawks, which flies the higher pitch;
Between two dogs, which hath the deeper mouth;
Between two blades, which bears the better temper;
Between two horses, which doth bear him best;
Between two girls, which hath the merriest eye;
I have perhaps, some shallow spirit of judgment,

are distinctly beyond the power of Shakespeare in 1592. The following scene, in which Mortimer bequeaths his claim on the crown to
Richard of York, is by no means so striking, but it too looks forward to
the later parts of the *Henry VI* trilogy. It is only in these scenes that

we find any reference to York's ambition; elsewhere he appears as the champion of England who at last conquers Joan. When Heminges and Condell sent their play-books to be printed in the Folio they naturally included this play, since they knew that their fellow, Shakespeare, had not only contributed scenes to its early form, but had later whipped it into shape as a sort of prologue to their popular two-part play on the Wars of the Roses, 'which oft our stage hath shown,' says the Chorus that closes *Henry V*.

Needless to say we look in vain for comedy in the scenes assigned to Shakespeare in *King Henry VI Part I*. The Talbot death scenes are poetic-pathetic; the York scenes are the work of a skilled playwright sewing a patch of new upon old material. What there is of comedy in the rest of the play is of the crudest sort. There is an early scene of riot (I. iii) where Gloucester's blue-coated serving-men 'beat out' Winchester's retainers in tawny coats, and the Lord Mayor of London enters to threaten the warring factions with the clubs of the city apprentices unless they promptly disperse. His pious ejaculation at the close of the scene:

> Good God! these nobles should such stomachs bear;
> I myself fight not once in forty year,

was, no doubt, good for a laugh. In fact, the scene was so effective that it was repeated at the beginning of the third act. Here a formal session of Parliament is disturbed by back-stage shouts of 'Down with the tawny coats!' and 'Stones! Stones!' and the Mayor enters again to complain to the King that the factions, debarred the use of arms, are knocking out each other's brains with 'pebble stones,' and, what is worse, are breaking the windows of London shops. After the Mayor the factions enter, 'with bloody pates,' and 'skirmish' in the very presence of the King until his Majesty's piteous entreaty persuades their masters to shake hands in a hollow peace. Thereupon the rioters disperse, some to the surgeon's to have their pates dressed, one cheerful soul to seek for 'physic' in the tavern. There is lively action of the same sort at Talbot's recapture of Orleans when the French 'leap o'er the walls in their shirts' and their leaders appear on the stage 'half ready and half unready,' i.e. half dressed. While they are completing their toilet an English soldier enters crying 'a Talbot! a Talbot!' and they fly, 'leaving their clothes behind,' which he picks up, and departs rejoicing in his loot.

If we turn from such slapstick action to look for comic matter in the dialogue we find nothing better than feeble puns: Rome, roam; dauphin, dolphin, dogfish; and pucelle, pussel (harlot). This last word-play (I. iv. 107) ties up with the charge repeated again and again that the Maid of Orleans was anything but a maid. When Orleans was retaken, for example, 'the Dauphin and his trull,' Joan, were seen running away, arm in arm,

> Like to a pair of loving turtle-doves
> That could not live asunder day or night.

The slander culminates in the shameful scene (v. iv) where Joan, condemned to the stake, attempts to save her life by pleading pregnancy and basely ascribes the paternity of her unborn child to one French lord after another. For her plea of pregnancy the author of this scene had, at least, the authority of Holinshed, who says that Joan, when condemned, 'Stuck not to confess herself a strumpet and (unmarried as she was) to be with child.' Joan's scornful renunciation of her old father, however, along with her shifting charges of paternity, is a deliberate and disgraceful invention of the playwright. One would be loath to ascribe this scene to Shakespeare; it is more in the manner of Peele, the slanderer of good Queen Eleanor.

There is no trace in any of the chronicle scenes of this play of Shakespeare's sparkling wit or of his gay humor, to say nothing of his poetry. After all, Shakespeare seems to have been a poet before he became a playwright and one might expect to find even in an early play some evidence of his poetic art. What we do find however, outside the scenes generally ascribed to him, is Marlovian rant alternating with verse of the most pedestrian description. In other early plays his humor and his wit shine through the action; in *Titus* he manages to introduce a typical English clown; in *Romeo and Juliet* the tragedy is enlivened by sprightly wit-combats. The final argument against Shakespeare's authorship of the whole of this incoherent and heterogeneous play is the complete absence of his genius for comedy. That one of the latest students of this play should extol it as 'an organic part of a vast design' is a startling proof of how far astray preconceived theory may mislead scholarship.

KING HENRY VI PARTS II AND III

Like *King Henry VI Part I,* the Second and Third Parts appeared in print for the first time in the Folio of 1623. But here the likeness ceases and a difference begins which has taxed the wits of scholars since the days of Malone in the late eighteenth century. There is no early form of Part I, but in 1594 a play was published with a long catchpenny title, abbreviated here to 'The First Part of the Contention betwixt the two famous Houses of Yorke and Lancaster . . . with the notable Rebellion of Jacke Cade.' The phrase, *The First Part,* promised a sequel, and it was not long delayed. In the next year it appeared with a long title abbreviated here to: 'The true Tragedie of Richard Duke of Yorke . . . with the whole contention betweene the two houses Lancaster and Yorke . . . acted by the . . . Earl of Pembrooke his servants.' The two plans were combined and published in 1619 as *The Whole Contention,* etc., to which title there was added the interesting information: 'Written by William Shakespeare, Gent.' This bit of information was no doubt supplied by the printer, Jaggard, who was planning to include them in a volume of plays, some by Shakespeare, some falsely ascribed to him. Jaggard, we know, was on good terms with Shakespeare's company; in fact it was to his shop that Heminges and Condell sent the company's play-books to be printed in the Folio. Presumably, therefore, it was from the company that Jaggard learned of Shakespeare's authorship of the early plays. Whether he was correct in his assertion or not is a point over which scholars have fought fiercely for a hundred years and more. The fact remains, however, that the two early plays, henceforth styled for brevity's sake *The Contention* and *The Tragedy,* bear a close and intimate relation to the Second and Third Parts of *King Henry VI.* The characters are the same in all four; the action runs along the same lines in practically the same sequence, and long passages in the early plays, particularly in *The Tragedy,* agree word for word with corresponding passages in the Folio plays.

A recent authority has stated three theories by which this relation may be explained.

I. *The Contention* and *The Tragedy* are early work by Shakespeare. This can hardly be right, for even in his earliest day Shakespeare cannot have written so careless, confused, and blundering a play as *The Contention. The Tragedy,* to be sure, is in a better state, but the two stand and fall together as parts of a whole; *The Tragedy* begins exactly where *The Contention* leaves off and would be unintelligible without its forerunner.

II. *The Contention* and *The Tragedy* are not by Shakespeare, but by another Elizabethan playwright, or by a group of playwrights. Nearly all the famous names of that time, especially Marlowe, Greene, and Peele, have been put forward, sometimes singly, sometimes in collaboration with each other, or in collaboration with Shakespeare. This theory, maintained with immense ingenuity in comparatively recent years, is beginning to lose supporters. Too many doctors disagree too violently over the facts of the case. One of the facts is the undeniable presence of Shakespeare's hand in both the early plays; yet it seems incredible that a young and unknown playwright, as Shakespeare was in the early 'nineties, should have been called in either to collaborate with, or revise the work of, such masters as Marlowe and the others.

III. *The Contention* and *The Tragedy* are merely abbreviated and garbled forms of an early two-part play by Shakespeare which appears in the Folio as the *Second and Third Parts of Henry VI*. This third theory seems now to be on the way to a fairly general acceptance, and an explanation of the abbreviated and garbled forms seems quite possible.

The title-page of *The Tragedy* states that it had been performed by Pembroke's Company; in that case *The Contention* also had belonged to them, for, as has been said, the two plays are inseparable. The suggestion is that certain actors of this company reconstructed from their memory of the two plays an acting version for a tour in the provinces in 1593 and that on their return, practically bankrupt, they sold this acting version to the publisher who brought them out in 1594 and 1595.[1]

Fortunately we are not bound here to discuss the pros and cons of this theory. It will serve at least as a working basis for an examination

---

[1] A careful study of *The Contention* and *The Tragedy* seems to fix the guilt, such as it was, of this memorial reconstruction upon two actors, one of whom played the part of Warwick, the other who doubled as Suffolk and the Cliffords, father and son. Their parts in the early plays are in remarkably close agreement with the true text of the Folio, whereas other actors, notably the boy who played Queen Margaret, often make a sorry mess of their lines.

of the Folio plays in order to discover what of Shakespeare's gift for comedy appears in them. We may dismiss the unmistakable echoes of other Elizabethan playwrights in the Folio as calm appropriations by the young Shakespeare of whatever seemed good to him in the current theater of his day.

A brief analysis of the two plays will serve to show how Shakespeare followed the technique of the contemporary chronicle play and, more especially how completely he submitted at this time to the dominating influence of Marlowe. We may begin with the Second Part of *King Henry VI*, always bearing in mind, however, that it is in reality the first part of a ten-act play *The Whole Contention of Lancaster and York.*

It opens with the reception of Margaret of France as Queen of England and the announcement of a treaty, ratified by her marriage to Henry, which ceded the counties of Anjou and Maine to the French. Treaty and marriage, denounced by Gloucester, Lord Protector of the young king, as a 'shameful league and fatal marriage,' turn out to be the efficient causes of the tragedy that follows. This is made clear in a speech by York which closes the scene. In a long self-revelatory soliloquy, much in the manner of Marlowe, he discloses the motives that urge him to press his claim to the throne, a claim that must, however, be deferred until the good Protector has fallen from power. This fall occurs in the third act when Gloucester, attacked by a group of nobles urged on by Margaret, is arrested and shortly after murdered. The fourth act is almost entirely devoted to Jack Cade's rebellion, incited by York, which exposes the utter weakness of the monarchy and shows York that his time has come. In the last act at the head of an army he proceeds to enforce his claim to the throne, and the play closes with the first bloody clash between the 'famous Houses' and the victory of York.

It is a play of action presented in strict chronological order, illuminated by occasional flashes of fine poetry, as in the parting of Margaret and Suffolk, and showing also a dawning power of characterization. York, the chief figure, is, it must be admitted, a character drawn after the Marlowe pattern; he is dominated by a single passion, desire for the crown, and is given to indulging in long declamatory tirades.

The deepening tragedy of the action is relieved, however, by occasional comic scenes which show that Shakespeare had not yet lost touch with the native tradition. One of these, the exposure of Simpcox, develops an anecdote recorded by Sir Thomas More. Pretending to have been born blind, Simpcox proclaims that his sight has been restored by prayer at the shrine of good St. Alban. The credulous King accepts this as a miracle, but Gloucester by a series of shrewd questions exposes the cheat. More ends his tale by saying that Gloucester set the rogue in the stocks. What follows in the play is Shakespeare's invention, helped out, perhaps, by his memory of Chaucer's *Merchant's Tale*. Noticing that the rogue is, or feigns to be, lame, Gloucester asks how he came to be so. By a fall from a plum tree, Simpcox replies, which he climbed to gratify his wife's longing for the fruit. Gloucester, well assured that the lameness, too, is a pretense, orders him to be whipped till he jump over a stool. In spite of the rogue's protest that he is not even able to stand alone, the Beadle begins to lay it on. 'After the Beadle hath hit him one jerke' reads the old stage direction, 'he leaps over the stool and runs away, and they, i.e. the crowd, run after him crying "A miracle, a miracle!"' This homely bit of native comedy must surely have provoked a laugh.

The second comic episode comes from Halle's chronicle. Horner, an armorer, was accused by Peter, his prentice, of having said that Richard of York was the true heir to the throne, and Henry a mere usurper. On Horner's emphatic denial of the charge, a trial by combat was ordained, not with the gentle weapons of swords and lances, but with sand bags strapped to the ends of poles. Horner accepts the combat willingly, but the faint-hearted Peter breaks down: 'Alas, my lord, I cannot fight!' he cries. 'For God's sake pity my case! . . . I shall never be able to fight a blow.' When the combat takes place Horner enters with his neighbors, 'drinking to him so much that he is drunk,' while Peter, urged to 'fight for credit of the prentices,' refuses a last cup, and, in fear of present death, bestows his few poor belongings, his apron, his hammer, and a little money, upon his friends. Yet when the fight begins Peter promptly hits his drunken master on the head, kills him, and kneels down to give thanks to God. This is another example of Shakespeare's ability to expand a mere hint into a comic scene. All he got from the chronicle was the fact of the duel with the defeat of the drunken armorer. The comic name of the prentice, Peter Thump, and all the words put into his mouth, with their revelation of the trembling coward, are Shakespeare's pure invention.

The long sequence of Cade scenes that fills up the greater part of the fourth act can hardly be called comic episodes; it is a structural part of the drama. Yet it seems clear that Shakespeare thoroughly enjoyed writing these scenes and that he let his gift of humor play lightly over this rising of the rabble. In fact for his own dramatic purposes he constantly misrepresents Cade's rebellion, a purely political movement, by mingling with it motives and incidents from the Peasants' Rising, communistic and equalitarian, in the preceding century. Cade's proclamation: 'When I am King . . . there shall be no money; all shall eat and drink on my score; and I will apparel them all in one livery, that they may agree like brothers,' is quite in the style of Parson Ball's sermons. Cade's short reply to Stafford, who calls him a shearman, 'And Adam was a gardener,' recalls Ball's famous rhyme,

> When Adam delved and Eve span
> Where was then the gentleman?

This confusion of the two revolts was not accidental. Shakespeare was too good an Elizabethan to sympathize with any sort of rebellion, and he deliberately stigmatized Cade's revolt with what were to Elizabethans the most foolish and repulsive features of the earlier rising. This is noticeable in the rabble's hatred of all sorts of learning; the Clerk of Chatham is hanged with his pen and inkhorn about his neck because he is found guilty of writing his name instead of signing with a mark, 'like an honest plain-dealing man'—Shakespeare's father for example. One of the capital charges against Lord Say is that he has 'traitorously corrupted the youth of the realm in erecting a grammar-school,' a ridiculous charge in Elizabethan eyes, for to the Elizabethans the grammar school opened a door to preferment of every kind in Church and State.

From Cade's first appearance his false brags of his high birth and hardihood are punctuated by ironic comments of his followers.

CADE: My father was a Mortimer—
DICK: He was an honest man, and a good bricklayer.
CADE: My mother a Plantagenet,—
DICK: I knew her well; she was a midwife.

. . .

CADE: Valiant I am.

SMITH: A' must needs, for beggary is valiant.

Something of the delightful illogical logic of the people appears in the clinching proof of Cade's statement that his father became a bricklayer in ignorance of his noble birth. 'Sir,' says the Weaver, 'he made a chimney in my father's house, and the bricks are alive at this day to testify it. Therefore deny it not.' This and much like it is genuine, if early, Shakespearean comedy and much of it appears often in a garbled form in *The Contention.*

It is worth noticing that Cade, a serio-comic figure, speaks prose pretty consistently. Even in his death scene, where another Elizabethan playwright might have let him indulge in heroics, Shakespeare holds him to good straightforward prose. 'Look on me well,' he says to Iden before the fight in which he falls, 'I have eat no meat these five days; yet come thou and thy five men, and if I do not leave you all as dead as a doornail, I pray God I may never eat grass more.' It is interesting and significant to find Shakespeare in this early play holding fast to the native tradition of realistic comedy expressed in idiomatic prose.

It is not possible to say so much of *King Henry VI Part III,* i.e. the conclusion of Shakespeare's two-part play on the Wars of the Roses. This long 'history' dramatizes that contention from a point immediately after the first triumph of the White Rose, through the defeat and death of York, the overthrow of the Lancastrians, the secession of Warwick the Kingmaker from the party of York, his temporary triumph, defeat, and death, to the final ruin of the House of Lancaster in the murder of King Henry by Richard of Gloucester. The play ends with Edward, son of the first York claimant, seated firmly on the throne, but a continuation of the story is implied here in the muttered threats of Richard against his brother's house. A long succession of scenes has dealt with the cruel bloodshed and shameful treason that mark this period of English history. It cannot be asserted that the young playwright has digested these scenes into a coherent whole; he has become too deeply involved in the factual history of the period, and his hand, like the dyer's, is subdued to what it works in.

This is not to say that the play lacks interest and value. It contains much really fine poetry, ranging from flyting matches, in which the champions of York and Lancaster hurl invectives at each other, to set rhetorical declamations like Margaret's oration to her troops at Tewkesbury. These speeches for the most part follow the pattern set by Marlowe, but occasionally Shakespeare escapes from this convention and strikes his own lyrical note. This rings clear and sweet in the long soliloquy of Henry withdrawn from the decisive test:

> This battle fares like to the morning's war,
> When dying clouds contend with growing light,
> What time the shepherd, blowing of his nails,
> Can neither call it perfect day nor night.
>
> . . .
>
> O God! methinks it were a happy life,
> To be no better than a homely swain;
>
> . . .
>
> Gives not the hawthorn bush a sweeter shade
> To shepherds, looking on their silly sheep,
> Than doth a rich embroider'd canopy
> To kings, that fear their subjects' treachery?
> O yes! it doth; a thousand-fold it doth.
> And to conclude, the shepherd's homely curds,
> His cold thin drink out of his leather bottle,
> His wonted sleep under a fresh tree's shade,
> All which secure and sweetly he enjoys,
> Is far beyond a prince's delicates.

This is true Shakespearean poetry with loving reminiscences of life in the fields about Stratford, but it has little bearing on the action, except to show, what had been shown clearly enough before, the utter inability of Henry to play the part of a true king. Shakespeare the poet has taken over the reins here from Shakespeare the playwright.

There are signs of the coming dramatist, however, even in this chronicle of blood. The most significant is the development, first by hints, later by long soliloquies, of the character of Richard Crookback. This characterization begins in the second scene of the play, where Richard urges his father to break an oath in order to win the crown, 'within whose circuit is Elysium.' It continues after the report of his father's murder when his fierce and unrelenting temper is contrasted with the softer nature of his brother Edward, and it finds full expression in the third act (III. ii) where Edward's disgraceful marriage awakes in Richard the first dream of the crown for himself. It is still only a dream, for there are many obstacles between him and the throne:

> And I, like one lost in a thorny wood,
> That rents the thorns and is rent with the thorns,
> Seeking a way and straying from the way;
> Not knowing how to find the open air,
> But toiling desperately to find it out,
> Torment myself to catch the English crown:
> And from that torment I will free myself,
> Or hew my way out with a bloody axe.

The second soliloquy comes at the very end of the play where, after his murder of the Lancastrian King, Richard turns deliberately against his own house of York. Harping on his bodily deformity, which Shakespeare, like the Elizabethan chroniclers, greatly overstressed, Richard exclaims:

> Then, since the heavens have shap'd my body so,
> Let hell make crook'd my mind to answer it.
> I have no brother, I am like no brother;
> And this word 'love,' which greybeards call divine,
> Be resident in men like one another
> And not in me: I am myself alone.

The last lines are the supreme and perfect expression, better perhaps than anything in Marlowe, of that overpowering egoism which characterizes the Marlovian hero.

Marlowe's influence is dominant in this play. There is not a single scene that can be classed as comic in its effect, such as those already noted in the Second Part of *Henry VI*. And this dominance of Marlowe continues, with a difference, in the play that follows and concludes the tetralogy of the Contention of York and Lancaster, Shakespeare's *Richard III*.

RICHARD III

Richard III, Shakespeare's first triumphant stage success, follows hard upon his two-part play on the Civil Wars. It may, perhaps, be dated *c.* 1593, but it can hardly have been performed until the reopening of the theaters with the cessation of the plague in the spring of 1594. The role of Richard was taken by Burbage, the great tragic actor of Shakespeare's company, who became, as contemporary records tell us, almost identified with the character he acted. A printed copy of the acting version appeared in 1597, another in 1598 with Shakespeare's name on the title-page, one of the first of his printed plays to bear his name, and a flock of reprints followed. Two of them, in fact, came out in 1629 and 1634 after the Folio had given the reading public a fuller and, on the whole, better text. Yet it is an interesting proof of the incompleteness of Elizabethan theatrical records that there exists but one notice of a performance of this popular play. That was at Court seventeen years after Shakespeare's death, when Charles I commanded it for the entertainment of his queen.

In *Richard III* Shakespeare completed the task he began in *The Contention of York and Lancaster*, and brought that long period of civil strife to a final close with the defeat and death of Richard, the last Yorkist King, and with the marriage of Richmond, the Lancastrian claimant, to Elizabeth of York. Richmond's oration at the end of the play gives full and formal utterance to the doctrine accepted by all loyal Elizabethans, Shakespeare among them, that the union of these 'true succeeders of each royal house' was destined to

Enrich the time to come with smooth-fac'd peace.

Only traitors, such as had plotted against Shakespeare's Elizabeth or had rebelled against her father, would dare to 'reduce these bloody days again.' Richmond's long speech, often omitted in modern performances, must have gone straight to the heart of Shakespeare's audience, who saw in the Tudor rose, with its blended red and white, a symbol of union and peace.

Dramatic exposition of an accepted political doctrine, however, does not make a play great, and this play's claim to greatness rests on Shakespeare's attainment of a more specifically dramatic end. He completes here the sketch drawn with swift vigorous lines in *King Henry VI Part III* of Richard Crookback; in *Richard III* he paints a Titian-like, full-length portrait. Shakespeare's Richard is the ideal tyrant of the Renaissance, the heroic villain who combines the natures of the lion and the fox, strong, ruthless, crafty, and cynical. Yet his Richard is a credible human character; he is saved from the monstrosity that degrades Marlowe's Barabas by clear intellectual superiority, by his genial delight in the triumph of his wit over bodily deformity, and not least, perhaps, by the fact that his victims were as deeply dyed as he in the bloodshed, treachery, and shameless self-aggrandisement of the Civil Wars. This last is true, to be sure, only up to the turning point of the play, where Richard contrives the murder of the young and innocent Princes. And it is exactly at this point that Richard's powers begin to fail him; he no longer owns 'that alacrity of spirit nor cheer of mind' that marked his triumphant progress to the throne. He drives his closest confidant into rebellion; he is suspicious of the adherents that still remain with him; he is haunted on the eve of battle by the ghosts of his victims, and is finally overthrown by an antagonist whom he despises.

Shakespeare has taken little pains to characterize this antagonist. It would, perhaps, have been impossible for him so early in his career to have put into one play two characters of rival greatness like Othello and Iago. Yet he has endowed Richmond with the one supremely necessary quality, the serene belief in himself as the instrument of divine vengeance on the enemy of God and man. This is the idea of *nemesis*, the judgment of the gods, or of God, and it is in the dramatic development of this idea that Shakespeare in this, the most Marlovian of his plays, rises above Marlowe. He has, in fact, incarnated this idea in the figure of Margaret, the Lancastrian Queen, whom, in defiance of history, he introduces early in the play to breathe a curse upon the triumphant house of York and again later to exult in the fulfilment of her prophecy:

> Bear with me; I am hungry for revenge,
> And now I cloy me with beholding it.

All the sins of the House of York, open violence, secret murder, and shameful treachery, are embodied in the figure of Richard, and it is upon him that the doom of Nemesis falls. This concentration of interest upon a single character gives to *Richard III* a firm dramatic unity that is wanting in the earlier chronicle plays. Here, as in Marlowe's *Edward II,* the chronicle play has been transformed into tragedy.

In a play that follows, even while it transcends, the pattern set by Marlowe, comic material would naturally be slight and scanty *Richard III* possesses much else of high poetic and dramatic value: passages, like the dream of Clarence, of vivid narrative, lines of almost lyrical description in the picture of the sleeping Princes, and an occasional flash of what Arnold called 'the grand style,' as in Richard's boast of the eminence of his House,

Our aery buildeth in the cedar's top
And dallies with the wind and scorns the sun.

There are highly stylized passages as in the stichomathy of the scene between Richard and Anne, and in the choral lamentation of the ladies—there is no Nurse present here to parody their complaints as in *Romeo and Juliet*. Shakespeare, it would seem, was in deadly earnest when he wrote this play.

The natural vehicle for the realistic comedy of the native tradition is prose, and there is almost no prose in *Richard III*. One scene (II. iii), where a group of citizens comment on the dangerous condition of the state, would probably have been thrown into prose with humorous touches in Shakespeare's later years; here he was so eager to forecast through their speech the impending storm that he failed to bring out the serio-comic nature of the common man's reflection upon the affairs of state. The one prose passage of any length, the talk of the two murderers before the assassination of Clarence, has an amusing comic description of the difficulties Conscience throws in the way of a man's pursuit of his ends: 'A man cannot steal, but it accuseth him; a man cannot swear, but it checks him; a man cannot lie with his neighbour's wife, but it detects him: . . . It made me once restore a purse of gold that I found; it beggars any man that keeps it.' This is excellent prose in the true comic vein, but in dramatic value it falls below the dialogue that Launcelot Gobbo imagines between his conscience and the fiend.

So far as Shakespeare relaxes the strain of tragic intensity in *Richard III*, the place of realistic comedy is supplied by flashes of wit, as in the chatter of the young Prince of York or in Richard's hypocritical and cynical comment on the situation as in his

O, do not swear, my lord of Buckingham

—a line, by the way, omitted in the Folio since the censor had deleted Buckingham's 'Zounds' which evoked it. Shakespeare laid a heavy burden on the actor who played Richard by the numerous asides with which he loaded that part. Yet given the conditions of the Elizabethan theater which made it possible for an actor to whisper, as it were, to the audience without the likelihood of being overheard by his fellow-actors, some of Richard's asides are extremely effective. They bring out more than once his keen enjoyment of the situation. Immediately after the death of King Edward, for example, while his head is full of his schemes for attaining the throne, he goes down on his knees to beg his mother's blessing. She gives it in full form with, perhaps, a certain foreboding:

> God bless thee! and put meekness in thy mind,
> Love, charity, obedience, and true duty.

'Amen' he answers and then in a swift aside,

> and make me die a good old man!
> That is the butt-end of a mother's blessing;
> I wonder that her Grace did leave it out.

One whole scene, Richard's wooing of Anne, a scene of pure invention on Shakespeare's part, since it lacks all historical foundation, might perhaps be considered comedy of a special type. Certainly Richard's audacity, his pretense of love, his feigned penitence, and his offer of atoning death strike comic rather than tragic notes. His summary of the situation after Anne has departed with his ring upon her finger demands of the actor the mimetic talent of a born comedian:

> Was ever woman in this humour woo'd?
> Was ever woman in this humour won?
>   . . .
> My dukedom to a beggarly denier
> I do mistake my person all this while:
> Upon my life, she finds, although I cannot,
> Myself to be a marvellous proper man.
> I'll be at charges for a looking-glass,
> And entertain a score or two of tailors,
> To study fashions to adorn my body.
>   . . .
> Shine out, fair sun, till I have bought a glass,
> That I may see my shadow as I pass.

Yet when all has been said and every grain of comic matter sifted out from *Richard III*, the fact remains that in this play Shakespeare is not quite himself. It is his supreme achievement in historical tragedy, but it is one in which he firmly suppressed his native bent for comedy. It is not until he emerges from the dominance of Marlowe that comedy begins again to play freely in his work. How slowly and how far he escaped from this dominance will appear in the next histories we have to consider.

KING JOHN

King John is by no means so good a stage-play as *Richard III,* but it is in some ways more interesting to the student of Shakespeare. There has been much talk of lost plays which Shakespeare is supposed to have rewritten for his company. Here, as in *The Taming of the Shrew,* we have an old play which he certainly rewrote, and it is possible to watch him at work on his job of adaptation. The old play is *The Troublesome Reign of John King of England,* already mentioned (p. 72). Published in 1591, this two-part chronicle play probably dates several years earlier; Shakespeare's adaptation can hardly be dated before 1594, as it was plainly written with an eye on the personnel of the Chamberlain's Company as organized in that year.

So much has been said of the superiority of *King John* to its source that it seems unnecessary here to go into the matter in detail. One or two points, however, may be briefly noted. Shakespeare reduced the lumbering two-part play to a drama of actable length, making, as he wrote, heavy cuts, especially in the long-drawn-out second part. Such cuts were the more necessary since, while following in the main the scenario of his source, Shakespeare expanded quite freely certain situations. Yet while preserving the old structure, he composed an almost entirely new text, taking over only a line or two of the old play, together with occasional words and phrases adapted to his purpose. He purged his source pretty thoroughly of the fierce anti-papal note, which, following the tradition started by Bale's *King John,* represented John as the Protestant champion of England against the tyranny of Rome, a note, of course, purposely struck to evoke response from a popular audience in the years just after the Armada. Reference has already been made (p. 73) to Shakespeare's elision of a comic scene in which the Bastard, ransacking English abbeys, discovers nuns and monks hidden where they had no business to be. Shakespeare omits also a deathbed speech by John in which the King prophesies the coming of a monarch, Henry VIII of course, who will put an end to papal usurpation. All that Shakespeare retains of the old anti-papal propaganda is found in two of John's speeches asserting the royal supremacy and denouncing the sale of indulgences. These, at least, were topics on which all Elizabethans of moderate liberal views were likely to agree.

It is in characterization especially that Shakespeare rises above his source. He deepens and darkens the character of John, particularly in the scene where he tempts Hubert to the murder of Arthur, a scene, by the way, of Shakespeare's invention, since he found no hint of murder either in his source or in contemporary chronicles. It is interesting to compare this scene with that in which Richard suggests to Buckingham the murder of the Princes, and to note the growing intensity of Shakespeare's tragic strain. Arthur in Shakespeare's hands changes from the somewhat commonplace and moralizing youth of the source to a helpless and pathetic child. The role of his mother, Constance, is greatly enlarged, perhaps to give the boy who had played Queen Margaret in *Richard III* a better part. Shakespeare's happiest and most effective transformation, however, is the part of the Bastard Falconbridge, but this demands a later and fuller consideration.

What strikes the sensitive reader most quickly in passing from *Richard III* to *King John* is Shakespeare's growing emancipation from the domination of Marlowe. He follows, to be sure, Marlowe's line in transforming the chronicle play into a stately tragedy; but in diction, in the handling of verse, and particularly in the free play of imagination, we see the young poet fighting his way back into drama. The declamatory tirades of Marlowe give place to bursts of imaginative poetry, decorated, at times too lavishly for modern taste, with a profusion of word-plays and fantastic conceits. Even a minor character is liable on occasion to break into such poetic fancies as

> To gild refined gold, to paint the lily,
> To throw a perfume on the violet,
> To smoothe the ice, or add another hue
> Unto the rainbow, or with taper-light
> To seek the beauteous eye of heaven to garnish,
> Is wasteful and ridiculous excess.

The last line might be applied by a captious critic to many a speech in *King John*. Shakespeare does better when he is briefer, as when Chatillon, announcing John's invasion of France, describes the youths of his army as

> fiery voluntaries,
> With ladies' faces and fierce dragons' spleens,

or in the rare direct dramatic utterance that reveals in a flash the character of the speaker as in the reply of Constance to the Cardinal blaming her excess of sorrow,

He talks to me that never had a son.

When we turn from a consideration of Shakespeare's poetic style in *King John* to compare the comic matter in the two plays, we see at once that *The Troublesome Reign* runs true to native form and mingles with its serious history and propaganda a fair amount of old-fashioned horseplay. In addition to the scene of the Bastard's discoveries in religious houses, there is another in which he chases Austria off the stage, picks up the lion skin the coward has dropped, and lays it at the feet of Lady Blanche. Just before the death of John, the old play has a scene in which the Abbot of Swinstead overhears a monk planning the murder of the King. Misunderstanding what he hears, the Abbot imagines that the monk is planning to kill him, and goes down on his knees to offer his post if the monk will spare him. When, however, he learns the monk's true intent, he blesses him and assures him that, if he succeeds, he will be canonized as a saint. Shakespeare has sometimes been blamed for not motivating more clearly the poisoning of John. Presumably he thought that his audience would demand no further motivation than the traditional enmity between John and the Roman Church, and that the comic scene of the old play struck a false note before the agonizing death of the King. All this comic matter disappears in Shakespeare's adaptation. What remains of the comic?

Not a great deal, to tell the truth, but enough to show that Shakespeare is moving away from the almost unmixed tragic tone of *Richard III*. If there is little or no horseplay in *King John,* there is from time to time a spice of comedy in the diction. The flyting of the ladies, Elinor and Constance, has none of the fierce invective of the flyting matches in Shakespeare's earlier histories. In one scene, for instance, Elinor calls on Arthur to come over to John's party; 'Come to thy grandam, child,' she says, and Constance answers for him:

> Do, child, go to it grandam, child;
> Give grandam kingdom, and it grandam will
> Give it a plum, a cherry, and a fig:
> There's a good grandam.

This surely was meant to provoke a laugh and the same may be true of Constance's mockery of Austria, bidding him doff the lion's hide and 'hang a calf's-skin on those recreant limbs.' The Bastard, at any rate, thought this a good jest, for he hurls the calf's-skin, so to speak, at

Austria again and yet again. These and the like jests, however, are only occasional flashes in what is for the most part a very serious play. Shakespeare's real contribution to comedy in *King John* appears in his characterization of the Bastard.

This character he found, to be sure, in his source, but the Bastard of the old play is a very different person from Shakespeare's hero. The old character is something of a swaggerer and a bully. In the first scene he indulges in a ranting aside to the audience intimating his certainty that he was the son of Richard Cœur de Lion and he holds a sword to his mother's breast to make her confess her amour with that king. He challenges Austria to a formal duel and stabs the Abbot when John is poisoned. In Shakespeare, on the other hand, the Bastard reveals himself at once as a mocking humorist. He is at heart aware of the secret of his birth, but he is resolute to hold on to his £500 a year despite this knowledge and the claim of his younger true-born brother. He mocks this claimant as the starveling image of old Sir Robert, supposed the father of them both. Yet he has sporting blood enough to renounce his patrimony and follow Queen Elinor's fortune. She bids him call her 'grandam,' and he answers with a jest on his birth:

> Something about, a little from the right,
> In at the window, or else o'er the hatch:
> . . .
> And I am I, howe'er I was begot.

On the appearance of his mother, whom Shakespeare has wisely kept off-stage during the inquiry into his birth, he elicits a confession from her, not by a threat, but by a broad jest:

> Sir Robert might have eat his part in me
> Upon Good-Friday and ne'er broke his fast

and by the bold assertion that he has denied his Falconbridge paternity

> As faithfully as I deny the devil.

The Bastard's soliloquy before his mother's entrance presents an amusing contrast to that of his namesake in the old play. Shakespeare's hero chuckles over his promotion—he has just been knighted by the King—fancies himself exchanging formal compliments with a traveler whom he has invited to dinner, and comments on the prevalence of 'observation,' i.e. obsequious flattery, in the world. The speech is a genial piece of social satire quite in the vein of the Clown-Vice of the Morals. And this vein of gay satire runs through the Bastard's speeches till the turning point of the play, John's plot against the life of Arthur. He mocks the ranting defiance of the Citizen of Angiers and parodies the Dauphin's conventional avowal of love for Blanche. It is not hard to see, by the way, in both these speeches Shakespeare's humorous mockery of his own early excesses of expression. The Bastard ends this strain by a jesting invective against

That smooth-fac'd gentleman, tickling Commodity,

i.e. self-interest, who has just brought about a disgraceful peace, instead of honorable war, between France and England. Commodity, he says, is the cause of many an evil in this ill-balanced world, and, then, with a sharp turn upon himself, he asks why he should rail upon Commodity. It is, perhaps, because he himself has not been tempted, so while he is a beggar he will keep on railing, but should he become rich, he'll declare 'there is no vice but beggary.' All this is so much in the manner of the Clown that a recent scholar has assigned the role of the Bastard to Will Kempe. Yet it is hard to see how Kempe could have acted the part that the Bastard is presently called on to play. When John keeps Arthur in prison and plots against his life, he ceases to perform the duty of a King, to do justice and to champion his country; he loses the hearts of his subjects, shamefully yields up his crown to Rome, and retreats before foreign invasion. Here the Bastard springs into the breach, and the son of Cœur de Lion takes over the role of the nation's defender that John has dropped. He confronts the angry nobles over the dead body of Arthur, denounces John's craven attempts to pacify the invaders by papal intervention, defies in the King's name the army of foreigners and rebels, and in the battle that follows alone upholds the day after the King has left the field. After John's death he rallies the returning English nobles around the innocent heir to the throne with words that have roused an echo in the hearts of his countrymen ever since:

This England never did, nor never shall,
Lie at the proud foot of a conqueror,
But when it first did help to wound itself.
Now these her princes are come home again,

Come the three corners of the world in arms,
And we shall shock them. Naught shall make us rue,
If England to itself do rest but true.

It is easier to imagine Burbage, the tragedian, than Kempe, the clown, voicing this proud boast.

The transition from the comic to the heroic in the character of the Bastard is neither impossible nor incredible. In the early scenes he is a realist, ready to swim with the tide and follow fortune, but there is nothing base or ignoble in him, and he rises like a man to meet the threat to his country. It is, of course, in the early scenes that this character marks Shakespeare's growing sense of independence. Here for the first time in his 'histories' he introduces a leading figure that has a truly comic value, a jester and a mocker, aware of the distorted values of the world, but content to take life as it is and to play out his hand. It would be hard even to imagine such a character in a Marlowe play. Shakespeare is still a long way from Falstaff, but he has now started on the road that leads toward him.

RICHARD II

The time relation between *Richard II* and *King John* cannot be precisely established. It is possible indeed that the latter play comes after *Richard,* but it is certain, none the less, that *Richard* represents an advance in the development of Shakespeare's art. It is, indeed, his first really independent historical drama. In *Richard III* he was still under the spell of Marlowe; in *King John* he had partly, but only partly, freed himself; in *Richard II* he shook off the chain and boldly challenged his master. For there can be little doubt that in writing *Richard II* Shakespeare had in mind Marlowe's *Edward II,* produced, we know, by Pembroke's Men, a rival company to Shakespeare's.

Marlowe's achievement in *Edward II* was the transformation of the conventional chronicle play, a thing of shreds and patches, into organic historical tragedy. To attain this end he toned down the resonance of his verse to an almost realistic dramatic dialogue and concentrated his attention upon the tragic career of his protagonist, the ill-fated King. Yet in one respect Marlowe accepted the old convention of the chronicle play, for the action of *Edward II* covers the whole reign of that monarch; it extends indeed beyond his death to the revenge exacted by his son. When Shakespeare sat down to challenge Marlowe's mastery, he deliberately selected a similar theme, the tragedy of another ill-fated English King, Richard II. The reign of Richard was, we know, of special interest to Elizabethans, since his deposition by his cousin, Henry of Lancaster, was the initial step in the long series of civil wars, happily ended by the union of the rival houses of York and Lancaster in the Tudor dynasty. And since this reign was of such special interest to his audience, Shakespeare felt free to break with the old convention and to limit the action of his play to Richard's last year, so as to bring out more fully the cause and the consequences of his fall. The cause of Richard's fall lay, Shakespeare felt, in the character of the King himself, and his portrayal of Richard's character, a strange blend of weakness, recklessness, and self-pity, combined with a charm capable of evoking passionate devotion from characters so different as his Queen, Aumerle, and the poor groom of his stables, is a masterpiece of psychological penetration compared with Marlowe's swift and somewhat superficial characterization of Edward. Marlowe's King never realizes that his fall has been brought about by his own folly; he continues to the end a self-pitying figure, and dies with a whimpering prayer for life. Shakespeare's Richard, on the contrary, comes to recognize himself as the sole author of his tragedy; he gives expression to this self-knowledge in one of the saddest lines in Shakespeare:

> I wasted time, and now doth time waste me,

and dies, as the son of the Black Prince should, sword in hand, fighting against odds. Moreover, our understanding of Richard's character is broadened and deepened by the contrast drawn throughout the play with that of his opponent, the tough-minded opportunist, Bolingbroke. It has been well said that in his creation of Richard, Shakespeare is on the way that leads to his supreme achievement in the character of Hamlet.

If Shakespeare's characterization of his protagonist differs from Marlowe's, the style in which he develops the dramatic action differs even more widely. Where Marlowe in *Edward II* curbed his tendency to rhetorical declamation, Shakespeare in his challenge gave free play to his lyric vein. It is hardly too much to say that it is the poetry rather than the action of *Richard II* that constitutes the chief charm of the play. The long speeches of Richard himself often seem like arias intended for the singing rather than the speaking voice. But it is not Richard alone who sings to us; such a minor character as Mowbray may at any time break out in song:

My native English, now I must forego;
And now my tongue's use is to me no more
Than an unstringed viol or a harp.

Even the realist, Bolingbroke, can sing:

O! who can hold a fire in his hand
By thinking on the frosty Caucasus?

. . .

Or wallow naked in December snow
By thinking on fantastic summer's heat?

and John of Gaunt's hymn of praise of England,

This land of such dear souls, this dear, dear land,

has come echoing down through the years.

There is plenty of music in *Richard II,* but a curious absence of anything like comedy. That there is no inherent opposition between dramatic lyricism and comedy is proved by the abundance of comic matter in *A Midsummer Night's Dream* and *Romeo and Juliet.* Why, one may ask, did Shakespeare so rigidly restrain his native gift for comedy in this historical play? The answer may perhaps be found in part in the relation of *Richard II* to another contemporary drama dealing with the reign of that king, a little-known chronicle play, first printed by Halliwell in 1870.[1]

This play is generally known as *Woodstock* from the chief character, Thomas of Woodstock, Earl of Gloucester, uncle of Richard, figuring here, in defiance of history, as Protector of the young King. Richard chafes under his control and finally contrives his arrest and secret murder. York and Lancaster, Shakespeare's John of Gaunt, take arms to revenge their brother's death and defeat Richard in a pitched battle. Here the mutilated manuscript breaks off, but as only a page or so is missing it seems apparent that *Woodstock* could not have included the final deposition of the King; it must have ended with some sort of reconciliation between Richard and his surviving uncles.

That Shakespeare knew *Woodstock* is proved not only by repeated

---

[1] Later and better editions than Halliwell's very rare publication are by Keller (*Shakespeare Jahrbuch,* 1899), and by Frijlinck for the Malone Society, 1929.

verbal parallels between it and *Richard II*, but by a similar conception of the character of Gloucester. Shakespeare makes John of Gaunt refer to him as

My brother Gloucester, plain well-meaning soul,—

and in *Woodstock*, Gloucester glories in the epithet of 'plain Thomas.' He opposes the greedy favorites of the Court, but is sincerely devoted to Richard. This, of course, contradicts the character of the historic Gloucester, a turbulent, ambitious, and intriguing noble. Another interesting point of contact between the two plays is the character of Richard's Queen. Shakespeare represents her as a grown woman devoted to her husband, while as a matter of fact Richard's second wife, Isabella, was a mere child of ten or so at the time of his deposition. What Shakespeare really did was to lift from *Woodstock* the character of Richard's first wife, the lovely and beloved Anne of Bohemia—'Ann a Beame' in the old play—and introduce her into his tragedy to add a touch of pathos to Richard's fall. Finally there are repeated passing references in *Richard II* to matters presented with lively detail in *Woodstock:* the 'leasing' of the kingdom 'like to a pelting farm'—the very phrase 'pelting farm' appears in the old play— the 'pilling' of the commons with grievous taxes, the new exactions by 'blanks.' Shakespeare seems to have assumed a knowledge of these things by his audience, just as in *Richard III* he assumed their knowledge of Richard's murders in an earlier play, *King Henry VI Part III*. All this goes to make the guess, hazarded by recent scholars, that *Woodstock* belonged to Shakespeare's company and that he himself acted in it, not only possible, but highly probable. It is otherwise almost incredible that Shakespeare could have known *Woodstock* so well.

Now *Woodstock* combines serious historic action presented in unadorned blank verse with lively realistic comedy in prose. In the comic scenes it introduces a Clown, Nimble, a direct descendant of the old Vice, a stupid Bailiff, Master Ignoramus, who seems to have stepped out of some Moral, and various foolish rustic characters, one of whom is arrested for 'whistling treason.' Even the protagonist plays at times a comic role, as when he walks the horse of a fantastically dressed courtier, who mistakes him in his plain garb for a groom and fees him with a tester. In spite of the murder of Gloucester and the spectacular appearance of the ghosts of Edward III and the Black Prince, *Woodstock* lacks the high seriousness of tragedy. In fact, it is not a tragedy at all but an old-fashioned chronicle play in the native tradition.

These two plays, *Edward II* and *Woodstock,* lie behind and largely condition the composition and the character of *Richard II.* Marlowe's play presented Shakespeare with a challenge, not only in the field of historic tragedy, but specifically in the theme, the downfall of an ill-fated English king. *Woodstock,* on the other hand, gave him only a starting point; Shakespeare's play, indeed, begins where that leaves off and conducts the action to the proper tragic catastrophe, the murder of the protagonist. But Shakespeare planned to give his company something more and better than a second part of their *Woodstock.* He would give them a poetic tragedy in the new fashion Marlowe had set, but one handled with a concentration of interest on the character of the king and a profusion of lyric poetry lacking in earlier plays of this genre. *Woodstock,* in fact, seems to have presented Shakespeare with something to avoid rather than to imitate; it would almost seem as if he had revolted from the crude archaic comedy of that play. To have incorporated anything of this sort into his deliberate challenge to Marlowe may well have appeared to him a retrogression to the old convention. Certainly he avoided it even when an opportunity presented itself, as in the Gardener's scene (III. ii). One can imagine what a later Shakespeare, the author of the two parts of *Henry IV,* for example, would have made of this character; he would have been a homely man of the people, commenting shrewdly in terms of folk wisdom on the action of the play, something like the Grave-digger in *Hamlet.* But the Gardener of *Richard II* is anything but a realistic character; he is a mere mouthpiece for uttering and elaborating in formal verse one of Shakespeare's favorite images in the play, the likeness of the realm of England to a garden, well-trimmed or overgrown with weeds, according as the master is diligent or careless and neglectful.

There is no other scene in *Richard II* where there is even an opportunity for genuine comedy. The scenes (v. ii & iii) in which York discovers and denounces the treason of his son and the youth's mother wrests a pardon from the new king have a rather ridiculous flavor to a modern reader. The jingling couplets destroy for us all sense of realism, and the pun with which York answers his wife's plea for pardon,

> Speak it in French, king; say, '*Pardonnez moy*'

is perhaps the very poorest quibble in all of Shakespeare's plays. Bolingbroke himself seems to suggest a certain comic quality in what follows the appearance of the Duchess:

> Our scene is alter'd from a serious thing,
> And now chang'd to 'The Beggar and the King.'

Yet it is hard to believe that an Elizabethan audience would have laughed at a scene in which a father and a mother plead alternately for the death and the life of their only son. Interposed between Richard's pathetic parting with his wife and his murder in the penultimate scene of the play, this incident is a mere filler to bridge over time; it must have been written in Shakespeare's most careless mood.

Richard II holds a unique place among Shakespeare's histories. It is an experimental play in which his growing mastery of dramatic characterization and his fully developed power as a lyric poet combine to the exclusion of his native bent for comedy. It is, no doubt, a charming experiment. *Richard II* has always been a favorite with readers, but it has never been a great stage success. The elaborate imagery in which theme after theme is caught up and interwoven in a new pattern is a sheer delight to the lover of Shakespeare's poetry; it is less effective as dramatic utterance. One feels in *Richard II* the controlling hand of the poet rather than the playwright, the poet of the *Sonnets* with their allusiveness, their verbal conceits, and their extraordinary command of poetic diction. On the other hand, one misses here the vigorous dramatic action of Shakespeare's other histories. More especially one feels the absence of comic scenes and comic characters. There is no scene in a tavern to contrast with high affairs of state; there is no character like the Bastard Falconbridge to comment with realistic irony on the behavior of his betters. Once he had written *Richard II*, Shakespeare picked up again in the great historic trilogy which follows, the *Henry IV* and *Henry V* plays, that strain that he for once had dropped. Lovers of Shakespearean comedy have reason to rejoice that the experiment of *Richard II* remained an experiment, and that Shakespeare promptly returned to the native tradition of blended grave and gay, and went on in the trilogy to create the character of Falstaff.

9

The Falstaff Plays

HENRY IV PARTS I AND II, AND HENRY V

IN THE trilogy, *Henry IV Parts I and II* and *Henry V*, Shakespeare reached the high-water mark of his work in the field of the chronicle play. The First Part of *Henry IV* must have been written and staged in 1597, for it was entered in the Stationers' Register on 25 February 1598 and published that same year with the catch-penny title-page: *The History of Henrie the Fourth; With the battell at Shrewsburie, betweene the King and Lord Henry Percy, surnamed Henrie Hotspur of the North. With the humorous conceits of Sir John Falstaffe.*[1] It was one of the most popular of Shakespeare's plays; four more quartos were published before the appearance of the Folio, 1623, and two more after that date; only *Richard III* attained a like success. The Second Part, probably written in 1598, was registered and published in 1600 with the following title-page: *The Second part of Henrie the fourth, continuing to his death, and coronation of Henrie the fift. With the humours of Sir John Falstaffe and swaggering Pistoll. . . Written by William Shakespeare.* In Shakespeare's day, as in our own, this play was far less successful than the First Part; one quarto sufficed the appetite of readers until the Folio, which offered a different and somewhat longer text. *Henry V*, we know, was on the stage by September 1599. Shakespeare's Company made an attempt to stop the publication of this play. It was entered, Stationers' Register, on 4 August 1600, along with three other plays of theirs: *Much Ado, As You Like It*, and Jonson's *Every Man in his Humour*, with the marginal note: *'to be staied,'* i.e. not to be printed. However, a pair of piratical publishers secured a 'stolen and surreptitious' report of a performance and gave it to the world in 1600 with the following title-page: *The Chronicle History of Henry the fift. . . Togither with Auntient Pistoll.* It is interesting to note that as Falstaff is absent from this play, his place as a humorist is supplied by swaggering Pistol. This is one of the 'bad' quartos, a shocking perversion of Shakespeare's

[1] The Second Quarto, 1599, bore Shakespeare's name on the title-page.

234

text, but as the company withheld the 'true and perfect' copy, it was all that the public could get to read, and two more quartos appeared in 1602 and 1619 before the Folio gave the play as Shakespeare wrote it.

The three Henry plays may be regarded as a unit to which *The Merry Wives of Windsor* is appended as a comic after-piece. The unifying theme is the career of Henry V, his evolution from the wild Prince into the hero King, and his achievement as the leader of a united nation against the old enemy France. A tradition beginning as early as the reign of Henry's son delighted to picture Henry as the wildest of young princes, a haunter of taverns, an associate for sport with highwaymen; he had struck, it declared, the Chief Justice upon his seat of office, and had lived at open enmity with his father. Equally, however, tradition affirmed that with his accession to the throne he experienced a sudden change of heart. He at once cast off the disreputable companions of his youth, called into council the wisest of English statesmen, among them the Chief Justice who had sent him to prison, and led an army to win against great odds the glorious victory of Agincourt. Sober Elizabethan historians accepted the tradition and repeated the scandalous tales of Henry's youth to contrast them with his unblemished behavior as a king. To Holinshed, for example, Shakespeare's chief authority for all his chronicle plays, Henry was 'the mirror of all Christian Kings.'

About the time that Shakespeare came to London this tradition, ratified by historians, took on dramatic form in one of the earliest of English chronicle plays, *The Famous Victories of Henry the Fifth.* This was a Queen's Company play, in which the famous comedian, Tarlton, distinguished himself in the role of Derick, the Clown; since Tarlton died in 1588 the play must have been on the boards before that year. It was entered, Stationers' Register, in 1594, but the oldest extant copy is a quarto of 1598, possibly a second edition brought out to compete with the sale of Shakespeare's play. This crude old play, which is preserved in a very badly mangled text, opens with a group of scenes representing the wildness of the Prince in the strongest light. It shows him counting up the money he has stolen from his father's tax-gatherers, laughing over the blows he has received from one of the men he robbed, going to an Eastcheap tavern where there is good wine and a pretty wench, striking the Chief Justice, and promising that office to one of his boon companions. It is only at his father's deathbed that he experiences a change of heart and declares himself new-born. Immediately after his coronation he rebukes and banishes his old companions, who have been exulting in their prospects—'we shall all be kings'—and the rest of the play deals with his war in France and his marriage with the French princess. Shakespeare certainly knew *The Famous Victories*, from which he caught several hints for his three plays. More particularly he took from it the name of Oldcastle, who appears there as one of the Prince's wild companions. This is, of course, a caricature of the historic Sir John Oldcastle, Lord Cobham, a famous soldier of that time and a friend of Prince Henry, later a Lollard and a rebel who was hanged as a traitor and burned as a heretic after Henry became king. Oldcastle plays a very minor part in *The Famous Victories;* Shakespeare took nothing but the name from the old play. His presentation of Oldcastle, however, as a drunken cowardly jester to the Prince gave great offense to the Cobhams, then a powerful family at Elizabeth's Court, and he was forced to change the name before the play appeared in print, a fact which the epilogue to Part II alludes to in the words: 'Oldcastle died a martyr and this is not the man.' The name Falstaff, which replaced that of Oldcastle, is a mere variation of Fastolfe, the Sir John who appears as a cowardly soldier in *King Henry VI Part I*. In spite of the change of name, however, both Shakespeare's comic character and the play in which he figures were long known as Oldcastle.

Shakespeare was too good an Elizabethan to reject the long-established tradition of Henry's wild youth and later change of heart. Moreover, *The Famous Victories* and a new play on Henry V successfully produced by a rival company, the Admiral's Men, in 1595, were a challenge to him to do something of the kind, but better, for his own company. It was only natural, too, that he should want to round off his series of plays on weak or wicked English kings with one which presented the last great and good Plantagenet. That some such notion had been in his mind before he finished writing *Richard II* is plain from a reference in the last act of that play to Hal's loose companions and reckless behavior. Yet even his unhappy father can still discern in him

> . . . some sparkles of better hope,
> Which elder days may happily bring forth.

Accepting as he did the native tradition of Henry's youth and manhood, it followed logically enough that Shakespeare should dramatize it in a play that belongs to the native convention of mingled mirth and sadness. Here he returns whole-heartedly to this convention with delightful results, especially for the modern reader, less interested in the political problems involved in the historical matter of these plays than in the sayings and doings of the major comic figure, the immortal Falstaff. Yet the student of these plays would do well to consider the nature of the dramatic problem that confronted Shakespeare. This was to make the evolution of Henry's character at once interesting and credible, to extenuate as much as possible the wild behavior of his youth, and to substitute his gradual realization of the duties and responsibilities of kingship for the sudden miraculous change of heart reported in the tradition. It is easy to see how Shakespeare toned down the reported excesses of Henry's youth. He allows him indeed to take part in a highway robbery, but only for the sake of a jest, and he is careful to restore the money. The most outrageous incident of his youth, the blow given to the Chief Justice —dramatized in detail in *The Famous Victories*—is carefully kept off the stage by Shakespeare and not even alluded to until the Second Part. But something more was needed, some charm to draw the Prince away from his duties and to make him for a time, at least, 'in love with vanity.' And for this purpose Shakespeare created the character of Falstaff.

It may be surmised that Shakespeare took over the name of Oldcastle from the old play with the idea, unconscious perhaps, of identifying the chief figure among Hal's boon companions with the historical soldier, rebel, and, as a heretic, scoffer at sacred things. When he was compelled to drop this name he substituted for it another which would at least suggest the character of a knight and a soldier. Certainly Falstaff stands on a higher social level than Hal's other companions, the bottle-nosed Bardolph, the sneak Gadshill, or even the younger brother, Poins. To an Elizabethan audience, far more sensitive than we to the difference in social rank, the association of the Prince's tempter with Sir John Oldcastle or Sir John Fastolfe had a significance that we are only too likely to overlook.

Falstaff, in other words, though the dominating comic character of two plays, is by no means the mere Clown, detached from the action, of earlier comedy. His role is essentially structural in the two parts of *Henry IV;* the attraction he exercised on the Prince, their gradual estrangement, and his final rejection are the dominating factors of the drama. To understand the play of forces in the drama it is necessary to understand the character of Falstaff.

Since the appearance in 1777 of Maurice Morgann's humorous and paradoxical essay on *The Dramatic Character of Sir John Falstaff*, enough has been written about the fat Knight to stock the shelves of a gentleman's library. And much of what has been written has been vitiated by a preconception that appears, perhaps for the first time, in Morgann's essay, namely that Shakespeare's characters may be fitly considered 'rather as historic than as dramatic beings.' Pushed to its logical conclusion this means nothing less than that we are at liberty to take Shakespeare's plays as veritable historic narratives, and that we are free to study his characters, interpret their motives, and divine their antecedents, as we might do with such historic figures as Napoleon or Abraham Lincoln. A witty author [2] has even in an essay, included in Birrell's *Obiter Dicta,* written a little life of Falstaff. But Falstaff has no life apart from Shakespeare's plays, and questions in regard to his cowardice, his veracity, and so forth, have no value, except so far as his words and actions contribute to our understanding of the drama in which he plays so great a part. To apologize for Falstaff's behavior in battle, to rail at the 'unthinkable inhumanity' of Henry in the rejection scene, is part and parcel of the moralistic sentimentality that has been the bane of literary criticism for a century and more.

For the modern reader, at least, the comic matter in the two parts of *Henry IV* far outweighs the historical, and the comedy is centered upon Falstaff and to a lesser degree upon a group of figures that revolve about him. It may be well, however, to bear in mind the fact that the two-part play is not a comedy, but a chronicle history, and that the character of Falstaff was created by Shakespeare not for itself alone, but for its bearing upon that of Prince Henry. With this in mind we may trace briefly the career of Falstaff through the two-part play and then, and not before, attempt an estimate of his character in its dramatic value and significance.

After an opening scene that tells of the King's alienation from his son whose brow, he says, is stained with riot and dishonor, Falstaff is introduced in company with the Prince, and it may be said here that in the First Part, Falstaff except for a brief moment never appears alone, but always along with Hal. This scene is of special importance since it gives us our first impressions of Falstaff's personality,

[2] Said to be George Radford.

and more particularly of his relation to the Prince. He appears yawning after a post-prandial nap, old, fat, a hard drinker, a gross eater, and yet a highway robber, a bundle of comic incongruities. He appears on intimate terms with Hal, yet this intimacy is hardly one of true friendship. Falstaff is the Prince's Jester; like the licensed Fool he presumes upon the humor of his master, and even in this first scene he evinces a purpose of exploiting his relation to Hal when the Prince shall have become king: 'Do not thou, when thou art king, hang a thief.' There is no sign that Falstaff is what Hal later jestingly calls him: 'a villainous misleader of youth'; on the contrary Falstaff complains that Hal, who is able to corrupt a saint, has done much harm upon him, and the Prince's tone throughout is one of humorous half-ironic condescension. Action begins when the Prince agrees to join Poins in a practical joke on Falstaff; 'the virtue of this jest,' says Poins, will be 'the incomprehensible lies' that Falstaff will tell them after it is over. Their plot, apparently, is not to expose Falstaff's cowardice—for compared with the true-bred cowards, his fellow-thieves, Falstaff is one who will fight, though not longer than he sees reason—but to exploit his inexhaustible fertility of invention and then put him to shame as an unconscionable liar.

In the scene where the practical joke takes effect, Shakespeare again calls attention to the incongruous contrast between Falstaff's person and his behavior. Old, fat, and broken-winded he is engaged upon a night attack upon a company of travelers, an action fitter for such young gentlemen as the Prince and Poins; but these two have deserted him to slip on their disguises of buckram overalls. As the travelers appear, Falstaff sets on them with wild shouts: 'Strike! down with them! cut the villains' throats!' Sharing the easily won booty with his fellows, Falstaff complains bitterly of his desertion by the Prince and Poins, 'two arrant cowards,' a remark that gives point to what happens a moment later. The disguised pair set upon the thieves and, according to the stage direction, written presumably by Shakespeare himself, 'they all'—i.e. Falstaff's fellows—'run away and Falstaff, after a blow or two runs away too.' The situation could hardly be plainer. Falstaff stays long enough to exchange a blow or two with his opponents and then, seeing himself deserted by his fellows and attacked by two vigorous young men, he takes to his heels. Yet how completely the situation has been misunderstood may be seen from Morgann's account of an eighteenth-century performance.

The players [he says] bring Falstaff . . . to the very front of
the stage, where with much mummery and grimace he seats
himself down with a canvas money-bag to divide the spoil.
In this situation he is attacked by the Prince and Poins, whose
tin swords hang idly in the air, and delay to strike, till the
player Falstaff . . . is able to rise; which is not till after some
ineffectual efforts and with the assistance . . . of one of the
thieves . . . after which without any resistance on his part,
he is goaded off the stage, like a fat ox for slaughter. . . I
think he does not roar—perhaps the player had never perfected himself in the tones of a bull-calf.

There is an amusing difference on the part of Falstaff's apologists in
regard to his 'roaring' as he fled. Morgann thinks 'the *roar* we should
take on the credit of Poins,' i.e. we should not believe it at all. Kittredge, in a recent edition of the play, asserts that Poins' words: 'How
the rogue roar'd,' refer to the shouts of Falstaff as he attacked the
travelers—this in flat defiance of Hal's statement (II. iv. 286) that Falstaff 'roar'd for mercy, and still ran and roar'd.' We must surely believe that Shakespeare coached the first actor of Falstaff to run bellowing off the stage. It is a bit of the broad comedy in action which
delighted the Elizabethans, and it has its bearing on what is to follow.

The scene of Falstaff's exposure (II. iv) becomes step by step one of
the maddest and merriest in Shakespearean comedy. It opens with a
bit of by-play between Hal, Poins, and Francis, a 'drawer,' from which
we learn incidentally that the waiters of the Boar's Head call Hal 'the
king of courtesy . . . no proud Jack, like Falstaff,' an interesting little
sidelight on Falstaff's behavior to his inferiors. Falstaff enters to the
Prince and Poins, who are on the watch for him, and, realizing that
the best defense lies in attack, begins with a general curse on all
cowards, passing on to a direct accusation of the two who have failed
to back him in the robbery. Challenged to tell what has happened, he
begins his stream of 'incomprehensible lies,' flourishing his sword,
'hacked like a hand-saw'—we learn later how it came that way—as
evidence of his battle with a host of foes. One fact alone is clear in
Falstaff's mind: he had really exchanged blows with 'two rogues in
buckram,' but as he continues his story the two become four, the
four seven, the seven nine, and the nine eleven. Somewhere in the
course of his recital Falstaff seems to sense that he is speaking to un-

believers, perhaps, indeed, to men who know the truth. Accordingly he caps the climax with a lie of Hitlerian proportions, the tale of three knaves in Kendal-green—Robin Hood's livery—who let drive on him from behind when it was so dark you could not see your hand. This is too much even for Hal's feigned credulity and he interrupts Falstaff with a plain tale of what really happened. Another than Falstaff would have been overcome with shame, but he is ready with the instant retort: 'I knew ye as well as he that made ye. . . Was it for me to kill the heir-apparent?' I was a coward on instinct, he confesses, but only because I instinctively recognized the true Prince. Nothing, however, not even this witty evasion, is more characteristic of Falstaff than the shameless good humor with which he forgets his disgrace, hails the Prince and Poins as hearts of gold, and proposes a play extempore to pass the night away.

Whatever play Falstaff had in mind is prevented by the arrival of a nobleman come to summon Hal to Court in the morning. Falstaff suggests that Hal had better practice an answer to the horrible chiding that he will get from his father, and this precipitates another witcombat between the Prince and his Jester. On Hal's suggestion Falstaff poses as the King seated on a stool for a throne, a dagger in his hand for a scepter, and a cushion for a crown on his bald head. He opens his reproof in King Cambyses' vein, but quickly shifts into pure Lylian prose, which seems to prove that, however low he had sunk, Falstaff had once been familiar with the flowery speech of the Court. Reproving Hal for his bad behavior he bids him discard the company he keeps, all but the virtuous Falstaff. Thereupon Hal deposes him and, playing in turn the role of the angry King, denounces 'that grey iniquity . . . that vanity in years.' Falstaff feigns ignorance of the royal meaning, but when Hal pronounces the name of Falstaff, he answers in a masterpiece of confession and avoidance: 'The man I know . . . but to say I know more harm in him than in myself were to say more than I know. . . If sack and sugar be a fault, God help the wicked! . . . If to be fat be to be hated, then Pharaoh's lean kine are to be loved.' Moved with self-pity, he breaks at last into verse: 'banish all the rest,' he cries, 'but for old Jack Falstaff,

> Banish not him thy Harry's company:
> Banish plump Jack, and banish all the world.

The merry play is interrupted by a knocking at the door. The sheriff has come in search of the highwaymen, one of whom has been reported as 'a gross fat man.' For Falstaff to be identified and seized means death; modern readers are apt to forget that the old penalty for robbery was the rope and the gallows. Falstaff's appeal to the Prince is not couched in the language of a frightened coward: 'If you will deny the sheriff, so; [i.e. that's all right!] if not, let him enter. . . I hope I shall as soon be strangled with a halter as another.' The Prince, of course, stands by him, bids him hide behind the arras, and lies like a gentleman in his behalf. After the departure of the sheriff, Hal lifts the arras to find Falstaff 'fast asleep . . . and snorting like a horse,' whereupon he picks the sleeper's pocket, finding nothing there but a supper bill for a capon, several gallons of sack, and a half-penny worth of bread. And so the scene ends as it began with a joke played on the jester.

This tavern scene has been dwelt on at what may seem inordinate length, but it is in fact of prime importance. Here we see Falstaff in his glory as a voluble liar, a witty dodger, a clever actor, and finally as the trustful dependent of his master, who can snore in his sleep while death stands at the door. The delight the reader finds in this scene goes far to account for the charm that Falstaff exercised upon the Prince. Yet lest we should fall too much in love with the fat Knight, Shakespeare rounds it off with the pocket-picking that prepares the way for a following scene. The apologists for Falstaff seem to consider him mainly, if not entirely, as he appears here; but there are other sides to his character than this genial humor which expands so happily under the sun of the Prince's favor, and Shakespeare does not delay to present them.

When next we meet Falstaff he is suffering, apparently, from a hangover; it is the morning after the night in the tavern. He is so testy to Bardolph as to evoke a curse from that devoted follower, and he picks a quarrel with the Hostess in order, it seems, to evade the debt he owes her: a dozen shirts of fine linen and £24 in coin of the realm. He abuses the Prince and vows to cudgel him like a dog if he repeats the slander about Falstaff's seal ring, but when Hal enters, Falstaff resumes his role of jester and entertains him with a furious war of words with the Hostess. With Hal's avowal that he had picked Falstaff's pocket, the Knight's good humor promptly returns: 'Hostess, I forgive thee'—for what, one asks?—'Go make ready breakfast. . . Thou seest I am pacified.' The Prince reports his reconciliation with his father and presents Falstaff with a captain's commission in the campaign against the rebels. This, of course, is Shakespeare's device to get the jester out of the tavern into the wars. Falstaff's first comment on his new post is highly characteristic: 'God be thanked for these rebels; they offend none but the virtuous: I laud them, I praise them.' The war which offers Hal the chance to regain the honor he has lost in his father's eyes is to Falstaff merely an opportunity to better his fortunes. We shall soon see how he does it.

In a witty soliloquy (IV. ii. 12ff.) addressed to the audience Falstaff confesses that he has 'misused the King's press damnably.' Following a practice familiar to Elizabethans he has pressed into service only the men most reluctant to fight, has allowed them to buy themselves off— he has made over £300 by the deal—and has filled their places with the scum of the country: 'You would think that I had a hundred and fifty tattered Prodigals, lately come from swine keeping.' He is much ashamed of his recruits; not at all of his behavior. To Hal's comment on these 'pitiful rascals,' he replies in words that came to have a sad significance in later years; 'food for powder; they'll fill a pit as well as better.' And fill a pit they do, for at Shrewsbury this wretched company perished, if we may trust Falstaff's word, almost to the last man.

The last act shows Falstaff in the King's camp and on the battle-field. Shakespeare puts him there to serve as a foil on the one hand to Hotspur's insensate pursuit of honor, on the other to Hal's steadfast loyalty to King and country. Falstaff's famous soliloquy on honor pricks the bubble reputation with a cynical realism; it ignores the call of duty with a callous indifference to all but self-preservation. This is serious enough, but since Falstaff is Falstaff there must always be a strain of the comic in his speech and action. We get it first in his petition to Hal to bestride him if he is down in the fight, a task, the Prince jestingly replies, that only a colossus could perform. As it happens it is Hal who calls on Falstaff for aid when his sword is broken in the battle, but Falstaff, who needs a sword in case Percy comes his way, offers him instead his holster, which contains, instead of a pistol, a bottle of sack, Falstaff's cure for all ills. Later Falstaff appears on the scene when Hal and Hotspur are exchanging blows. He cheers on his patron as if he were in the ring at a prize fight, but he is quickly turned from a spectator into a performer by the sudden on-slaught of Douglas. 'Falstaff falls down as if he were dead,' reads the old stage direction. This is simply putting into practice Falstaff's resolve: 'Give me life; which if I can save, so.' There is no need to turn his action into such buffoonery as Morgann saw on the stage. 'The painful comedian,' he writes, 'lies spread on his belly and . . .

covers himself all over with his robe as with a shell . . . in addition to which he alternately lifts up and depresses and dodges his head and looks to the one side and the other.' Shakespeare surely instructed his Falstaff to lie 'as if he were dead,' for the Prince turns from the corpse of Hotspur to speak his epitaph:

> Poor Jack, farewell!
> I could have better spar'd a better man.

As Hal goes out Falstaff rises from the dead with a speech of self-congratulation: 'The better part of valour is discretion; in the which better part, I have saved my life.' Suddenly a horrible suspicion crosses his mind: what if Hotspur had practiced this same discretion and should rise to confront him. To prevent such a misfortune Falstaff gives the corpse another wound and resolves to claim for himself the honor of the famous rebel's death. He hoists the body on his back and is waddling off when he is met by Hal and Prince John. To Hal's exclamation: 'Why, Percy I kill'd myself, and saw thee dead,' Falstaff replies, with his characteristic trick of turning the tables: 'Lord, Lord, how this world is given to lying.' Both Percy and he, Falstaff asserts, were down and out of breath, but both rose together and 'fought a long hour by Shrewsbury clock.' That he expected Hal to believe this lie is doubtful; Prince John certainly is skeptical, but Hal with his careless disdain of personal glory laughs it off. In fact, if the lie will help Falstaff along, he will back it up, and Falstaff ends his part in this play with the words: 'He that rewards me, God reward him! If I do grow great . . . I'll purge, and leave sack, and live cleanly, as a nobleman should do.' How he keeps his vow we shall see in Part II.

The comedy of this serious chronicle play has been furnished by the action, the words, and the character of Falstaff. There are scenes where Falstaff's behavior: his bellowing flight from the scene of the robbery, his snoring sleep while his pocket is picked, his feigned death, and his lugging off of Percy's body, is designed to provoke laughter, more readily, perhaps, from the spectator in the pit than from the reader. Such business, however, is but a minor factor in the comedy of this play. Falstaff's speeches are far more amusing than his actions. It is worth noting that for this speech Shakespeare employs the proper comic vehicle of prose. Compared with the complete absence of prose in the preceding histories, *King John* and *Richard II,* the proportion of prose to verse in *King Henry IV Part I* is quite remarkable; it amounts to nearly half of the play, and with a few exceptions—Hotspur speaks prose at times with serio-comic effect—it is confined to the Falstaff scenes. And in these the prose of Falstaff attracts into its circle, so to speak, the diction of his interlocutors; Hal, for example, always speaks prose to Falstaff as he does verse in his serious scenes.

The comic value of Falstaff's speech depends far less on the puns, the malapropisms, and the threadbare clichés of earlier Clowns than on its inexhaustible flow, its unexpected turns, its deliberate parodies of courtly speech or scriptural language. All this, of course, reveals, as it is meant to, the character of the speaker. 'No prose,' says a critic, who yet maintains that Falstaff is a liar, a coward, and a butt, 'is so heavily charged with the magnetism of a personality.' It is just this personal magnetism that charms Prince Henry in the play as it does the reader in the study. Falstaff's sins of omission and commission are forgotten in view of his absurd pretensions, his fluent self-excuse, his whimsical melancholy, and the quick wit which extricates him from apparently inescapable dilemmas. He so abounds in good cheer, good fellowship, and inextinguishable good humor that we take him home to our hearts. This is the Falstaff of Part I. Had the rejection scene come at the end of this play we could hardly have forgiven Henry or the author who wrote the words for him to speak.

The progress of Falstaff through Part II might well be characterized as his decline and fall. He enters on his first scene attended by a tiny page—the smallest boy, probably, in Shakespeare's company—staggering under the weight of Falstaff's sword and buckler, a child who has been presented to Falstaff by the Prince in mockery of his new gentility. The contrast with his first scene in Part I is very plain; instead of consorting with highwaymen Falstaff is living at his ease in London sending his water to a doctor to get a diagnosis of his ailments, trying to wheedle a merchant out of twenty-five yards of satin for new clothes, and writing familiarly to Prince John, the Earl of Westmoreland, and old Mistress Ursula, whom he had long since promised to marry. Confronted by the Lord Chief Justice, who has a bone to pick with him over the robbery, Falstaff's behavior is an amusing compound of evasion and effrontery. He has the insolence to remind the Judge of the blow that Hal had given him, declares—believe it who list—that he has rebuked the Prince for it, and ends by asking the grave senior to lend him £1,000. Falstaff is never wittier nor more fluent, but the sunny good humor of the tavern scene in

Part I has changed to a complacent attitude of exploitation. He apparently thinks that on the strength of his renown in battle—even the Judge thinks that he has done well at Shrewsbury—he can, as the phrase goes, get away with murder.

This is very evident in his next scene. Worn out by Falstaff's continual drain on her purse—he owes her, she declares, about £65— Mistress Quickly, the Hostess of Part I, arranges for his arrest by a bum-bailiff and his man. Falstaff is in no mood to submit to these minions of the law; he and Bardolph draw on them, and a scuffle ensues in the best tradition of horseplay on the Elizabethan stage. The bailiff bawls for help; Mistress Quickly dances and screams about the fighters, and the page paddles her backside—'catastrophe' is the word in the text—with the hilt of his little dagger. The brawl is stopped by the Chief Justice, who enters guarded, and Mistress Quickly pours out her woes to him in a torrential flow of words. We learn from it among other things that Hal had lately broken Falstaff's head for comparing the King to a singing man at Windsor. The point of this comparison is no longer obvious, but it must have been most offensive to provoke Hal's action; Shakespeare did not let Falstaff take such liberties with his patron nor Hal react in this manner in Part I. Furthermore Mistress Quickly declares that when she dressed his wound on this occasion, Falstaff promised to marry her, kissed her, and borrowed thirty shillings more. Falstaff's reply is a characteristic evasion of the issue; 'My lord,' he says, 'this is a poor mad soul; and she says up and down the town that her eldest son is like you.' There is a trace of malice in this speech, a new note in Falstaff; but it fails of its effect upon the Judge. Under his sharp rebuke Falstaff draws Quickly aside and makes his peace with her in such a way that the intended arrest ends in a further loan of £10 and an invitation to supper with Doll Tearsheet, a lady whose profession is indicated by her name. We have heard before of Falstaff's imposition on the Hostess and of his familiarity with loose women, but now we see this behavior in action, and seeing is believing. The scene ends with the Judge's summary dismissal of Falstaff with the words: 'Now the Lord lighten thee! thou art a great fool.' Falstaff has been called many names in Part I, but never before a fool. Yet that is how he appears to a dignitary charged with the affairs of the kingdom.

The next scene introduces Hal for the first time in the play. He is back from the war, weary, and depressed by the news of his father's grave illness. To the cynical remark of Poins that as heir-apparent he could hardly regret the King's condition, Hal replies with a little outburst of temper: 'Thou thinkest me as far in the devil's book as thou and Falstaff for obduracy and persistency: let the end try the man.' This is a significant forward-looking speech; Hal has never before spoken of or to Falstaff without a good-natured jest. In this mood he receives an impertinent letter from Falstaff and, learning that the Knight is to dine at the Boar's Head with Mistress Quickly and Doll, he proposes that he and Poins surprise them in disguise. The parallel to the surprise at Gadshill in Part I is evident; the result of the encounter is very different.

The tavern scene which follows shows Falstaff at his best and worst. Never is he wittier or more self-possessed; never before has he appeared in such low company as that of the harlot, Doll, and the drunken Pistol. The row in which Pistol gets involved with Doll is stopped by Falstaff, who with Bardolph's aid hustles him from the room. Some of Falstaff's lovers have cited this action as a proof of his innate valor, but after all it does not take much courage for a captain backed by a corporal to dispose of a drunken subordinate. As a reward Doll sits on Falstaff's knee, kisses him, and tries to pump him about the Prince and Poins. They're both pretty much of a muchness, answers Falstaff; young fellows of a weak mind and a strong body, better for boy's games than for anything else. Hal and Poins who have entered unobserved, disguised as drawers, overhear this unflattering description and advance to charge Falstaff to his face with slander. But Falstaff as ever is adept at evasion; he has indeed dispraised the Prince, but it was before the wicked, that the wicked might not fall in love with him. This was the part of a true friend and the King owes him thanks for it. Falling in with the jest, Hal asks if the present company, the 'virtuous gentlewoman,' Doll, the Hostess, and honest Bardolph, are to be accounted wicked. Falstaff, of course, is ready with an answer and manages deftly to shift the question to Dame Quickly's violation of a sumptuary law. At this moment a messenger enters with news of the King's arrival at Westminster and of the dozen captains he had passed searching every tavern for Sir John Falstaff. There is a quick revulsion in the Prince's mood; he blames himself for wasting precious time in a jest, and bids Falstaff an abrupt good-night. This is the last time the two are on the stage together till the rejection scene, and it might well be asserted that Hal's break with his old jester comes just at this point. Falstaff, to be sure, does not think so; he brags of his merit to the women, prepares to follow the captains, who have at last tracked him down, but, apparently, takes time out for a last session, off-stage, with Doll.

The scene now shifts to the country estate of Master Shallow, Justice of the Peace, who is preparing to receive Falstaff and furnish him with his little quota of men for the King's war. The main purpose of the scene is to show Falstaff in action as a recruiting officer. Under the eye of Shallow he picks four likely men, but as soon as he is off the stage the two best men buy themselves off with a couple of pounds apiece slipped into the hand of Corporal Bardolph, which that faithful retainer dutifully hands over to his master. As a result Falstaff dismisses the two, presses in their place the ragged Wart, whom he had scornfully rejected on first inspection, and prepares to leave, one man short of his prescribed quota but with money in his pocket. The parallel with the King's press scene in Part I is palpably designed by Shakespeare, but he knows that to see Falstaff in action would carry deeper conviction than to listen to his jesting account of his behavior. We might laugh off the first scene; the second is a bit too bad. There is, moreover, a sting in the tail of this scene. Shallow, who has flooded Falstaff with tales of their old wild life in London—'and every third word a lie'—now proposes to visit him at Court. Falstaff cheerfully agrees, but on the old man's departure indulges in a satiric description of Shallow's former life in London in as witty and malicious a speech as any in the play, and goes off with a vow we know he will keep to return and make his profit of the old fool.

Before Falstaff's return to Shallow a scene intervenes on which some stress has been laid by his apologists, his capture of Coleville of the Dale, described by Falstaff as 'a most furious knight and valorous enemy.' We need not take Falstaff's word for it; Coleville, a fugitive from the dispersed rebel army, apparently decided to take a chance by surrendering to so renowned a soldier as Falstaff. The interview between Prince John and Falstaff which follows is marked by cool disapproval on the Prince's part and unblushing effrontery on Falstaff's. He recognizes that this sober-minded boy does not love him and compares him most unfavorably with Hal, whose courage he ascribes to frequent potations of good sherris sack.

With the beginning of the last act we find Falstaff back again with Shallow, but, be it noted, after the gravely beautiful scenes of the fourth act which present the final reconciliation between the dying King and his repentant son. Falstaff's boast that he will 'devise matter enough out of this Shallow to keep Prince Harry in continual laughter' shows that he still plans to play his role as the Prince's Jester. But this Prince has already become King; this 'fellow that never had the ache in his shoulders' has solemnly accepted the heavy weight of the crown. Before this news reaches Falstaff, however, we have another interposed scene which shows Henry as King, calming the fears of his brothers and adopting the Chief Justice, who had some reason to doubt his reception, as a father to his youth and his chief councilor. This alternation of scenes is, of course, carefully designed to contrast the grave reality with Falstaff's vain dreams.

At an after-supper banquet in Shallow's orchard where his fellow-justice, Master Silence, makes the night merry with song, Pistol appears with the great news: 'Sir John, thy tender lambkin now is king.' Falstaff's response is immediate and determined; he will no longer be the Jester to a wild prince, but 'Fortune's steward,' a ruler in the kingdom: 'Master Robert Shallow, choose what office thou wilt in the land, 'tis thine.' He and Shallow will ride all night to London: 'I know the young king is sick for me. Let us take any man's horses; the laws of England are at my commandment. Happy are they which have been my friends, and woe unto my lord chief justice!' This is an exhibition of *hubris,* the over-weening insolence that, according to old belief, brings inevitably in its train *nemesis,* the vengeance of the angry gods. Such an exhibition is, perhaps, more fitting to tragedy than to comedy, but we should remember that, in spite of Falstaff, the two-part play of *Henry IV* is not a comedy. Certainly the mad exultation of Falstaff is meant not only to prepare us for, but to justify, his rejection by the King.

Before the rejection there is a brief scene of lively action in which Dame Quickly and Doll Tearsheet are dragged to jail as accomplices of Pistol in a case of manslaughter. The laws of England which Falstaff thought were at his commandment are here seen in active operation against his old associates. The scene looks forward to what follows, for when Pistol tells Falstaff that his Doll is in 'base durance,' the Knight confidently replies: 'I will deliver her,' a boast that immediately precedes his own arrest and despatch to prison. To us there is nothing very funny in this scene, but it is in the true pattern of the old Morals, where at the end the wicked were haled off to condign punishment amid the laughter of the audience.

The rejection scene has been so often discussed as if it were a historic event like the surrender at Yorktown, Henry's rebuke has been so bitterly condemned as 'ungenerous and dishonest,' that it may be well to look at it for a moment as it was played on Shakespeare's stage. It opens with two grooms strewing rushes; the Company wants the stage to look fresh and clean, for they are about to put on the best show possible. And that should be rather a good show. Some years later at the Globe their new play, *Henry VIII*, was 'set forth,' says a contemporary, 'with many extraordinary circumstances of pomp and majesty.' Falstaff and his party enter on the empty stage and Falstaff bids Shallow stand by him: 'I will make the King do you grace.' There is a roar of voices backstage and the royal party enters from the King's coronation. It consists, the old stage direction tells us, of King Henry, his three brothers, and the Lord Chief Justice, with, probably, the whole strength of the company following in the procession. Falstaff hails the King with a cheer as 'my royal Hal!' reinforced by a yell from Pistol. In a vain effort to avoid a public scandal, Henry bids the Chief Justice speak to Falstaff, but the Knight shoulders the old man aside and addresses the King in terms of intimate familiarity. Then and only then comes the famous—or as some modern critics have it 'infamous'—rebuke:

> I know thee not, old man: fall to thy prayers.

Halfway through his speech Henry seems to catch a glimpse of one of Falstaff's witty evasions rising to disarm him, but he crushes it back sharply:

> Reply not to me with a fool-born jest.

It is hard to see how in a drama anything but so severe and public a rebuke could have clinched the fate of Falstaff. Bradley suggests that Henry might have broken with him in a private interview; Charlton that Falstaff might have been 'allowed a death-bed scene' before the coronation. These are devices that a novelist might employ in re-telling the story; they are essentially undramatic. The old tradition, reinforced by the stage presentation in *The Famous Victories*, declared that the King broke with his loose companions at once and publicly. It was Shakespeare's task to make this breach as dramatically effective as possible.

One feature especially in the scene has deeply grieved the tender-hearted modernists, that Falstaff should be carried to the Fleet by his old enemy, the Chief Justice. But consider again the situation on the stage. The King and his train sweep out; far from being stunned by the rebuke, Falstaff turns to Shallow to assure him that all was but a pretense: 'I shall be sent for soon at night.' Action added to public reproof is needed to demolish Falstaff's cloud-castle, and the King's last word has ordered the Chief Justice to take action. The Fleet, moreover, was not in Shakespeare's time the filthy jail of later years; it was, on the contrary, a place of detention to which Queen Elizabeth occasionally sent courtiers and even ladies who had offended her. In *The Famous Victories*, in fact, Prince Hal himself is sent there for striking the Chief Justice. Nor need we think that Falstaff was long detained there: 'I will hear you soon,' says the Judge as he cuts short Falstaff's wild protest. Henry's sentence involved not imprisonment, but banishment from the Court. The Fleet, so Shakespeare's hearers must have thought, would hold Falstaff until the conditions were arranged. Shakespeare's audience needed to be assured that there would be no more such scenes between the King and Falstaff.

Finally in Shakespeare, as in *The Famous Victories*, the King's speech holds out a promise of 'competence of life' along with 'advancement' in case of reform. Reform in Falstaff's case one fears is hopeless. Shakespeare certainly had no intention of letting Falstaff die in prison. Indeed there is reason to believe that when Shakespeare finished this play he intended to bring Falstaff back on the stage again: 'If you be not too much cloyed with fat meat,' says the dancer who spoke the Epilogue, 'our humble author will continue the story, with Sir John in it, and make you merry with fair Katharine of France: where, for anything I know, Falstaff shall die of a sweat.' This surely implies that Shakespeare at one time meant to take Falstaff to the French war along with the King and, perhaps, let him die there, of a sweat, of over-exertion in battle or, more likely, of the so-called sweating sickness. The implied promise was not fulfilled; it may be that Shakespeare came to realize how far Falstaff would be out of place in the heroic-epic play of *Henry V*. Certainly another Falstaffian discourse on honor at Agincourt would clash harshly with Henry's words:

If it be a sin to covet honour,
I am the most offending soul alive.

Another more realistic explanation has been proposed. Kempe, it is suggested, as the leading comedian of Shakespeare's company, would normally have played the part of Falstaff. He and Burbage as Prince Hal, playing up to each other in the tavern scenes, would surely have brought down the house. Accordingly when Shakespeare

half-promised to take Falstaff to France in his next play, he expected
Kempe to play the Knight's part again. But sometime in 1599 before
Henry V was staged, Kempe suddenly for some unknown reason deserted Shakespeare's company. An audience accustomed to seeing
the famous clown as Falstaff would, perhaps, have resented the appearance of an inferior actor. If this be true, it is clear that Shakespeare quickly changed his plan, deleted the part of Falstaff from his
manuscript, and wrote in the famous death scene of the old favorite.
And that scene demands a brief consideration.

Falstaff's name is not even mentioned in the first act of *Henry V,*
which deals with preparations for the war in France. The second act
opens with a comic quarrel between Pistol and a new character, Nym,
a man of few words and stock phrases. It is interrupted by the entrance of Falstaff's page, who reports that his master is very sick
and desires the attendance of Mistress Quickly. This estimable woman,
who once looked forward to becoming Lady Falstaff, has declined into
a marriage with Pistol, now installed as Host in her tavern. It is here,
not in the Fleet or another prison, that Falstaff is attended by his old
mistress in the bed from which he never rose. The received opinion
seems to be that Falstaff died there of a broken heart, and this seems
soundly based upon Shakespeare's text. Dame Quickly says: 'The
King has killed his heart,' and Pistol re-echoes, 'His heart is fracted and
corroborate.' Unfortunately for the sentimentalists the phrase, 'to
kill the heart,' is an Elizabethan expression meaning little more than
to dishearten, to abash. Autolycus, while picking the Clown's pocket,
says to him: 'Offer me no money . . . that kills my heart,' and in
Love's Labour's Lost we are told that the ladies' contempt will 'kill
the speaker's heart,' i.e. put the page off his memorized speech. It is
a mistake to translate Elizabethan into modern English. Pistol's words,
moreover, simply repeat Quickly's in his own bombastic manner of
speech. Quickly's diagnosis of Falstaff's complaint as a 'burning
quotidian tertian' seems a more likely one. Perhaps it was a consequence of the pox or the gout which Falstaff long since had confessed
to be troubling him.

Whatever the disease was, the old sinner made a good end. He called
on God, blamed his errors on sack and women, and babbled of green
fields, perhaps recalling the green pastures of the Psalm he had
chanted as a choir boy. He 'went away an it had been any christom
child . . . ev'n at the turning o' the tide.' His epitaph is spoken by
Bardolph, his follower for more than thirty years: 'Would I were

with him, wheresome'er he is, either in heaven or in hell!' That, we may take it, is Shakespeare's farewell to the greatest comic character he ever created, a farewell not without a trace of pathos and regret.

The presence of the farce comedy, *The Merry Wives of Windsor*, at this point in a discussion of comedy in Shakespeare's histories is due, of course, to the reappearance of Falstaff, who has here moved out of the field of war and courtly life into the bourgeois atmosphere of an English country town. An old tradition, generally accepted today, gives a good and sufficient reason for his reappearance. Queen Elizabeth, we are told, was so delighted with the character of Falstaff in the two parts of *King Henry IV* that she commanded Shakespeare to write a play showing him in love; and she was, moreover, so eager to see this play that she ordered Shakespeare to finish it in a fortnight. We need not accept this time limit literally; but there can be little doubt that this play, so different from the romantic comedies of about the same time, was written in haste to gratify the royal whim.

The generally accepted date for *The Merry Wives* is 1598-9. Whether it precedes or follows *King Henry V* is uncertain. There is some reason to believe that it follows and that the Queen's disappointment in not finding her favorite alive in *Henry V* led to her demand. Falstaff's reported death in *Henry V* would no more preclude his reappearance on the stage than the reported death of Sherlock Holmes at the Reichenbach Fall forbade his return to life in time to solve the mysterious murder of the Hon. Ronald Adair. It is quite impossible to fit Falstaff's doings in *The Merry Wives* into any reconstructed story of his life. In *Henry V* he dies just before the King's invasion of France; in *The Merry Wives* we find him living at his ease in Windsor some time, apparently, after his rejection by the King. But, as has already been said, Falstaff is not a historical person calling for a biography, but a character in a play, and this play, *The Merry Wives,* should be judged on its own merits, not as a chapter in a biography of Falstaff. A study of this play as a unique specimen of Shakespearean comedy with special reference to the characterization of Falstaff should be more profitable than an argument over its exact date.

The task that Majesty imposed on Shakespeare, if we accept the tradition, presented a double difficulty. To show Falstaff in love, in any true sense of the word, was probably impossible even for Shakespeare. To show him engaged in an amorous intrigue with a woman, or women, of somewhat better class than Doll Tearsheet was quite possible, but this would involve the construction of a complicated plot, never Shakespeare's forte, and the time allowed him, even if we reject the fortnight of tradition, was short enough. If we know anything of Shakespeare's method of work, we may imagine him under the stress of the Queen's demand racking his brain for material of a sort which he could dramatize in such shape as to satisfy his royal mistress.

There is no known source for *The Merry Wives,* but the interesting suggestion has been made that under this stress Shakespeare pulled out from the archives of his company the manuscript of a play they had performed some years before, *The Jealous Comedy,* produced as a new play at the Rose on 5 January 1593. This he is supposed to have rewritten to meet his immediate need. Unfortunately *The Jealous Comedy* has vanished into the dark backward and abysm of time; we know nothing of it but its name. A few years earlier, however, c. 1590, there had been published a little collection of stories, *Tarlton's News out of Purgatory,* one of which, *The Two Lovers of Pisa,* bears a striking resemblance to the main plot of *The Merry Wives.* In this tale a young gentleman falls in love with a married woman and confides his passion to an old doctor, unaware that the doctor was the lady's husband. The jealous doctor encourages him to push his suit, hoping to catch him in the act. He does, in fact, surprise the lover thrice in his wife's company, but the lover is saved by the quick wit of the lady, who conceals him once in a dry-vat, once between two ceilings, and the third time has him carried out in a chest supposedly full of valuable papers. In each case the lover tells the husband how he had escaped and that he means to try again. At last the doctor gets him to relate his adventures at a family dinner, so as to expose the intrigue, but, tipped off by the lady, the lover ends by declaring the whole story a fiction invented to mock the jealous husband. Soon thereafter the doctor dies, apparently of mortification, and the lover enjoys the lady. This tale, we know, is an adaptation of one of the stories in Straparola's *Piaccevoli Notti,* itself, apparently, a retelling of an older tale in *Il Pecorone.*[1] It is, of course, possible that *The*

[1] In *Il Pecorone* the lady hides the lover under a heap of dried clothes and the husband, who has learned this from the lover, attacks the clothes and pierces them with his sword—compare the behavior of Ford in *The Merry Wives.*

Jealous Comedy was a dramatization of this Tarlton story. If so, we may be fairly sure that the denouement was different. Italian stories made a jest of adultery; the Elizabethan dramatic code, while allowing married women to skate over very thin ice, brought them in the end safe to shore and left their suitors struggling in the water. If *The Jealous Comedy* was indeed a dramatic version of the Tarlton tale and ended in this fashion, it would just have suited Shakespeare's purpose; it would have let him present Falstaff embarked in amorous intrigue to please the Queen, and yet exposed in the end as the laughing-stock of the company, even as on his first appearance he is exposed and mocked by the Prince and Poins.

One other guess may be hazarded about *The Jealous Comedy.* Any dramatization of the Tarlton story would naturally set it against a background of middle-class London life in an atmosphere of realistic comedy. This type of play, deriving ultimately from the comic scenes in the old Morals and Interludes, was very popular in Shakespeare's day, and was especially cultivated by his contemporary, Ben Jonson. It seems that Shakespeare, on the other hand, disliked this type of play; he preferred to set his comedies in the forest of Arden or in some vague Illyria. He would naturally therefore shift the scene of action from the streets of London to the pleasant country town of Windsor. Here he could indulge his own love of country life and country sports: deer-stealing, hawking, and greyhound racing, as is shown by one allusion after another in *The Merry Wives.*

Wherever Shakespeare found the material for his new play, he contrived to fashion it into a comedy that was an instant stage success. So successful was it, in fact, that it was promptly pirated. In January 1602 John Busby, who two years earlier had published a scandalously bad version of *Henry V,* entered a claim to *The Merry Wives* in the Stationers' Register. He at once transferred his rights, such as they were, to Arthur Johnson, who in the same year published the play with a flourish of trumpets on the title-page:

A Most pleasaunt and excellent conceited Comedie, of Syr John Falstaffe, and the merrie Wives of Windsor. Entermixed with sundrie variable and pleasing humors, of Syr Hugh the Welch Knight [sic!], Justice Shallow, and his wise Cousin M. Slender. With the swaggering vaine of Auncient Pistol, and Corporall Nym. By William Shakespeare. As it hath bene

divers times Acted by the right Honorable my Lord Chamber-
laines servants. Both before her Majestie, and else-where.

That flourish should have sold the book like hot cakes, but it apparently failed to do so; this quarto text had to wait seventeen years before it was reprinted. Probably the reading public soon recognized
that it was a travesty rather than a true report of Shakespeare's play.
It is the shortest and most corrupt of the stolen and surreptitious
copies; it omits some of the most entertaining passages, and appears
to be a badly memorized version of a text cut down for a special performance by one of the actors who took part in it. Yet this wretched
quarto contains more than once genuine Shakespearean lines which
for some reason had dropped out of the company's play-book when it
was published in the Folio. The most interesting thing about the
quarto version is that it seems at times to throw back to a comedy of
London life such as we imagine *The Jealous Comedy* to have been.
Perhaps the pirate actor had once taken part in that play and eked
out his imperfect memory of *The Merry Wives* by what he remembered of the earlier work. It contains also a distinct allusion to Count
Mumpellgart's visit to England, which would have been good for a
laugh in 1592, but was old stuff when Shakespeare wrote *The Merry
Wives*.

The Folio text itself is not altogether reliable. It has apparently
been revised from time to time; the profane oaths with which the
quarto is plentifully garnished have been elided, and one curious
change must be due to the interposition of the Master of the Revels.
In the quarto when the disguised Ford first calls on Falstaff, he sends
in his name, along with a cup of sack, as Master Brook, and Falstaff
replies: 'Such Brooks are welcome to me that o'erflow such liquor.'
But Brooke was the family name of the Lord Cobham who had already
taken offense at Shakespeare's use of the name of Oldcastle. Perhaps
Shakespeare forgot this in his haste; but when the play was rehearsed
before the licenser for a Court performance that official remembered
it and insisted upon a change. Accordingly in the Folio the name always appears as Broome. That spoils Falstaff's pun; but the licenser
cared less for a joke than he did for the susceptibility of Lord Cobham.
Modern editions, of course, restore Brook to the text. The poetic
eulogy of the Order of the Garter in the final scene appears only in the
Folio text; it was probably written for a special performance at

Windsor Castle, where the choir boys of the Chapel could be impressed to play the singing fairies.

There has been much, and mostly derogatory, comment on the character of Falstaff as he appears in *The Merry Wives*. Charlton, indeed, allows himself to say that in this play Shakespeare slaughters his own offspring in a spirit of cynical revenge. A brief comment upon the scenes in which Falstaff appears may serve to show how far his falling-off is due to the exigencies of a borrowed plot, how far, perhaps, to Shakespeare's careless haste.

Falstaff enters in the first scene to answer the charge preferred by Justice Shallow that he has killed the judge's deer and beaten his game-keepers.[2] Here, certainly, is the Falstaff that we know, a jolly, shameless rioter, quick of speech and clever in evasion. The kiss he gives to Mrs. Ford upon her entrance is quite in keeping with his character. This scene must have been written while the old Falstaff was still fresh in Shakepeare's mind, before he began to transform him into the dupe required by the plot. It may be noted in passing that nothing further is made of the Shallow-Falstaff quarrel; Shakespeare drops it as he passes on to the main action.

When this action, Falstaff's pursuit of the merry wives, starts in the third scene, a change seems to have come over the Knight. He begins by discarding his followers to save his expenses at the Windsor inn. This does not seem like the Falstaff whom *Henry IV Part II* introduces swaggering along with a page at his heels, buying a horse at Smithfield, and bargaining for twenty-two yards of satin, although at the time he has but seven groats and twopence in his purse. Nor is it easy to believe that such rascals as Pistol and Nym would loftily decline to carry Falstaff's love letters. The scene reads somewhat like a hasty rewriting of an old play in which a London gentleman, reduced to poverty, plans to better his estate by tapping the purses of two merchants' wives, while his honest serving-men refuse such base employment. This suspicion is strengthened by the Host's request to Falstaff: 'Speak scholarly and wisely.' Scholarly speech is the last that one would

[2] The deer-stealing business has long been connected with the tradition of Shakespeare's own youthful poaching, and there can be little doubt that Shakespeare's assignment to Shallow of the arms of Sir Thomas Lucy, three luces argent, was meant to raise a laugh from a courtly audience at the expense of a puritanical country gentleman, well known for his interest in preserving game. This does not mean, however, that Shallow in this play, still less in *King Henry IV Part II*, is a deliberate caricature of Sir Thomas. It is a passing jest driven home by Parson Evans' pronunciation of 'luce' as 'louse.'

expect from the mouth of Falstaff, and the last person to expect it of him would be the Host, who had known him in his hours of ease at his inn. Can there be here a trace of the *Pecorone* tale in which the suitor is a student, a character who may have found his way into *The Jealous Comedy?* A like suspicion is roused by Mrs. Ford's account of Falstaff's earlier behavior to her: 'He would not swear; praised women's modesty; and gave such orderly and well-behaved reproof to all un-comeliness, that I would have sworn his disposition would have gone to the truth of his words.' This is Shakespeare's familiar device of characterizing one person in a play by the words of another, and certainly this bit of characterization better suits the figure of a hypocritical scholar than such a tavern-haunter as Falstaff. The disguised Ford strikes the same note when he addresses Falstaff with the words: 'Sir, I hear you are a scholar,' and later declares: 'You are a gentleman . . . generally allowed for your many war-like, court-like, and learned preparations.' In this interview Ford seems to predominate; Falstaff responds for the most part with brief phrases and queries, save for his strangely pedantic reply to Ford's request: 'Methinks you prescribe to yourself very preposterously.' Only at the end of the interview does the true Falstaffian strain break out in his tirade of abuse: 'Hang him, mechanical salt-butter rogue! I will stare him out of his wits; I will awe him with my cudgel: it shall hang like a meteor o'er the cuckold's horns.'

We do not see Falstaff again till the third scene of the third act when he pays his first call on Mrs. Ford. He salutes her with a line from *Astrophel and Stella,* a little out of character, perhaps, but he drops into his old role again in his abuse of the absent Mrs. Page. He hides behind the arras to avoid her as he had done to escape the Sheriff at the Boar's Head Tavern. His creeping into the buck-basket might be compared to his playing dead at Shrewsbury, but there is a difference between his natural fear of the doughty Douglas and his panic at the approach of Mr. Ford. His mode of escape comes from the old tale, but it is elaborated here for comic effect when Ford stops the servants who are carrying him out. In the story the suitor escapes while the jealous husband sleeps, but Falstaff is not allowed to escape unharmed; the servants throw him into the Thames 'with as little remorse as they would have drowned a blind bitch's puppies.' In Falstaff's soliloquy (III. v) where these words occur and later, in his account to the disguised Ford of his experience, we get the true Falstaff, glorying in the eloquence with which he describes the event and chuckling as of old over his corporosity. The unquenchable humor of the fat Knight shines through every line.

There is a sad relapse when Falstaff visits Mrs. Ford the second time and greets her with a strangely formal speech: 'Your sorrow hath eaten up my sufferance. I see you are obsequious in your love.' He has little time, however, for such speeches, for Mrs. Page runs in again to announce the approach of Ford with a search party. Here we get a bit of business, apparently derived from the *Pecorone* tale, introduced to ridicule Ford's causeless jealousy. As the servants once more carry out the basket, Ford stops them, believing that Falstaff is again hidden there, and with wild cries pulls out all the clothes in a vain search for his wife's lover. Meanwhile the merry wives dress up Falstaff like the old fat witch of Brainford and escort him solicitously from the house; they do not save him, however, from a sound beating at Ford's hands, a beating administered by the very man over whose head Falstaff had boasted that his cudgel would hang like a meteor.

This scene is followed shortly (IV. iv) by a conference between the wives and their husbands, in which the ladies reveal Falstaff's attempts upon their honor and plot with their husbands to give him a third rendezvous and there expose him openly, a denouement that probably derives from the lost play. Before this, however, another scene shows Falstaff at his inn where he has stripped off his disguise and talks in his own person with Slender's man Simple and with Mistress Quickly. Here Falstaff is himself again both in his mockery of the foolish Simple and in his speech to Quickly. She has come, she says, 'from the two parties' with a letter; 'The devil take one of the parties and his dam the other!' answers Falstaff, and he goes on to brag that only his 'admirable dexterity' in playing the part of the old woman had saved him from public shame in the town's stocks.

We learn in the first scene of the last act that Falstaff has fallen for the wives' plot and has agreed to meet them in Windsor Park at midnight disguised as the ghost of Herne the hunter, with horns on his head, symbolic of the horns of cuckoldry he planned to set upon the husbands. That the wily old Knight should have been so easily trapped into such an absurd plan is inherent in the plot; it is quite out of keeping with the Falstaff of earlier plays. There follows a brief interview with Ford, still disguised as Brook, in which Falstaff tells him of his past misfortune and his expected success in his new venture. Once more we hear the accents of the true Falstaff, more especially in his old trick of scriptural allusion: 'He beat me grievously, in the shape of a woman; for in the shape of man, Master Brook, I fear not Goliath with a weaver's beam, because I know also life is a shuttle.'

The denouement has been carefully planned for stage effect. Falstaff enters with a stag's head on his shoulders, which may have reminded some of Shakespeare's audience of the 'translation' of Bully Bottom. The wives meet him as arranged and he begins to make love to them, when suddenly—according to the old stage direction—there is a 'noise of horns' and the women run off. Instantly Falstaff is surrounded by a crowd of boys, twenty at least, dressed like fairies. As he cowers in fright they test his innocence by putting the tapers they carry to his fingers' ends. He howls with pain and they dance about, singing and pinching him—the scene closely resembles one in *Endimion*—till at a 'noise of hunting within,' i.e. a flourish of horns back-stage, they run off. Falstaff rises and pulls off the stag's head only to be confronted by the wives and their husbands. The public exposure is complete and the quartet mock Falstaff in a running fire of jests and laughing abuse, which is, perhaps, a little long drawn out. What is remarkable in this scene is the complete collapse of Falstaff's morale. One recalls how once he had laughed himself out of the dilemma in which the Prince and Poins had pinned him and how he had held his head up after his rejection by the King. Now he can only falter: 'And these are not fairies? I was three or four times in the thought they were not fairies; and yet the guiltiness of my mind . . . drove the grossness of the foppery into a received belief. . . See now how wit may be made a Jack-a-lent, when 'tis upon ill employment!' Neither the sentiment nor the words befit the true Falstaff; they are more suitable to the scholar of the old story. The comedy then ends, as a comedy should, in reconciling mirth. Ford renounces his humor of jealousy, and Page, the good-natured husband, joins his wife in an invitation to Falstaff to go home with them all to eat a posset and to 'laugh this sport o'er by a country fire.'

This analysis of the character of Falstaff as he appears in scene after scene of *The Merry Wives* seems to show clearly enough a striking inconsistency in characterization. In action Falstaff is almost always the butt and dupe, a very different character from the domineering Falstaff of *King Henry IV Part II*. In speech, on the other hand, barring the few exceptions noted when he seems to fall out of his role, he constantly recalls the Falstaff of the histories. It is hardly possible to account for this inconsistency except on the hypothesis that Shakespeare rewrote hastily and under pressure an old play in which some form of the Tarlton story was presented in dramatic form. The Queen's demand forced Shakespeare to present Falstaff as an amorous suitor; the borrowed plot and the Elizabethan convention forced him to show this suitor as a baffled dupe. But since the suitor was Falstaff, Shakespeare, being Shakespeare, could not but endow him with that gift of speech, fluent, witty, allusive, and rhythmical in which the fat Knight excels all other Shakespearean creations. And, finally, it cannot be too emphatically affirmed that the inconsistency apparent to the student in the study is practically nonexistent to the auditor in the theater. The role of Falstaff is in more ways than one a fat part for the actor; *The Merry Wives* has been from the beginning a success upon the stage, and its success is mainly due to the comic character of Falstaff.

MINOR FIGURES IN THE FALSTAFF PLAYS

Falstaff once remarked with perfect truth: 'I am not only witty, but the cause that wit is in other men.' Sir John might, in fact, be likened to a central sun around which revolve various comic characters, witty and witless. His influence actually seems to stretch beyond his proper sphere, for there are certain characters, especially in the last two plays discussed in this chapter, that touch tangentially upon the Falstaff system, although they stand in no direct personal relation to Sir John.

In *King Henry IV Part I* the comic scenes are in the main filled by the bulky figure of Falstaff, either alone or in conjunction with Prince Hal. Of Falstaff's immediate retainers in this play only one is definitely portrayed, and he rather by external appearance than by internal qualities. This is honest Bardolph, 'the Knight of the Burning Lamp.' The actor who played this part must have been so made up that the very sight of him tickled the risibilities of Shakespeare's audience. 'I never see thy face,' says Falstaff, 'but I think upon hell-fire and Dives that lived in purple; for there he is in his robes, burning, burning.' Fluellen in *King Henry V* describes him more specifically: 'his face is all bubukles, and whelks, and knobs, and flames o' fire; and his lips blows at his nose, and it is like a coal of fire, sometimes plue and sometimes red.' This ridiculous figure must have made an instant hit upon the stage; otherwise Shakespeare would hardly have retained him through all this group of plays. Falstaff, it seems, 'bought him in Paul's' thirty years before the action of this play begins, and he is Falstaff's closest companion to the very end. He defends his master against arrest, drinks with him in Justice Shallow's orchard, and shares his dream of future favor with the young king: 'I would not take a knighthood for my fortune.' He sticks to Falstaff after the rejection scene and speaks his epitaph. Later he joins the army in France, where he distinguishes himself as a petty plunderer rather than a fighter. He once stole a lute case, carried it twelve leagues, and sold it for three half-pence, and he and Nym together stole a fire shovel. His thefts, however, were too open; he was at last condemned and hanged for stealing 'a pax of little price,' a sorry end for so faithful a servant. He comes to life again with Falstaff in *The Merry Wives,* still with the old red face, for it is by this that Slender identifies him among the rogues who picked his pocket. Discharged by Falstaff, he enters the service of the Host and drops out of the action. Possibly Shakespeare was getting a little tired of him.

Mistress Quickly, the hostess of the Boar's Head Tavern, is another character who enters in Part I and continues throughout this group of plays. She first appears in the great tavern scene, but here she gives little taste of her quality; she only stands in open-mouthed wonder at Falstaff's impersonation of the King: 'O Jesu! he doth it as like one of these harlotry players as ever I see!' She has but one more scene in this play, that of her indignant denial of responsibility for Falstaff's loss in her inn. Here she has only a few lines to speak, but Shakespeare puts across in those lines a convincing sketch of a voluble, irritable, yet easily pacified woman. The guess might be hazarded that the hit made by the boy actor in this scene led Shakespeare to enlarge the sketch into a life-size portrait. In Part II Mistress Quickly's irritability becomes a passionate invective against the man who has eaten her out of house and home; her volubility a torrential flow, and her placability such an easiness of temper that her attempted arrest of Falstaff ends in a further loan and an invitation to supper. That this invitation includes Doll Tearsheet is a side-glance at Mistress Quickly's easy morality. This trait she shares with Juliet's Nurse along with the inability to tell a plain tale plainly—compare for example the Nurse's account of baby Juliet's fall with Quickly's story of her dressing Falstaff's broken head. It is probable that the two roles were played by the same actor. One trait, however, barely indicated in that of the Nurse, becomes an outstanding feature with Mistress Quickly, a magnificent capacity for malapropisms. No character in Shakespeare, not even Dogberry, has such a gift for abusing the King's English: 'indite' for invite, 'honeysuckle' and 'honeyseed' for homicidal and homicide, are but a few in the long list of her verbal misdeeds. Mistress Quickly carries over into *Henry V* as the newly wed wife of Ancient Pistol. Her part is but a small one here, but it is precious beyond rubies for her report of Falstaff's last hours. All in all Mistress Quickly in these plays is a superb achievement in comic characterization, a convincing testimony to Shakespeare's loving study of the eccentricity in speech and behavior of hostesses he had encountered in his life as a wandering actor.

When Mistress Quickly reappears in *The Merry Wives* a change has come over her. She is now Dr. Caius's maid of all work: 'I keep his house; and I wash, wring, brew, bake, scour, dress meat and drink, make the beds, and do all myself . . . up early and down late.' How this change came about it is idle to inquire; this chapter of Mistress Quickly's life can no more be fitted into a formal biography than can the doings of Falstaff in this play. In addition to her 'great charge' as housekeeper she plays the 'she-Mercury' between Falstaff and the merry wives, and as an extra task she supervises the wooing of pretty Anne Page. That young lady has three suitors, and Mistress Quickly divides her sympathies almost impartially among them: 'I would my master had Mistress Anne; or I would Master Slender had her; or, in sooth, I would Master Fenton had her. I will do what I can for them all three, for so I have promised, and I'll be as good as my word; but speciously for Master Fenton.' She still retains her gift of malapropism: 'allicholy' for melancholy, 'canary' for quandary, 'infection' for affection, are some of her jewels of speech. In general, however, she seems toned down a bit from the shrill Hostess of Part II. That she should play the Queen of Fairies in the last scene and should speak in prettily rhymed couplets seems quite out of character. Perhaps the boy who played her part in the earlier scenes was chosen and coached for this quite different role.

In *King Henry IV Part II* comedy triumphs over history. We miss here the character of Hotspur and his rivalry with the Prince; the rebels in this play are dull uninteresting figures, and the verse which tells of them is cold and formal. It is not until near the end when Shakespeare comes to deal with the dying King and his reconciliation with his son that the verse catches poetic fire again. To compensate in part for this lack of interest in the historic scenes, Shakespeare not only enlarges the role of Falstaff, he surrounds him also with a fresh group of comic characters more varied and more fully realized than his associates in Part I.

The first, though the least important of these, is Falstaff's page.

This lad has but a small part to play; like the pages in Lyly's comedies his chief function is to mock his master. His diminutive figure, fantastically dressed, 'transform'd an ape,' affords on his first entrance a comic contrast to that of the fat Knight who walks before him 'like a sow that hath overwhelmed all her litter but one,' and his attack on Dame Quickly in the scuffle with Snare and Fang is an absurd parody of his master's resistance to arrest. He mocks his fellow-servants as well as his master, and cracks a joke on Bardolph's face which wins him a crown from Hal and, perhaps, a cuff from Bardolph later. That his eyes were open to the seamy side of London life appears from his demure description of Doll Tearsheet as 'a proper gentlewoman, sir, and a kinswoman of my master's,' a remark which paves the way to a coarse jest by the Prince. In *King Henry V* he appears first as Falstaff's page, later as attendant 'boy' to the three rogues, Bardolph, Nym, and Pistol in Henry's army. Shakespeare uses him here to comment sharply on the greed and cowardice of the three and later to interpret the French of Pistol's prisoner to the ignorant audience in the pit. He shares his old master's preference of the tavern to the battlefield; 'Would I were in an alehouse in London,' he says at the storming of Harfleur, 'I would give all my fame for a pot of ale and safety.' He did not, however, share Falstaff's luck in escaping danger, but perished when a French mob broke into Henry's camp; ' 'Tis certain,' reports Captain Gower, 'there's not a boy left alive.' Re-baptized as Robin, Falstaff's page, he has a small part in *The Merry Wives*. He is handed over to Mrs. Page to serve as an innocent go-between 'for 'tis not good,' Mistress Quickly remarks, 'that children should know any wickedness.' Jealous Master Ford, however, is by no means sure of the boy's innocence and thinks his presence in Page's house another argument for the guilt of the merry wives. Robin's part in the play is so small that we may suspect he doubled as little William Page to recite his Latin lesson to a running fire of Quickly's punning commentary. He was also, no doubt, one of the fairies in the final scene.

Another character of far greater importance than Robin appears for the first time in Part II, Master Justice Shallow, the only comic figure in these plays that, for the few scenes in which he appears, can stand side by side with Falstaff. The character of the country Justice of the Peace is drawn with masterly realism. We can both see and hear him. He is so thin that Falstaff, if properly divided, would make 'four dozen of such bearded hermits' staves' as he. He is an incessant babbler with a peculiar trick of constant repetition; 'certain, 'tis certain;

very sure, very sure.' An active and diligent landlord, he is interested in the price of bullocks and ewes, and knows the right kind of wheat to sow on the headland. Yet his thoughts keep turning back to the days he spent in London, when, like many an Elizabethan country gentleman, he lived for a year or two in one of the Inns of Court to learn a little law. How much law Shallow learned may well be doubted; that he has little sense of justice appears from his readiness to back William Visor, 'an arrant knave on my knowledge,' he admits, against Clement Perkes o' the hill. These proper names have been traced in Elizabethan days to a district in Gloucestershire not far from Stratford, and they suggest a suspicion that Shallow is drawn from life. Perhaps some country squire once crammed the ears of young schoolmaster Shakespeare with tales of great doings in London when he roamed the streets with other swinge-bucklers, fought Samson Stockfish, a fruiter, and lay all night in the windmill in St. George's Field. Young Shakespeare may have guessed that there was hardly a word of truth in these tales, but they would have whetted his desire to see the great city, and he recalled them when he drew Justice Shallow's portrait. Shallow's officious serving-man, Davy, and the frightened recruits that Shallow assembles for Falstaff's inspection go back likewise, no doubt, to Shakespeare's memory of his life in the country. A simple country gentleman like Shallow is an easy mark for Falstaff, who borrows £1,000 of him and carries him to London to share his coming fortune. The King's rejection of the man in whom Shallow had placed his fond hopes was a sore blow to the worthy Justice. His one thought is to get his money back, half of it at least, if possible, and to Falstaff's confident assurance that Henry's speech was but a 'colour,' he replies with the ominous prediction: 'a colour that I fear you will die in, Sir John.'

There is no place for Shallow in the heroic play of *Henry V*, but he reappears with other characters from the histories in *The Merry Wives*. He is, however, not quite the old Shallow; his comic luster, like that of Falstaff, is somewhat faded. He no longer indulges in his old repetitive trick of speech, nor recites tall tales of his youth in London. It is true that he reverts occasionally to the time when with his long sword he would have made four tall fellows skip like rats, but this is an incidental flourish, not an habitual boast. He has no very definite function in *The Merry Wives;* his quarrel with Falstaff is dropped as soon as it is well begun, and thereafter he confines himself mainly to backing his nephew's suit to Anne Page. In the received text, that of the Folio, he disappears before the end of the play; in the words of a modern editor he is 'dropped unnoticed in a ditch,' that is in the castle ditch, where he hides with Page and Slender to wait for the fairies. In the quarto, however, he enters with the ladies and their husbands after the fairies' song, and is the first to begin mocking Falstaff. This, it seems plain, is what Shakespeare planned: Shallow, who opened the play with an attack upon Falstaff, should be in at the end when his enemy is put to shame. His single speech in this last scene must have been dropped by accident or been canceled by a careless reviser.

A third comic figure appearing for the first time in Part II is the swaggering Pistol. This is a 'humor' character, if not the first, at least the most extreme, of the kind in Shakespeare's plays. The word 'humor,' originally a medical term for one of the fluids in the human body, had become in Shakespeare's day a popular catchword to denote any individual whim. Shylock, for example, when asked why he desires the pound of flesh, replies briefly: 'it is my humour.' Jonson, however, in a play produced by Shakespeare's company in 1598, defined a humor as 'a monster bred in a man by self-love and affectation.' This exactly describes the humor of Pistol. His 'monster' is compounded of a fine conceit of himself and an absurd affectation of spouting bits of verse, parodies and half-remembered fragments of old plays. Thus on his first appearance he thrusts himself, half drunk, into Falstaff's supper party with Doll and Dame Quickly. Rebuffed in his attempt at familiarity, he breaks into high astounding terms:

> Shall packhorses,
> And hollow pamper'd jades of Asia,
> Which cannot go but thirty miles a day,
> Compare with Caesars, and with Cannibals,
> And Troyan Greeks? nay, rather damn them with
> King Cerberus, and let the welkin roar!

He next appears at the banquet in Shallow's orchard, where the great news he brings so inflates his conceit that he is unable to deliver them like a man of this world. He rants of 'Africa and golden joys,' insults Shallow and Slender, and then turns to Falstaff with the words:

> Sir John, thy tender lambkin now is king;
> Harry the Fifth's the man. I speak the truth.

In the last scene just before the King appears he uses the same stilted language in telling Falstaff of Doll's imprisonment, and when he is dragged off to prison he consoles himself with an Italian proverb on fortune and hope.

That this experiment in comic characterization met with success appears from the fact that Shakespeare continued and elaborated the character of Pistol in *Henry V*. Here he first appears in a noisy quarrel with Nym, whose terse staccato phrases provoke him to wild outbursts:

> O braggart vile and damned furious wight!
> The grave doth gape, and doting death is near.

Later at Agincourt he gets the scene with a French prisoner which in *The Famous Victories* belonged to Derick, the Clown, but for the horseplay of his source Shakespeare substitutes the 'killing words' of Pistol:

> I will fetch thy rim out at thy throat
> In drops of crimson blood.

The clever Boy who takes part in this scene compares Pistol to the 'roaring devil i' th' old play,' and knows that he is a coward at heart. After the battle Fluellen, who had once been deceived by Pistol's 'brave words,' exposes the coward and forces him to eat a Welsh leek under the blows of his cudgel. This punishment, along with Gower's rebuke which follows, drives Pistol out of his humor. He sneaks back to England to live as bawd and cutpurse there, boasting the while of his brave deeds in France. This type of the braggart pseudo-veteran, evidently well known in Elizabethan England, had already appeared on Shakespeare's stage in the person of Jonson's Bobadil, but Bobadil lacks the fine flow of Pistol's decorated speech.

This should be the end of Ancient Pistol, but he reappears, with his fellows, Nym and Bardolph, in *The Merry Wives*, as a follower of Falstaff *redivivus*. He keeps his trick of bombastic utterance and answers Falstaff's suggestion that he carry love letters to the ladies with an indignant

> Shall I Sir Pandarus of Troy become,
> And by my side wear steel? then Lucifer take all!

He has one speech which alone is enough to make him immortal:

> The world's mine oyster,
> Which I with sword will open.

He takes little part in the plot and, after denouncing Falstaff to Master Ford, he drops out altogether. His name, indeed, appears as a speaker in the fairy scene, but it is probable that the actor who played Pistol was impressed here for the role of Hobgoblin.

Pistol is not the only 'humor' in *Henry V;* his fellow Nym is another, but Nym's humor consists mainly in running the poor word out of breath in almost every speech he makes: 'and that's the humor of it.' It is as if Shakespeare were ridiculing the widespread abuse of the word. Like Pistol Nym passes on to *The Merry Wives,* but his role there is even less than Pistol's. He attempts to discuss the humor of his master's love for Mrs. Page to the lady's husband, but honest Page turns a deaf ear to the drawling affected rogue, and Nym disappears from the scene. That is no great loss, for Nym is one of the few comic characters in Shakespeare that do not come alive; he is only a character part for a clever actor.

It is quite another story with Captain Fluellen. He has, to be sure, his humor, a pedantic devotion to 'the true disciplines of the wars—the disciplines of the pristine wars of the Romans.' But he is not enslaved by it; he is more than a pedant; he is a brave soldier with a keen sense of a soldier's honor and a fine pride in his native Wales. The King himself is Welsh, he declares, by virtue of his birth in Monmouth. He is a long-winded and repetitive talker and delivers all he has to say with a strong Welsh accent. Alexander the Great, for example, becomes in his mouth Alexander the Pig, and he is more than little vexed when his accent is corrected: 'Is not pig great?' he asks, 'The pig, or the great, or the mighty, or the huge, or the magnanimous, are all one reckonings.' This trick of raising a laugh by means of an alien's distortion of English seems to have been especially effective on the Elizabethan stage about this time; numerous examples might be cited, and in this very play Shakespeare adds to his Welshman a stolid Scotch and an irascible Irish captain to ring the changes on mispronunciation. To this type of comedy we may assign also the English lesson which Princess Katharine takes from her lady-in-waiting. This scene fulfils the promise to the audience in the Epilogue to *King Henry IV Part II,* to 'make you merry with fair Katharine of France.' The blunders of the little princess, no doubt, got a laugh even from those of the audience who knew no French, while better scholars chuckled over the *double-entendre* in the last words of her English lesson.

Scraps of French are mingled with the English of the final scene in

which Henry courts the princess. The King's behavior here has been
harshly condemned by certain critics, who persist in regarding the
scene as a historic document rather than a bit of drama. Shakespeare,
it seems clear, planned to wind up his heroic play with a dash of
comedy; his warrior king is to win the love of a French princess. How
was he to represent Henry as acting? To make him affect the lover
à la mode and court his lady in the language of a Romeo would be
absurdly inconsistent with all that he had so far shown of Henry's
character. On the other hand, to let Henry lay violent hands upon
his prize and claim her as the captive of his bow and spear would be
rather brutal, certainly not comedy at all. Shakespeare avoids both
extremes and here presents Henry endowed with the same easy and
masterly familiarity he had shown with the drawers in the tavern
and the soldiers in the camp. He laughs with and at the frightened
girl till he persuades her that the terrible conqueror of France is
after all 'the best king of good fellows.' The friendly violence with
which he breaks down her demure resistance and kisses first her hand
and then her lips completes his conquest. The scene is hardly high
comedy, but it is good 'theater' and provides a sunny ending to a
stormy play.

Returning to a final consideration of *The Merry Wives* we may
note that while various characters in that play, one of course of prime
importance, Falstaff, enter it from the histories, others appear here
for the first time. Two of these, Sir Hugh, the Welsh dominie, and
Dr. Caius, the French physician, are humor characters, more or less
of the Jonsonian type. Sir Hugh, a man of peace, is all for precision
and exact statement. A true schoolmaster, he is something of a pedant,
but he is a friendly soul on good terms with his neighbors, ready to
compose a quarrel or promote a marriage. His strong Welsh accent
must have given an additional comic touch to his rendering of Marlowe's 'Passionate Shepherd,' with an interpolated line from the Psalms
in meter, which he sings to keep his courage up while waiting for an
encounter with the Doctor. Probably this part was played by the actor
of Fluellen in *Henry V*. Dr. Caius is the slave of a humor composed
in equal parts of vanity and choler. His broken English, poured out at
hot speed, would raise a laugh, and his frequent misunderstanding of
what is said to him would get another. His suit of Anne Page is on
the face of it ridiculous, and in the fairy scene '*un garçon,* a boy; *un
paysan,* by gar, a boy,' is palmed off on him instead of the lady. It
has been plausibly suggested that this character is Shakespeare's **satiric**

portrait of the foreign physician popular in the highest circles of Elizabethan society.

Master Ford is another humor character, but of a very different type. The jealous husband had been from of old a comic figure; but there is a strain in Ford's passion that is not far removed from the tragic. His humor is, indeed, a monster; it drives him to such irrational action as his offer of a bribe to Falstaff to corrupt his wife. His outburst of anger when he hears that the lady has already granted Falstaff a meeting is a piece of almost insane rant, and he is ready to proclaim himself publicly a cuckold provided he can catch his wife's lover and expose her guilt. It is only Shakespeare's deft handling of the buck-basket and the wife of Brainford business that brings the whole matter back to the plane of comedy, even of farce comedy. Ford is, presumably, purged of his humor by his discovery of the truth and his reconciliation with his wife, but it would demand the best effort of the actor of the part to make this quite clear. Jonson had quite recently, 1598, embodied this humor of jealousy in the Thorello-Kitely character of his first great comedy, but the suspicion of Jonson's husband is as ridiculous as groundless. Shakespeare saw more deeply into the tragic possibility of this passion; not long after *The Merry Wives* he developed it to the full in what is, perhaps, the most poignant of his tragedies.

It is a relief to pass from the dark figure of Ford to that of Master Slender, a pure and altogether delightful comic masterpiece. Barring his counterpart, Sir Andrew Aguecheek, a role composed, no doubt, for the same actor, Slender is the most complete and hopeless fool in all Shakespeare's plays. He is, indeed, not far removed from what the Elizabethan's called an 'innocent,' a feeble-minded person. A gentleman born with a handsome income, he is from the worldly point of view a fit match for Anne Page, and at his uncle's request he is willing to wed her. Yet he cannot pretend a passion: 'If there be no great love in the beginning, yet heaven may decrease it upon better acquaintance . . . I hope, upon familiarity will grow more contempt.' As he comes to know her, however, something like real affection develops in his simple heart, and he sighs repeatedly: 'Ah, sweet Anne Page.' His wooing of her by proxy when he begs Shallow to tell her the jest how his father stole two geese out of a pen is, perhaps, the most inept method of courtship in all literature, and when he is forced to speak for himself he can only stammer: 'Your father and my uncle hath made motions: if it be my luck, so; if not, happy man be his dole!' It is no wonder that Mistress Anne declares she would sooner be 'set quick i' th' earth, and bowl'd to death with turnips' than marry such a fool. Like her other suitor, Dr. Caius, Slender is fubbed off at last with 'a great lubberly boy' and when he discovers the cheat 'if it had not been i' the church, I would have swinged him or he should have swinged me.' We may dismiss Slender with Hazlitt's label round his neck, 'a very potent piece of imbecility.'

It is the abundance, variety, and lifelikeness of the comic characters, moving as they do about the central figure of Falstaff, that atone for the trivial plot of *The Merry Wives*, make the play a delight to the judicious reader, and account for its age-long success upon the stage. Certainly no one would select this play as a characteristic example of Shakespearean comedy; written almost entirely in prose, it lacks the music of his verse; its realistic background of Elizabethan life has nothing of the other-world atmosphere of his romantic comedies. Yet when all this is confessed, this play, much maligned by closet critics, affords a notable example of Shakespeare's art. It is a striking proof of what a master craftsman can do with a theme forced upon him and accomplished in a stinted time. For *The Merry Wives* is a capital stage-play, lively in action, crowded with amusing and actable characters, and breathing in every scene Shakespeare's whole-hearted delight in the follies of his fellow mortals.

10

The Tragic Period

WITH the turn of the century Shakespeare begins to enter upon what is generally known as his tragic period, the time of *Hamlet, Othello, Lear,* and *Macbeth.* Yet we must not think of this period as a watertight compartment, enclosed within fixed dates, and shut off from all that preceded or followed it. The periods of Shakespeare's dramatic activity are like the seasons of our year when winter slowly melts into spring and autumn hardens into winter. A time comes when we can say spring has finally arrived or winter is here at last. The tragic period had definitely arrived when Shakespeare's company produced *Othello* in 1604; but before that date there was for some time what we may call debatable ground. Shakespeare's perfect comedy, *Twelfth Night,* overlaps *Hamlet,* and *Julius Caesar* serves as a link between his histories and his tragedies.

There has been endless and in the main idle debate concerning the underlying cause of this tragic period. Romantic critics have been inclined to assign it to a change in Shakespeare's temper and outlook on life, a sudden shift from the carefree gaiety laughing through *As You Like It* to the skepticism of *Hamlet,* the anguished pity of *Othello,* and the black darkness of *Lear.* This conception has crystallized in the catchword 'Out of the Depths,' applied to this period. The phrase was borrowed from the first words of Psalm cxxx—*De profundis clamavi*—and the great tragedies were interpreted as Shakespeare's cries of distress from a pit of despair. The trouble with this conception is that we have no justification in what we know of Shakespeare's life for such a shift in tone and temper. He was at this time triumphantly successful, not only in his art, but in the practical aspects of his life. His company was honored by the direct patronage of King James; Shakespeare and his fellows had been made Grooms of the Chamber, robed in liveries of royal scarlet, and repeatedly commanded to perform at Court. Shakespeare himself may have been shocked by the treason and death of Essex and by the condemnation of his friend, Southampton, but with the accession of James, Southampton was freed from prison and restored to royal favor. The only evidence for the alleged tragic gloom of Shakespeare is the tragedies themselves; Shakespeare, it is assumed, must have been in a tragic mood to write such plays, and the plays are what they are because of the mood in which he wrote them—a curiously circular method of proof.

A more realistic explanation of the underlying cause points to the waning of the national spirit of romance and adventure in the last years of Elizabeth's reign and to the pacifistic policy of James. This change was, as a matter of fact, reflected in contemporary drama where romantic gives place to realistic satiric comedy, and the chronicle play, long the dear delight of the public, to a new-born tragedy. One has but to examine a list of plays produced over the turn of the century to realize this fact. Yet to attribute Shakespeare's tragic period to this change in theatrical fashion is to make the poet little better than a reed shaken by the wind of popular favor.

A truer explanation, perhaps, may be gained from a consideration of Shakespeare's dramatic development. It is interesting to observe in a survey of the chronology of his plays his shifts from one type of drama to another. He rises step by step to mastery in each type and then passes on to another. His early experiments in comedy culminate in the great trio of plays that overlap the end of the century; his work in the field of historic drama comes to a heroic end in *Henry V*. In tragedy, however, his early efforts, *Titus* and *Romeo and Juliet*, left him, we may believe, so dissatisfied that for a stretch of years, while he was occupied with comedy and history, he made no further attempt in this genre. Now the time had come for him to venture boldly with full self-assurance into the high field of tragedy. Shakespeare was first of all a playwright; he was concerned, of course, with the public response to his plays, but he trained and guided rather than followed popular demand. He was no philosopher to wrestle with the problem of evil, but his eyes had been at last opened to the existence, below the brilliant world of Renaissance culture, of evil, treacherous, and cruel powers. He was now prepared to deal with them in his own way by means of his own art.

Yet since Shakespeare was an Elizabethan playwright, accepting, as has been shown, the Elizabethan convention of mingled mirth and sadness, we may expect to find a strain of comedy in the tragedies of this period, along with a serious and at times a bitter note in the few comedies that fall within its limits. It may repay the student to examine both genres in some detail.

JULIUS CAESAR

Julius Caesar, 1599, at once a history and a tragedy, represents Shakespeare's transition from the lower to the higher field. It has been said that to write of the comic matter in this play would be to repeat the laconic report on snakes in Ireland. This, however, would not be quite accurate; the genius of comedy shows his head even here for a brief moment only to vanish under a stronger spell, as Irish snakes did at the voice of St. Patrick. The 'commoners' of the first scene are not Roman citizens at all, but English craftsmen, a carpenter and a cobbler, out for a holiday in their Sunday best. The cobbler, with his impertinent behavior to his superiors and his evident enjoyment of his own foolish prattle, is a direct throwback to the peasants that followed Jack Cade in Shakespeare's first chronicle play. He is, however, less irrepressible than they, and the eloquent reproof of the tribunes sends him and his fellows 'tongue-tied' from the stage. They do not appear again; the citizens who listen to the speeches of Brutus and Antony are mere conventional types, representatives of the 'many-headed multitude.' Their insensate fury appears in the scene of the murder of Cinna the poet, a scene which may have wrung a gasp but hardly a laugh, even from the most brutish members of Shakespeare's audience.

A like quick shift away from comedy appears, it would seem, in the characterization of Casca. On his first appearance he speaks as a caustic commentator on Caesar's behavior when the crown was offered him and on the reaction of 'mine honest neighbors . . . the rag-tag people' who clapped and hissed the great man 'as they use to do the players in the theatre.' Casca speaks plain blunt prose, a designed, perhaps a comic, contrast to the grave poetic dialogue between Brutus and Cassius which precedes his appearance and continues when he departs. Curiously, however, when he reappears in the next scene he swings over into verse and from then on becomes simply another of the conspirators, with no specially distinguishing characteristic. His last lines:

> Why, he that cuts off twenty years of life
> Cuts off so many years of fearing death,

might as well be spoken by Cassius, to whom, in fact, they are assigned by certain editors. The character of Casca is practically a new creation by Shakespeare; in the source there is only a passing reference to him as one of the group who slew Caesar in the senate house. It would seem as if Shakespeare had at first conceived this character as a possibly amusing contrast to the sober dignity of the play's protagonist. As Shakespeare proceeded, however, in the composition of *Julius Caesar*, he discarded this idea and merged a comic Casca in the group of determined and serious conspirators.

There is, we may be sure, a reason for this disappearance of comedy from *Julius Caesar* after so brief a showing in the opening scenes. This reason may be found in the source of the play, Plutarch's *Parallel Lives of the Noble Greeks and Romans*. This great series of biographies, long lost during the Middle Ages, was discovered and reassembled in the dawn of the Renaissance, and had become by Shakespeare's day one of the darling books of Renaissance humanists. Plutarch's extraordinary skill in the portraiture of heroic characters specially recommended his work to an age in which, with the breakdown of the class and guild organization of the Middle Ages, the individual was becoming more and more important. In addition Plutarch's ethical earnestness endeared him to the promoters of the New Learning, who, one and all, laid special stress on moral edification. Henry of Navarre, for instance, congratulating his young wife on her study of Plutarch, tells her that his mother, one of the chief patrons of Humanism in France, had put this book into his hands when he was still a child; 'it has been, as it were my conscience,' he continues, 'and has whispered in my ear many fair virtues and excellent maxims.' Henry's reading seems to have been confined to the *Lives;* had he taken to heart the moral maxims of Plutarch's *Advice to the Married,* he might have lived a quieter and, probably, a happier life.

Since the original Greek of Plutarch was difficult even for scholars of that time, translations had been made, not only into Latin, then the universal language of scholars, but into all the vernaculars of Western Europe. One of the best of these, Bishop Amyot's French translation, 1559, quite probably the book that Marguerite of Navarre put into her son's hands, served, it is known, as the basis for the English version of Sir Thomas North.

Shakespeare's debt in *Julius Caesar* to North's translation has been so fully demonstrated by editors that it would be idle to repeat it here. Of more importance, perhaps, than specific borrowings is the immediacy of North's impact upon the sensitive and receptive mind and art of Shakespeare. There is no reason to believe that he had read Plutarch in school; Plutarch's *Morals* may sometimes have been read in Elizabethan schools; his *Lives* certainly were not. There is no trace in Shakespeare's earliest plays of his having even a bowing acquaintance with this work. In *A Midsummer Night's Dream*, however, *c.* 1594-5, there appear allusions to the amours of Theseus which he can have drawn only from Plutarch's life of that legendary hero. Now 1594 is the year in which *Lucrece*, the second of Shakespeare's narrative poems, was given to the public; and the printer of *Lucrece* was Richard Field, Shakespeare's fellow Stratfordian, who a year before had both printed and published his *Venus and Adonis*. Shakespeare seems to have read the proof of his poems with a care that he never lavished on the printed copies of his plays, and he must often enough have been in Field's shop in these years. It happens that in 1594-5 Field was busily engaged in printing the second edition of North's *Plutarch,* and it is more than a mere guess that Richard called William's attention to the work, possibly even let him see some of the sheets damp from the press. The account of Theseus from which the *Midsummer Night's Dream* allusions were taken stands at the very head of the great collection of the *Lives*. Shakespeare certainly could not have been satisfied with a casual glance at the proof sheets. He must soon have purchased a copy; his intensive study of North's work, shown in *Julius Caesar* by his selection of material from three separate lives, those of Caesar, Brutus, and Mark Antony, proves that he used Field's edition as only an owner could do. Before long Plutarch's *Lives* came to replace Holinshed as a source book for Shakespeare. Yet Plutarch was to him much more than a mere source book; for the *Lives*, it is clear, Shakespeare cherished a veneration he had never felt for Holinshed. With the English chronicler Shakespeare allowed himself considerable liberty: in defiance of history he brought Queen Margaret back from France to hurl curses at the Yorkist Court, and he pushed Prince Hal to the front to slay Hotspur in single combat. The work of the old classic, however, seems to have been to him almost sacrosanct. From the behavior of the tribunes in the first scene to Antony's words over the body of Brutus in the last, *Julius Caesar* is true to history as recorded by Plutarch.

It would, of course, be wrong to assert that Shakespeare followed Plutarch slavishly. Closely as he kept to the main lines of the narrative in his source, he selected, omitted, and expanded what he found there for his dramatic purpose: to enact on the Elizabethan stage one of the most famous scenes of ancient history, the murder of Caesar, and to present the grandeur that was Rome, in a setting of contemporary realism. Republican Rome comes to life again in Shakespeare; his Roman nobles act and speak like Elizabethan gentlemen. This was the very opposite of Jonson's dramatic method of detailed archaic verisimilitude, and a spectator who saw the Roman plays of both dramatists testifies that the audience listened to Shakespeare's play 'ravish't with wonder,'

> When some new day they would not brook a line
> Of tedious though well-labour'd Cataline.

This absorption in the temper of Plutarch, this determined effort to revive the past in terms of the present, exerted a profound effect upon Shakespeare's art in the composition of *Julius Caesar*. He may once have meant, as traces in the first scenes seem to show, to present the old story in the form of an Elizabethan chronicle play. As he proceeded in his task, however, he became more and more imbued with the tragic significance of the fall of the mightiest Julius and the fate of the noblest Roman of them all. There was no place for the laughter of comedy in such a play as this.

HAMLET

With *Hamlet*, probably on the stage in 1600, Shakespeare moves from the middle ground of historical tragedy in *Julius Caesar* into the realm of high tragedy. There is, to be sure, something in common in these two plays; repeated references in *Hamlet* to the story dramatized in *Julius Caesar* show that memories of that play still lingered in Shakespeare's mind. Polonius, for example, declares that he performed the role of Caesar in a university play, and Horatio compares the portents that foretold the fall of the mightiest Julius to the apparition of the Ghost with its warning to the state of Denmark. A certain likeness might even be traced between the protagonists of the two plays; Brutus and Hamlet both are tragically frustrated idealists. Yet on a larger view there is more difference than likeness between these plays; *Julius Caesar* is dominated not only by the story but by the spirit of Plutarch's *Lives*; *Hamlet*, on the other hand, is Shakespeare's adaptation, one might better say transfiguration, of an old play in the hands of his company. So long as he preserved the main outline of a play familiar to his public, he was free to introduce new matter, to reshape characters, to heighten poetic expression, and intensify the psychologic values of the tale: in short, to transmute an archaic melodrama into a tragedy for all time. It would be out of place here to discuss at any length the evolution of *Hamlet* from its earliest source to the crowning result in Shakespeare's play, yet a brief restatement of the results of scholarship may help us better to understand what Shakespeare attempted and achieved.

There is reason to believe that shortly before 1589 Thomas Kyd, author of the successful *Spanish Tragedy,* composed a play called *Hamlet.* This play, the *Ur-Hamlet,* to use the accepted scholarly term, is lost apparently beyond redemption; so far as we know, it was never printed; the discovery of a possibly existing manuscript would be of the greatest value to our knowledge of early Elizabethan drama and our understanding of Shakespeare's methods of work. We do know, however, that the ultimate source of Kyd's play was an old Northern saga, preserved in the medieval Latin of Saxo Grammaticus, *c.* 1185, and popularized in the Renaissance by the French translation in Belleforest's *Histoires tragiques,* 1582. This saga told the tale of a wise young prince who feigned madness to escape death at the hands of an uncle, the murderer of his father, thwarted various attempts upon his life, and finally achieved a complete and satisfactory revenge. Such a simple and savage story needed, apparently, considerable modification to fit it for the Elizabethan stage. Taking into account Kyd's dramatic technique in *The Spanish Tragedy* and drawing upon a German play, *Der Bestrafte Brudermord oder Prinz Hamlet aus Daennemark,* generally accepted as a late and debased version of the *Ur-Hamlet,* we may safely assume certain important changes that Kyd made in his dramatization of the story. He altered the method of the fratricide from open violence to secret poisoning, brought in the Ghost of the murdered man to reveal the secret and demand revenge, and wound up his play with a general massacre in which the revenging Prince perished along with his guilty uncle. This would have made a stirring melodrama with a strong dash of the Senecan element which Kyd so much admired. We can probably trace the general outline and many of the incidents of the lost *Ur-Hamlet* in the surviving German play.

A *Hamlet,* presumably Kyd's play, was acted by the combined Admiral's and Chamberlain's players in the suburban theater at Newington Butts in 1594. Someone in the Chamberlain's Company, perhaps Shakespeare himself, recognized the dramatic possibilities of the old play and his company took the play-book with them when they moved to the Theatre. Two years later, 1596, we hear of a performance there when Lodge sneered at the Ghost 'which cried so miserably at the Theatre, "Hamlet revenge." ' Lodge's remark proves that an acting version of *Hamlet* was in the possession of the Chamberlain's Company close to Shakespeare's hand when he was ready to work a miracle upon it.

And herein lies one of the main differences between *Julius Caesar* and *Hamlet*. The former was written under the direct influence of Plutarch's noble narrative; in the old *Hamlet*, on the other hand, Shakespeare found, indeed, an actable scenario, but a text for which he had no particular respect, perhaps even a certain contempt. It is evident that in his recasting of the old *Hamlet* Shakespeare felt free to give rein to his native instinct for comic incidents and humorous characters in a tragic action. We have seen this instinct at work in *Romeo and Juliet* and noticed the cause for its temporary check in *Julius Caesar*. In *Hamlet* it comes to life again; there is more than a little comic matter in this tragedy, much more, perhaps, than is realized by a modern reader. We may begin with the famous graveyard scene, which opens the last act.

The Grave-diggers, 'those favorites of the public,' as Garrick called them, were ruthlessly struck out of the play in his notorious alteration of *Hamlet*. These characters had, no doubt, endeared themselves to the public by a good deal of comic business. Till well into the last century, for example, it was customary for one of them to peel off a whole series of waistcoats, 'an operation,' says Halliwell, 'which always created great merriment.' Such buffoonery, no doubt, was the main reason that prompted Garrick, strongly influenced at that time by French censure of Shakespeare's indecorum, to eliminate these characters. Yet there is no need for such buffoonery in the scene as Shakespeare wrote it. The Grave-diggers, 'Clowns' the old text calls them, are genuine humorous English countryfolk, free of speech, critical of their betters, fond of riddles and the tag-ends of old songs. The professional indifference of the Clown who has been grave-digger, man and boy, for thirty years contrasts comically with the sensitivity and skepticism of the hero, and there is bitter irony in Hamlet's jests with the Clown at the grave of the girl he himself has driven to madness and death. There is a touch of shrewd folk wisdom in the Clown's remark that Christian burial would have been denied any but a gentlewoman who had committed suicide. The audience knows that this gentlewoman was Ophelia, but Hamlet does not, and it is the

shock of his sudden discovery of the fact that drives him to the sudden
outburst of rage and grief which shortly follows. The term 'comic relief' is out of fashion, but the scene with the Grave-diggers is one of
low tension; it brings us literally back to earth again in the midst of
a high-flown action. More, surely, is lost than gained by the excision
of this scene as in Garrick's acting version and in a modern New York
production. Cuts in the long text of *Hamlet* are apparently necessary for a modern performance, but it is dangerous to tamper with
the structure erected by a master. The scene with the Clowns is
Shakespeare's invention for his designed dramatic purposes; there is
nothing like it in the German play, and Kyd himself could not have
written anything like it if he had lived to Methuselah's age.

Nowhere else in *Hamlet* does Shakespeare bring in his beloved
shrewd and simple countryfolk. There are other characters, however,
who serve to lighten the gloom of tragedy with a ripple of laughter.
The fop Osric, who appears for the first time just before the final
catastrophe, is one of these. This 'water-fly' is a Jonsonian humor, a
cousin-german of Fastidious Brisk in *Every Man Out*, a play produced
by Shakespeare's company in the same season as *Hamlet*. Jonson himself describes Fastidious as 'a neat spruce affecting courtier, one that
wears clothes well and in fashion . . . speaks good remnants,' a very
pat characterization of Shakespeare's Osric. On the modern stage this
character is usually extravagantly overdressed; in Shakespeare's day it
was hardly possible for a gallant to be too extravagant in dress. The
laugh that Shakespeare was playing for in this scene would be provoked rather by the absurd affectation of the courtier's speech. Much
of it is barely intelligible today; comedy that depends on mere tricks
of speech is apt to lose its savor as time passes. Yet we may well believe that when *Hamlet* was first played, the affected speech of Osric
and its mocking parody by the Prince drew approving smiles from
the gentlemen and louder laughter from the groundlings at the
Globe. Like the graveyard scene, moreover, this colloquy has something higher than a mere comic purpose. It shows the hero immediately before the treacherous fencing match in which he meets his
death, no longer subject to the 'sore distraction' that so long had
punished him, but cool, clear-headed, ready even to laugh at the fop
despatched by the King to lure him into the trap. Garrick in his haste
to drop the final curtain cut Osric out altogether, but in so doing he
lost just the effect of mingled mirth and sadness that Shakespeare
aimed at here.

Osric is, no doubt, a purely comic character; does Polonius belong in this class? Certainly the role has often been so interpreted on the stage. Even before Garrick's day the part of Polonius had usually been played as low comedy, and Garrick's attempt to restore a certain dignity to the part was quite unsuccessful. As late as 1836 after the great *Hamlet* performances of Kean and Kemble, Morgann declared that Polonius was always 'buffooned' for the delight of the common spectator. Even at the close of the nineteenth century the French actor who took this part in Sarah Bernhardt's production of *Hamlet* retained this stage tradition. Sarah, as Hamlet, caught a fly off his nose as she pronounced the words: 'Buz, buz,' and later detected him foolishly popping his head out through the back curtain to overhear the conversation of Hamlet and Ophelia. It is, however, more than doubtful if this was Shakespeare's conception of the part. Hamlet, it is true, calls Polonius a tedious old fool, but Hamlet is a bitterly prejudiced witness; Polonius, after all, is Lord High Chamberlain of the Court of Denmark, an office somewhat above the capacity of a tedious fool. A brief review of the scenes in which Polonius appears may enable us to determine more exactly Shakespeare's conception of this character.

We first see Polonius in the court scene of the first act where the King pays high tribute to him as a valued servant of the state. The 'few precepts' that he delivers, at considerable length, in the next scene to his son probably heighten the reader's opinion of his character, for they are undoubtedly sound, practical, moral maxims. Shakespeare's audience, however, would be quick to recognize them as current commonplaces, the sort of good advice that Euphues gave his friend Philautus and Lord Burghley passed on to his son. In the interview with Ophelia that follows, Polonius appears as a shrewd, somewhat cynical man of the world, a conventional and rather peremptory father.

The first trace of comic characterization appears in the charge he gives Reynaldo at the beginning of the second act. Here Polonius is not only prolix and tedious; he actually loses the thread of his discourse: 'What was I about to say? By the mass I was about to say something.' The thread must be picked up and handed respectfully back to him by his servant. There is, it would seem, a deeper implication than the merely comic in this; Polonius is about to play a leading part in determining the state of Hamlet's mind and the necessary measures for controlling his supposed madness. If he is

unable to hold the thread in such a petty business as arranging for
private espionage on his son, what will he do in this greater matter?
We soon get the answer.

No sooner has Reynaldo left the stage than Ophelia runs in af-
frighted to report the alarming appearance and behavior of Hamlet,
who, in defiance of her refusal to receive him, has broken into her
boudoir. Polonius is not for a moment in doubt in regard to the
cause: 'This is the very ecstasy of love,' he exclaims. An instant and
erroneous impression becomes an *idée fixe* which endures till the
moment of his death at the hands of the Prince he had so misjudged.
Unlike Hamlet, who knows not 'seems,' Polonius judges and acts on
appearances.

In the long scene (II. ii) that follows, Polonius has three parts to
play. To the King and Queen already disturbed by Hamlet's behavior,
he reports at great length with a precise medical diagnosis the cause
of the Prince's 'lunacy.' Audience and reader know well enough that
Hamlet is not mad, but has only 'put an antic disposition on'; we
gain, no doubt, a certain comic satisfaction in seeing this positive and
wordy wiseacre go so far astray. This comic strain continues in the
following colloquy with Hamlet. Here for the first time we see the
Prince acting his antic disposition before us. This, no doubt, is one of
the scenes in which, according to Dr. Johnson 'the pretended madness of Hamlet causes much mirth.' The mirth, such as it is, springs
from the game of cross purposes that takes place here; Polonius takes
Hamlet to be a lovelorn madman and Hamlet plays up to him with
words that at once confirm his opinion—'He is far gone, far gone:
and truly in my youth I suffered much extremity for love,'—and yet
rouse an uneasy suspicion that 'Though this be madness, yet there
is method in 't.'

If Hamlet mocks Polonius in this colloquy, he does so even more
openly and brusquely in the episode that follows. Polonius breaks
in upon the talk of Hamlet with his old friends, Rosencrantz and
Guildenstern, to announce the arrival of the actors, 'the best actors
in the world, either for tragedy, comedy, history, pastoral,' et cetera,
et cetera. The old man sets up for a literary and dramatic critic; he
applauds Hamlet's delivery of the rugged Pyrrhus lines, and he finds
the actor's recitation too long. This unhappy interruption provokes
Hamlet's bitter comment: 'He's for a jig or a tale of bawdry'—the dear
delight of the tired businessman today—and finally stops the informal
rehearsal. His condescending patronage of the actors contrasts sharply

with Hamlet's genial familiarity, a trait that would be recognized by Shakespeare's audience, aware as they were of the gap between the friendly interest in the theater of such young aristocrats as Essex and Southampton and the indifference or hostility of the bourgeois city officials. The three episodes of this scene bring out more clearly than anything else in the play the comic aspects of the character of Polonius; they need no buffoonery of stage business to over-accentuate them.

After this we see little of Polonius until his untimely end. He arranges an interview between Hamlet and his daughter to convince the King of the truth of his diagnosis. The two plotters overhear Hamlet's fierce denunciation of all womankind in the person of his once-loved lady, and the King shrewdly guesses something near the truth:

> Love! his affections do not that way tend;
> . . . There's something in his soul
> O'er which his melancholy sits on brood.

Polonius, on the other hand, clings to his fixed idea:

> But yet I do believe
> The origin and commencement of his grief
> Sprung from neglected love.

Consequently he arranges one more test, a final and, as it proves, a fatal one. Let the Queen, he suggests, have a heart-to-heart talk with her son; he will overhear and report on it, since a mother's version would naturally be too partial. His final injunctions to Gertrude just before this interview, delivered in a tone pardonable only in so old a friend and counselor, proclaim him still assured of the truth of his opinion and still addicted to privy espionage. But while the scene with Reynaldo was rather comic, the present turns into sheer tragedy. Hamlet overhears his cry for help, kills him like a rat, and speaks his epitaph:

> Thou wretched, rash, intruding fool, farewell!

Can we, too, dismiss Polonius so briefly and bitterly?

There is, surely, little evidence of a foolishly comic Polonius in most of the scenes in which that character appears. Yet there are lines spoken by him and thrown at him which have a distinct comic value. Perhaps the best conclusion we can form is that Shakespeare meant to draw and set in action here a serio-comic figure, an aging, not to say senile, politician and official. Dealing with routine matters Polonius behaves quite creditably; confronted with an extraordinary situation, the heir to the throne gone mad for love of his daughter, he is hopelessly at sea. Yet he is confident of his ability to deal with this case as with anything in the usual day's work, and it is this vain self-confidence that exposes him to mockery. There is, of course, a strong dash of satire in this portrait of an old official. We need not rack our brains to puzzle out which of the elder statesmen who guided Elizabeth's ship of state Shakespeare was thinking of when he conceived Polonius. Vanity, verbosity, a strange blend of servility and loyalty, a strong bias toward intrigue and espionage characterized more than one of the Queen's great servants. And these were traits that the eager young nobles, Shakespeare's special patrons, would be quick to detect in the Lord High Chamberlain of Denmark. They would laugh at Polonius, but not, perhaps, without a touch of malicious envy. This local and contemporary satire is lost for us. What remains is a lasting portrait of an old wheel horse in state affairs: respectable and well-meaning, but over-confident and prone to expose his own weakness and folly. It is so, it would seem, that the role should be played today, evoking at times a pitying smile, seldom, if ever, a contemptuous laugh.

A rather difficult question presents itself in regard to comic matter once present in the tragedy of *Hamlet* that is unrecognized today. This question is suggested by Dr. Johnson's comment on the 'mirth' caused by Hamlet's feigned madness. To us it seems almost impossible to think of the scenes in which Hamlet plays the madman as a source of mirth, and this impossibility may be owing to a different tradition or convention in the stage presentation of the role. We know little of the way in which it was acted by the first performers, Burbage, Shakespeare's fellow, or Taylor, who succeeded him. It seems probable that in the scenes in question Hamlet assumed the familiar role of the Elizabethan malcontent, and the unknown author of an Elegy on Burbage pays tribute to the realism of his acting:

> Oft have I seen him leap into the grave,
> Suiting the person which he seem'd to have
> Of a sad lover with so true an eye,
> That there I would have sworn, he meant to die.

More specific testimony comes later from those who saw Betterton play the part, 'the best part, I believe,' says Pepys, 'that ever man acted.' Now Betterton had been coached by D'Avenant, who had seen Taylor as Hamlet before the theaters were closed. Presumably, therefore, Betterton carried on the Elizabethan convention and of Betterton's conception of the character we have explicit testimony. Of his last performance, 1709, Steele says that though then about seventy he 'appeared through the whole drama a young man of great expectation, vivacity, and enterprise.' There is no trace here of the irresolute and melancholy Hamlet of later days. Nor is there in what we hear later of Garrick's impersonation, realistic, vigorous, even blamed at times as too 'rough and loud.' A marked change comes with the dawn of the romantic movement and the famous interpretation of Hamlet by Kemble as an introspective melancholy prince; Kemble was, in fact, accused of exhibiting in the role a 'fixed and sullen gloom.' His successors, Kean, Booth, Irving, and Forbes-Robertson, all contrived to shake off this funereal aspect, but all clung, more or less, to the conception of Hamlet as emotional and melancholy.

It seems quite possible that the earlier vivacious and enterprising Hamlet could so play the scenes of his feigned madness as to delight the spectators, move them, perhaps, to laughter, by the clever manner in which he tricked his enemies, particularly the foolish Polonius. Today with our stage tradition of a Hamlet trembling on the narrow bridge that leads from sanity to madness, such an impersonation seems hardly conceivable.

Is it possible to determine the Elizabethan conception of these scenes? We know, of course, that the Elizabethan attitude toward madness was very different from ours; Shakespeare's contemporaries looked on insanity as something comic rather than tragic. They entertained idiots as domestic fools and paid visits to the mad cells in Bedlam by way of an afternoon's party of pleasure. It would seem to follow that mad scenes in Elizabethan drama were essentially comic, and some, no doubt, were so. In *The Spanish Tragedy*, the hero, Hieronimo, is sane and mad by fits and starts. In a scene (iii. xi) with a pair of visitors his insane rant moves them to laughter; 'Ha, ha, ha!' they cry, and he re-echoes: 'Why, ha, ha, ha, Farewell, good ha, ha, ha!' This surely was a cue to the audience to burst into laughter. Yet in an earlier scene (iii. viii) the hero's wife, Isabella, a prototype of Ophelia, driven mad by grief, speaks lines revealing a vision of her murdered son in heaven, which are almost tragic in their simplicity and beauty. If such discrimination in the dramatic conception of madness was possible by so primitive a playwright as Kyd, what may we not expect of Shakespeare?

It may, in fact, be questioned whether so sensitive a poet as Shakespeare shared the common Elizabethan attitude toward madness. Certainly he never tried to raise a laugh in his theater by bringing an idiot on the stage, as more than one of his fellow playwrights did, and his professional Fools are usually more intelligent than their masters. Ophelia in the German version of the *Ur-Hamlet* is an insane nymphomaniac. This may be a vulgarization of Kyd's conception, but some such strain was probably present in the original play. Shakespeare, on the other hand, handles Ophelia's mad scenes with a most poignant pathos. That there may be no misunderstanding, that the spectators in the Globe may not be tempted to laugh at the mad girl, he warns them in lines spoken by other spectators, the actors on the stage with her. She is, indeed, 'distract,' but 'her mood will needs be pitied'; 'alas, sweet lady'; 'this is the poison of deep grief.' He crowns her with her brother's apostrophe:

O rose of May!
Dear maid, kind sister, sweet Ophelia!

and dismisses her from the stage with Laertes' comment on her actions:

Thought and affection, passion, hell itself,
She turns to favor and to prettiness.

It is interesting that Shakespeare uses Ophelia herself earlier in the play (III. i) to comment in somewhat similar fashion upon one of Hamlet's scenes of feigned madness. For the benefit of those 'lawful espials,' the King and Polonius, Hamlet works himself up to a pitch of frenzy in his abuse of women. Such a diatribe would be more amusing to the mainly masculine audience in Shakespeare's theater than it is to us. It might even set them laughing, but Shakespeare warns against it by the words he puts into the abused girl's mouth as she laments

that noble and most sovereign reason,
Like sweet bells jangled, out of tune and harsh.

Here, certainly, is a scene of feigned madness which was not intended to cause mirth.

There are, of course, other scenes in which Hamlet plays the madman to which no such warning is attached. In addition to his mockery of Polonius at their first interview we have his interjected comments during the performance of 'the Mouse-trap,' culminating in the wild outburst that sends Claudius flying from the stage. Immediately thereafter Hamlet rises to a climax of emotional excitement; he laughs and rhymes with Horatio, pushes a recorder into the hands of his false friends, and quizzes Polonius about the cloud that is alternately shaped like a camel, a weasel, and a whale. He may not be playing the madman throughout the whole scene; in the passage with Polonius he surely is; the old man's prompt acquiescence in his assertions about the cloud must be taken as an attempt to humor a dangerous lunatic. After his killing of Polonius Hamlet's wild and whirling words to Rosencrantz and Guildenstern, and later to the King, serve as a smoke screen to shield him from the immediate consequences of his rash act. It is quite possible that in the old convention of acting Hamlet's behavior in these scenes was calculated to produce a comic effect; it is also possible that the mirth to which Dr. Johnson refers was caused by such overacting as we know took place in early impersonations of Polonius. Be that as it may, the modern reader has still to reckon with the fact that till well into the eighteenth century there persisted a strain of comedy in *Hamlet* which has now completely vanished.

Insanity, real or feigned, made perhaps something of the same appeal to an Elizabethan as drunkenness does to a modern audience. The quickest way to get a laugh, as every playwright and producer knows, is to bring a drunken man upon the stage—witness the peals of laughter that greeted the buffoonery of the drunken butler in a modern production of *The Tempest*. Yet a sensitive dramatist of our century dared to present a drink-sodden artist in a fantastic pathetic play, and Gillette's memorable rendering of Will Dearth in *Dear Brutus* was more likely to evoke a sigh than a laugh. A large and heterogeneous audience is, of course, quick to respond to an actor's appeal, and it is permitted us to question whether the mirth provoked by actors playing the mad Hamlet was always, if ever, in accord with Shakespeare's original intention.

There is, as has been shown, a considerable body of comic matter in *Hamlet*—a far larger and more varied body than we found in *Julius Caesar;* larger and more varied, perhaps, than we shall find hereafter in any of Shakespeare's tragedies. And the reason for this is clear: of all Shakespeare's tragedies, *Hamlet,* his miraculous transformation of an old and well-known stage-play, is most completely in the native tradition of mingled mirth and sadness. Perhaps it is for this reason, among others, that through succeeding centuries *Hamlet* has remained the most successful of Shakespeare's plays.

OTHELLO

Othello, the second of Shakespeare's tragic masterpieces, follows close upon *Hamlet.* It was probably written during the period of theatrical inactivity forced upon him by the terrible outburst of the plague in the year 1603-4. The theaters were closed even before Queen Elizabeth's death in March and were not reopened till April 1604. During this period Shakespeare's company made occasional short trips in the provinces, but it is unlikely that he accompanied them. He seems about this time to have withdrawn more and more from acting—the last play in which he is known to have taken part was Jonson's *Sejanus,* probably a Court performance late in 1603—in order to devote himself to his true calling as a tragic dramatist. At home in London Shakespeare seems to have begun seeking material for new plays in a collection of Italian *novelle,* Cintio's *Hecatommiti,* a book he may have borrowed from Florio, a protégé of Shakespeare's friend, Southampton. Here he found the story of the Moor of Venice, and, as we shall see later, the first source of another play, *Measure for Measure,* produced in the same year as *Othello.* The first record we have of *Othello* is of a Court performance 1 November 1604; but it had probably been played with success in public before it was commanded for presentation by King James, who in May 1603 had taken the company under his direct patronage as His Majesty's Servants.

It was possible to see *Othello* on the stage long before it could be read in print. Apparently the company was withholding this play along with others for publication in the Folio of 1623. Just a year before that date, however, Thomas Walkley, a publisher who had somehow secured a transcript of an acting version, brought it out in quarto form with the following title-page:

> The Tragœdy of Othello, the Moore of Venice. As it hath beene diverse times acted at the Globe, and at the Black-Friers by his Maiestie's Servants. Written by William Shakespeare.

Walkley had, of course, no right to print this play, but he remarked with shameless assurance that, since the poet was dead—Shakespeare had been in his grave for six years—he took the liberty of writing the usual prefatory epistle. He need not, he said, praise the play; 'the author's name is sufficient to vent [sell] his work.' Where Walkley procured his copy of the play we do not know; it must have been a fairly old one, for the text he printed abounds in profane oaths. The editors of the Folio, on the contrary, in obedience to the Act of 1606, 'for the preventing and avoiding the great abuse of the Holy Name of God in stage plays,' carefully deleted them from the acting version which they sent to the press. Occasionally this censorship has weakened the force of Shakespeare's language, notably in Emilia's cry of horror at her discovery of Iago's villainy (v. ii. 218), but on the whole the Folio presents not only a longer, by about 150 lines, but a better text.

Close as *Othello* stands to *Hamlet* in time, it is as different from that play as *Hamlet* is from its immediate predecessor, *Julius Caesar*. In *Hamlet* it was Shakespeare's task to fit his own conception of the tragic hero into the framework of a well-known melodrama; his hands were to some extent tied by his public's acquaintance with the old story. In *Othello,* on the other hand, his source was an unfamiliar Italian tale; his difficulty here was to transmute a rather revolting narrative of sexual jealousy and brutal murder into a tragedy that explored the depths of evil in the soul of man and revealed man's temporary defeat and final triumph in conflict with this power. To do this it was necessary for Shakespeare to make a fairly complete recast of his material. Cintio's story of the Moor of Venice is told with more or less detail in every edition of *Othello;* it need not be repeated here. We need only observe that while he preserved various minor details, Shakespeare altered the motivation and the whole atmosphere of his source. The great first act of *Othello,* with its admirable exposition, including the elopement and secret marriage of Desdemona, the charge of sorcery brought against Othello, and his defense before the Senate, is Shakespeare's pure invention; there is no trace of these incidents in Cintio. So, too, the masterful dramatic catastrophe, with its revelation of Desdemona's innocence and Othello's remorse and atonement, is a complete departure from the long-drawn-out and unsatisfactory conclusion of the *novella*. Such a reworking of his material must have cost Shakespeare time and thought in careful planning. The result is that in *Othello* he achieved what is generally recognized as the most nearly perfect in construction of all his tragedies.

There is yet another and more striking difference between *Hamlet* and *Othello*. *Hamlet* still bears the marks of its origin in the Senecan tragedy of Kyd. The action is started by a supernatural agency, and it involves the members of a royal family and with them the fate of a kingdom, for 'something is rotten in the state of Denmark' which demands purgation. *Othello,* on the other hand, resembles more closely than any other Shakespearean tragedy the popular Elizabethan genre of domestic tragedy. The distinguishing feature of this form was an uncompromisingly realistic presentation of contemporary life, discarding alike supernatural machinery and romantic appeal. Superficially *Othello* has something in common with this genre. The Italian *novella* purported to be a true story of an almost contemporary event; there is no trace in it, or in Shakespeare's play, of the supernatural. The action involves the fate of private persons only; the state of Venice is not threatened by the tragic ruin of its alien soldier. Yet Shakespeare was too much of a poet to be bound by the petty conventions of domestic tragedy. The world in which he set the action of his play is one of dignity, adventure, and romance. Into a tragedy of private life he has infused a note of universality; the tragic theme of *Othello* appeals very directly to men of all climes and ages; and into this theme he has breathed a poignant sense of the pathos of things mortal—'the pity of it, Iago, O, Iago, the pity of it!'

It seems possible that these two factors, the intellectual effort involved in Shakespeare's transformation of his source into effective dramatic form and the inner compulsion that drove him to transmute a sordid narrative into poetic drama, were, in part at least, the cause of the almost complete absence of comedy in *Othello.* Shakespeare, it would seem, was too busy with the architectonics of his play, and too deeply moved by the passion and pity which he read into his source, to have either time or inclination for comedy.

Compared with *Hamlet* the lack of comic matter in *Othello* is peculiarly remarkable; there is no scene of incidental comedy like that in the Danish graveyard; there are no satiric comic characters like Osric and Polonius. There is, indeed, a Clown, a professional Jester attached to the household of Othello in Cyprus; but he is so insignificant a figure that he is omitted without loss in most, if not in all, performances, and barely noticed, if not quite forgotten by the reader. He has no functional part, like that of King Lear's Fool, in the action of the play; he appears briefly in two short scenes to crack some dirty jokes and stammer a few feeble word-plays.[1] One wonders,

1 Granville-Barker (*Prefaces to Shakespeare,* v. II. p. 141) notes that the Clown 'with his conventional jokes (coarse for the minstrels, innocuous for Desdemona)' furnishes the only completely contrasted 'relief' to the intense strain of the action. His two brief appearances come just after the downfall of Cassio and after sen-

in fact, how he got into the play. Perhaps the answer may be found in Shakespeare's relation to his fellow-actors. One of them, Armin, had won marked success in the role of a Jester in *As You Like It* and in *Twelfth Night,* and we may imagine his shrill cry of protest, 'Where do I come in?' when *Othello* was first read to the company and parts were being assigned. If his protest were backed by other members, Shakespeare may good-naturedly have yielded and indicated certain scenes before the grip of tragedy tightened on the action in which the Clown might strut his stuff upon the stage. Shakespeare may even have allowed Armin to write his own lines; one would be glad, certainly, to take the Clown's silly talk away from Shakespeare and attribute it to such a mediocre writer as Robert Armin.

It was not for Armin only that Shakespeare was obliged to create parts in his new play. There are only four or five characters in Cintio's story, a quite insufficient number for a play in which every full member of the company naturally expected a part. The characters of the Duke, Brabantio, Roderigo, Montano, the two walking gentlemen, Gratiano and Ludovico, as well as the courtesan Bianca, are all invented by Shakespeare not only to give variety and background to his action, but also to accommodate his fellow-actors. All these characters are deftly woven into the pattern of the play; there is no underplot, no diffusion of interest in *Othello.*

Is it possible to find anything of comic value in these new figures? Certainly not in the grave Duke, the grieved father of Desdemona, or the passionate Montano. Something might, perhaps, be made of the foolish Roderigo, that 'poor snipe' as Iago calls him. This, however, is doubtful. Shakespeare, as a rule, seems to show a certain sympathy, not to say affection, for his simpletons, but for Roderigo the contempt Iago expresses for his dupe passes over to our attitude toward him, and is presumably that of Shakespeare himself. Roderigo is, in fact, presented as evil-minded as well as weak; he takes part in the plot to arrest Othello in the first act, hopes in vain to seduce Desdemona, and ends by attempting a midnight murder. His function in the play seems to be to illustrate the extraordinary influence that 'honest' Iago exercised over his associates from the noble Othello down to this poor wretch.

Emilia, a capital acting part, is not exactly a new creation of

tence of death has been passed on Desdemona. This is the best that can be said for the part, but stage performances seem to have shown that such 'relief' is hardly needed.

Shakespeare's. In the source the Ensign, who corresponds to Iago, has a wife who is the friend and confidant of Desdemona. This woman, however, is an entirely passive character; she lives under such fear of her husband that, although she knows of his plot against Desdemona, she dares not reveal it to her, and can only warn her not to give the Moor any cause for suspicion. It is only after the death of her husband that she tells the whole story; she is the supposed source of Cintio's tale. Emilia, on the contrary, does not wait for her husband's death to denounce him; she does so to his face, with a fair certainty that her disclosure will bring about her own death at his hands. She lays down her life, in fact, to establish the innocence of her slandered and murdered mistress. Shakespeare might easily have made Emilia a comic character, an easy-going, vulgar-minded waiting maid set off against the innocence and purity of her mistress. There is, indeed, a contrast between these two in the play, but it is not comic; we are not expected to laugh at Emilia's realistic view of married life expressed at a time when her mistress is flooded with the rising tide of her husband's jealousy. That Shakespeare refrained from such a facile comic contrast is one proof among many of his intense concentration upon his tragic theme.

There remains Iago. Is it possible to discover in this incarnation of hatred and malice and all uncharitableness any trace of the comic? The answer would seem to be a flat negative. Yet, curiously, there is an old tradition to the effect that the role had at one time certain comic values. Gildon, a minor writer of the late seventeenth century, declares: 'I'm assured from very good hands that the person who acted Iago was in much esteem for a comedian, which made Shakespeare put several words and expressions into his mouth . . . to make the audience laugh.' Gildon does not name this 'comedian,' and, possibly, his statement is little more than stage tradition. Taylor, the tragic actor who played Hamlet, is known also to have played Iago. Later, however, Colley Cibber, comic playwright and comedian, took the part, and it is hard to think of Cibber as a tragic Iago. In the last generation of heroic actors Edwin Booth played alternately the roles of the protagonist and the villain in *Othello,* and his memorable impersonation of Iago was marked by a 'sardonic, cruel, veiled humor.' Such humor is, of course, poles apart from comedy, and those who still recall the 'glare of hateful glee' with which at the very end Booth as Iago started forward to gloat upon the tragic loading of the bed can hardly believe that this great interpreter of Shakespeare found anything comic in the character. Yet the gifted young actor, José Ferrer, who played in this part in the record-breaking New York run of *Othello*, 1943-4, performed it in such a way as to win more than one laugh from his audience. There are, perhaps, two scenes where a laugh might be permissible; the first is that where Iago, to while away the time of Desdemona's waiting for her lord, entertains her with a string of Elizabethan commonplace satires on women. They are not remarkably witty; in fact Shakespeare himself has stigmatized them in Desdemona's comment as 'old fond paradoxes to make fools laugh i' th' ale-house'—or, let us say, in the theater. The second is the drinking bout which brings about the discharge of Cassio. Iago's false gaiety in this scene is, as audience and reader know, a crafty trap to ensnare his trusting friend. What there is of comedy in these scenes should not be overstressed, for from the very beginning of the play Iago's function has been revealed as that of the villainous intriguer. To play Iago as if his plot were just a game light-heartedly begun for the gratification of his conscious intellectual superiority would contradict the plain evidence of the text and misinterpret Shakespeare's purpose.

It has, perhaps, seemed strange to scrutinize this most pathetic of tragedies to discover some trace of the comic element, familiar in Shakespeare's as in other Elizabethan tragedies. The result of the scrutiny seems to be that this trace is barely visible, and the question at once arises why in *Othello*, of all others, Shakespeare's native strain of comedy has shrunk to such minute proportions. An answer has in part already been attempted: the raw material with which Shakespeare here was dealing demanded tense intellectual effort before it could be cast into finished dramatic form, and, at the same time the bitter pathos of the story as Shakespeare read it fastened a close grip upon his emotions.

There is, perhaps, another reason, indefinable in exact terms yet suggesting itself to the student of Shakespeare's work during this period. It is impossible to pry into his mood and temper and to assert that his plays at this time are cries *de profundis.* Yet when we consider that in the year of *Othello* his fellows called on him for a new comedy and got *Measure for Measure* with its tragic overtones we may, perhaps, be right in thinking that in the plague year of 1603-4 Shakespeare was in no mood for mirth.

KING LEAR

King Lear, the supreme revelation of Shakespeare's power as a tragic poet, comes next to *Othello*, in order of succession. It has, however, little in common with its predecessor. Apart from a certain number of similarities in diction, showing that words and phrases from *Othello* still lingered in Shakespeare's mind, the one point of contact is the intrigue of the underplot in *Lear*. Here the Bastard Edmund deceives a credulous father and an unsuspicious brother somewhat in the way in which Iago imposes upon Othello. Yet even here there is a marked difference. In *Othello* Shakespeare took all possible pains to make Iago's charges credible and convincing; in *Lear* Edmund's accusation is unreasonable and his success impossibly easy; Shakespeare presumably was unwilling to write the Iago intrigue over again. More important still, there is a wide gap between *Othello's* unity of theme and close-woven texture and *Lear's* double plot and complicated action with its numerous inconsistencies and improbabilities. The difference is due, in part at least, to the material with which Shakespeare was working; in *Othello* it was a brief compact narrative, in *Lear* a legend that had been told and retold for centuries until it assumed dramatic form in an old Elizabethan play. And to make his task as a dramatist still harder, Shakespeare added to the original action of the legend and the old play a subplot drawn from a wholly different source, the *Arcadia* of Sir Philip Sidney.

In some ways *King Lear* seems like a throwback to *Hamlet*. Both deal with legendary history; *Lear* was, in fact, first published as a 'true chronicle.' Both involve the tragic fate of a royal house and an ancient kingdom, and both find their immediate source in plays still on the boards in Shakespeare's day. Moreover, as we shall see, *Lear* like *Hamlet* is closer to the Elizabethan conception of tragedy than the intense concentration of *Othello* allowed. It is easier, therefore, to find even in the tragic gloom of *Lear* those gleams of comedy which were barely discernible in *Othello*.

The date of *Lear* can be fixed with comparative accuracy. Entered in the Stationers' Register 26 November 1607, 'as yt was played before the Kinges maiestie . . . upon Sainct Stephen night at Christmas Last,' it was published in quarto form in 1608. Repeated performances at the Globe had, presumably, preceded the call to Shakespeare's company to show this play at Court; we may be sure, therefore, that *Lear* was on the stage in the autumn or early winter of 1606. It cannot have been written much before that time, for, as has been said, its immediate source is an earlier play, *The True Chronicle History of King Leir and his three daughters,* published in the summer of 1605.

This old play has a rather curious history; Henslowe notes that a *King Leare* was played at the Rose in April 1594, and a *History of Leire, Kinge of England,* no doubt the same play, was entered in the Stationers' Register in May of that year. We do not know if it was published at that time; certainly no copy of an early edition has ever been recorded. In 1605, however, this play was again entered in the Register and published 'as it hath bene divers and sundry times lately acted.' Possibly Shakespeare saw this late revival; there can be no doubt whatever that he read the book. The actual composition of his *Lear,* then, must have occurred between the summer of 1605 and that of 1606.

A summary of the old *King Leir* will serve to show the nature of Shakespeare's raw material.

> Leir, a pious Christian King of England, decides to lay down his crown, marry off his three daughters, and divide his kingdom into equal parts for their husbands. The two older girls, Gonerill and Ragan, are already courted by neighboring princes, but Cordella shows no inclination to marry. To overcome her reluctance Leir devises the love-test; Cordella, he knows, will vow she loves him best, and this will give him the chance to bid her show her love by accepting at his hand a princely husband. Unfortunately the 'stratagem,' as Leir calls it, goes quite awry. The older daughters make a great parade of their love, but Cordella, who detects their flattery, responds coolly that she loves him as the child should love the father. Hereupon the pious King breaks into rage, cuts off her protests with 'Peace, bastard imp, no issue of King Leir,' and turns her out to shift for herself. A good old lord, Perillus, speaks up for her, but is told to hold his peace on pain of death. Leir now decides to marry off Gonerill to the King of Cornwall and to take up his residence with her. Meanwhile the Gallian King, who has heard much of the beauty of Leir's daughters, comes to Britain, disguised as a pilgrim, to see if the report be true, and, if so, to win one of them for his wife. On the way to Leir's Court he meets Cordella, who has thrown

off her princely robes, and resolves to earn her living as a seamstress. As pious as her father she exclaims: 'It is the pleasure of my God: And I do willingly embrace the rod.' The Gallian King promptly falls in love with her and tells her that a young and lusty King of France would gladly marry her, but Cordella, who seems quite an up-and-coming sort of girl, bids the disguised pilgrim, 'Cease for thy King, seek for thyself to woo.' He reveals his identity and they hurry off to church.

The action now shifts to the court of Cornwall where Leir is mocked and abused by Gonerill, but bears all as 'the mirror of mild patience.' Finally, pretending that he is making trouble between her and her gentle husband—the Cornwall of *King Leir* resembles Shakespeare's Albany—Gonerill bids him go pack and seek another lodging. Leir breaks down and weeps, but, on the advice of Perillus, who has joined him in disguise, he sets off to Ragan, now married to the King of Cambria. Gonerill despatches a messenger after Leir with instructions to abuse him to Ragan, and, if her sister agrees, to make away with him. Ragan at first pretends to welcome her father, but after an interview with the messenger she bribes that villain to murder both Leir and Perillus. He comes upon the two old men asleep in a wood, wakes them, and bids them prepare to die. After a long-drawn-out pathetic scene in which they rebuke his wickedness and each of them offers to die for the other, a thunderstorm breaks over them. Between fright at the storm and remorse of conscience, the messenger throws up his job, remarking, 'Here I found you, and here I'll leave you.'

Leir now decides to try Cordella. He and Perillus arrive in France penniless, having been held up and robbed by foot-pads. On the way they are about to die of hunger when in the nick of time they find assistance. Cordella, who, in spite of a happy marriage, is grieving over her father's unkindness, has been persuaded by the King to go on a picnic with him and Lord Mumford disguised as countryfolk. Perillus sees them sitting at food and leads Leir to the table. Cordella delays revealing herself until she has induced Leir to tell his sad tale, upon which she kneels to ask his blessing. In turn he kneels to beg forgiveness; the French King kneels to vow revenge upon the wicked daughters. The French army lands unopposed in England, for the watchmen set to fire the warning beacon had deserted it and gone to watch a pot of ale and a rasher of bacon at Goodman Jennings'. The scene in which they excuse themselves for abandoning their post is in the true style of native realistic comedy, as is a later one in which they stagger from the alehouse to encounter their angry captains. The battle that follows is apparently a bloodless combat; the trumpets sound, and Leir is once more King.

It is interesting to consider what Shakespeare has made of this old play. It would, of course, be wrong to limit his knowledge of the legend to the old play alone; there is evidence that he knew more than one of the many other versions; he found it told as sober history in his favorite Holinshed, and Spenser's *Faerie Queene* gave him the lovely name Cordelia. Yet his debt to *King Leir* is undeniable. Among minor details like the occasional borrowing of a word or phrase, he found there, as nowhere else, the prototypes of Kent and Oswald, the storm that breaks over the outcast King, and a recognition scene between father and daughter. It goes without saying that he completely changed the tone of the action, and converted a naive chronicle play into a tremendous and elemental tragedy.

Shakespeare's conception of the tragic import of filial ingratitude and his presentation of this conception in dramatic form have been admirably discussed by Bradley, and, from the point of view of the theater, even better by Granville-Barker. What concerns us here is Shakespeare's use of comic elements in this supreme tragedy. It is evident at once that in this matter he owes nothing to the old play; there is no scene of incidental comedy like that of the drunken watchmen. There is, in fact, nothing in *Lear* that can be described as comic action. What there is of comedy is embodied in two characters, both of them Shakespeare's addition to the story, the Fool and Edgar.

We may begin with Edgar, for this character made such an impression on Shakespeare's first audiences that the publisher of the quarto used him as a selling point by calling attention on the title-page of this edition to his 'sullen and assumed humor of Tom of Bedlam.' It is only in this assumed humor that the role of Edgar calls for consideration here; we may disregard his early appearance as the credulous dupe of his brother and his later return as the champion of truth and justice. These are tragic strains derived from the *Arcadia* which Shakespeare has woven into the larger pattern of *King Lear*.

What is here of prime importance is Edgar's behavior in his disguise as a mad beggar. Something has already been said in the discussion of *Hamlet* on the Elizabethan attitude toward madness. That the common Elizabethan was apt to laugh at the behavior of madmen is certainly true; that Shakespeare rose above the common Elizabethan in his ability to discriminate between the comic and the tragic phases of insanity seems equally obvious. And this power of discrimination appears even more clearly in his treatment of insanity in *Lear* than in *Hamlet*. The King himself goes mad, a new feature in the story, by the way, but Shakespeare takes pains that there shall be nothing laughable in Lear's madness. The superb poetry of the scenes in which his wits begin to turn precludes any tendency on the part of the audience to laugh at the old King's sorry plight. One scene, that in which two joint stools, representing the 'she-foxes,' Goneril and Regan, are arraigned before a royal commission composed of the Fool, the Bedlam, and Kent, was deliberately struck out of the later acting version of the Folio. It is not unlikely that this scene overtaxed the restraint of an early audience and that the groundlings broke into guffaws at the catches of the Fool and the babble of the Bedlam. In the last scene of Lear's madness, where he enters 'fantastically dressed with flowers'—a modern stage direction—his incoherent raving might well have provoked a similar outburst in the pit, but Shakespeare guarded against this by comments he put into the mouths of actors on the stage with Lear. Edgar greets the King's appearance with 'O thou side-piercing sight!' and a Gentleman echoes this phrase as Lear leaves the stage:

> A sight most pitiful in the meanest wretch,
> Past speaking of in a king!

With Edgar, however, Shakespeare has deliberately introduced feigned madness into the action to lighten the tragic strain of the scenes of Lear's genuine insanity. There is nothing like this assumed role in the *Arcadia* episode from which the subplot of *Lear* is derived. There the slandered brother flies from the kingdom to escape his father's wrath, serves abroad as a mercenary soldier, and returns to save his blinded father from self-destruction. Edgar, on the contrary, having escaped immediate pursuit, and knowing that the ports are barred against him—a true Elizabethan touch—determines to disguise himself as a Bedlam beggar. These strolling vagabonds were familiar figures in Elizabethan life. We met one of them, the comic figure of Diccon the Bedlam in *Gammer Gurton's Needle*. But Diccon is more rogue than fool; there is little sign of madness in his trickery. The role that Edgar plans to play is of a wilder sort, that of the Abraham-man, described by Dekker in his *Belman of London,* 1608. The Abraham-man swears, writes Dekker,

> he hath been in Bedlam and will talk franticly of purpose; you see pins struck in sundry places of his naked flesh . . . only to make you believe he is out of his wits: he calls himself by the name of *Poor Tom,* and coming near any body cries out *Poor Tom* is a cold. Of these Abraham-men some be exceeding merry and do nothing but sing songs fashioned out of their own brains . . . others are dogged and so sullen . . . that spying but small company in a house, they boldly and bluntly enter compelling the servants through fear to give them whatever they demand.

Dekker's language is so close to that of Edgar in Act II. iii as to suggest that he had attended a performance of *King Lear* and picked up some of the most telling phrases. There can be no doubt, however, that he has given us a vivid realistic picture of a well-known type. Now it is exactly this type of madness, half real, half deliberately assumed, that was most certain to provoke the Elizabethan sense of humor. That this provocation continued long past Elizabethan times is shown by the report of an actor who took part in Booth's production of *King Lear.* 'Playing Edgar,' he said, 'in Texas and other places remote from civilization, I was often laughed at, though I spared no effort to bring out its tragedy.' It is, perhaps, a question whether the well-meaning actor with his reverence for the Bard did not mistake the playwright's purpose. In his fierce concentration on the tragedy of the King, Shakespeare had no time to spare for the temporary misfortune of Edgar. The patter that he puts into his mouth as the Bedlam has no real relation to his fall from prosperity to wretchedness. Like one of Dekker's Abraham-men, Edgar calls himself *Poor Tom* and sings songs of his own devising. He plays, however, a special role not mentioned in Dekker's pamphlet, that of a man possessed by devils. His first word when he bursts from his hovel upon Lear and the Fool is 'Away! the foul fiend follows me!' and he strikes this note again and again: 'Poor Tom whom the foul fiend hath led through fire and through flame . . . poor Tom whom the foul fiend vexes. . . Five fiends have been in poor Tom at once.' To give a touch of contemporary realism to this demoniac possession Shakespeare drew on a tract supposedly written by Samuel Harsnett, chaplain to Archbishop Bancroft, *A Declaration of Egregious Popish Impostures*, 1603. From this work, an exposure of some alleged Jesuit feats of exorcism, Shakespeare drew all the names of the devils who haunted poor Tom: Obidicut, Hobbididance, Mahu, Modo, Flibbertigibbet, and so on. At the Court performance of *Lear*, King James, no doubt, with his keen interest in demonology, chuckled audibly at this hit at Jesuit pretensions, and the King's mirth would be caught up and redoubled by fawning courtiers.

Later on Edgar plays another comic part. He is, to be sure, introduced to his blind father as a mad beggar who will guide him to Dover, but by the time they get there his voice is altered and he speaks 'in better phrase and matter.' When they are challenged by the wicked Steward, however, Edgar at once assumes the role of a peasant and speaks the few lines of his dialogue with Oswald in the sort of Southern dialect which was conventional on the Elizabethan stage for the speech of a country boor: 'Keep out, che vor ye, or ise try whether your costard or my ballow be the harder.' This is no doubt a comic touch. There was no reason for Edgar to play the peasant, but Shakespeare's audience must have been amused and pleased to see a country fellow armed only with a cudgel, Edgar's 'ballow,' knock down and kill the overweening retainer of a great lord, a type heartily disliked by London citizens. Edgar, speaking as poor Tom, had already described this type in Shakespeare's best prose: 'a servingman, proud in heart and mind; that curled my hair, wore gloves in my cap, served the lust of my mistris' heart, and did the act of darkness with her.'

Certainly the 'humor' of Edgar, both as the sturdy peasant and as the mad beggar, had comic values for the Elizabethans. Yet there is more in this role than mere entertainment. Shakespeare confronts his fallen monarch with the utter degradation of the Bedlam and uses this horrid spectacle first to push Lear over the border line between impotent anger and complete insanity, and then to bring home to him the mocking unreality of all the trappings that had adorned his state as King: 'Thou art the thing itself; unaccommodated man is no more but such a poor, bare, forked animal as thou art. Off, off, you lendings!'

The character of the Fool in *Lear* has been the theme of such ecstatic eulogy by romantic critics that it is not easy to discuss this role with any degree of sobriety. Yet there is something that needs to be said of the Fool's appearance in the play, his function in the action, and his stage history. The introduction of a professional Jester into the tragedy of *Lear* may possibly be due in the first place to Shakespeare's personal relation to his company. After the somewhat shabby way in which he had treated Armin in the allocation of parts in *Othello,* Shakespeare certainly owed his fellow-actor something and he paid the debt with interest by creating for him the part of the Fool in *Lear.* Another not improbable cause for the introduction of the Jester here may be found in Shakespeare's persistent interest in experiment and variation. It was a commonplace of Elizabethan criticism that decorum demanded the separation of tragedy and comedy and that, in particular, the appearance of the Fool in tragedy was the gravest of sins against decorum. Shakespeare must have known, for example, Sidney's protest against plays that mingled kings and clowns, where, in Sidney's phrase, the clown was 'thrust in by head and shoulders to play a part in majestical matters.' But Shakespeare's indifference to conventional criticism was probably on a par with his knowledge thereof. He had never yet, it is true, introduced a professional Jester into the company of a king, but he had not been far from this breach of decorum when he brought Falstaff into the royal council of war at Shrewsbury. A slight variation of this attempt would, he thought, not offend his uncritical audience; it would certainly be an interesting experiment.

We need not suppose that Shakespeare introduced the Fool into *King Lear* merely to satisfy the claim of a fellow-actor or to indulge his own desire to flaunt a received convention. There must have been a deeper underlying purpose. Shakespeare alone, of all who had told the tale of Lear, realized to the full the insensate folly of the King's behavior and its inevitable tragic consequences. To bring this home directly to his audience he needed a commentator upon the stage to play a part something like that of the Greek tragic chorus. Only something like, for the impersonal classic chorus was wholly at variance with the accepted tradition of the native stage, for which, after all, Shakespeare was writing. The commentator must be one of the characters of the play; yet one qualified by his very nature only to remark upon, not to take part in, the action; a nobleman would not serve the purpose. In the first scene of the play Shakespeare shows how the imperious temper of Lear resents and rejects a councilor's advice; Kent's opposition results only and immediately in his banishment on pain of death. The Court Jester, on the other hand, because he was at once the all-licensed Fool and yet impotent to act, was free to comment at will in a tone of jesting mockery and so to contrast the fantastic illusion in which his master lived with the bitter truth of things as they were. No other character could serve so well what seems to have been Shakespeare's purpose.

Yet because of Shakespeare's intense and abiding interest in human nature, the Fool in *Lear* is something more than a choric commentator. He is a real and very human person. Before ever he comes upon the stage we hear that he has pined away since Cordelia left the Court, an admirable stroke that reveals at once his loving nature and his discernment of the truth of the daughter to which Lear was so wilfully blind. He is cowed by Goneril's frown and only chirps aside his comments during the quarrel between her and Lear. He follows his master with doglike fidelity when most of his train have forsaken him: 'I will tarry; the fool will stay.' In the storm he 'labours to outjest' Lear's sense of his wrongs; but he shivers in the cold rain to which the tempest in the King's mind makes Lear oblivious. He runs screaming from the hovel where he has encountered the Bedlam and clings to Kent for help. Reassured, he recovers sufficiently to play his part with Lear and Edgar in the arraignment scene, but he is physically exhausted. His last words, when Lear falls asleep, 'I'll go to bed at noon,' seem to have a symbolic significance; we might render them: 'I've played my part and can go to rest now, even though the action is but half completed.' Critics have asked why we get no more of this lovable, whimsical character, but the answer is implied in the words just quoted; the Fool's role as commentator is completed. Shakespeare did not introduce him until Lear's troubles had actually begun; he retained him until they had reached their peak, and then dismissed him. The rest of the action deals with what has been called the redemption of Lear; there was no place for this realistic humorous critic in the scene of reunion between father and daughter, even less in the tragic catastrophe which Shakespeare invented to bring this play to its tremendous close.

Was this daring experiment, this thrusting in of the Clown 'to play a part in majestical matters,' justified by success? It smacks of heresy even to ask the question. In Shakespeare's time, certainly, the familiar figure of the Fool had a comic value for the audience which it has lost today. Yet even on Shakespeare's stage there seems to have been some uncertainty as to the Fool's role, or at least as to the extent of his role. His lines differ from time to time in the two old texts which represent two different acting versions. His trick of exiting with a scrap of doggrel suggests the improvisation of the Clown accustomed to speak more than was set down for him. The obscene jest with which he closes the last scene of the first act may charitably be ascribed to Armin rather than to Shakespeare; it got a laugh, which was enough to keep it in both versions. On the other hand the rhymed prophecy which he speaks in Merlin's name before he follows Lear to the hovel (III. ii) appears only in the later text. It is little more than an expansion of a few lines falsely ascribed in Shakespeare's day to Chaucer, and is absolutely undramatic with no bearing either on the situation or on the character of the speaker. It is the Clown's direct address to the audience and must have got into the text after Shakespeare severed his connection with the company and retired to Stratford.

If there was this uncertainty about the Fool's role in Elizabethan times, what was to be expected later when the decorum that Shakespeare had defied once more prevailed upon the stage? The role was ruthlessly canceled in Tate's famous, or infamous, adaptation of *King Lear* in 1681, and Tate's version held the stage for a century and a half. Even Kean, who restored the tragic ending in 1823, did not dare to bring back the Fool. Macready, who in 1830 replaced the contaminated Tate-Shakespeare version by the true text, hesitated to restore the part of the Fool. He feared, he said, lest that character would 'weary, or annoy, or distract the spectator,' and finally he handed over the part to a young actress. This was at least logical, for Macready conceived Shakespeare's Fool as a 'fragile, hectic, beautiful, half-idiot-looking boy,' a conception that still lingers in Bradley's picture of the Fool as a 'timid, delicate, frail being,' as remote a figure from the boisterous, romping Elizabethan Clown as possible. The groundlings at the Globe would have pelted Macready's girl off the stage with nuts and bitten apples. It was not till 1845 that Phelps restored the role to a male actor, a practice retained in later productions.

What are we to make of this long-continued repugnance of the profession to the role of the Fool? Certainly no reader would wish to cancel the part; a text of *Lear* without the Fool is inconceivable. Quite apart from his satiric commentary, the Fool's songs, jests, scraps of folklore and folk wisdom go far to lighten the tension of some of the most painful scenes. On the other hand it would appear that on the stage the role has lost the comic values it once possessed. The experiment was, perhaps, successful in Shakespeare's day, but a modern audience is readier to take its tragedy straight than the folk for whom Shakespeare wrote. Ibsen and O'Neill see no need of introducing clowns into *Ghosts* and *Mourning Becomes Electra.*

Shakespeare's use of comedy in *Lear* differs widely, it seems, from his practice in the immediately preceding tragedies. Comedy here is not incidental entertainment, realistic, naive, or satiric. It is embodied in two characters intimately associated with the main action of the play. Whatever we may think of the Bedlam and the Fool, to the Elizabethans they were comic characters. In Shakespeare's hands, however, they serve not merely to amuse his audience, but to emphasize, to contrast with, to comment upon the tragic fate of his great protagonist. We may discover later that he made a somewhat similar use of such figures, though indeed in less striking fashion, in his later tragedies.

TIMON OF ATHENS

It would take an eye sharper than that of Lynceus to discover any genuine Shakespearean comic matter in the confused and incoherent play included in Shakespeare's works as *Timon of Athens.* Its first inclusion, in the Folio, seems to have been something of an accident. There is convincing evidence that while the Folio was going through the press, the play of *Troilus and Cressida* was actually being set up directly after *Romeo and Juliet.* Trouble of some sort arose—the matter will be more fully discussed hereafter—and the printing of *Troilus* was stopped. To fill the gap left by its disappearance, Heminges and Condell handed the printers the play-book of *Timon,* a reprint of which now appears in the Folio between *Romeo and Juliet* and *Julius Caesar.* There seems at least the possibility that if it had not been for the trouble over *Troilus,* the strange and troublesome play of *Timon* might never have found its way into print. That, surely, would have been unfortunate, for we should have lost some magnificent Shakespearean poetry. On the other hand, his fame as a dramatist would stand quite as high, perhaps higher, if this hapless failure had never come to light.

Even after the labor of editors for two centuries and more, *Timon* remains a failure on the stage and a vexatious problem in the study. This applies even to the comparatively intelligible form in which the play appears in modern editions. An attempt to read it in the original text will leave the student swamped in a Serbonian bog of misprints, misnomers, inconsistencies, and contradictions, a confusion worse confounded, well symbolized by the mystic word, Ullorxa (III. iv. 112), carefully elided by editors, which has somehow crept from the copy into the original text. The copy from which this text was set up must have been something very different from those scarcely blotted 'papers' which Shakespeare's old friends, Heminges and Condell, declared he habitually handed them to be arranged for stage performance. One of the characteristics of the Folio text is the fullness and specific character of the stage directions. This would seem to show that the manuscript had been carefully annotated for performance, and it seems unlikely that a play so prepared should not have had at least a tryout on the stage. There is, however, no record of any performance before the closing of the theaters, and it is quite possible that the failure of *Timon* on the stage was so complete that the playbook was thrust away among the archives of the company, where it lay until it was hauled out to serve as a stopgap in the Folio. Such a presumed performance will, perhaps, prove later a practical explanation of the condition of the text.

The peculiar condition of the text of *Timon* is that long passages reveal Shakespeare at the top of his form as a dramatic poet, while others, almost inextricably intermingled with these, fall below what we may believe him capable of at any stage of his career. Various explanations have been attempted to account for this discrepancy. The earliest, most elaborately expounded by Delius, a German scholar, is that we have here Shakespeare's hasty and incomplete revision of an older play. This theory will not, however, stand the test of careful examination. We know something of Shakespeare's fashion of dealing with old plays; we have seen him at work in *King John, The Taming of the Shrew*, and even in *King Lear;* in each case an old play lies behind Shakespeare's finished work, but his work in each case is finished. It is incredible that Shakespeare at the height of his power—all critics agree that *Timon* belongs somewhere toward the close of his tragic period—should have stooped to hand over such an undigested mass of matter to his fellow-actors.

Another theory, long ago proposed, abandoned, and again revived, seems more nearly to explain the facts of the case. Stated briefly as a working hypothesis, it would run about as follows. Encouraged by the striking success of *Lear* (performed as we know at Court in the

Christmas season of 1606), Shakespeare began another play in which Burbage could repeat the hit he had made as the mad and misanthropic King. The misanthrope, *par excellence*, in Renaissance literature was Timon of Athens, whose story was told in part by Plutarch in his *Life of Antony* and more fully in dialogue form by Lucian. Timon, it seems, was a rich Athenian of the age of Pericles who squandered his fortune in gifts to false friends, but when reduced to poverty, experienced only base ingratitude from those he had assisted. Thereupon he turned misanthrope and cursed mankind. Later, while toiling as a peasant, he discovered a great treasure of gold and was at once besieged by flatterers whom he repelled with threats and blows. He died and was buried on the seashore and, says Plutarch, 'the sea setting in, compassed his tomb round about so that no man could come at it.'

Here was raw material for a play in which a misanthrope might figure as protagonist. It seems not unlikely that Shakespeare began his work at the point where his sources were fullest, that is with the fourth act. This opens with the ruined Timon's tremendous curse on Athens and his stripping himself naked, like Lear, as he flies to live a hermit in the woods. It continues with his discovery of the gold and his dealing it out to soldiers, thieves, and harlots to aid them in wreaking his vengeance on mankind, an original and tragically Shakespearean note. The last act, apparently hastily thrown together, shows Timon's angry refusal of a recall to Athens, including Plutarch's anecdote of the fig tree on which he gave the citizens leave to hang themselves, and finally the report of the misanthrope's lonely death. It is a curious proof of the unfinished state of this act that Shakespeare copied from Plutarch the two epitaphs on Timon's tomb, uncertain, apparently, which of them to retain.

If Shakespeare, as seems to have been the custom, read these last acts to his fellows, he was, no doubt, urged to go on and finish a regulation five-act play; Burbage, the foremost tragedian of the company, would naturally be delighted with the resounding tirades that Shakespeare put into the mouth of the protagonist. When, however, Shakespeare took up his pen once more, he found himself confronted with serious difficulties. It was incumbent on him to devise a dramatic exposition showing Timon in his glory, a rising action dramatizing his fall into poverty, the climax, and his final plunge into misanthropy. Now Shakespeare's forte was never outright invention of incident and action, and we may imagine him laboring over this task. It was while he was turning over these things in his mind and writing, perhaps, some isolated fragments of the first three acts that the call came to him to compose at once and speedily a Scottish play for the entertainment of King James and his royal visitor, Christian of Denmark. This call was equivalent to an imperative command, and Shakespeare, we must suppose, turned over his unfinished manuscript to his fellows, and attacked the problem of *Macbeth*. He may have meant to return to it later and finish the play; he may have recognized that for once he had tackled an almost impossible task. That we shall never know. What does seem clear is that after the strenuous effort involved in *Macbeth*, he abandoned *Timon* and turned to the easier task of dramatizing Plutarch's fascinating narratives of Antony and of Coriolanus.

It must have been years later, perhaps after Shakespeare's death, that the leading members of the company in need of a new play for Blackfriars bethought themselves of Shakespeare's manuscript, drew it from their archives, and handed it over to one of their associated playwrights to doctor up for the stage. And that is exactly what this unknown playwright did; [1] he had no thought of attempting the probably impossible task of completing a fragmentary Shakespearean tragedy. His business was to supply what was wanting in the fragment to make it a good Blackfriars show: bustling action, low comedy, spectacle, and music. These he added in ample measure. To him belong, for example, the second dunning scene (III. iv) where Timon enters in a rage to be assailed by the vociferous servants of his creditors, the mock banquet scene (III. vi), the Fool, and the flyting match between Timon and Apemantus. Most noticeable, perhaps, is the elaborate Masque of Cupid and the Amazons 'with lutes in their hands, dancing and playing' in the second scene of the play. Directions for music, a specialty of Blackfriars plays, are scattered throughout the text; they include calls for trumpets, hautboys, lutes, and the fife and drum of a marching army. One brief scene (v. iii) has apparently been inserted to tell the audience that Timon is really dead and buried.

What has here been put forward is a hypothesis only, yet it seems to be a good working hypothesis; it explains better than another the

[1] Various guesses have been made on the identity of this playwright. In an address delivered before the British Shakespearean Association in 1923 the present writer urged the claims of Chapman plus some hack playwright, cutting and supplementing Chapman's work. Today he would feel less certain of Chapman and inclined to substitute the name of Middleton, who, it seems certain, was called on to smarten up *Macbeth*. After all, it does not greatly matter.

discordant and heterogeneous nature of the present text. And it does more than that. If Shakespeare turned to the story of Timon the misanthrope directly after finishing his work on *Lear*, it accounts for the mood of the play and its likeness to the darkest of all Shakespeare's tragedies. *Timon* shares with *Lear* an insistence on the tragic consequences of ingratitude, a fierce invective against the corruption of modern life, and a special abhorrence of sexual vice. In such a play there was no room for the happy genial note of true Shakespearean comedy. The rough horseplay of certain scenes may well be attributed to the reviser rather than to Shakespeare. The character of Apemantus, introduced in the first scene by Shakespeare, may have been designed as a cynical commentator on the action; he would probably have been an even bitterer Fool than Lear's Jester. Unfortunately in the reviser's hands he has become little better than a scurrilous buffoon. If, as has been suggested, the play was a failure on the stage, one reason may be this absence of comedy. The Shakespearean fragments are the shards of a broken vessel into which the poet poured all the bitterness that had been accumulating in his heart during the period of his great tragedies. We may say of the play what the faithful Steward says of his master:

> Trouble him no further, thus you still shall find him,

and close our comment with Timon's own farewell to life:

> Come not to me again; but say to Athens,
> Timon hath made his everlasting mansion
> Upon the beached verge of the salt flood;
> Who once a day with his embossed froth
> The turbulent surge shall cover: thither come,
> And let my grave-stone be your oracle.

MACBETH

Pre-eminent among Shakespeare's tragedies for the rapidity of its movement, *Macbeth* is the latest in time of his four tragic masterpieces. It is also the shortest, running to only a little over 2,000 lines as compared with nearly 4,000 in *Hamlet* and over 3,000 in *Othello* and in *Lear*. Its swift action springs from its brevity, and its brevity in turn was probably determined by the occasion that called it into being. There can be little doubt that *Macbeth* was written in headlong haste to comply with a royal demand for a new play by Shakespeare's company, 'His Majesty's Servants,' for presentation at Court during the festivities that attended the visit of the King's brother-in-law, Christian IV of Denmark in the late summer of 1606. The call must have found Shakespeare almost exhausted by the tremendous effort he had just expended upon *Lear,* to say nothing of his unfinished *Timon,* but like a loyal subject and a faithful co-worker with his fellow-actors, he bent himself to the task. The first step, of course, was to find a plot, a subject that would please his royal master, a speedy action that would meet the actors' need for brief rehearsals, and, we may perhaps add, a theme in accord with his own mood, brooding as he had been for years on tragic issues. Shakespeare was in no humor at this time to write another *Merry Wives of Windsor* to stir the laughter of the Court. Fortunately a suitable subject lay close at hand.

In August 1605 James had paid a formal visit to Oxford, where he was entertained with various shows and spectacles. Among others he was met at the gate of St. John's College by three youths costumed like Sybils, or the three weird sisters of the legend, who had prophesied power without end to the race of Banquo. They greeted James as descended from Banquo and hailed him with a threefold *salve* as King of Britain, Ireland, and France. This 'conceit,' we are told, 'the King did very much applaud.' Shakespeare, a member of the King's Company, must have heard of this pageant and of the King's applause. When the call came to him for a new play at Court, he would have remembered it and realized that here was a theme that would please the King if it could be worked up into full dramatic form. He recalled reading in his favorite Holinshed something about a prophecy by the weird sisters to Banquo and his brother-in-arms Macbeth; he would look it up again to see if it offered material for a royal tragedy. A reperusal of Holinshed's chronicle must have been at once stimulating and unsatisfactory. He found there, to be sure, something to please the King: the prophecy to his ancestor Banquo, the reference to wizards and a certain witch—sure to interest the witch-hating James— and the overthrow of the usurper Macbeth by the true heir to the throne. On the other hand Holinshed made Banquo an accomplice with Macbeth in the murder of King Duncan. That would never do at Court; the King's view of the abhorrent nature of regicide was well known. The murder itself was told in a brief phrase: 'he slew the King at Inverness'; but a murder which placed Macbeth on the throne should be the central and most exciting scene of a tragedy. Evidently the story in Holinshed would have to be recast, but that was not impossible.

We can almost see Shakespeare at work reshaping the plot. In the first place he changes the conspiracy against Duncan and his death, apparently in battle, to a secret midnight murder. Earlier in the chronicle he had found the story of the secret murder of the sleeping King Duff by his host, Donwald, Captain of the Castle of Fores. The substitution of a secret murder for an open slaughter would permit Shakespeare to make Banquo innocent of any knowledge of the deed, and as a result Banquo becomes in the play a loyal subject profoundly shocked by the murder of Duncan. The various tempters of the chronicle—the weird sisters who hailed Macbeth as King to be; the wizards who warned him against Macduff; the witch who told him that no man of woman born should kill him—are united in a single group whom Shakespeare identifies with the witches of popular superstition. In addition, to increase the supernatural horror of his play, he calls up Banquo's ghost, of which there is no earlier mention, to confront Macbeth at the royal banquet.

There are signs of hasty composition in *Macbeth*, in the brevity and swift succession of the scenes. No single situation is developed so fully as is the scene between Hamlet and his mother or the temptation scene in *Othello*. In spite of his haste, however, Shakespeare succeeded in converting a rather arid chronicle into one of the world's greatest tragedies. He has done this by centering attention on the protagonist and tracing the progressive degeneration of a noble soldier into a regicide and a tyrant under the influence of the power of evil embodied in those emissaries of the devil, the Witches. *Macbeth* is a great psychological drama; the hero, like Satan in *Paradise Lost,* has wilfully chosen evil for his good, and the result of his choice is bitter disillusion and the torture of the mind. No other hero in Shakespearean tragedy makes this fatal choice and no other suffers such an irretrievable fall.

Our task at present, however, is not to discuss the relation of *Macbeth* to other Shakespearean tragedies, but rather to ascertain what trace there is of comic matter in this dark and bloody drama. To do this it is necessary first to consider the state of the text, for it is quite certain that *Macbeth* has not come down to us as Shakespeare wrote it. There is but one text of the play, that of the Folio, and this text was evidently printed from a late prompt-copy prepared for a performance some time after Shakespeare had retired. There is a general agreement among scholars that certain passages in the text are un-Shakespearean: viz, the Hecate scene (III. v) ending with the stage direction for a song, 'Come away,' and two passages in the cauldron scene (IV. i): (a) that when Hecate appears again with 'the other three witches,' and the stage direction for the song, 'Black spirits,' et cetera; and (b) lines 125-32, where the Witches, now apparently six in number, dance to music.

There is, further, a general agreement that these interpolations are the work of Thomas Middleton, a dramatist occasionally writing for Shakespeare's Company. It was for them that he wrote among other plays, *The Witch,* a tragi-comedy performed at their Blackfriars theater. This play seems to have been a complete and, it may be added, a well-deserved failure. It was withdrawn and never got into print, but a transcript of the play-book was discovered and printed in 1778. Here there appeared not only the character of Hecate, a mistress of the witches, but the full text of the songs called for in the stage directions in *Macbeth.* The exact date of *The Witch* is not known, but it was certainly later than *Macbeth* and before the Folio of 1623. It seems plain, therefore, that Middleton lifted the character of Hecate and a couple of songs from his unsuccessful play and inserted them into Shakespeare's work when he was called on to smarten it up for some revival.

The question naturally arises why Shakespeare's fellow-actors felt any need of revising this masterpiece of tragedy. The answer may probably be found in the stage history of *Macbeth.* It may have been successful at the Court performance for which it was composed, but apparently it did not please the general public. There are very few allusions to *Macbeth* in contemporary literature and but one record of a public performance before the closing of the theaters in 1642. After the Restoration, D'Avenant felt called on to rewrite *Macbeth* from beginning to end. He cut out the Porter scene as improper in tragedy, and greatly enlarged the songs and dances of the Witches, who now flew through the air on 'machines.' This new version exactly hit the taste of the time; Pepys, who may be allowed to speak for that age, calls D'Avenant's *Macbeth:* 'a most excellent play in all respects, but especially in divertisement . . . which is a strange perfection in a tragedy.' These singing and dancing Witches held the stage well into the nineteenth century; in the famous Kemble-Siddons production one of the Witches was costumed as a Court lady with powdered hair, rouge, and point lace. It was not till the time of **Phelps, 1847,** that Shakespeare's weird sisters, 'so wither'd and so wild in their attire,' once more regained the stage.

It would appear, therefore, that *Macbeth* in its original form was too unrelieved a tragedy for the taste of a public which, even in Shakespeare's day, was turning to the more sensational form of tragicomedy with its spectacular and masque-like effects accompanied by music and dancing. This was especially true of the sophisticated audience at Blackfriars, and there seems reason to believe that the prompt-copy on which the Folio text is based was prepared for a revival at that theater.

Now it is just this spectacular effect with music and dancing that Middleton introduced into *Macbeth*. He promoted the vulgar witch Hecate of his own play to the classical Goddess of Hades and made her rebuke the weird sisters and bid them meet her at the pit of Acheron. Into the grim cauldron scene he interpolated another sort of 'divertisement.' Here while the weird sisters are stirring the filthy ingredients of their charm, Hecate enters, this time 'with the other three witches,' a stage direction that is omitted or altered in many modern editions. These extra witches were presumably wanted for the song and dance that immediately follows. Hecate bids the assembled company

> Now about the cauldron sing,
> Like elves and fairies in a ring.

It is hard to think of Shakespeare's 'black and midnight hags' dancing like fairies, but Middleton did not mind the incongruity so long as he could stage a bit of a show. This is not the last of Middleton's interpolations, for after the ghostly procession of the eight Kings followed by the blood-bolter'd Banquo, a sight which sears the eyeballs of Macbeth, the First Witch proposes to the others to 'cheer up his spirites' by a little song and dance:

> I'll charm the air to give a sound,
> While you perform your antick round,
> That this great king may kindly say
> Our duties did his welcome pay.

Could anything be less appropriate?

Divertisement, such as Middleton inserted and Pepys admired in *Macbeth,* is comedy of a sort, amusing entertainment, but it is certainly not Shakespearean. A search for traces of true comedy in the play yields but a scanty harvest. The Witches in their original form must have been repulsive rather than amusing. Other gleanings are suspect as later additions to the text. The Doctor's quavering cry,

> Were I from Dunsinane away and clear,
> Profit again should hardly draw me here,

seems like an appeal to the audience for a laugh and may perhaps be the extemporization of an actor. A passage of prose dialogue between Lady Macduff and her son (IV. ii. 37-63) appearing in the middle of a verse scene sounds suspiciously like an interpolation. There is no reason why the Lady, who has just shown the greatest concern for herself and her boy, should suddenly begin to jest with him about buying husbands in the market. The lines that follow this feeble bit of fun (ll. 44-64) are apparently a thrust at the 'equivocators' already alluded to in the Porter scene. We may cancel the prose passage and yet retain a coherent text. After the boy's innocent speech,

> Poor birds they are not set for, (IV. ii. 36)

his mother takes him in her arms with the sigh,

> Poor prattler, how thou talk'st! (IV. ii. 62)

only to be roused by the entrance of the messenger with his warning of danger near at hand. That D'Avenant cancelled the passage suggests that he felt it presented a comic aspect improper in a tragedy. It may have been inserted in an early version of the play to fatten the parts of the two boys who played the Lady and her son. Whether the more or less comic insertion derives from Shakespeare or not may be left to the judgment of the reader; certainly it seems out of place in a pathetic scene designed to bring out the innocence of Macbeth's last victims.

The famous comic scene of the drunken Porter has been a stone of offense from early times. D'Avenant, of course, struck it out. Coleridge declared that the 'low soliloquy of the Porter [was written] for the mob by some other hand, perhaps with Shakespeare's consent; and that finding it take, he with the remaining ink of a pen otherwise employed, just interpolated the words, *I'll devil-porter it no further: I had thought to have let in some of all the professions that go the primrose way to the everlasting bonfire.* Of the rest not one syllable has the ever present being of Shakespeare.' The gentle Schiller was so shocked by the Porter that he replaced him in his adaptation of *Macbeth* for the Weimar theater by a pious old man who comes on singing a morning hymn and bids the impatient knockers at the gate attend till he has finished the more important business of prayer. Shakespeare has been called 'myriad-minded,' but it is hard to picture the chamber of his mind in which such a character as Schiller's sentimental Porter could have been conceived.

No scene or part of a scene in a play by Shakespeare should be rejected because it transgresses the code of the classicist or offends the sensibilities of a romantic poet. The tests to be applied are dramatic fitness, realism of character, and Shakespearean diction, and the Porter scene will assuredly meet all three. In the first place an intercalary scene like this is needed to give Macbeth time to retire to his chamber, wash his bloody hands, and put on his nightgown, before he meets the lords who have come to rouse King Duncan. In the D'Avenant version there is only a patch of a dozen lines between Macbeth's exit with the groan: 'Wake Duncan with thy knocking! I would thou couldst!' and his re-entry, calm and self-possessed, to await the dreadful discovery that impends. But there is a stronger reason for this scene than mere theatrical necessity. De Quincey, in a famous passage of poetic and imaginative criticism, long ago pointed out that the knocking on the gate symbolizes the return of the real and human upon the fiendish world in which the murderer and his wife are moving. Now the knocking at the gate implies a porter to attend and open it. Even D'Avenant saw this and introduced here a nameless Servant, who speaks one meaningless line, ·to perform this necessary task. Shakespeare knew better; his Porter is a lifelike figure with a character of his own. He has been drinking hard with the King's retainers and now staggers into the courtyard in the reluctant performance of his duty. He is in no hurry; the gentry at the gate can wait till he is ready to admit them, and in the meantime he will play the part that his drunken fancy suggests, that of the Porter of Hell-gate. Shakespeare, and no doubt many in his audience, had seen in youth some old Miracle Play in which a devil-porter summoned lost souls to Hell; perhaps some well-read auditor at the Court performance recalled the 'good master Porter' of *The Four PP,* who admitted the Pardoner in search of Margery Corson. Certainly it was no unfamiliar role that Macbeth's man imagined himself playing.

The lost souls whom the Porter invites to enter are no very dreadful criminals: a greedy farmer who had guessed wrong on the grain market and hanged himself when prices fell; a conspirator who had tried in vain to equivocate himself out of a charge of treason —the allusion to the trial of Father Garnett is fairly obvious—and a tailor who had committed petty larceny on the stuff sent him to make his patron's hose. A far greater crime has been committed behind the Porter's back, the murder of a sleeping guest who was both king and kinsman. It has been well said that 'in pretending to be the porter of hell-gate he is terribly near the truth.' The scene serves a double dramatic purpose: the Porter's patter no doubt pro-voked laughter even in the Court circle; the dreadful irony of the scene must have come with startling force to the more sensitive of Shakespeare's audience. The Porter in *Macbeth* plays a role like that of the Grave-digger in *Hamlet* or the Clown who brings the worm of Nilus to Cleopatra; he is a visitor from the common kindly world into the realm of tragic circumstance.

Finally, despite Coleridge's emphatic assertion, there is nothing in the Porter's speech, down to a certain point at least, that war-rants us in discarding it as un-Shakespearean. The dominant idea that the Porter should imagine himself as the keeper of Hell-gate is a stroke of genius, far beyond the reach of Middleton or any other possible reviser of Shakespeare's text. Once given this idea, the language of the Porter is both appropriate and effective. The short, broken rhythm, the vigorous realistic phrasing are what might be expected of a man roused from uneasy sleep with the fumes of a late debauch still swirling in his head. And when the chill of the morning recalls him to the situation and his duty, he responds to the insistent knocking with 'Anon, anon,' the familiar answer of waiters in a tavern to the call of impatient guests, 'Coming, sir, coming!' His 'remember the porter' is a characteristic and rather impudent request for a tip.

Here, or a line or two lower, it seems possible that the speech of Shakespeare's Porter ends. We surely must allow him the words, 'carousing till the second cock,' but this phrase seems to have sug-gested to a reviser, possibly indeed to Armin, who played the Porter, the vulgar dissertation of the effects of drink which follows. There is not a gleam of Shakespeare's wit in these lines; on the contrary their grossness probably caused Coleridge to brand, too hastily, the whole scene as 'disgusting.' The passage is not unlike the fooling of the Vice in the old Morals, with which, of course, an actor like Armin would be familiar. It seems unlikely, moreover, that the impatient Macduff would linger on the threshold of the castle and play the stooge to the Porter's jests. If we cancel lines 27 to 46 of this scene, we may get, as in a passage already discussed, a quite coherent text. To the Porter's excuse for his delay, that he had been drinking late, Macduff replies sharply: 'Is thy master stirring?' and then turning from him sees Macbeth entering, and exclaims: 'Here he comes.' Some such cut as this, it may be noted, is made in most acting versions. With this excision we get a scene of true Shakespearean ironic humor, the only one of the kind in the whole play.

Of all Shakespeare's tragedies *Macbeth* alone was written for a special performance at Court. Perhaps this explains why there is so little of comedy in the original version; Shakespeare may have felt that there was plenty of mere entertainment, some of it notably transgressing the bounds of propriety and even decency, in other Court performances at that time. Nor was there any need for him at Court to appeal, as he was bound to do to the groundlings of the Globe, by the antics of a clown. Moreover he seems in *Macbeth* to have been absorbed in his task of tracing the soul's tragedy of the hero, as in *Othello* he had been absorbed in the problem of transmuting the brutal narrative of his source into poetic drama. While at work on *Othello* he may have yielded to Armin's protest and allowed him to interpolate the brief and trivial passages for the Clown; in *Macbeth* what he wrote for Armin to speak has theatrical and ironic as well as comic value. There is nothing in *Macbeth*, however, to compare with the interwoven comedy of character and action that runs through the tragic tissue of *Hamlet* and *King Lear*. *Macbeth* stands apart as an example of concentrated and headlong tragedy.

ANTONY AND CLEOPATRA

With *Antony and Cleopatra* Shakespeare emerges from the valley of the shadow in which he had been sojourning since he wrote *Julius Caesar*. It is a curious, perhaps a significant, fact that a Roman play marks his entrance into this realm of night and another of the same type heralds his escape. There is a bond of likeness between these two plays; both are historical tragedies and both draw heavily upon North's translation of Plutarch. Yet there is also a marked difference; *Antony and Cleopatra* is not only a tragedy, it is also a great love poem. This mutual pair are two of the famous lovers of history and romance, and as such they had been celebrated in poetry and drama long before Shakespeare turned his eye upon them. In the dawn of English poetry Chaucer gave Cleopatra the first place among the good women whom he enrolled in his 'Legend of Cupid's Saints,' for there 'was never unto her love a truer queen.' When the Revival of Learning brought Plutarch back to Western Europe, Renaissance playwrights in Italy, Germany, and France drew upon him for the tragic story of Antony and Cleopatra's love and death. The theme was caught up in England, where Sidney's sister translated Garnier's tragedy, *Marc Antoine*, 1590; Daniel, a poet of her circle, wrote a *Cleopatra*, 1594, as a companion piece; and an otherwise unknown Brandon in his *Virtuous Octavia* hymned the chaste wife of Antony as opposed to his Egyptian mistress. These are cold and lifeless dramas of the Senecan school; they preceded Shakespeare's play, but meant nothing to him, unless, perhaps, in revolt from their formal frigidity he decided to retell the classic story in terms of the native romantic drama.

Of all the poetic versions of the tale of Antony and Cleopatra, Shakespeare's play is by far the noblest, but it is more than that. It is a great historical play, a dramatic panorama of the conflict in the ancient world which determined the supremacy of Rome for centuries to come. Shakespeare reverts here to something like the technique of the chronicle play; in construction *Antony and Cleopatra* more nearly resembles *Henry V* than the closely woven texture of *Othello* or the swift pace of *Macbeth*. The action follows the sequence of historical events as Shakespeare found them in Plutarch; a ten years' period of history is condensed into the five acts of the play, with some omissions but with few additions or changes in the historical scenes. Shakespeare took none of the liberties with his revered author that he had dared to take with Holinshed's Scottish chronicle. In the treatment of character, however, he felt free to interpret as he chose the data that Plutarch gave him.

The editors of the Folio rightly included *Antony and Cleopatra* among the tragedies. Yet no thoughtful reader of the play can escape the feeling that this drama differs from the great tragedies that precede it not only in degree, but in kind. There is no trace here of the inner struggle, the combat in the hero's soul with the power of evil, which rises to its climax in *Macbeth*. There is no scene in the play that shows Antony deliberately making the fatal choice to desert Rome and duty and return to the East where his pleasure lies. Yet the choice is made and his ruinous flight from Actium is the inevitable consequence, for his heart was tied to Cleopatra's rudder. We see his consciousness of shame and dishonor afterwards, but nothing of the conflict before; his flight indeed seems to have been unpremeditated, the result of an instant and irresistible impulse. In a sense, to be sure, Cleopatra incarnates the power of evil; it is her dominion over the hero that brings about his fall. Yet evil in Cleopatra appears in quite another form than it had taken in the inhuman malignity of Iago or the devilish arts of the weird sisters. Cleopatra is all too human, a queen 'whom everything becomes, to chide, to laugh, to weep.' Even in death her charm remains. Caesar exclaims as he bends over her body:

> She looks like sleep,
> As she would catch another Antony
> In her strong toil of grace.

Shakespeare himself seems to have been caught in her toil; certainly he transfigured and exalted the character that he found in Plutarch. For such a miracle of beauty, grace, and infinite variety a man might well give all for love and, to borrow the subtitle of Dryden's play, count 'the world well lost.' There is no sense of tragic waste in the catastrophe of this tragedy, rather a feeling that the lovers have triumphed over external forces and that they rightly preferred death to life in a world of turmoil and treachery dominated by the cold-blooded Caesar Augustus.

Antony and Cleopatra, in fact, is not so much a soul's tragedy as a drama of external action, a conflict of opposing forces for world empire, in which the lovers are caught and hurried to their deaths. In the slow unfolding of this contest, ranging over a period of years and shifting the scene from Egypt to Rome, to Parthia, and back to Egypt, there is ample room for a greater variety of incident than in the tense concentration of such tragedies as *Othello* and *Macbeth.* And this variety of incident is heightened and enlivened by a generous admixture of the comic in action, word, and character. *Antony and Cleopatra* has been called 'the most spacious' of Shakespeare's plays, and in this vast canvas there is ample room for comedy. This, of course, is in accordance with the native tradition to which Shakespeare has now returned, and this strain of comedy running through so serious a play springs directly from Shakespeare's reawakened joy and interest in the brighter side of life so long obscured by his tragic vision; certainly he found no suggestion for the comic in his sober and sententious source.

Shakespeare seems to use this comic strain by way of contrast with the serious matter of the historic scenes. It serves as a commentary, whimsical, satiric, almost naive at times, on the characters and the motives involved in the tragic struggle for power. We catch this note of contrast and of comment in the opening scenes. In the first the triple pillar of the world is presented, in the eyes of his Roman soldiers, transformed into a strumpet's fool. Rather than hear the ambassadors he prefers to wander through the streets with Cleopatra to 'note the qualities of people,' hardly a fit task for a ruler of the world. In the scene that follows we get a back-stage view of this Court of Egypt for which Antony has turned away from Rome, an idle, frivolous, and sensual Court. After a state dinner the soldier Enobarbus settles down to serious drinking, and Cleopatra's maids call in a soothsayer to tell their fortunes. The graceless Charmian puts into his mouth the fortune she desires: 'Let me be married to three kings in a forenoon, and widow them all; let me have a child at fifty, to whom Herod of Jewry may do homage.' It may well be that the three kings of Charmian's wish would recall to Elizabethan minds memories of the three Kings of Orient who followed the star in the old Miracle Plays, and the child would recall the infant King of the Jews whom Herod professed himself ready to worship. The irreverent jest would go home to Shakespeare's audience with a force that is quite lost to us today. Iras next holds out her hand with the smirking assurance: 'There's a palm presages chastity, if nothing else,' on which Charmian comments: 'E'en as the o'erflowing Nile presageth famine.' The two rogues then unite in a prayer to Isis for a fortune befitting the courtier Alexas: May he have one wife after another,' worse following worse, 'till the worst of all follow him laughing to his grave, fifty-fold a cuckold!' 'Lo, now!' says Alexas, 'if it lay in their hands to make me a cuckold, they would make themselves whores, but they'd do't.' Yet these wanton girls are the devoted servants who later die of heartbreak and the aspic's bite beside their mistress.

Upon this scene of idle frivolity Cleopatra enters in search of Antony, who has left her, struck, she says, by 'a Roman thought!' What caused this thought we learn at once; civil war in Italy and foreign invasion in Asia summon him imperatively to break these strong Egyptian fetters, and he confides his purpose to Enobarbus. In the dialogue that follows, Enobarbus plays the part of a humorous and mocking chorus. It was for this role that Shakespeare created the character from a name and an incident in Plutarch. According to the historian, Enobarbus, an old comrade of Antony's, tried in vain at the crisis of the war with Caesar to persuade him to send Cleopatra back to Egypt. When he failed in this 'being sick of an ague . . . he went and took a little boat to go to Caesar's camp. Antonius was very sorry for it, but yet he sent after him all his carriage, train, and men.' Shortly thereafter Enobarbus died, prob-ably of the ague, though the moralizing Plutarch suggests that it was as though he gave Antony 'to understand that he repented of his open treason.' This is not Shakespeare's Enobarbus, who stands by his master even after Actium and deserts him only when he perceives a diminution in his mind as well as in his fortune. Shake-speare, to be sure, picked up the hint that Plutarch had dropped, and lets Enobarbus finally die in a ditch, of mingled remorse and shame. Until his end, however, he functions as a satiric commentator on the action. In this scene, for example, he answers Antony's 'I must with haste from hence,' with the cool: 'Why, then, we kill all our women,' and continues cynically: 'Under a compelling occasion let women die; it were pity to cast them away for nothing.' To Antony's half-hearted expression of regret that he had ever seen Cleopatra, Enobarbus replies with perfect honesty: 'You had then left unseen a wonderful piece of work.' That, in truth, is what Cleopatra is to this Roman realist, a splendid spectacle, as he demonstrates later in his famous report of her first meeting with Antony. To his master's announcement of the death of Fulvia, his trouble-making wife, the reply of Enobarbus is short and frank: 'Give the gods a thankful sacrifice . . . the tears live in an onion that should water this sorrow.' He ends the colloquy with a bawdy jest that provokes even Antony's patience, and is cut short with a 'no more light answers' and an order to prepare a prompt departure.

It is, perhaps, a question how much of comedy there is in the fol-lowing scene, the parting of Antony and Cleopatra. Certainly the Queen does not behave like a tragic heroine in distress. For that we must turn to a parallel scene in Dryden's *All for Love;* but Dry-den's Cleopatra, who asserts that Nature meant her for 'a wife; a silly, harmless, household dove,' is of another order of creation from Shakespeare's serpent of old Nile. Shakespeare's Cleopatra runs here the gamut of emotions from an appeal for sympathy, through angry defiance,

> I would I had thy inches; thou shouldst know
> There were a heart in Egypt.

to open mockery of Antony's anger,

> Look, prithee, Charmian,
> How this Herculean Roman does become
> The carriage of his chafe.

closing with a farewell that rings like a call to arms,

> Upon your sword
> Sit laurel victory! and smooth success
> Be strew'd before your feet!

It would take a versatile actress to do justice to these swift changes of temper. We can only wonder what the boy was like to whom Shakespeare dared entrust the lines. He must have been capable of great things to have played this defiant, mocking, applauding Cleopatra to the burly Antony of Richard Burbage.

Later, in the closing scene of the first act, there is surely a flash of comedy in the Queen's threat to give her servant bloody teeth if she persists in singing the praise of Julius Caesar as opposed to Cleopatra's man of men. Yet this mock threat of physical violence looks forward to the Queen's actual assault on the messenger some few scenes later.

The second act is mainly occupied with the meeting of the Trium-virs, the marriage of Antony and Octavia, and the pacification of Sextus Pompey. This is serious historic matter, but it is shot through with comic implications. Enobarbus continues his role of realistic commentator. He rejects the request of the futile peacemaker Lepidus that he entreat Antony to use 'soft and gentle speech' at the coming conference. He expresses the cynical wish that all men might have such cross-grained wives as Fulvia so that 'the men might go to war with the women.' Rebuked by Antony for his blunt speech, he replies in a phrase that recalls the words of Lear's Fool: 'That truth should be silent I had almost forgot'—compare 'Truth's a dog must to kennel; he must be whipp'd out' (*Lear*, I. iv. 124-5)—and relapses into the silence of a stone, mute but observant. The gorgeous description of Cleopatra on her barge, paraphrased in verse from the prose of North, is assigned to Enobarbus with a definite dramatic purpose. He is the proper character to remind the audience of the absent Cleopatra, and that he speaks here for the first time in verse enhances the fascination of her magic. This realist has come to a very firm conclusion. The politicians who have arranged the marriage of Antony and Octavia may believe, or pretend to believe, that Antony must now abandon Cleopatra; Enobarbus knows better:

> Never; he will not:
> Age cannot wither her, nor custom stale
> Her infinite variety.

And as an example of her varying moods he recalls a time when he saw this magnificent Queen 'hop forty paces through the public street,' an incident apparently invented by Shakespeare for this purpose; there seems to be no trace of anything like it in classic literature. To the pirate Menas, with whom he is at once on the friendliest terms, Enobarbus expresses himself even more vigorously; Antony, he says, 'will to his Egyptian dish again; then, shall the sighs of Octavia blow the fire up in Caesar.'

The act closes with the banquet scene on Pompey's galley and here Shakespeare gives full play to the comic spirit. The humorous details of the scene are his own invention; he caught from Plutarch only a hint that the guests 'fell to be merry with Antonius love for Cleopatra,' a phrase that suggests a gay, but not exactly a riotous party. One other incident in this scene Shakespeare also drew from Plutarch, the whispered proposal of Menas to cut the cable and kidnap the Triumvirs. This was too good for Shakespeare to lose. Pompey's reply: 'This thou shouldst have done, and not have spoke on't' neatly corresponded to Shakespeare's conception of this ineffectual heir of a great name. Even more important, perhaps, is the fact that this brief episode reveals the close juxtaposition of tragedy and comedy, a murder plot in the midst of a banquet, and so provides the note of contrast recurrent in this play.

Apart from these brief borrowings, the long scene is Shakespeare's own. It begins with the servants' mockery of Lepidus,[1] and continues with his foolish questions about the crocodile until he sinks in a

[1] Lepidus is no doubt meant for a comic character. The captains' later mockery (III. ii) of his alternating enthusiastic praise of Antony and of Caesar deepens the impression left by the banquet scene.

drunken stupor and is carried ashore by a strong slave, who, in the words of Enobarbus, 'bears the third part of the world.' With his departure the banquet ripens toward an Alexandrian feast. The reluctant Caesar is dragged into the dance of the Egyptian Bacchanals and the party breaks up with loud music and a boy's drinking song, to which the revelers bawl out the chorus. The great men go ashore with a flourish of trumpets and a roll of drums, but Enobarbus, the insatiable drinker, throws his cap in the air with a shout, and staggers off to the cabin of Menas for more wine. The scene is one of broad and riotous comedy. Dryden would have been ashamed to include anything like it in his heroic play; but it serves Shakespeare's purpose. It offers something for the pit to laugh at, while in the contrast between Antony, who would be 'a child o' th' time,' and Caesar, who would 'possess it,' he gives the judicious spectator a preview, as it were, of the approaching catastrophe.

The two scenes between Cleopatra and the Messenger who brings her the news of Antony's marriage are widely separated; the first precedes the banquet scene; the second follows the departure of Antony and Octavia from Rome. Between the two there appears in all modern editions an act pause, but we do well to remember that there is no such interruption in the play as first printed. In the Folio after the heading, *Actus Primus, Scena Prima,* the text runs on unbroken, as, perhaps, the action did on Shakespeare's stage. Shakespeare has his own technique of shifting time and place back and forth, something like the technique of a modern cinema play with its changes of place and flash-backs in time. Yet if we are to consider Cleopatra's character presented, as here, with a certain comic slant, we should read the two scenes in quick succession.

In the first of these we see Cleopatra in idleness indulging in fond memories of her revels with Antony. Her mood is broken by the entrance of the Messenger, whose gloomy face makes her suspect at once that he brings bad news. She will hardly let him speak, but at last he utters his message bluntly enough: Antony is 'bound unto Octavia . . . for the best turn i' th' bed . . . he's married.' She turns furiously upon him, strikes him, hales him up and down, and draws a knife on him. Shakespeare reverts here for a moment to the old convention of physical violence as a comic note. There is no source for this business in Plutarch, but Shakespeare caught a hint for it from Plutarch's account of Cleopatra's treatment of her servant Seleucus [2] in her last interview with Caesar. Cleopatra, says Plutarch, 'was in such a rage with him that she flew upon him and took him by the hair of the head, and boxed him well-favoredly. Caesar fell a laughing and parted the fray.' The groundlings in the Globe, no doubt, got a good laugh to see the slender boyish Cleopatra manhandling the sturdy cowering Messenger. Her behavior is not exactly royal, but, as Plutarch had shown, it was quite in keeping with Cleopatra's character. Here it is a momentary outburst of fury; Cleopatra, in fact, is a little ashamed of herself and calls the poor man back with a promise of safety:

> Though I am mad, I will not bite him.

She tries in vain to get him to retract his message, and dismisses him unfee'd, but at least unharmed. Yet she is not through with him, for she sends after him to get full details on Antony's new wife: her face, her age, her temper, the color of her hair, her height; all this, of course, in preparation for the second interview.

Of that scene, Granville-Barker says: 'It is pure comedy and of the best.' There is no physical violence here; it is comedy of contrasted character: a frightened, but pliant Messenger, a collusive serving-maid, above all a deserted mistress determined to get such an account of her rival as will give her assurance of regaining her lover. An elaborate cross-examination elicits to Cleopatra's satisfaction the facts that Octavia is: dull of tongue and dwarfish, a widow, some thirty years of age, and round-faced—'for the most part, too, they are foolish that are so.' If the Messenger is a true reporter, and 'three in Egypt,' Charmian asserts, 'cannot make better note,' Cleopatra has no great cause to fear her rival: 'this creature,' as she calls her, is, after all, 'no such thing.' The accommodating Messenger is dismissed with thanks and gold instead of blows, as Cleopatra reflects: 'All may be well enough,' and Charmian echoes her thought: 'I warrant you, madam.' It would be hard to find elsewhere anything approaching this scene of wilful self-delusion; over it the comic spirit hovers gently smiling.

After this there is little comedy in *Antony and Cleopatra* until the very end. The scene shifts from courts to the camps of war, and there is no Falstaff in this play to mock at military glory. Antony is not fighting for honor like Hotspur, but for empire and even for

---

[2] In the corresponding scene (v. ii) of the play, Shakespeare omitted Cleopatra's assault on Seleucus; he knew better than to pull off this old trick twice.

life. This is a serious matter, and comedy for a time is crowded off the stage. There is no scene to mark Antony's return to Cleopatra; we only hear from Caesar (III. vi) that the lovers are together again and are 'levying the kings o' the earth for war.' We first meet them when war has actually begun. Enobarbus now plays the part assigned him in Plutarch, opposing Cleopatra's wish to be present at the decisive battle, but his coarse jest on the folly of putting stallions and mares in the same troop of cavalry is, of course, Shakespeare's own, another stroke of the brush for fuller characterization.

In the reconciliation scene after Actium (III. xi) there is a bit of lively realistic dialogue and action before the lovers are in each other's arms, but the effect of the whole is rather pathetic in the hero's hopeless enslavement when a kiss of Cleopatra's repays all he has lost. Later (III. xiii) Enobarbus plays again the part of mocking chorus, commenting on the folly of Antony's challenge to Octavius, but he becomes an agent in the action when he brings Antony in to catch Cleopatra giving her hand to Caesar's messenger to kiss. There is nothing comic in the whipping of Thyreus as in the earlier beating of the messenger; this bit of physical violence occurs off-stage, and our attention is fixed on Antony's burst of wrath against his mistress and on his desperate determination to fight it out to the last. The scene ends with the choral comment of Enobarbus on the mad valor that preys on reason.

The fourth act preserves a unity of place wanting in what has gone before. The action occurs in and near Alexandria and deals with Antony's last fight, his betrayal by the Egyptian fleet, and his suicide on the false report of Cleopatra's death. Shakespeare keeps close to his source here, and the closer he keeps to Plutarch the less likelihood is there of comedy breaking in. The episode of the desertion and death of Enobarbus is a mere enlargement of an earlier bit of narrative in the source and adds a deeper shade to the now impending catastrophe. When Antony's case is so hopeless that a stout fellow like Enobarbus leaves him, we know that the end is near; Antony's success in the sally from the town can only be a gleam of the setting sun. It is interesting that in the report of this skirmish, which Shakespeare exalts into a real victory, there occurs the only spot of humor in the act. The veteran Scarus, one of the few invented characters in the play, jokes about his wound which has been enlarged from a T to an H shape, brags that he has 'room for six scotches more,' and swears that he and Antony will beat the

Romans 'into bench-holes,' i.e. into their camp latrines. Needless to say this jest does not come from Plutarch.

The last act is devoted to Cleopatra and this is as it should be, for the story does not end with Antony's death. Dryden, in his effort to preserve the unities of time and place, brings Cleopatra and her maids to the dying Antony and lets them die beside him. Shakespeare, one feels, would not have taken such a liberty with Plutarch. Certain minor liberties he did, indeed, allow himself. He omitted Plutarch's pitiful description of Cleopatra on the occasion of Caesar's visit. She rose from 'a little low bed' and 'fell down at his feet'—'naked in her smock' and 'marvelously disfigured: both for that she had plucked her hair from her head, as also for that she had martyred all her face with the nails . . . moreover they might see the most part of her stomach torn insunder.' Shakespeare would never have degraded his Eastern star to this abject state. He omits also Cleopatra's long pathetic prayer at the tomb of Antony; he can do better than this in fewer lines.

The meeting of the victor and the vanquished in the last scene is a pure battle of wits; Caesar seeking by kindly promises to keep her alive for his triumph in Rome, Cleopatra feigning complete submission until she learns his purpose. It is Cleopatra who wins, and here, perhaps, Shakespeare caught a hint from North's marginal note: 'Cleopatra finally deceiveth Octavius Caesar, as though she desired to live.' Shakespeare's Queen has no such desire; she turns to her maids as Caesar leaves with

> He words me, girls, he words me, that I should not
> Be noble to myself.

The means of death are already provided (v. ii. 195), a fact which has escaped the notice of some critics, and Charmian is despatched to hasten their arrival. Meanwhile Cleopatra bids her women attire her like a queen; she is 'again for Cydnus, to meet Mark Antony.'

And now there follows one of the most daring exploits of Shakespeare, the Elizabethan playwright. Into the presence of the death-doomed Queen he introduces a Clown, played, and doubtless well played, by Robert Armin. As often Shakespeare elaborates a mere hint from Plutarch, who reports that a countryman came to Cleopatra's monument with a basket of eggs and jested with the soldiers that stopped him. That is all; of his talk with Cleopatra there is not a word in Plutarch. But in Shakespeare's hands this countryman becomes a Warwickshire peasant who has somehow strayed into the Court of Egypt. He is a blood relation of Christopher Sly and Hamlet's Grave-digger. He has the old tricks of the country Clown, his malapropisms, the worm's bite is 'immortal' and 'this is most fallible, the worm's an odd worm.' His easy good humor is quite unabashed by royalty; he would like to gossip with Cleopatra about 'a very honest woman, but something given to lie' who died of the worm's bite only yesterday. Cleopatra thrice bids him farewell, but he is thoroughly enjoying himself and lingers on to tell her that the worm will do his kind, that it 'is not to be trusted but in the keeping of wise people,' and that she must give it nothing, 'for it is not worth the feeding.' A little impatiently, perhaps, she asks jestingly, 'Will it eat me?' a question that unlocks a flow of rustic moralizing eloquence: 'You must not think I am so simple but I know the devil himself will not eat a woman; I know that a woman is a dish for the gods, if the devil dress her not,' and so on and so on. To a last imperative, 'get thee gone,' he answers quite politely: 'Yes, forsooth; I wish you joy of the worm.'

Was there ever a graver breach of decorum, and was there ever a greater effect gained by such a breach? Something has been already said of Shakespeare's use of comedy in *Antony and Cleopatra* as a contrast and foil to high romantic tragedy. Here is the supreme example, the guileless peasant chatting cheerfully with the Queen to whom he brings the means of death. 'I wish you joy of the worm,' he says, and he speaks truer than he knows for he has brought Cleopatra her last joy in life, the key to liberty through death

As sweet as balm, as soft as air, as gentle.

And now on the rustic prose of the Clown's speech follows the matchless poetry of the death scene:

Give me my robe, put on my crown; I have
Immortal longings in me; now no more
The juice of Egypt's grape shall moist this lip.
. . . husband, I come:
Now to that name my courage prove my title!
I am fire, and air; my other elements
I give to baser life.

Even the slave girl Charmian catches the fire of inspiration:

Now boast thee, death, in thy possession lies
A lass unparallel'd. Downy windows, close;
And golden Phœbus never be beheld
Of eyes again so royal!

Shakespeare's Cleopatra is wafted to meet her Antony 'where souls do couch on flowers' upon the pinions of immortal verse.

Antony and Cleopatra has seldom been a success in the theater.[3] It must have been produced at the Globe in Shakespeare's lifetime, but there is no record of any performance before 1642, and after the Restoration it was driven from the stage by Dryden's *All For Love*. Attempts have been made from time to time to revive it, but the difficulties of a performance on any but the Elizabethan stage are almost insuperable. Yet it has been for centuries the delight of readers, and critics from the time of Dr. Johnson to the present have extolled its variety of incident, its vivid characterization, and its happy audacity of style. It would seem, however, as if insufficient regard had been paid to the strain of comedy running throughout the action which gives to *Antony and Cleopatra* a liveliness, a refreshing contrast to the statelier main theme, and a sense of common humanity that is wanting in Shakespeare's earlier and profounder tragedies. The Messenger, the Clown, and Enobarbus are essentially comic figures. Take them away and the play sinks to a cross between a chronicle history and a heroic drama. It is among other things Shakespeare's native turn for comedy that makes *Antony and Cleopatra* what it is, the most delightful of his tragedies.

CORIOLANUS

Coriolanus, probably the last tragedy that Shakespeare ever wrote, must have followed *Antony and Cleopatra* very shortly in the season of 1608-9, and it is in many ways closely connected with that play. Both are historical tragedies, and both draw from Plutarch's *Lives* as their one essential source. *Coriolanus* in fact depends even more than *Antony and Cleopatra* upon the old biographer; Shakespeare must have known Plutarch's life of his hero almost by heart; in fact, it seems at times as if he had written with North's translation open on the desk before him, and had been mainly engaged in turning North's vigorous prose into resounding blank verse. This is not to say, how-

---

[3] The production in which Katharine Cornell starred in 1947-8 is an exception.

ever, that he failed to add in almost every case his own characteristic distinctive touch; a comparison of the great speech of Volumnia's plea to her son in its two forms, prose and verse, will show not only Shakespeare's fidelity to his source, but also his sudden flashes of poetic dramatic inspiration. Her last words:

> This fellow had a Volscian to his mother;
> His wife is in Corioli, and his child
> Like him by chance. Yet give us our dispatch:
> I am hushed until our city be a-fire,
> And then I'll speak a little,

with its implied threat of a mother's curse is pure Shakespeare; there is nothing in the least like it in Plutarch.

Like *Antony and Cleopatra, Coriolanus* is a play of action rather than of inner conflict. It has already been noted that in the first of these plays Shakespeare deliberately omits a scene which would show Antony weighing in the balance the mortal choice between Roman duty and Egyptian pleasure. So in *Coriolanus* he fails to write a scene to show his hero struggling between his thirst for revenge and an in-born love of country. The omission is the more remarkable in *Coriolanus* since the hero departs to exile apparently in a mood of philosophic resignation; he comforts his weeping wife and mother, and promises them

> While I remain above the ground you shall
> Hear from me still; and never of me aught
> But what is like me formerly.

We next find him in an enemy town prepared to sell his services to hereditary foes at the price of revenge upon his country against which he swears he will fight 'with the spleen of all the under fiends.' That, at least, is most unlike what he was formerly.

This sudden desertion of a Roman soldier to the enemy makes Coriolanus an almost repellent figure, perhaps the least sympathetic of Shakespeare's tragic heroes. Even Macbeth, by reason of his struggle before the crime and his remorse thereafter, wins a fuller understanding and greater sympathy than this traitor to his country. The question, then, arises why Shakespeare should have chosen such a character as the protagonist of his last tragedy. There is, perhaps, a twofold answer. In the first place, the story of Coriolanus as told by Plutarch presented to the aging playwright a drama, ready made, so to speak: the rise and fall of a heroic figure in irrepressible conflict with his environment. This is not to say that Shakespeare took over the framework of his play unchanged; he condensed the action, shifted events about to suit his dramatic purpose, and even made minor alterations in the story. In Plutarch Coriolanus is not actually chosen consul, but only promised the people's votes; in the play the nullification of his election by the commons, instigated by the demagogic tribunes, is an insult and a bitter wrong, which excuses the hero's outburst of anger and leads directly, as it does not in Plutarch, to civil strife and the decree of exile. A like outburst of anger in the play, though not in Plutarch, is the immediate cause of his death at the hands of the Volscians. Shakespeare derived from his source the conception of Coriolanus as 'a man too full of passion and choler,' but he exploited this conception with great dramatic effect at the crisis and at the catastrophe of the action. Even if the tragic impulse was waning, Shakespeare was still a past master of his art. *Coriolanus* is as superior to *Antony and Cleopatra* in construction as it falls below it in poetry.

There is, perhaps, another reason why Shakespeare turned from *Antony and Cleopatra* to *Coriolanus*. In both of Plutarch's narratives he found a striking example of a woman's decisive influence upon a hero's destiny. In *Antony and Cleopatra* it is the mistress who brings about the hero's fall; in *Coriolanus* it is the mother. The unchecked control of a good woman over a man's life may be as fatal, Shakespeare seems to say, as that of a courtesan. The influence of Volumnia upon her son's career is exaggerated by Shakespeare above what appears in his source. He is her good soldier; she sent him forth while still a boy, and exulted to see him return 'his brows bound with oak' for saving a comrade's life in battle. In the most critical points of the action the influence of Volumnia tips the scales. It is she who first suggests the 'one thing wanting,' the consulship, to her son who, with better knowledge of his temper and capacity, replies:

> I had rather be their servant in my way
> Than sway with them in theirs.

Again it is she who with mingled persuasion, entreaty, and reproaches, drives him against his better convictions to the humiliating appeal to the commons; and finally it is her intercession that induces him to renounce his purpose of destroying Rome. This last instance occurs in Plutarch and is, indeed, an essential part of the story, but the others are invented by Shakespeare to account for Volumnia's final success. It is a success that, as Coriolanus well knows, will prove dangerous, 'if not most mortal to him.' The mother, in fact, ruins her son's career quite as certainly and with as little knowledge of what she does as Cleopatra wrecked the empire and caused the death of her lover.

Coriolanus has never been a popular stage-play; but it has afforded a debatable ground for critics. Their judgments have been curiously diverse; Eliot ranks it along with *Antony and Cleopatra* as Shakespeare's 'most assured artistic success'; Barrett Wendell, on the other hand, calls it almost cynically cold, betraying a weakening of Shakespeare's creative energy. Perhaps one reason for this discrepancy of judgment is that *Coriolanus* has too often been regarded as dominated by a definite political bias. Hazlitt, a staunch republican, insists that 'Shakespeare . . . seems to have spared no opportunity of baiting the rabble.' Stopford Brooke, a liberal Victorian, declares: 'We are made to feel . . . the sympathy of Shakespeare with the struggle of the people.' A truer verdict than either might perhaps be found in Coleridge's note on 'the wonderfully philosophic impartiality of Shakespeare's politics.'

It is, perhaps, possible today, when we have come to know something more of the Fascist mind, to attain a deeper insight into this play and to wonder at Shakespeare's anticipation of the temper and behavior of that type of politician. For Coriolanus is not so much a conservative aristocrat as an incarnation of the Fascist spirit. On his first appearance he avows his notion of the best way to deal with a hungry mob: let the Government only permit him to use force and he would 'make a quarry with thousands of these quarter'd slaves,' very much as Bonaparte, that pre-Fascist, swept away a Parisian mob with a whiff of grapeshot. He objects strenuously to the established custom which forced candidates for office to stand in the market place and plead for votes; it might well, he thinks, be annulled. In the tumult that follows his rejection as consul he bids the Senate depose the tribunes, the regularly appointed representatives of the people. Just so Mussolini and Hitler abolished all forms of representative government. The tribunes call him with perfect justice 'a traitorous innovator,' an exact description of the Fascist. And finally he leads a foreign army against his country, as Franco brought his Moors from Africa to overthrow the Republican government of Spain. It is somewhat late in the day to speak of *Coriolanus* as a biased dramatic presentation of the struggle between aristocrats and plebeians; the aristocrats in this play, like good Englishmen, are willing to compromise; the plebeians are ready to follow a leader who will appeal to them as brothers. It is the self-willed Fascist who denounces both 'the dastard nobles' and 'the mutable rank-scented many.'

A humorless Harvard professor once explained what seemed to him the monotony of *Coriolanus* by stating that it lacked the relief of underplot and comedy, such as appears in Shakespeare's English chronicle plays. It would be interesting to ask what sort of an underplot this scholar found in *Henry V*, or what fiend blinded his eyes with the pin and web to the comedy in *Coriolanus*. Dr. Johnson was more discerning when he pronounced this play 'one of the most amusing of our author's performances.' As a matter of fact, the comic element in *Coriolanus* exceeds that in *Antony and Cleopatra*. This appears from the relative proportion of prose, the usual vehicle of Shakespearean comedy; in the earlier it runs to about 8 per cent; in *Coriolanus* to about a quarter of the whole play. Moreover, the comic element in *Coriolanus* is not only larger, but more pervasive than in its predecessor. There is nothing, to be sure, in *Coriolanus* like the comic violence of Cleopatra's mistreatment of the Messenger, the riotous extravagance of the banquet scene, or the surprising entrance of a Clown into Cleopatra's chamber. What we find is, in fact, something in the nature of comic relief, a repeated lowering of the tension in the more serious scenes.

There is little of comic action in *Coriolanus;* the hero's beating of the impertinent Third Servant is briefly passed over; another bit of violence, the boy's 'mammocking' of a butterfly, is narrated, not presented. The scene in which it occurs is one of quiet conversation between three Roman ladies. There is indeed a flavor of domestic comedy in this scene, interposed between scenes of war, particularly in the character contrast between the boastful mother, the gentle, reticent wife, and the laughing visitor who tries in vain to lure her out for a social engagement.

If there is little of the comedy of action in *Coriolanus* there is plenty of the comedy of speech. The sudden outburst of the boy Marcius in the grave intercession scene,

A' shall not tread on me:
I'll run away till I am bigger, but then I'll fight,

accompanied, probably, by an attempt to escape from the restraining hand of his grandmother, was no doubt good for a laugh, a moment's relaxation at this tense crisis. This is only a sudden flash of the comic spirit, but there are long passages where it shines with a steadier glow. Such, for example, is the scene of the citizens' revolt at the beginning of the play. Here the First Citizen—possibly played by Armin—is a serio-comic character who mingles incitements to riot with poor puns. Menenius characterizes him as 'the great toe of this assembly,' the lowest, basest, poorest, yet ever the first to run into mischief. He appears again in the scene where the hero solicits the votes of the people; he has here, indeed, a smaller part to play than his fellows, but Shakespeare puts into his mouth one of the key speeches of the play. When Coriolanus asks with a sneer what price he is expected to pay for their voices, the First Citizen answers: 'The price is, to ask it kindly.' Had Coriolanus taken this reply to heart, the whole issue of the action would have been different. Throughout this scene these Roman citizens are, in effect, decent Elizabethan Englishmen, homely of speech, properly respectful of a great lord, but conscious of their own place in the commonwealth, and naturally resentful of the aristocrat's arrogance. It is this resentment that makes them the easy victims of the machinations of the tribunes; since the hero will not prove a kindly leader, they fall in behind the demagogues who talk a language they can understand.

There is a similar example of Shakespeare's knowledge of simple folk and his humorous enjoyment of their behavior and speech, in the chatter of the serving-men at the house of Aufidius. Before the hero is recognized by their master, they are snobbishly abusive of the 'poor gentleman' who has intruded, an uninvited guest, upon the feast. Their sudden change of tone when Coriolanus is welcomed by the Volscians is a comic presentment of popular fickleness. The servant who had thought to have beaten Coriolanus like a dog is now convinced that he 'knew by his face that there was something in him.' Coriolanus is a better man than their master, but the two will go together and 'sowle the porter of Rome gates by the ears.' The servants break out in a chorus of praise of war that recalls Falstaff's blessing on the rebels who 'offend none but the virtuous.' War, they say, 'exceeds peace as far as day does night; it's spritely, waking, audible, and full of vent.'

The various citizens and serving-men who appear in these scenes are minor figures; they furnish amusement by their racy talk rather than by action or by individualized characterization. There is one

character, however, engaged in the action from the beginning to the
end, who stands high among Shakespeare's comic figures, the old
Senator, Menenius. That his role is comic there can be no doubt.
Johnson, indeed, bluntly calls him a buffoon; but the Doctor must
have been in one of his combative moods when he wrote these words.
His own definition of a buffoon is harsh indeed: 'a man whose profession it is to make sport by low jests and antick postures, a jack-
pudding,' or 'a man who practises indecent railery.' The attorney
for the defense would certainly assert the innocence of Menenius on
either charge, and corroborative proof of the accusation would be
hard indeed to find. No buffoon could have stopped a hungry crowd
of rioters; no jack-pudding could play the sober and dignified part
in the Senate that Menenius does. There is, in fact, much in the
character of Menenius that lifts him above the role of the professional
Clown or Jester. We may see his devoted love of Coriolanus, a love
quite free from any such implication of self-interest as taints Falstaff's
attachment to Prince Hal. He calls Coriolanus 'son' and makes his
final plea to him in the character of a distressed old father. He is
courteous and hospitable to the ladies of the hero's family, both in
the time of their exultation and in their sorrow. A frank and out-
spoken politician, he is yet recognized by the mob as 'one that hath
always loved the people.' This fits him well to play the part of com-
promiser and mediator. At the height of the civic tumult he calls on
Coriolanus to lay down his sword, and a moment later the tribunes
appeal to him to act as the people's officer and bring the accused hero
to a judicial trial in the Forum. So too at the last hour of Rome's
distress the tribunes again implore him to avert the threatened de-
struction of the city by interceding with Coriolanus for mercy.

If this were all that could be said about Menenius he would only
be another of the wise and kindly old men who appear so often in
English drama, favorite parts for the character actor. But there is
much more to him than this; he is a highly individualized character.
Among other things he is well known as a *bon-vivant;* the tribunes
taunt him with being a 'perfecter giber for the table than a necessary
bencher in the Capitol,' and he readily admits that he 'loves a cup
of hot wine with not a jot of allaying Tiber in't.' Cherishing a firm
conviction of the mollifying power of a good meal upon a man's
temper, he explains the rebuff Cominius received from Coriolanus
by the fact that the hero had not yet dined:

and then
We pout upon the morning, are unapt
To give or to forgive.

Accordingly he makes careful inquiry of the sentry before his own
interview with Coriolanus: 'Has he din'd, canst thou tell? For I
would not speak with him till after dinner.' Even more characteristic,
however, is his frank and fluent speech: 'what I think, I utter, and
spend my malice in my breath.' It is this absence of malice that lets
him rail at the people and their tribunes without offending either;
he is an accepted and licensed humorist. His talk is garnished with
proverbs, homely sayings, and quaint similes: Coriolanus, he says,
'no more remembers his mother now than an eight-year-old horse';
'there is no more mercy in him than there is milk in a male tiger.' Yet
he can be serious enough when the occasion calls for it, as when he
implores the tribunes to forbear rash action against Coriolanus and

Proceed by process;
Lest parties—as he is belov'd—break out,
And sack great Rome with Romans.

The very sentries who jeer at him for his failure to persuade their
general recognize him as 'a noble fellow.'

Now this delightful character, like Enobarbus in *Antony and Cleopatra,* is a sheer creation by Shakespeare. Plutarch, to be sure, once
more gave him the name and a hint to work on. To the rebellious
plebs, Plutarch says, the Senate sent 'certaine of the pleasauntest olde
men and the most acceptable to the people.' Among these was Menenius Agrippa who recites 'an excellent tale . . . to pacifie the people,'
the fable of the belly and the members, which Shakespeare took
over, borrowing, as he versified it, some additional details from Cam-
den's fuller version. With this excellent tale Menenius drops out of
Plutarch's narrative; all that endears him to us in the play is pure
Shakespeare. Like Enobarbus he was created to serve, in part at
least, as a contrast to the passionate tragic hero, and Menenius has
some likeness to his predecessor. Both are fond of a cup of wine;
both are realists who see the situation and its remedy more clearly
than the hero does. That, in fact, is the chief function of Enobarbus,
who often plays the part of a cynical, commenting chorus. But there
is nothing cynical in Menenius; and nothing so realistic that we could
imagine him deserting Coriolanus to win the favor of the plebs. Nor

is there anything of the tragic in him; he does not die broken-hearted, of shame and remorse, like his predecessor. His last words are in praise of the mother who has saved Rome

> This Volumnia
> Is worth of consuls, senators, patricians,
> A city full; of tribunes, such as you,
> A sea and land full.

Shakespeare ends the role of Menenius on this note of serio-comic exultation, as he began it with the serio-comic fable of the belly.

With *Coriolanus* Shakespeare completes his escape from the shadow that overhung his tragic period. We have seen the beginning of his emergence in *Antony and Cleopatra;* here he is in the open again. The theme of this last of his tragedies must have tempted his craftsmanship; the hero, certainly, could not have deeply appealed to his sympathy. In fact the most sympathetic figure in the play is the genial, free-living, free-spoken, thoroughly human comic character of Menenius. Shakespeare's genius in the field of comedy has regained its former freedom and creative power.

11

The Problem Comedies

A TRIO of comedies falls exactly within the limits of the tragic period. They form a unique group in the canon of Shakespeare's plays, differing alike from the supreme comedies that immediately precede them and from the so-called 'romances' that follow. They have long been a stumbling block and source of confusion to scholars and critics. They have been called 'bitter' comedies, 'cynical pseudo-comedies,' and interpreted as proof of Shakespeare's compliance with the satiric spirit dominant in Elizabethan literature in the first decade of the seventeenth century. Perhaps the best label, if one is needed, is that of 'problem comedies,' which Lawrence affixes to the group in his admirable study of the three.

Problem plays they are indeed, and each presents its own peculiar riddle. Yet there seems to be a formula that may serve to group them under one head. They are all by-products of the tragic vein in which Shakespeare was at this time working. Pressure of one sort or another seems to have diverted him for a time from his more serious labors. The diversion, however, was neither great nor permanent; there are but three of these problem plays, and there is little trace of their peculiar spirit in the plays that follow. It would seem, moreover, that Shakespeare's heart was not deeply engaged in this effort to handle a psychological problem in the form of comedy. The last acts of these plays are hurried and confused as if he were in haste to wash his hands of the business.

Yet in any consideration of Shakespearean comedy this trio demands special attention. Even if here Shakespeare's heart is not wholly in his work, his native gift of humor has not deserted him. It takes, indeed, new forms; instead of the happy laughter of earlier plays we get farcical situations, satiric portraiture, cynical comment on heroic themes, and comically realistic presentation of lower and baser sides of human nature. The stream of Shakespeare's humor is still flowing, even if with a peculiar and not always palatable flavor.

TROILUS AND CRESSIDA

Troilus and Cressida, the first of the comedies that fall within the tragic period, has been called the most puzzling of Shakespeare's plays; 'a puzzle we found *Troilus and Cressida,*' says a modern critic, 'and a puzzle we must leave it; our best comment must be guess-work.' Things are not quite so bad as that; thanks to the labor of some contemporary scholars, our guesses need not be made at random; they have a fairly sure foundation to build on. Yet the fact remains that much about this play is still puzzling: its publication, its treatment of the story, its inconclusive ending, and its strangely discordant tone.

We may begin with the circumstances of the publication. On 7 February 1603 Roberts, the regular printer for Shakespeare's company, filed a claim to this play in the Stationers' Register: *Entired for his copie . . . The booke of Troilus and Cresseda as yt is acted by my lord Chamberlen's Men.* There is reason to believe that this is what is called a 'staying entry,' i.e. one intended to prevent the printing of the play by any other person; Roberts, at least, made no attempt to print it. Six years later, however, 28 January 1609, another entry appears in the Register. Bonian and Walley, two young booksellers, filed a claim to it as follows: *under th' handes of Master Segar deputy to Sir George Bucke and under master warden Lownes a booke called the history of Troilus and Cressida.* Evidently the lapse of time since the Roberts' entry emboldened this pair to attempt to overrule his claim. To do this they managed to secure a special license from the deputy of Buck, since 1606 Master of the Revels. Perhaps Roberts protested; but if so, it was in vain, for Bonian and Walley published the play that same year with the following title-page: *The Historie of Troylus and Cresseida. As it was acted by the King Maiesties servants at the Globe. Written by William Shakespeare.* Then a strange thing happened. Possibly the publishers received some information about the performance at the Globe; at any rate within the year, with business enterprise worthy of a twentieth-century publisher, they stopped the sale, cut out the title-page of the book, and substituted two new leaves. The first of these bore a more attractive title: *The Famous Historie of Troylus and Cresseid. Excellently expressing the beginning of their loves, with the conceited wooing of Pandarus Prince of Licia. Written by William Shakespeare.* No reference is made here to any performance of the play, and special attention is called to Pandarus, one of the chief comic characters, apparently a good selling point. The second new leaf was occupied with an epistle from 'a never writer to an ever reader,' extolling the merits of the play. This amusing anticipation of the modern 'blurb' is too long to be reprinted here—it may be found in Tatlock's introduction to the Tudor edition of the play and elsewhere—but certain phrases need to be noted and interpreted. It begins by telling a prospective buyer that here is 'a new play, never stal'd with the stage, never clapper-claw'd with the palmes of the vulger.' This has been generally understood to mean that the play had never been performed on the stage. Yet both the Roberts' entry and the first title-page distinctly refer to a performance, and the preface-writer does not mean to contradict them. Here, he says in effect, is a new play, though it was really at least six years old, that has not become stale by repeated performances and has not been patted on the back by the groundlings of a public theater. The writer goes on to assert that this book is the work of a most witty playwright, and that among all his comedies there is none more witty than this. The time will come, he says, when Shakespeare's plays will be out of print—fortunately that time has not yet arrived—you had better spend your sixpence on it now; in fact you may be glad you have the chance to do so, 'since by the grand possessors wills, I beleeve, you should have prayd for them [Shakespeare's plays] rather then beene prayd [to buy].' The 'grand possessors' are, of course, Shakespeare's fellow-actors, the owners of his plays, who are deliberately holding them back from the reading public. The preface is, in fact, an ingenious appeal to buyers sophisticated enough to enjoy a play that was caviar to the general. Clever as it is, the appeal seems to have failed; no further editions of *Troilus and Cressida* were called for until the Folio of 1623. When the Folio was being printed, the editors secured a copy of the quarto, corrected it by checking with a manuscript in their possession, and sent the corrected quarto off to Jaggard's shop.

An ingenious hypothesis, now generally accepted, has been advanced to explain the facts just recited. Stated briefly it comes to this: *Troilus and Cressida* was not originally designed for the public theater; a playwright as successful as Shakespeare must have known that a play so lacking in action, weighted down with so many long, political, and ethical speeches, and so often bitter in tone, would not go down at the Globe. For a private performance before a cultured and literate audience such a play might well succeed, and it was for such an audience that *Troilus and Cressida* was written, perhaps at the request of the governors of one of the Inns of Court who had heard of, or witnessed, the success of *Twelfth Night,* played at a feast in the Middle Temple. A comedy would be preferred for such an entertainment, but a comedy, if possible, on a literary theme with a freightage of moral 'sentences,' seasoned with the Attic salt of Shakespeare's wit. Certainly *Troilus and Cressida* would nicely correspond to such a request.

But a question may be asked about the performance at the Globe referred to on the first title-page of *Troilus and Cressida* and also about the manuscript from which the printed quarto was corrected for the Folio. It seems most unlikely that the publishers were mistaken in this reference; plays at the Globe were as much a matter of common knowledge in London then as plays brought out on Broadway are today. In that case we must assume that in some slack season, *c.* 1607-8, Shakespeare's fellows, now the King's Company, persuaded him to revise it, equip it with a resounding Prologue, found only in the Folio text, write some new battle scenes, and stage it at the Globe. For such a performance, of course, an official book of the play would be needed, and it was this manuscript, no doubt, that was used in 1623 to correct the quarto. That such a public performance was a failure seems almost self-evident, especially if it took place at the theater where such hits as *Hamlet* and *Othello* were being repeated again and again. Such a failure, it seems, would explain the action of the publishers. No sooner had the first issue of *Troilus and Cressida* appeared on the bookstalls of the Spread Eagle in Paul's Churchyard where they offered it for sale, than some wiseacre of the theater world hurried to them to suggest that the less said about the Globe performance the better for the sale of the book. Like shrewd businessmen they took the tip, canceled the original title-page with this unlucky reference, and hired a clever writer to compose a preface which might persuade the better sort of book buyers that a play 'never stal'd with the stage' was just the dish for their nicer palates. This, at least, seems a simple and plausible solution of the whole matter.

These bibliographical details are, no doubt, of less interest to the general reader than the theme of *Troilus and Cressida* and Shakespeare's treatment of it. The theme, of course, is the age-old story of the Siege of Troy, handed down from generation to generation since Homer's day. But the main stress of the story as Shakespeare dramatized it was less on the Trojan War than on the unhappy love affair of Prince Troilus. Now this affair is not Homeric at all; it is an invention of medieval poets who consistently romanticized the old epic to bring it up to date, since to the medieval minstrel a warrior without a ladylove was almost inconceivable. Chaucer's beautiful treatment of this love story had made it familiar to all English readers; but no English writer after Chaucer shared that gentle poet's pity for the unhappy lady. Henryson, a Scotch poet, a century or so later, went so far as to punish the faithless Cressida with leprosy, and this punishment became part of the popular version of the story. Shakespeare himself refers to it when his Pistol calls the harlot, Doll Tearsheet, a 'lazar kite of Cressid's kind.' Shakespeare could no more have presented a true and loving Cressida on the Elizabethan stage than he could have introduced a cowardly Hector. What he did was to portray with unerring hand the folly of a generous youth's passion for a wanton. Shakespeare's Cressida is far more realistically characterized than Chaucer's gentle lady; readers who prefer sentiment to bitter truth may be advised to turn back to Chaucer's poem, a kindlier piece of work than Shakespeare's play.

This love story is the central core of *Troilus and Cressida*, as indeed the title shows. The action opens with Troilus bewailing his hopeless passion to his friend, the go-between Pandarus; it closes [1] with the dismissal of this 'broker, lackey' with ignominy and shame. But Shakespeare was quick to perceive that there was too little of drama in the story of this love affair to furnish matter for the conventional five-act play. He therefore set it against a background of the Trojan War, recounted in such detail that it seems at times to overshadow the central theme. This background, too, is as un-Homeric as the love story. The characters that move about in it are not Hellenic heroes, but chivalric knights and lovers. Achilles sulks in his tent, not because of wrath for a bitter wrong, but because his lady, Polyxena, old Priam's daughter, has sworn him to refrain from battle. Hector offers to meet the bravest Greek in single combat to maintain his assertion that

> He hath a lady, wiser, fairer, truer,
> Than ever Greek did compass in his arms,

[1] One would gladly believe with certain modern scholars that the revolting Epilogue put into the mouth of Pandarus was not by Shakespeare, but the work of some theater hack written to raise a laugh at the Globe when this comedy of disillusion and failure had come at last to an end.

and Agamemnon answers the challenge with the declaration that
Hector shall be met for We are soldiers;

> And may that soldier a mere recreant prove,
> That means not, hath not, or is not in love!

All this comes from Shakespeare's sources; he had never read Homer
in the original, but he had steeped himself in Lydgate's *Troy Book*
and in Caxton's *Recuyell,* a translation of a French narrative of the
Siege of Troy. Both writers throw over the Greek epic a spangled
veil of medieval romance; both stress the noble virtues of the Trojans;
both insist on the insolence and treachery of the Greeks. This was
the orthodox Renaissance conception, and Shakespeare, a child of his
age, accepted it.

Yet there is much more in the background of *Troilus and Cressida*
than this afterglow of medieval romance. Into the mouth of his
Greek and Trojan knights Shakespeare puts some of his own pro-
foundest reflections upon topics still familiar today: on the relation
of the individual to the state, on the clash of private and political
ethics, on the dominance of Time over the life and work of man. One
passage from the great speech of Ulysses on Degree, which means
Law and Order, reads like an ominous prophecy of events in our
own century:

> Take but degree away, untune that string,
> And, hark! what discord follows . . .
>   . . .
> Force should be right; or rather, right and wrong—
> Between whose endless jar justice resides—
> Should lose their names, and so should justice too.
> Then everything includes itself in power,
> Power into will, will into appetite;
> And appetite, a universal wolf,
> So doubly seconded with will and power,
> Must make perforce a universal prey,
> And last eat up himself.

It must have been of such speeches that Goethe was thinking when
he advised Eckermann to read *Troilus and Cressida* if he would discover the 'free spirit of Shakespeare, working unhampered by the
requirements of the stage.' If Shakespeare wrote *Troilus and Cressida*

for a private performance, as seems likely, he had no need to think of these requirements.

There is, of course, another aspect of this strange play than the romance of chivalry and the reflective speeches of the heroes. This is the steady stream of satiric comment on the two themes of love and war which make up the body of the play. Over against the idealizing raptures of Troilus is set the frank realism of Pandarus, whose conception of love is merely physical; he can praise Cressida to Troilus and Troilus to Cressida, but his one purpose is to put the lovers to bed together. To Diomed, the rivalry of Paris and Menelaus for Helen is little better than the strife between a cuckold and a lecher. And that is how Thersites views the Trojan War: 'all the argument is a whore and a cuckold—a good quarrel to draw emulous factions and bleed to death upon.' This is the underside of love and war. Yet, in fact, this underside is so obtrusive, portrayed so often in such repellent colors, that it produces something like a discord between the heroic and the comic elements of this play; Thersites does not blend into the picture as Falstaff does in the war in *Henry IV*.

The denouement of *Troilus and Cressida* has been sharply criticized as a conclusion in which nothing is concluded. The faithless Cressida is left unpunished, the gallant Troilus turns into something like a fighting savage, and the noble Hector is treacherously murdered. Dryden felt this so strongly that when he adapted the play for the Restoration stage, he wrote a new fifth act; but what he really did was to change an Elizabethan comedy into a 'regular' neo-classic tragedy. An easy explanation of the unsatisfactory close of the play is to reject the last six scenes as un-Shakespearean. Yet traces of Shakespeare's hand are everywhere visible in them, except in the scurrilous Epilogue. It is hard to assign the prose of Thersites in the first of these suspected scenes, or the verse of Nestor in the fifth scene, to any other hand than Shakespeare's. It seems possible, at least, that Shakespeare meant to end his play earlier; the love story comes to a definite close when Troilus tears the guilty Cressida's letter at the end of the third scene of the last act. One might guess that Shakespeare had planned to write one more scene, the death of Hector, to bring the war story also to an end, and that in rehearsal it was found, or fancied, that a lively bit of action, packed with alarums and excursions, with Thersites skipping on and off the stage between the fighters, would better please the audience. Whereupon Shakespeare, always willing to oblige his fellows, dashed off what was wanted in his hastiest, most careless fashion, drawing heavily upon his reading of Lydgate and Caxton for the battle scenes; it would seem as if he had lost all interest in the play by this time. Yet, strange as it may seem, these suspected scenes when performed by the Players' Club in 1932, ended the play in most effective fashion. For the student the play comes to an end when Shakespeare's interest in it seems to stop.

There is little of hearty laughter in *Troilus and Cressida*. Written, as it probably was, for a select audience, there was no need for Shakespeare to respond to the groundlings' demand for horseplay on the stage. The comic element here consists less in action than in characterization and in the diction that Shakespeare uses to individualize his comic characters. There are three of these which call for brief comment.

The heroic Ajax of Homer becomes in *Troilus and Cressida* a lumbering, boastful bully, with 'not so much wit as would stop the eye of Helen's needle.' In this treatment of his character Shakespeare was only following post-Homeric tradition, which consistently degraded the sturdy Ajax in comparison with the crafty Ulysses. By Shakespeare's time Ajax had become a mere symbol of brawn without brains, a comic caricature of the old hero. The Elizabethan pronunciation of his name, Ajakes, gave the last touch to this figure of fun, very much as if in some G.I. review a French soldier should be introduced as Captain La Trine. Yet this Shakespearean Ajax turns out to be a capital acting part; he is, after all, a bluff, honest, single-minded fighting man, which is more than can be said for his fellow Greeks.

Shakespeare's Pandarus is a similar degradation of the humorous and sympathetic character of Chaucer's poem. This was, of course, an inevitable consequence of the debasement of the love story in popular tradition. If Cressida became a wanton, it followed as a matter of course that the uncle who promoted her intrigue with Troilus should become a bawd. His proper name, Pandarus, had become in Shakespeare's time the common noun, pander, i.e. a go-between in amours of the baser sort. Shakespeare himself alludes to this shift of meaning when he makes Pandarus say as he joins the lovers' hands: 'If ever you prove false to one another, since I have taken such pains to bring you together, let all pitiful goers-between be called to the world's end after my name; call them all Pandars.' Yet Shakespeare's Pandarus is not wholly base; he is after all a gentleman, Lord Pandarus, and a courtier on friendly terms with Paris and Helen. Apparently past the fighting age, since he alone of the main characters never appears on the battlefield, he still feels an old man's sympathy for young lovers. He can tease Troilus about Cressida, but he praises him to her as a better man than Hector. His sly jokes when the lovers meet to consummate their passion, his broad jests on the morning after, betray the superannuated rake, but he sheds real tears at the forced separation of the lovers, and later carries a letter from 'yond poor girl' in the Greek camp to the lover she has betrayed; there is nothing to show that he knew of her treason. To Shakespeare's audience he must have been a most amusing character and as such he was chosen to dismiss them with his Epilogue.

There can be no question of the degradation of a heroic or of a kindly character in Shakespeare's Thersites. All Shakespeare did here was to deepen and darken the lines of the figure he found in Chapman's 1598 translation of the *Iliad*. Thersites, Chapman says, was

> The filthiest Greek that came to Troy
> A man of tongue, whose raven like voice a tuneless jarring kept,
> Who in his rank mind copy had of unregarded words,
> That rashly and beyond all rule used to oppugn the Lords.
>
> • • •
> To mighty Thetides
> And wise Ulysses he retain'd much anger and disease
> For still he chid them eagerly; and then against the state
> Of Agamemnon he would rail.

With this last line compare the very first words that Thersites utters in the play (II. i). In Homer he is silenced by the cudgel of Ulysses, but in Shakespeare the blows of Ajax only quicken the flow of his railing vein. Thersites, to be sure, plays the part of the Fool, but he is not the household Fool of other comedies; 'I serve here voluntary,' he says; he is a free man, and though he seems at first attached to the service of Ajax, he promptly quits him to hang about the tent of Achilles, where he chants a catalogue of the members of his profession: 'Agamemnon is a fool to offer to command Achilles; Achilles is a fool to be commanded by Agamemnon; Thersites is a fool to serve such a fool; and Patroclus is a fool positive.' He is the most foul-mouthed rogue in Shakespeare's plays. The courteous farewell of Hector: 'Goodnight, sweet Lord Menelaus,' becomes in his mocking echo: 'Sweet draught: . . . sweet sink, sweet sewer.' He dwells with special fondness upon loathsome forms of disease, particularly upon those connected with sexual excess. Yet we do well to remember that language which disgusts the modern reader would sound to well-read gentlemen in Shakespeare's audience like snatches from the contemporary satire of Marston and Ben Jonson. Each age has its own standard of taste in such matters. Certainly the virility, vivacity, and quenchless stream of Thersites' speech testify to the delight with which Shakespeare created this epitome of all abuse; it must have been a wonderful part for his fellow-actor, Armin.

It is extraordinarily difficult to arrive at a final judgment of *Troilus and Cressida*. After all this is not surprising, for it occupies a unique position among Shakespeare's plays; there is no other in the body of his work that at all resembles it. It has too often been called a 'bad play,' but no one who saw the performance given by the Players' Club would for a moment accept this verdict. On the stage Shakespeare's characters came to life with amazing force and freshness; reviewers at the time praised especially the impersonation of the comic characters: Ajax, Pandarus, and Thersites. The grave and lovely poetry of the play rang like music from a distant past and the whole was a revelation of dramatic power and beauty to those who had up till then known the play only from the pages of a book. The success of various performances, professional and amateur, on the Continent, in England, and America, shows that *Troilus* still retains its appeal for a select audience.

Unhappily few readers of Shakespeare are at all likely to see *Troilus and Cressida* in action. What advice can be given to the student desiring a fresh approach to this strange play? One thing, at least, may be said. He should dismiss the wrangle of critics over the nature of the play and discard whatever memories he may retain of Homer and Chaucer. Let him approach it with an open mind as an Elizabethan drama, retelling in Elizabethan terms a famous age-old story. Yet he should realize also that the story is the least important thing in the play. What is of prime importance is the criticism of life that it embodies, a criticism vigorous and realistic, yet never cynical. And this criticism is mainly directed against two ideals that tend to dominate and direct man's course of life, those of love and of war. It is against mistaken ideals that the attack is directed, against the folly of love lavished on an unworthy object, against the folly of war pursued for unjust ends. The discord between ideals and realities is audible at times in jarring notes, like sweet bells jangled. Yet above the discord we often catch the clear voice of what Goethe called Shakespeare's 'free spirit,' rising at times to heights of almost unmatched eloquence. In the end, perhaps, we may be content to abide by the verdict of Swinburne, who calls this 'wonderful play one of the most admirable among all the works of Shakespeare . . . as also and naturally, the least beloved of all.'

ALL'S WELL THAT ENDS WELL

All's Well that Ends Well, the second of this group, is one of the least read, as it is one of the least pleasing, of Shakespeare's plays. There are good reasons for this. In the first place the sole text that has come down to us, that of the Folio, is in a most unsatisfactory state. It is marred by misprints, mis-assignment of speeches, and unintelligible passages that have baffled the skill of editors. It seems to have been printed from a hasty and careless transcript of the company's play-book. There is a fairly general agreement that *All's Well* is not a homogeneous piece of work, but a revision by Shakespeare about 1603-4 of a play that he had written some years before, plus, possibly, still later additions by another hand.

When Meres drew up his catalogue of Shakespeare's plays in 1598, he included among the comedies a play called *Love labours wonne.* No comedy with that name exists today; either the play has been lost, which seems unlikely considering Shakespeare's reputation as a playwright and the evident desire of his fellow-actors to publish all his plays, or it is still extant under another name. There is nothing at all unlikely in this. Shakespeare, it seems, took little or no trouble to name his plays; he let two of them go on the stage under the meaningless titles of *As You Like It* and *Twelfth Night; Othello* was performed at Court as *The Moor of Venis,* and *Henry IV Part I* as *The Hotspur. All's Well* itself was labeled *Monsieur Parolles* by Charles I in his copy of the Second Folio. Of all surviving Shakespearean comedies *All's Well,* with its dominant theme, the recapture of a reluctant husband by a loving wife, seems most likely to have once been called *Love's Labours Won;* the original name, in fact, seems alluded to in almost the last words that Helena addresses to Bertram:

Will you be mine, now you are doubly won?

There is no need to discuss in detail the crying discrepancies of style in *All's Well* that point to Shakespeare's revision in Jacobean times of his earlier comedy. For one thing there is a far greater proportion of rhyme than we should expect in a play dating *c.* 1603. On the other hand, much of the blank verse is in Shakespeare's grave later manner. A factor pointing to revision which has escaped the notice of most critics is the presence in the play of the professional Jester, Lavache, a part that must have been written into the original play for Armin, the creator of Touchstone and Feste, who only joined the company in 1599. It would be a thankless task to analyze the play with a view to discovering possible non-Shakespearean additions to his own revision, but attention might be called to the prose dialogue between Helena and Parolles on the topic of virginity (I. i), foisted in between two passages in verse, a passage that has been rightly denounced as a blot on the play, inconsistent with the character of the heroine, and an interruption of the action. It looks like a late addition written in to pad the part of Parolles with a supposedly witty attack on chastity. The Fool's part also probably contains some un-Shakespearean lines, but it is quite possible that here, as elsewhere, Armin wrote them into the text.

There is, however, a graver reason than the unsatisfactory text of *All's Well* for the general dislike of this play. Its plot involves a girl's pursuit of a gentleman above her in social station, her winning him as a husband by royal decree, and finally establishing herself as his wife in fact as well as in name by perpetrating what has been called the bed-trick. All this is naturally offensive to modern sensibilities, and it has been too easily assumed that Shakespeare shared our modern feelings and that he revised his early play and renamed it *All's Well that Ends Well* in a spirit of bitter irony. This, however, is fanciful and subjective criticism; after all, Shakespeare was an Elizabethan and he wrote for an Elizabethan audience, whose sensibilities, though quick and responsive, were far less nice than ours. An examination of the material on which Shakespeare worked may help to clear the air.

As has long been known, the source of *All's Well* is Boccaccio's story of Giglietta di Nerbona, a translation of which was included by Painter in his *Palace of Pleasure,* 1566. A summary of Painter's version will suffice to give the essentials of the plot.

> Giletta of Narbona, the orphan daughter of a famous physician, fell in love with Beltramo, the Count of Rossiglione, in whose house she had been brought up. When he left home for the Court of France she followed him. There by means of an inherited medical secret she healed the sick King, whom his

doctors had given up as incurable. As a reward she was given her choice of a husband and chose Beltramo. Although the young lord strongly objected to wedding a doctor's daughter, the King insisted on the marriage. Immediately after the ceremony, however, Beltramo deserted his wife and fled to Italy. Giletta returned to Rossiglione, where she ruled the Count's estate so well that all the people loved her. Later she wrote her husband saying that if he lived in exile on her account, she would leave the country. He replied that she might do as she pleased, but that he would never live with her until she got a ring off his finger and a child in her arms by him begotten. Determined to fulfil these conditions, Giletta put on a pilgrim's robe and went to Florence, where she learned that Beltramo was trying to seduce a poor but honest girl. She arranged with the girl's mother to have the girl pretend to receive Beltramo, only first demanding as a love-token the ring he wore on his finger. This ring would then be handed to Giletta, who would take the girl's place in bed. The plan was carried out; Giletta got the ring, slept with her husband, and before long found herself with child. Beltramo was called home by his vassals, but Giletta stayed in Florence till she was brought to bed of twin boys. Then she followed Beltramo to France and found him giving a great feast to many lords and ladies. She entered the hall with his sons in her arms, and his ring on her finger, fell down before him and claimed with tears the fulfilment of his promise. Moved by the suit of all the ladies present, Beltramo embraced Giletta, acknowledged her as his lawful wife, and from that time forth loved and honored her.

Here is material for a serious domestic drama. It is interesting to see how Shakespeare used it and what he added to it to impart a flavor of rather bitter comedy.

Shakespeare, it is clear, followed the plot of Boccaccio's story step by step until the very end, but allowed himself the liberty of altering the conclusion of his source to correspond with his sense of dramatic fitness and theatrical effect. He changed the simple appeal of Giletta to her husband into the elaborate intrigue of the last scene of *All's Well*, with its charges and counter-charges and the sudden appearance of Helena to clear up the situation. It is a fair question whether this change improved the old story. It prolongs the interest, to be sure, and amuses the audience with a *coup-de-théâtre,* but the shifty and deceitful behavior of the virtuous Diana is hardly credible and the sudden conversion of Bertram from a slanderous rascal into a loving husband is one of the conventions of Elizabethan comedy that moderns find hard to accept. It is less convincing, certainly, than the conversion of Beltramo, which is motivated not only by his wife's plea, but also by the general petition of the ladies of his Court.

Possibly an underlying, half-conscious reason for Shakespeare's alteration of the denouement was his desire to spare his heroine the scene of humble and tearful petition with which the source closes. Shakespeare's lady makes no petition, but boldly claims her husband her rightful due, 'doubly won' by the King's gift and by her own fulfilment of his conditions.

Shakespeare's main interest in dramatizing the story of Giletta seems to have been the character of the heroine, whom he rebaptized Helena. We can see him at work developing her from the first scene of the play in which she gives full and frank expression of her hopeless love for Bertram:

> It were all one
> That I should love a bright particular star
> And think to wed it, he is so above me.

Shakespeare clearly sympathizes with this passion, in marked distinction from Boccaccio, who remarks that Giletta loved Beltramo 'more than was meet for a maiden of her age.' Helena's defense of her love for Bertram to his mother, and her prayer for pity, win over the apparently indignant lady, who dispatches her on her mission to cure the King, with her love and blessing. The old Countess is a new figure in the story, invented by Shakespeare to heighten the character of Helena by her approval and praise. In the heroine's interview with the King she shows a fine confidence of success, and it is worth noting that she demands as her reward for the completed cure a husband of her choice from the nobles of the Court. There is a pretty scene at Court in which Helena passes the young nobles in review, more than one of whom seems quite willing to take her in marriage, until she pauses before Bertram with the words:

> I dare not say I take you; but I give
> Me and my service, ever whilst I live,
> Into your guiding power. This is the man.

On Bertram's indignant refusal to take her as his wife, Helena's confidence falters for a moment and she says to the King:

> That you are well restor'd, my lord, I'm glad:
> Let the rest go.

But the King's pride is roused and he denounces the 'proud, scornful boy' as 'unworthy this good gift'; he recognizes the union of youth, beauty, wisdom, and courage in Helena as a fitting counterpoise to the lord's rank. This is good Elizabethan doctrine.

In the scene of Bertram's abrupt departure from his newly wedded wife, Helena shows at once her quiet obedience and her love-longing when she begs in vain for a parting kiss. Shakespeare suppresses the lady's wise rule of her husband's estate, and speeds up the action by having her receive Bertram's letter imposing the apparently impossible conditions immediately upon her arrival at his home. There she is confronted by his mother, who renounces Bertram and adopts Helena as her only child. But she is not content to stay at home while her beloved is exposed to all the dangers of war abroad; she will depart,   although

> The air of paradise did fan the house,
> And angels offic'd all!

She steals away as a pilgrim, leaving behind a pretty sonnet letter in which she begs the Countess to call Bertram home and intimates, clearly enough, that she will embrace Death to set him free from what he has disdainfully called his 'clog.'

This, it must be confessed, is the end of Shakespeare's Helena. In the scenes at Florence she walks through the part allotted her in the source without special distinction; it is hard to imagine the Helena of the earlier acts stage-managing the complicated business of intrigue and deception that ends the play. Did Shakespeare, perhaps, grow weary of the imposed task of turning out a comedy for his fellows; was he eager to get back to the more serious business of *Othello*? None the less the portrait that he drew of Helena while his interest was still fresh is at once so clear and so sympathetic that it should stop the mouths of modern critics who denounce her as untrue to her sex, selfish, indelicate, and lacking in decorum. We may be fairly sure that Shakespeare's audience accepted the performance as an entertaining example of the old saying: 'all's well that ends well.' To ask whether the marriage of such an ill-matched pair was likely to be a happy one is to confuse drama with contemporary life, much in the fashion of a small boy at a performance of *Hamlet* who asked his father why Mr. Evans didn't marry Ophelia.

There are not enough characters in the source to furnish roles for the members of Shakespeare's Company. Naturally, therefore, he invents new persons to give background to the action; he even devises a subplot, the exposure of the braggart Parolles, to enliven it with comic matter. Mention has already been made of the old Countess and her function in the play. She is a charming old lady, as wise as she is kind-hearted. Lafeu, another invented character, also plays a part in the action. He is the friend as well as the councilor of his ailing King, and introduces Helena to him with a jest as a 'Dr. She,' who has come to bring the health-restoring grapes within the reach of his 'royal fox.' He is a humorous, though not exactly a 'humor' character, but he is shrewd enough to recognize the virtue of Helena and to detect the worthlessness of Parolles. It seems, indeed, somewhat out of character that he should offer his daughter as a second wife to Bertram, but this is the first move in the intrigue Shakespeare devised to end the play, and consistency of character is thrown to the winds here in favor of amusing complication.

Two other characters unknown to the source were invented by Shakespeare to add a dash of comedy to a rather serious plot. The first of these is Lavache, the Clown. Like Touchstone and Feste, he is a part created directly for Armin. Like them he is the professional Jester, the domestic Fool. His relation to the Countess is like that of Feste [1] to Olivia, but the good old lady, who bluntly terms him a foul-mouthed rogue, is hardly so patient of his follies as Olivia is of her merry servant's. The epithet that his mistress applies to Lavache is not without justification, for a good part of his wit consists of indiscreet, if not indecent, jests. Yet it hardly seems as if Shakespeare took any such pleasure in creating this character as he had done with the earlier parts he wrote for his fellow-actor. From time to time, indeed, we get a flash of the true Shakespearean wit, as when Lavache comments on the puritan hypocrite who wears 'the surplice of humility over the black gown of a big heart,' or contrasts his own preference of 'the house with the narrow gate' with that of the many who are for 'the flow'ry way that leads to the broad gate and the great fire.' On the

---

[1] Like Feste, Lavache has been bequeathed to a noble household by a master who took much delight in him.

whole, however, Lavache is a poor specimen of the Fool, and he takes little part in the action but drifts in and out to crack his jokes with whoever happens to be on the stage. His last appearance (v. ii) is to heap a final measure of contempt upon the dejected and beggarly Parolles; a man has indeed sunk low in the world when a domestic Fool stops his nose at him.

Parolles is a more original creation than Lavache. In fact he is so original, so unlike a stock figure in Elizabethan comedy, as to puzzle many critics. Quiller-Couch calls him 'about the inanest of all Shakespeare's inventions,' while Kittredge acclaims him as 'one of Shakespeare's masterpieces.' This diverse reaction is probably due to an inability to recognize Shakespeare's purpose in the creation of this character. Taking a hint from his friend Jonson's practice of satirizing contemporary figures, Shakespeare drew in Parolles a portrait that was probably recognized by his audience. Parolles is, or claims to be, a veteran of foreign wars; he has built up a reputation which imposes upon the inexperienced Bertram, who takes him for a soldier 'of very valiant approof.' The shrewd old Lafeu, on the other hand, sees through his pretensions and, while he is willing to endure him for a time as a teller of traveler's tales, warns Bertram against him as an empty nut: 'The soul of this man is in his clothes,' he says. On Shakespeare's stage Parolles was probably fantastically dressed; Diana calls him 'that jack-an-apes with scarfs,' and Lafeu comments on the scarfs and the bannerets about him. He makes pretensions to wit and courtly manners as well as to valor, accompanies Bertram to Court, coaches him in his behavior to his noble acquaintances there, and urges him to seek honor in foreign wars rather than dally with a wife at home, since 'a young man married is a man that's marr'd.' He has so wormed his way into Bertram's confidence as to boast that he is the young lord's companion rather than his servant, and addresses him familiarly with the endearing term of sweetheart. All this, it would seem, adds up to a lively portrait of a special type in the class of hangers-on who clustered about a young English lord like Shakespeare's friend, Southampton. Back from the wars in France or the Low Countries, such a pretender to valor could amuse by his stories, dominate by his supposed experience, and yet prove a dangerous influence by exciting his patron to risk his life abroad rather than to live in quiet orderly fashion at home. Unlike Lavache Parolles has a definite part to play in the action. The dominance of such a worthless fop and braggart over Bertram is designed to show the young

lord's blindness to real worth in Helena. It takes the complete revelation of the cowardice and treason of Parolles to open Bertram's eyes,
and it seems a pity that this recognition of his error was not somehow causally connected with Bertram's final reunion with his wife.
But by the fifth act Shakespeare had lost interest in everything but
the closing intrigue.

Shakespeare may have modeled Parolles after Bobadil in Jonson's
Every Man in his Humour, in which Shakespeare himself took part;
but Parolles is both a more complex and a more realistic character than
Jonson's Elizabethan Miles Gloriosus. It is as hard to believe that a
living Bobadil ever walked the streets of Old Jewry as to accept the
presence of an actual Sam Weller polishing boots at the Old George.
The technique of Shakespeare's rival playwright is not unlike that of
the great Victorian humorist, one of exaggeration and caricature. That
is not Shakespeare's way. Even in a satiric portrait of an unlovely
contemporary type Shakespeare recognizes the essential humanity of
a liar and a coward. The exposure of Parolles is a scene of broad
farce; the rogue is tricked and laughed at, but he is spared the shame
and pain that Bobadil suffered under the cudgel of Downright. Parolles
slinks off with something like repentance in his heart; he will let his
idle sword rust and try to live by 'fooling': after all—and here we may
catch Shakespeare's own voice—'There's place and means for every
man alive.' And a place, as a matter of fact, is reserved for him at
Lafeu's table; the honest lord, who was the first to see through him,
is willing to entertain and make sport with him; 'though you are a
fool and a knave you shall eat.' Shakespeare has none of Jonson's
bitter indignation at fools and knaves.

Apart from Parolles and Lavache there is little of comedy in this
problem play. Yet neither the stupid Jester nor the vain braggart add
greatly to the gaiety of nations. Shakespeare, it seems, had little heart
for comedy when he took pen in hand to recast *Love's Labours Won*
into a new play for his company; he wrote in a new role for Armin to
set the groundlings laughing; enlarged and heightened the satiric
comic character of Parolles; and let it go at that. There is less true
Shakespearean humor in *All's Well* than in any other of his comedies,
and we may dismiss this play as we began our study of it, with the
verdict that it is one of the least pleasing of Shakespeare's works.

MEASURE FOR MEASURE

There are certain links between *Measure for Measure*, the last of this group, and its immediate predecessor, *All's Well that Ends Well.* Both exist in but one text, that of the Folio, and in each case this text is so bad as to suggest that it was printed from a careless transcript of the official play-book; moreover, it is at least probable that this play-book had been revised before or after Shakespeare's death. Apart from this, however, there is a further and more important link between these two plays. Both attain a solution of the dramatic complication by an elaborate intrigue involving the so-called bed-trick, the substitution in the villain's bed of his wife or his betrothed for the lady whose honor he has attacked. In *All's Well* this substitution is an integral part of the story; in *Measure for Measure* it is a deliberate addition to the original, quite plainly lifted by Shakespeare from his own earlier play.

Bad as the text of *Measure for Measure* is, it does not obscure the main action of the play, and this action is of such a nature as to present a double problem, esthetic and ethical. In sharp contrast to the almost universal neglect of *All's Well*, *Measure for Measure* has been one of the most debated of Shakespeare's comedies. In *All's Well* Shakespeare's apparent indifference to all but the heroine and a pair of minor characters has, naturally enough, left his critics and commentators cold; in *Measure for Measure*, on the contrary, the noble poetry, the strong characterization, and the lively realism of the background go to show that Shakespeare was keenly interested in the tale that he was dramatizing, and his interest has naturally provoked a constant stream of interested and would-be interpretative comment. The strange thing is that no two critics seem to agree in a final judgment on his work. There is, in fact, an extraordinary variation of critical opinion. *Measure for Measure* has been denounced as 'a most inconsistent drama' with a 'clumsy plot'; on the other hand it has been praised as 'a deliberate artistic pattern of certain pivot ideas.' Some say that it can best be understood as a satiric comedy, more or less along Jonsonian lines, directed to the unmasking of a pretentious hypocrite; on the other hand it is interpreted as a dramatic exposition of the Gospel maxim: 'Judge not that ye be not judged.' The denouement 'baffles the strong indignant claim of justice': the marriage of Isabella to the Duke is 'a scandalous proceeding': *per contra* this union may be understood as the 'marriage of tolerance with moral fervour' and the pardon of Angelo exemplifies the central theme of the play, that justice should be tempered with mercy.

The verdicts passed upon the main characters vary with the ethical and esthetic preconceptions of the judges. One of them condemns the Duke as too timid or irresolute to enforce his own laws; he deputes his duty to another, 'plunges into a vortex of intrigue,' and ends by 'falling into love with a votary'—a heinous crime indeed. A more clement judge finds that the Duke's sense of human responsibility is delightful and that 'within the dramatic universe he is automatically comparable with Divinity'; while a third affirms that he is not a live man at all, but 'essentially a puppet, cleverly painted and adroitly manipulated.' Angelo 'appears to have been conceived as a villain by nature,' or he was first designed 'to serve as an object of ridicule,' or he is 'virtuous because untried.' Perhaps the extremes of clashing judgments are found in the verdicts upon Isabella; in one she is 'Shakespeare's first wholly Christian woman'; another, acknowledging her 'self-centered saintliness,' declares that she 'lacks human feeling'; while a third, who here might qualify as a hanging judge, roars against the 'rancid chastity' of a seeming saint who saves her own soul by turning into 'a bare procuress.' There must be something wrong with the play, it is affirmed, since critics so violently disagree upon the action, the conclusion, and the chief characters.

It might be suggested that there is something wrong with the critics. Certainly few of them have taken into account the conditions under which the play was written and the material of which Shakespeare composed it. It may be profitable to consider both these matters.

All that we know with any particular certainty about the date of *Measure for Measure* is that it was performed at Court on St. Stephen's Day, 26 December 1604; but it had been preceded in that year by *Othello,* played at Court on 1 November. *Measure for Measure* falls thus in the very center of Shakespeare's tragic period; it is a comedy that goes hand in hand with his most perfectly finished tragedy. Perhaps the wisest comment on the relation of Shakespeare's tragedies to his comedies was made by one of the sanest of modern critics, Sir Walter Raleigh: 'Shakespeare's Comedy is akin to his Tragedy, and does not come of the other house. . . If they [his fellow-actors] asked for a comedy while he was writing his great tragedies, they got *Measure for Measure* or *Troilus and Cressida.*' In other words, when Shakespeare sat down to comply with the request of his fellows for a comedy in 1604, his head was full, his heart, perhaps, still wrung with the agony of *Othello*. It is not likely that he would have written one of his laughing comedies in that year. There is yet another link, moreover, between *Othello* and *Measure for Measure*. The source of both plays lies in Cintio's *Hecatommiti*.

The story of Epitia's sacrifice of her honor to save her brother's life, as told by Cintio, is probably not original with him. The actual occurrence that seems to underlie his novel has been preserved in a letter written by Macarius, a Hungarian student, in 1547.

> A new story has come to us [he writes] from a town near Milan. There in a quarrel a gentleman killed his opponent; he was arrested and condemned to death. His beautiful young wife begged the chief magistrate (who goes by the name of the Spanish Count) for mercy. Charmed by her beauty the Count offered to release the prisoner if she would sacrifice her honor to him. She refused at first but, after consulting her relatives, she accepted, yet with such reluctance that the adulterer's pleasure in the act was ruined by her tears. Next day she learned that her husband had been beheaded and thus indeed had been set free from prison. The lady reproached the Count for his breach of faith, but he only mocked her. Thereupon she went to Ferdinando Gonzago, the Emperor's vicegerent in Milan, and told him her story. Ferdinando called the Count to Milan, rebuked him for his cruelty, and ordered him to pay the lady a dowry of 3,000 ducats and marry her at once. A priest was called who wedded them with the exchange of rings. Then Ferdinando ordered the Count to lose his head. The sentence was carried out, and approved by the Emperor, Charles V.[1]

Several versions of the story, says Macarius, are already in circulation.

Cintio worked up the version that came to him into an *exemplum* of injustice and ingratitude, adding various sensational effects: the prisoner is a youth of sixteen years condemned to death for rape; the interceding lady, Epitia, is his sister; urged by her brother and on a vague promise of marriage, she sacrifices her honor to Juriste the judge. He not only fails to keep his promise but sends her the corpse of the prisoner. She complains to the Emperor, who forces Juriste to marry

---

[1] Condensed from the translation of the Hungarian letter in *Notes and Queries*, 29 July 1893.

her and condemns him to immediate execution. Epitia, however, realizing that, if she consented to the death of her husband, she would be condemned as acting in a spirit of revenge, begs for and obtains his pardon.

Some years later Cintio composed *Epitia,* a dramatic version of his own tale. To bring about a happy ending more psychologically probable than that of his tale, he introduced a startling variation. In the last act after Epitia has refused to beg the pardon of her condemned husband, she learns from the Captain of Justice, who had brought her the corpse, that he had spared her brother's life and substituted the body of a lately executed criminal who closely resembled her brother. Upon this discovery, Epitia relents, and begs for and obtains her husband's life. This play, we may observe, was never performed, and was not published until 1583, ten years after Cintio's death.

Five years before the publication of Cintio's play a dramatic version, *Promos and Cassandra,* 1578, of his novel appeared in England. This was the work of George Whetstone, a typical Elizabethan scholar, traveler, and poet. That his play was designed for the stage is plain from the careful stage directions, but four years later when he rewrote it as one of the prose tales in his *Heptameron,* 1582, he admitted that it had never been performed.

It is customary to dismiss *Promos and Cassandra* as a clumsy two-part play whose only significance is that it served as a source for Shakespeare. Such a verdict disregards the historical evolution of Elizabethan drama. *Promos and Cassandra* antedates any Elizabethan play ordinarily read today; it is earlier than the first efforts of Lyly and Peele, and belongs to the period of the late Morals and the early romantic comedies. What Whetstone tried to do was to present in dramatic form a tragic story of contemporary life against a background of English realism, and to remold it toward a happy ending.

The direct source of Whetstone's play is, of course, the Cintio story; he handles his source, however, with a freedom that shows he had the instinct of a true playwright.

> He enlists our sympathy for Andrugio, the prisoner, by changing his offense from rape to a fall 'through force of love'; love made Polina, Shakespeare's Juliet, grant him 'even what he would request,' an offense lightly enough regarded in Elizabethan England. Urged by her brother, Cassandra implores mercy of Promos, but only succeeds in firing him with lustful

passion. She at first refuses his demand that she surrender her honor as the price of the captive's life, but in a scene in prison she is moved by her brother's entreaty and agrees to forsake her 'virgin's weeds.' Whetstone allows the villain to hesitate and at last to decide on the execution for fear that he be charged with partial performance of his office. In the scene where the Jailer brings the prisoner's head to Cassandra, Whetstone erects a little sign-post to bid his audience look forward to a happy ending, for the Jailer intimates that if she knew what he knows, she would be pleased with his present. The secret comes out in the next scene, where the Jailer avows that it was compassion rather than a bribe that moved him to substitute the head of a lately executed criminal. Cassandra, on seeing what she took to be her brother's head, thinks first of suicide, but later she makes her public appeal to the King of Hungary, who at once orders Promos to marry her and to lose his head the next day. Andrugio hears by chance of the sentence passed on Promos, and returns in disguise to witness his execution. He learns of his sister's vain plea to the King for mercy and resolves to reveal himself, at the risk of his life, and second her appeal. His interview with the King takes place off-stage, but after a pathetic parting scene between husband and wife the good news comes of a royal pardon both for Andrugio and Promos. In a final scene brother and sister are reunited; the King marries Andrugio to Polina, grants Cassandra's plea for her husband's life, and replaces him in office with a charge henceforth to 'measure Grace with Justice.'

Such is the main plot of *Promos and Cassandra,* but many scenes are filled with rather dull realistic comedy, some of it rough horseplay of the conventional early-Elizabethan type. Whetstone is a moralist as well as a playwright and takes occasion to inveigh against the vices of his time, not sexual vice only, but more particularly against the injustice and corruption of minor officials. All this is excised in the prose version [2] which Whetstone included in his *Heptameron.*

[2] This version is often spoken of as a translation of Cintio's tale, by scholars who should know better; it is nothing of the sort; it differs from Cintio in many details exactly as Whetstone's play does. It is narrated by a Madam Isabella—the name evidently stuck in Shakespeare's mind—who is congratulated when she ends it on her 'good conclusion,' for, says one of her hearers, 'had you ended with the sorrow

It has seemed worth while to review these early works in some detail so as to have a clear conception of the material on which Shakespeare went to work when the call came to him in 1604 to write a new comedy for his company. There is reason to believe that he knew both the Cintio and the Whetstone versions, but he did not follow any one of them exactly. Indeed, the changes that he made are such as largely to impair the unity of the originals. *Measure for Measure* is an incomparably greater play than either *Epitia* or *Promos and Cassandra,* but it may be questioned whether it preserves, as they do in their different ways, an essential harmony, and it is this lack of inner harmony that has provoked the violently differing verdicts upon Shakespeare's comedy.

Shakespeare, we may suppose, saw at a glance the dramatic possibilities of a tale that presented a virgin sister pleading for her brother's life and confronted with the condition of saving him by the sacrifice of her honor. Yet he probably realized that compliance on her part as in the early versions would be a virtual impossibility on the stage of the Globe. There are instances enough in Elizabethan drama of rape followed by revenge, or of seduction atoned for by marriage; no case that seems at all comparable to this violation enforced by threat and followed by the violated maiden's acceptance of the villain as her husband. Such a course of action would be all the more impossible if Shakespeare originally conceived the character of Isabella as she appears in his play, a novice about to take the vow of chastity; she is a very different character from the philosophical Epitia or the pliant and rather featureless Cassandra. Isabella, Shakespeare must have decided, should at all costs be spared the sacrifice of her honor, and the substitution of another's head for that of the condemned brother perhaps suggested to him the device he employs to save her. But again a difficulty arose. It was all very well for the masterful Helena of *All's Well* to initiate the intrigue that won her a husband; it would violate all dramatic probability to have a novice of the order of Poor Clares seek out a substitute to take her place in Angelo's bed. A substitute must be found not only for Isabella's body but, so to speak, for her mind, as the directing force of the intrigue that would circumvent the villain.

For this substitute Shakespeare resorted to a device as old as the

you began, we had all like to have been drowned in tears.' That is a sentence worth bearing in mind when we come to pass judgment on the happy ending of Shakespeare's *Measure for Measure.*

Arabian Nights, as modern as Stevenson's Prince Florizel, the disguised ruler moving unknown among his people, observing their desires, directing their actions, and passing final judgment upon them. In all earlier versions of the tale the supreme ruler, Emperor, King, or Viceroy, is absent from the scene; the wronged lady goes to him to seek for justice, and he appears like the *deus ex machina* to administer it. In Shakespeare's play, on the other hand, the Duke is the first person to appear upon the stage, and though he feigns withdrawal, we learn before the first act is over that he is remaining in disguise to watch the actions of his deputy. Even to an auditor unfamiliar with the story, this secret presence of the all-powerful ruler would give a sense of security; Isabella could not lose her honor nor Claudio his life while the Duke was still in Vienna to protect them. In his disguise as a friar, he plays the part of an overruling Providence; he dispels Claudio's fear of death, voluntarily takes charge of Isabella's case, and provides just the substitute, Angelo's betrothed bride, whose replacement of Isabella at the rendezvous would satisfy Elizabethan *mores.* That in this role he tells one lie after another, culminating in the cruel deception that lets Isabella believe her brother has perished, need not shock us. The Duke is not a character from real life, like Angelo, Claudio, and Isabella, but a dramatic device for the manipulation of the plot, and this device of Shakespeare's invention is the final touch that converts an old, true, and tragic story into a tragicomedy.

Here, perhaps, is the reason why so many critics have been baffled by *Measure for Measure.* The original theme is essentially tragic, and Shakespeare, dealing with it in his tragic period, takes it seriously enough; Isabella's plea, Angelo's fall, Claudio's petition for life are all in his profoundly tragic vein. From the moment, however, that the Duke intervenes in the action there is a complete change of tone, marked by the sudden shift from noble verse to stylized prose in the first scene of the third act. In particular, the character of Isabella, as it has so far been developed, suffers a complete collapse. The Friar-Duke bids her promise Angelo satisfaction, she at once consents, and we learn later that she has visited him and arranged all the details of their meeting. We learn it only from her report; Shakespeare did not write the scene; dare we say that he could not write it? Later in the long-drawn-out and artfully involved judgment scene she tells the lie the Duke has put in her mouth, and accuses herself in open court of carnal intercourse with Angelo. This is a little hard to believe of the novice of the order of St. Clare. It is only at the very end when she joins Mariana in a plea for mercy on her brother's supposed murderer that Isabella comes to life again; and that plea at once redeems her and enforces the central idea of the play. After that we need not quarrel with her marriage to the Duke. Some disposition must be made of this central character, and Shakespeare's Protestant audience would hardly have been content to see her shipped back to the convent. Certainly her marriage with the kindly Duke is more in accord with modern as well as Elizabethan taste than that of Cassandra with Promos.

Measure for Measure, then, is in effect a tragi-comedy; in Fletcher's well-known definition: 'it wants death which is enough to make it no tragedy, yet it brings some near it which is enough to make it no comedy.' It employs in the main action all the conventional devices of this genre: disguise, mistaken identity, complex intrigue, and the surprise ending. There is no more striking instance of the *coup-de-théâtre* in Elizabethan drama than the discovery of the Duke when his friar's hood is pulled off by the jesting Lucio and the guilty Angelo beholds his master face to face. And this discovery is purely for theatrical effect; the Duke could have passed an earlier sentence upon his deputy while sitting on the judgment seat *in propria persona;* but, then, of course, the suspense which Shakespeare has been so artfully building up would have been destroyed. The free pardon of Angelo, which 'baffles the strong indignant claim of justice,' is in the strict convention of tragi-comedy; there can hardly be a case in Elizabethan tragi-comedy where the villain gets his due reward.

Between this tragi-comic manipulation of the main plot and the background against which it is set, there is another lack of harmony that has provoked the outcries of the critics. For this background is that of contemporary realistic comedy, a genre rapidly gaining favor in the early years of the seventeenth century. To be frank, it is not a particularly savory background, yet we should not blame Shakespeare too severely; it is in these scenes of low comedy that the hand of the reviser is strongly suspected. And those who blame Shakespeare for presenting in *Measure for Measure* 'without disguise or extenuation a world of moral license and corruption' might turn their eyes to *Henry IV Part II* and consider whether there is any scene in *Measure for Measure* that compares with the Falstaff-Tearsheet episode in an unfaltering exhibition of drunkenness and lechery. The scene at the Boar's Head Tavern is funnier, no doubt; Shakespeare's laughter is less hearty in these comedies of his tragic period. Yet it is far from extinct; he still retains his sympathetic interest in the follies of his fellow mortals, and the low comedy characters who offend the critics are quite effective on the stage.

There is no underplot in *Measure for Measure*. The comedy, such as it is, consists in the characterization of those figures of the underworld against which the tragic characters of Angelo, Isabella, and Claudio stick fiery off. Prominent among these is the bawd, Pompey, a good-natured realist, whose reaction to the old law against fornication, revived and enforced by Angelo, might be paralleled by the comment of an honest bar-keep against law enforcement in the days of our own noble experiment: 'if you head and hang all that offend that way but for ten year together, you'll be glad to give out a commission for more heads.' His cheerful acceptance of a new trade, the 'mystery' of the official hangman, is matched by his genuine pleasure in recognizing in prison so many of Mistress Overdone's old customers: 'Master Starve-lackey the rapier and dagger man, and young Drop-heir that killed lusty Pudding . . . wild Half-can that stabbed Pots, and, I think, forty more.' A new acquaintance he makes there is the hardened prisoner Barnardine, a character invented for the sole purpose of suffering death as a substitute for Claudio. Shakespeare, however, fell so in love with Barnardine on his brief appearance that he let him stagger back to his cell to sleep off his hangover, and included him in the Duke's general pardon at the end of the play. His place is taken by the recently defunct pirate Ragozine,

> A man of Claudio's years; his beard and head
> Just of his colour.

This is perhaps the most shameless theatrical trick that Shakespeare ever allowed himself to pull on his audience.

The shifty, easy-going, and adaptable Pompey is a new type of Clown; if Armin took the part, he must have laid aside for the time his favorite role of the licensed Jester. Elbow, on the other hand, is an old acquaintance, a second cousin at least to Dogberry. Like his predecessor, Elbow is a constable, head of that often ridiculed body, the city watch. Like Dogberry too, he is a pompous ass, abusing the Queen's English with repeated malapropisms; a wise officer who hales to court two 'notorious benefactors . . . void of all profanation in the world that good Christians ought to have.' One of them, it appears, has made improper advances to his wife and he naturally seeks redress, but he is quite incapable of stating his case, and is left stranded in the flood of Pompey's irrelevant argument for the defense. The scene in this local police court is, no doubt, Shakespeare's travesty of occasional proceedings in his own London, where city magistrates sat to handle cases dealing with a controversy of three-pence, such as came, according to Menenius, before the Roman tribunes. Elbow's simple explanation of how he came to hold his office for seven years and a half throws an interesting light on the policing of Elizabethan London, and some prospect of reform is suggested in the implication that he is about to be relieved of his burdensome duties.

Lucio belongs to a higher social class than that of Pompey and Elbow. He is a gentleman born, a friend of the unfortunate Claudio and a reverent admirer of his chaste sister. But he is the type of club-man closely in touch with the underworld, one of Mistress Overdone's customers and the seducer of Kate Keepdown under promise of marriage. His peculiar quality is a zest for social scandal, which he practices to great effect by telling his disguised master 'pretty tales' of the 'old fantastical Duke of dark corners'; it must have especially delighted the Elizabethan groundlings to see this worldly-wise man giving himself away with every word he utters in this scene. The final sentence passed on him that he should marry his 'punk' has been denounced as 'harshness unrelieved,' but nothing is more common in Elizabethan comedy than the marriage by force or fraud of a rogue to a prostitute. To Shakespeare's hearers this sentence, no doubt, seemed rather in the nature of a practical joke. The justifying line, 'slandering a prince deserves it,' may have been written in for the Court performance to get a.hand from the nobles about the throne of James, as avid of flattery as he was averse to criticism, but it also served doubly to justify the Duke's decision.

A final judgment on the problem play *Measure for Measure* is, perhaps, impossible, but what has been said here may at least explain the puzzle that it presents. Shakespeare was called on to write a comedy; the theme that presented itself to him was essentially a tragic one with effective situations. It had, however, already been modified in the direction of tragi-comedy, and he gave it the final touch by sparing his heroine the sacrifice imposed in earlier versions. To effect this he lifted from his own earlier play the device of the bed-trick and disposed of Isabella by marrying her to the Duke in strict accordance with Elizabethan convention. *Measure for Measure* is by no means a triumph of Shakespeare's art; the incongruity between the tragic theme, the tragi-comedy technique, and the realistic background is too harsh. On the other hand, the play affords, as few other of his comedies do, a direct insight into Shakespeare's mind and heart, a mind working along the lines of Christian ethics and a heart full of sympathy for even the lowest forms of human life.

12

The Sunset

SOMETHING has already been said about the mistake of dividing Shakespeare's plays into watertight compartments, each labeled with an appropriate catchword. For the last period of his creative activity the familiar title, On the Heights, seems to carry with it a suggestion that here Shakespeare attained the summit of his art. That, most certainly, is not true; no play of these last years is comparable in comic mirth or tragic force with the masterpieces of his great creative periods. They have, to be sure, a charm and value of their own. Their beauty is that of evening when the slowly sinking sun has lost its power and heat, but still sheds light over the earth and dyes the heavens with radiant color. Whatever else is missing in this last period, Shakespeare's poetry remains, endowed at times with a special magic. And there is something more in these last plays than his poetry.

Shakespeare seems to have moved into this last period about the year 1608. After Coriolanus, c. 1608, he wrote no more tragedies or, with the exception of Henry VIII, chronicle plays. He still wrote comedies, but those of his last years are so different from those of his prime that they have sometimes been styled romances, a rather misleading term. We find him collaborating more than once with a younger playwright, a practice that he had avoided in earlier days, and there is a marked weakening of his former constructive power. Shakespeare's reworking of the old play of Pericles serves as an introduction to this period, which includes Cymbeline, The Winter's Tale, and The Tempest.[1] These plays form a distinct group and represent a shift in technique and a change of tone in Shakespeare's art.

There has been much speculation regarding the cause of this change. Probably no single event, external or internal, was the sole cause. We may dismiss, for example, the suggestion that in 1608 Shakespeare suffered something like a nervous breakdown. We know too little of

[1] Two plays written in collaboration with Fletcher belong in this period. They are not discussed here because Shakespeare's share in them is uncertain and there is no trace of his comic vein in either.

his life to accept this hypothesis; certainly *Coriolanus* shows no weakening of Shakespeare's constructive power. Yet the strain under which he had been living for the last ten years, as actor, playwright, and man of business, must have been very great, and there is evidence that about 1610 he began to withdraw from London to live in Stratford. It is not impossible that a weakening of the association with his fellow-actors may have played a part in the failing of his dramatic power.

More to the point, perhaps, as a partial explanation of the change in tone and technique of Shakespeare's latest plays, is the acquisition by his company of a new playhouse, the private theater of Blackfriars. A company of children who had been playing there for some years fell into disgrace at Court, and their manager was glad to surrender his lease of the property to Burbage. The King's Men took over in August 1608, probably with happy hearts as they recalled the bitter winter of 1607-8 and their hardships while playing at the open-air Globe to a shivering audience. Their new theater was roofed in, heated with seacoal fires, and lighted with cressets. It seems to have been better equipped with machinery for the production of the masque-like stage effects dear to an audience which in part had witnessed, and all had heard of, the elaborate spectacles presented in the masques at Court. For with their new theater Shakespeare's company acquired also a new audience, more select than the groundlings of the Globe, rather sophisticated and trained to delight in sensational romantic plays, such as Beaumont and Fletcher had lately been offering them. It was for such an audience, for performance in such a theater, that Shakespeare's latest plays, except for *Pericles* and *Henry VIII*,[2] were written.

Shakespeare was a practical playwright, working in the theater, with fellow-actors, for an Elizabethan audience. Yet even more: he was a poet endowed with a poet's vision of life. And this vision is revealed to us, if not directly, yet unmistakably, in the emotional emphasis of his plays. It cannot be denied that in the plays of his last period this emphasis changes. The bitterness of *Troilus*, the misanthropy of *Timon*, are no longer heard. Instead we catch a strain of acceptance of the world order. It is no enforced and gloomy resignation, rather a cheerful and smiling recognition of the rightness of things as they are. And this for the reason that the world order now seems to Shakespeare to be governed by divine powers. It is, perhaps, too much to say that the implicit philosophy of Shakespeare's latest

2 Both Globe plays. That *Henry VIII* was performed at the Globe we know from a contemporary statement by Sir Henry Wotton.

plays is Christian, yet there is something akin to the Christian faith in this willing acceptance of divine control. Man may hoist the sails, but the vessel is borne 'even where the heavenly limiter pleases.' It is remarkable how often in these plays divine interposition directs the action: Diana guides Pericles to the recovery of his lost wife; the oracle of Delphos proclaims the innocence of Hermione; Jupiter descends from heaven to rebuke the complaining ghosts and to promise the reunion of their 'low-laid son' to Imogen; and in *The Tempest* Prospero is the incarnation of Providence to guide, to punish, and to reward. The closing note is often, as in *Cymbeline*, one of grateful acceptance of this divine control:

> Laud we the gods;
> And let our crooked smokes climb to their nostrils
> From our bless'd altars.

A sunset glow, beneficent, serene, spreads over the world that had been ravaged by the storm of *Lear*.

What part has the Muse of Comedy to play in this world that ends in peace and beauty? Certainly there is no room here for Puckish mockery, for the realistic comment of Lear's Fool, or the chuckling cynicism of Thersites. Yet comedy is never wholly absent from Shakespeare's work, and a study of the plays of this period may help to determine both the quantity and the quality of Shakespearean humor in his latest years.

PERICLES

Pericles, Prince of Tyre, the first of this group, is a dramatization in characteristic Elizabethan fashion as a chronicle play, enlivened by dumb shows and spectacle, of a widespread medieval legend; the *Historia Apollonii regis Tyri* is still preserved in some hundred Latin manuscripts. A version found its way into the *Gesta Romanorum,* that popular collection of entertaining and edifying stories, and it was translated and imitated in almost every European language. It came early to England, where a fragmentary Anglo-Saxon version antedates the Norman conquest. In Chaucer's day his friend, the moral Gower, told it at great length in his *Confessio Amantis,* adding a sententious conclusion in regard to the happiness of lawful as opposed to unlawful love. With the dawn of the Renaissance in England, Wynkyn de Worde, Caxton's apprentice and successor, published, 1510, Copeland's translation of a French version. And while Shakespeare was still a boy at Stratford, Laurence Twine, an Oxford scholar, and an 'ingenious poet,' wrote a 'simple pamflet' entitled *The Patterne of Painefull Adventures,* which converted the Latin of the *Gesta Romanorum* into Elizabethan prose. His pamphlet, entered in the Stationers' Register in 1576, exists in two editions, one undated, the other a reprint in 1607, a date which may have some bearing on that of *Pericles.*

This brings us up to the play itself. On 20 May 1608, 'a booke called the booke of Pericles prynce of Tyre' was entered in the Register by Edward Blount, an Elizabethan publisher of genuine literary taste, and one of the syndicate that later brought out the first Folio. Presumably the *Pericles* that he entered was that which passes today as Shakespeare's, though the possibility remains that it may have been the old play which, according to modern scholarship, Shakespeare revised for his company. If so, a publisher of Blount's fine taste may well have refrained from publishing his copy after Shakespeare's revision, appearing on the stage, had made it worthless. Be that as it may, the fact remains that Blount never published an edition of *Pericles.*

The stage success of Pericles tempted a minor man of letters, George Wilkins, who in 1607 had written a domestic tragedy for Shakespeare's company, to attempt a quite unprecedented feat in Elizabethan literature. Many an Elizabethan play had been derived from a novel; Wilkins seems to have been the first to novelize, if the word may be permitted, an Elizabethan play. The title-page of Wilkins' novel, *The Painfull Adventures of Pericles Prince of Tyre,* 1608, frankly admits that it is 'the true History of the Play of *Pericles,* as it was lately presented by the worthy and ancient Poet John Gower,' and Wilkins begs the reader 'to receive this Historie in the same manner as it was . . . by the King's Maiestys Players excellently presented.' Neither here nor in Blount's entry is there any reference to Shakespeare, but here at least we learn that *Pericles* had been performed by Shakespeare's Company.

This novel by Wilkins is a curious specimen of hack work; he evidently had on his desk a copy of Twine's pamphlet, upon which he made liberal drafts. On the other hand, his connection with the players possibly allowed him a sight of their prompt-copy, for verse passages of *Pericles* appear repeatedly with slight or no change in the prose of Wilkins. It seems certain that the novel was a mere attempt to exploit the stage success of the play. So long as the play itself was withheld from publication, there might be a market for a prose ver-

sion in a fresher and shorter form than Twine's long-winded narrative. This was probably the view of Wilkins' publisher, Nathaniel
Butter, but if he hoped for repeated editions of the novel he must
have been sadly disappointed; for in the very next year, 1609, there
appeared a text of the play itself. Henry Gosson, a young bookseller
who had recently begun to publish cheap and popular books, issued
in 1609 a quarto edition of *Pericles* with a grand flourish on the title-
page:

> The Late, And much admired Play, Called Pericles, Prince of
> Tyre. With the true Relation of the whole Historie . . . of the
> said Prince: As also The no lesse strange, and worthy acci-
> dents in the Birth and Life of his daughter Mariana [sic]. As it
> hath been divers and sundry times acted by his Maiesties
> Servants, at the Globe on the Banck-side. By William Shake-
> speare.

Gosson seems to have got his 'copy' by sending a notetaker to the
Globe and, as might be expected from such a method, the text of
Pericles is very bad indeed. None the less it was the only text to be
had, and there was a strong demand for it; two editions were called
for in the same year, another followed in 1611, a fourth in 1619, and
two more in 1630 and 1635, when it became apparent that it was
not to be read in either of the early Folios. Only two other Shakespearean plays, *Richard III* and *King Henry IV Part I*, were so
eagerly sought for by Elizabethan book-buyers.

Pericles was not included in the first Folio. The reason for its exclusion is not at once apparent. The company must have possessed an
acting version, since they had played it at Court as late as 1619. The
editors could hardly have decided to exclude it because of the presence
of non-Shakespearean matter in the text, for they did include such
plays as *Henry VIII* and *Timon of Athens*. It seems they judged that
Pericles belonged in another category than these, that it was, in fact,
not a Shakespeare play. Perhaps their judgment was influenced by
that of Ben Jonson, who was in close touch with the editors and
contributed to the Folio the long poem, 'To the memory of my beloved the author.' Now *Pericles* seems to have been of all Elizabethan
plays the object of Jonson's very special dislike. In the *Ode to Himself*, written after the failure of his new play, *The New Inn*, 1629, he
vows to leave a stage where 'some mouldy tale like *Pericles*' is received with applause. It is hard to believe that Jonson would have

spoken of this play in such terms had he believed it the work of the playwright he had praised as the peer 'of all that insolent Greece or haughty Rome sent forth.' In 1623, when the Folio was being printed, Jonson's reputation and influence were at their highest, and his contempt of the faulty construction, the jigging choruses, and the antiquated dumb shows of *Pericles* may well have tipped the scales against this play.

Whatever the reason, *Pericles* did not appear in the first Folio, nor was it included in the second of 1632. After the Restoration there was a change of attitude. *Pericles* still held the stage and Betterton was 'highly applauded' for his acting as the protagonist. In an attempt to complete the collection of Shakespeare's plays the editors of the third Folio, 1664, added to the second impression of that volume *Pericles, Prince of Tyre* and six other plays, 'never before Printed in Folio,' all of which had been ascribed to Shakespeare, or, at least to W.S., during his lifetime. These six are now universally discarded as apocryphal; they need not even be named here.

The fourth Folio included *Pericles* and the other six; so did Rowe, Shakespeare's first editor. Pope, who followed Rowe, excluded them all from his edition, 1725, and his example was followed by later editors until in 1790 Malone included *Pericles* in his edition of Shakespeare. Since then the play has appeared in practically all editions of Shakespeare's works.

As late as 1874 Dr. Furnivall, the great English scholar, admitted to Lord Tennyson that he had never read *Pericles*, but that he had been told by good judges that it was doubtful whether Shakespeare had any part in it. 'O no! that won't do,' replied the Laureate; 'he wrote all the part relating to the birth and recovery of Marina and the recovery of Thaisa. I settled that long ago. Come upstairs and I'll read it to you.' Tennyson's reading began with the speech of Pericles: 'Thou God of this great vast' (III. ii) and continued to the end of the play, omitting, we happen to know, the brothel scenes of the fourth act. It is hardly too much to say that this subjective division of the play by a poet corresponds rather closely to the general results of later scholarship.

It is needless to recite here the varying views of modern scholars; it may suffice to state briefly what seems to be the best conclusion in regard to the genesis and authorship of *Pericles*. Some time in the first decade of the century, perhaps near the year 1607 when Twine's pamphlet was reprinted, an unknown author [1] dramatized the story of Apollonius of Tyre, basing his work mainly upon the Gower version, and using Gower as the 'presenter' of the play. This old play seems to have been such a stage success as to warrant its acquisition by the King's Men, who turned it over to Shakespeare for a revision. One may imagine Shakespeare looking over the copy submitted to him and finding little or nothing to arouse his interest in the first two acts. The dull old-fashioned verse, the flat narrative-dramatic technique, the imparting of necessary information by dumb show rather than by dialogue are all so unlike Shakespeare's manner at any period of his career that scholars generally agree he left these acts practically untouched. As he read on, however, his interest quickened. The tale of the early loss and late recovery by Pericles of wife and daughter struck in Shakespeare's mind a chord which is heard again and again in his latest plays, the chord of separation and reunion. Here, to be sure, it was not creation, but restoration, that he undertook; the facts were already given him, but they deserved, he must have thought, a loftier, more poetic expression, than had been given them in the prosaic measures of the old play. Shakespeare suddenly caught fire and he began to write fresh matter into the text. From the point where Tennyson began to read, Shakespeare's voice is heard intermittently throughout the rest of the play, sometimes ringing full and clear, sometimes distorted by hasty and unintelligent reporting. It is, indeed, in the Shakespearean scenes that the text of the quarto is most confused and corrupt, as if it were beyond the power of the notetaker to transcribe with any degree of accuracy the swift, vigorous, yet at times curiously involved, Shakespearean dialogue.

Yet it cannot be asserted that the last three acts are wholly and solely the work of Shakespeare. The choruses come from the old play, though Shakespeare may have given some of them a touch or two; that which introduces the fifth act reads very like Shakespeare. The fiercest battle of the critics, however, has been fought over the brothel scenes.

The prudery of Victorian scholars led them for the most part to reject these scenes on moral and esthetic grounds; a late reaction ascribes them to Shakespeare, insisting on a supposed likeness to corresponding scenes in *Measure for Measure*. Insufficient consideration,

[1] This author has sometimes been identified as Wilkins, but a better case can be made out for Heywood, many of whose plays, he tells us, were lost 'by shifting and change of companies' and got into print without his knowledge.

it would seem, has been given by either school to the position of these scenes in the Apollonius legend. They are an essential part of the tale and develop a situation dear to medieval storytellers and moralists, a virgin's preservation of her chastity under the most untoward circumstances. Some such scenes must surely have been in the text which was handed to Shakespeare for revision. He could not have deleted them without destroying a striking feature of an already popular play, and Shakespeare was no Victorian prude. The proper question is not whether Shakespeare wrote these scenes, but whether he rewrote them as completely as he did the storm scene (III. i) or the reunion of Pericles and Marina. The answer to this question would seem to be in the negative.

The first of these scenes, written almost entirely in prose, is, to speak frankly, as dull as it is dirty, without a gleam of the humor that enlivens matter of this sort in *Measure for Measure*. Pompey, in that play, is a genuine comic character; Boult in this is a featureless puppet, merely the slave of the brothel keeper, who appears in all versions of the legend. The second is so brief, some ten lines of prose, as to defy stylistic tests. It is, however, a rather important sign-post scene, pointing forward to what immediately follows, Marina's successful repulse of the Governor's attack upon her virtue. There is nothing like this interview in Gower, but in Twine the Governor is the first visitor to Marina in the brothel. Now to suggest, as this short scene does, that he had been anticipated by others who came to sin and went away converted by Marina's eloquence, is a little stroke of dramatic art. We may well imagine Shakespeare writing these few lines into the old text. The last of the three presents a more difficult problem. It is a long scene, over two hundred lines, mostly in prose, in which one may perhaps occasionally suspect the quickening hand of Shakespeare. It breaks into verse with Marina's appeal and the Governor's reply. This verse has a true Shakespearean ring, but it is so rough and broken as to suggest that the speeches have been heavily cut, or badly reported. The novel at this point puts into the mouth of Marina a long and passionate speech in which one may perhaps detect reminiscences by Wilkins of Shakespearean lines he had heard at the Globe.

Perhaps a fair conclusion on these disputed scenes might be that Shakespeare found the brothel business in the old play and retained it, that he left the first scene untouched, wrote in the brief second, and in the third smartened the prose with an occasional touch, and wrote for Marina and Lysimachus speeches in verse which have come down to us in damaged condition, how badly damaged no one can even guess who has not looked at them in the quarto, where, in fact, they are printed as prose. After all, Shakespeare's main interest in the play was in the recovery of Marina, and both medieval tradition and Elizabethan convention demanded that she should be recovered a virgin. Shakespeare could hardly have refrained from making her speak in her own defense at this most critical moment of her life.

If the foregoing attempt to determine Shakespeare's contribution to *Pericles* is approximately correct, it remains to ask what comic matter can be found in his share of the play. The answer seems to be little or nothing. There are but two situations in this spectacular romantic play where anything comic may be looked for. The first of these is the scene with the fishermen (II. i). Here we might, perhaps, expect an occasional Shakespearean interpolation, but while a current of homely humor flows through the scene, there is nothing that can be assigned with any degree of assurance to Shakespeare; nor is there any such discrimination of character between the actors as Shakespeare draws, for instance, between the Grave-diggers in *Hamlet;* Patchbreech, the third fisher, seems to have been planned as a rustic Clown, but he soon drops out of the action. The chief argument, however, against Shakespeare's presence in the scene is the lamentable quality of the verse assigned to Pericles. Surely if Shakespeare had touched this scene in his revision he would have done something better for his distressed hero. The whole scene is a dramatic elaboration in early Elizabethan fashion of a brief incident in the legend where the shipwrecked prince meets a good fisherman who, like St. Martin, shares his poor cloak with him. There is nothing in the scene beyond the reach of any one of a number of Elizabethan playwrights; the general tone and style suggest, perhaps, Heywood rather than another.

The second of these situations occurs in the brothel scenes. This dirty linen has, let us hope, been already sufficiently washed and shifted. The only trace of humor that a microscopic inspection can detect in them would be in some few prose speeches of the third scene. We may, it seems, rest assured that Shakespeare did not rewrite this group to bring out whatever of comedy the situation offered.

The conclusion of this 'tedious brief' examination of *Pericles* may now be stated. Shakespeare's contribution to the play was limited to a hasty revision of the last three acts. Even there his interest was aroused mainly by the Marina story, and there was nothing in this old romantic tale to quicken his sense of humor. On the other hand, some of the verse that he wrote into the old play shows him at the height of his power. We have only to compare the lovely recognition scene between Pericles and Marina with Gower's version to realize the gulf that lies between a good old-fashioned teller of tales and a great dramatic poet.

CYMBELINE

Cymbeline, 1609, probably the first play that Shakespeare wrote for his company at Blackfriars, did not appear in print until it was included in the Folio. There it was placed at the very end of the book, the last in the group of tragedies. This was not a happy disposition of the play, for there is nothing truly tragic in Cymbeline. Probably the editors were as much puzzled where to place it as they had been with Troilus and Cressida, which they crammed in between the histories and the tragedies. Cymbeline could not well go into the histories, for the historical subplot is of very minor importance, while on the other hand the main action is quite too serious for the play to be grouped with the comedies. The truth is that Cymbeline is a tragi-comedy of the newly developing genre, but for this type of drama the editors of the Folio had allowed no place in their collection.

In writing Cymbeline Shakespeare, it seems, was trying his hand in a new type of drama, the romantic, sensational, and spectacular play, which Beaumont and Fletcher had introduced with great success upon the stage. Some scholars have even asserted that in Cymbeline Shakespeare was imitating their much applauded Philaster, but it is by no means certain that Philaster preceded Cymbeline, and Shakespeare himself, as early as 1604, had written a play best described as a tragi-comedy, Measure for Measure. Cymbeline, however, shows a marked advance over that play in the technique of tragi-comedy; it discards the frank realism of Measure for Measure and substitutes for it a high-flying romanticism that verges at times on the sensational. In addition, as might be expected of a play aimed at a Blackfriars audience, it stresses the scenic and spectacular.

The plot of Cymbeline is a multicolored web, woven of strands drawn from diverse sources. The main plot, which has to do with a husband's wager on the chastity of his wife, goes back to a widespread medieval folk tale. Of the many versions of this story, the closest to Shakespeare's play is found in the Decameron. It may be summarized as follows:

At an inn in Paris some Italian merchants are mocking the idea of wifely virtue. Bernabo of Genoa, however, firmly maintains the chastity of his wife, Ginevra. One of the company, Ambrogiuolo, declares that he could win her as he has won others, and provokes Bernabo into a wager on her virtue. The tempter goes to Genoa and at once discovers that he has undertaken a hopeless task. Unwilling, however, to lose the wager, he gains admittance to the lady's bed-chamber concealed in a chest. While she sleeps he creeps out, notes the furniture and pictures of the room, steals a ring, a purse, and a girdle, and remarks on her breast a mole with a group of golden hairs. He returns to Paris and convinces Bernabo that he has won the wager. The husband then returns to Italy, sends a servant to bid Ginevra meet him outside the city, and orders him to kill her on the way. Overcome by her tears and protestations of innocence the servant spares her, takes her dress to show his master as proof of her death, and leaves her his hat and doublet.

From this point Boccaccio's story diverges widely from Shakespeare's plot. Briefly it runs as follows:

Disguised as a man Ginevra becomes at last the trusted servant of the Soldan. One day she sees on a stall in the market place her own purse and girdle exposed for sale. She hears from the owner, Ambrogiuolo, that they had been given him by his mistress, the wife of Bernabo. Using her influence with the Soldan she brings the two merchants together, and forces the slanderer to confess his trick and the husband to admit the murder of his wife. Ginevra then reveals herself and pardons her husband. Ambrogiuolo is impaled and stung to death by wasps and flies.

It is interesting to consider how closely Shakespeare followed his source in certain details and yet what important changes he made with a view to heightening the romantic note. He lifts the action from the bourgeois atmosphere of Boccaccio by turning the slandered lady into a British princess, secretly married to a noble gentleman, but separated from him by the anger of her royal father. He arranges to have the wager thrust upon the exiled husband in such a way that he is bound in honor to accept it. The great dramatic scene between Imogen and Iachimo (I. vi) is invented by Shakespeare; in the story the slanderer does not even try to seduce the lady. Shakespeare discards the long-drawn-out conclusion of the story and substitutes for it the romantic adventures of the wandering princess: her encounter with her unknown brothers, her passion over what she believes to be the body of her murdered husband, and her reunion with him after a British victory over the invading Romans.

Since the heroine of the wager story was changed in Shakespeare's hands into a British princess, it was incumbent on him to provide her with a background. For this he turned to his old stand-by, Holinshed, and drew from him all the matter of the Roman war against King Cymbeline. It need hardly be said that this is quite fictitious, since Holinshed got it from Geoffrey of Monmouth, the fabulizing historian of ancient Britain. An old play, *The Rare Triumphs of Love and Fortune,* may have given Shakespeare a hint for the banished Belisarius and the visit of the princess to his cave. By way of good measure Shakespeare wove into his pattern other strands drawn from folklore: the wicked step-mother, the drug that causes a death-like sleep, the supposed death of the heroine, and her later awakening.

What judgment can be passed upon this strange tissue of improbabilities? There have been many widely divergent sentences. That it pleased its first audience is probable; certainly when performed at Court some twenty-five years later it was 'well likte by the Kinge.' In the age of reason, Dr. Johnson was very severe in his comment on 'the folly of the fiction, the absurdity of the conduct . . . and the improbability of the events in any system of life.' At the close of the Victorian era Shaw railed at 'this silly old *Cymbeline*' and reproached his beloved Ellen Terry for squandering her talent on Imogen, 'an old mechanical thing with a few touches of simple nature,' when she might be playing Ibsen or even G.B.S. With this contemptuous dismissal of the heroine we may compare the verdict of another playwright and critic of our time, the lamented Granville-Barker, whose subtle analysis of the character of Imogen presents her as 'a pleasantly human paragon,' 'a princess to the marrow,' 'gallant, generous, royal, and innocent.' Swinburne called her 'the woman above all Shakespeare's women,' and the greatest of Victorian poets died with *Cymbeline* open in his hands at the lines where Posthumus again has his lady in his arms:

> Hang there like fruit, my soul,
> Till the tree die!

De gustibus non disputandum is a sound old maxim. Those who prefer realistic action and modern dramatic technique to fairy tale romance and Elizabethan poetry may side with Johnson and Bernard Shaw, but there are, fortunately, others.

After all it is perhaps doubtful whether Shakespeare himself is solely to blame for the many faults of *Cymbeline*. The text is far from satisfactory and has long been an open field for emendators. One of the longest of Shakespeare's plays, over 3,000 lines, it could not have been played in its entirety upon Shakespeare's stage. Cuts must have been made, marked in the prompt-book, but not elided from the text. Worse still passages seem to have been written in by another hand than Shakespeare's. The most patent of these is the choral chant of the ghosts who circle about the sleeping Posthumus in prison (v. iv). It is incredible that Shakespeare at his weariest and weakest could have written such pitiful stuff. So bad is it, in fact, that many scholars have rejected the whole business of the vision as a later insertion. This, however, is impossible; we hear the unmistakable voice of Shakespeare in the speech of Sicilius which follows the vision:

> He came in thunder; his celestial breath
> Was sulphurous to smell; the holy eagle
> Stoop'd, as to foot us; his ascension is
> More sweet than our bless'd fields.

This speech certainly implies that Shakespeare had planned, or at least accepted, the vision of Jove on the eagle, and wrote these lines to comment on it. And why not? There is a like bit of spectacle in *The Tempest* where Ariel enters 'like a harpy' to denounce 'three men of sin.' Both are instances of Shakespeare's exploitation of the mechanical apparatus of his new theater to entertain an audience who wanted masque-like effects in drama. Quite apart from the vision, however, there are various signs of later additions to the text: the tedious expository soliloquies of Belarius (III. iii. 79-107) and of Posthumus (v. i). Shakespeare, one feels, had long outgrown this crude dramatic device. There are frequent rhyme-tags inserted into blank verse; Ellen Terry was ready to swear that the tag:

O Imogen!
Safe mayst thou wander, safe return agen!

was written by the actor who spoke them, 'the clever fellow.' Many a
dull platitude rounds off a passage of true Shakespearean verse. It
is noticeable that most of these instances occur in the latter part of
the play; perhaps a reviser after Shakespeare's death undertook to
smarten it up—and spoiled it—for some revival at Blackfriars. It is
dangerously subjective to comb the text for faults and attribute them
to such a reviser, yet it seems plain that the original text has been
more or less rewritten.

Yet when all allowance for such revision is made, the conviction
remains that Shakespeare was not quite at ease in the new dress he
had donned for his first appearance at Blackfriars. There is an air
of artifice in much of his movement through the action; a sense of
unreality in the happenings of the play. He is most himself when
dealing with Imogen, whose story he took very much to heart, and
whose character he developed from the bare outline of his source
with genuine interest and sympathy. Yet even in her case he strains
all probability to provide her with one great sensational scene, her
discovery of the headless corpse. In this new garb even his grip on
character seems less firm. The Queen is a monster, whose villainies, as
related by the good Cornelius in the last scene, are barely credible.
Iachimo, so firmly drawn in the first acts, becomes a sentimental peni-
tent in the last, begging his death at the hand of the man he has
wronged. His final pardon is part of the convention of tragi-comedy.
Cloten, apparently conceived at first as a comic character, the butt
of flattering and mocking lords, turns first into a bold Briton and
then into a melodramatic villain intent on rape and murder, and he
is conveniently despatched—a breach of tragi-comic convention—to
provide the necessary corpse for Imogen's great scene.

In the composition of *Cymbeline* Shakespeare, it would seem, was
mainly preoccupied in weaving into a vivid pattern the divergent
threads he had collected. Invention as such was never his forte; his
general practice was to select a source and manipulate it for his own
dramatic ends. Here, however, as the foregoing summary of the Italian
story shows, he abandoned his source half way through the action.
Practically all that happens in the play after Imogen's escape from
death is Shakespeare's own invention.

It may be that this preoccupation with invented and romantic plot served to block the flow of Shakespeare's native humor. Something like this seems to have happened before in *Othello,* where his fierce concentration on the dramatic development of action from character absorbed his thought to the exclusion of all comic matter. Certainly there is little comedy of situation or speech in *Cymbeline.* Elizabethan audiences may have smiled at the foolish brags of Cloten; the asides of the Second Lord in the early scenes seem like a hint to them to laugh; but Cloten's shift into the role of villain strips him of comic values; we can hardly laugh at a man who proposes to rape a royal princess. There is, however, one truly comic character, the Jailer who chats in the prison scene with the condemned Posthumus. The position in the play of this scene (v. iv) is not without interest. It follows the spectacular vision and immediately precedes the final elaborate *éclaircissement* with its surprising shifts and revelations. Shakespeare seems to pause here for a moment to pen the sort of scene he would like to write when not bound to play up to stage spectacle or meet the requirements of a tragi-comic denouement. For the Jailer is one of the common folk whom Shakespeare loved, a blood relation of the First Grave-digger, and of the Porter in *Macbeth.* Like them he speaks straightforward prose; like them he is a realist, the only one in this romantic play. His conception of death is that of the man in the street; it puts an end to earthly ills, but it is a leap in the dark: 'How you shall speed in your journey's end,' he says to his prisoner, 'I think you'll never return to tell one.' The romantic Posthumus is determined to sacrifice his life in atonement for his crime against Imogen, but the sensible Jailer cannot understand such eagerness to die; he comments on it with good-humored irony: 'Unless a man would marry a gallows and beget young gibbets, I never saw one so prone.' Most men, he thinks, 'die against their wills; so should I, if I were one.' He ends with an expression of common humanity's wish, as applicable in our troubled world as ever it was in Shakespeare's time: 'I would we were all of one mind, and one mind good. O! there were desolation of gaolers and gallowses!'—also of concentration camps and military executions. With this character the fresh air of common sense briefly blows through the rarefied atmosphere of tragi-comedy.

This, after all, is but a scanty gleaning of comic grain from Shakespeare's first venture into a new field. A possible reason for this has already been suggested. As we shall see, however, Shakespeare moved on to a freer play of his native turn for comedy as he came to feel more at home in his new surroundings. After *Cymbeline* comes *The Winter's Tale* and then *The Tempest*.

THE WINTER'S TALE

There is a pause between *Cymbeline* and *The Winter's Tale* during which Shakespeare seems to have rested and gathered strength for his next attempt at fashionable tragi-comedy. *Cymbeline* was apparently written in 1609; *The Winter's Tale* is, certainly, considerably later. We know from Sir Henry Herbert's office-book that it had been licensed by Sir George Buck, who became Master of the Revels in August 1610; on the other hand Dr. Forman saw it at the Globe on 5 May 1611. If, as has been suggested, the dance of the satyrs in the fourth act was borrowed from Jonson's *Masque of Oberon*, 1 January 1611, *The Winter's Tale* must fall between January and May of that year; but this dance may have been interpolated for a Court performance of the play; it is not essential to the action, in fact the 'men of hair,' three of whom had danced before the King, seem somewhat out of place at a rustic sheep-shearing festival. Late in 1610 or early in 1611 seems a safe date for *The Winter's Tale*, which puts it at least a year or more later than *Cymbeline*. Shakespeare had once been in the habit of writing two plays a year for his fellow-actors, but that was over now; it was possible for him to take his ease at Stratford. Yet when the call came to furnish another play for the company's new theater, he buckled on his harness and set to work.

Even though Forman saw *The Winter's Tale* at the Globe in May, there can be no doubt that the play was written for Blackfriars and shifted to the Globe when, in the warm spring weather, the actors returned to their open-air playhouse. Even if there were no other reason, the last scene of *The Winter's Tale*, the unveiling of the statue, was evidently planned for the indoor theater where the possibility of brilliant lighting on the inner stage of a darkened house would make the discovery most effective. There are, moreover, other reasons; *The Winter's Tale* is a true Blackfriars comedy of sensations and surprises. It is certainly a better play of its kind than *Cymbeline*. Perhaps one reason for its superiority is that here Shakespeare returned to his old method of working; he selected a story and proceeded to shape it for his stage.

The story that Shakespeare chose as the basis of his new play is Greene's *Pandosto: the Triumph of Time*, one of the most popular of Elizabethan novels. Originally published in 1588, it appeared again in 1607 and in 1609 with the running-title of *Dorastus and Fawnia* on the title-page. Possibly this revival of his old enemy's work attracted Shakespeare's attention; certainly *The Winter's Tale* is as much a dramatization of Greene's novel as *As You Like It* is of Lodge's *Rosalynde*. A summary of a long and often tedious tale will show both Shakespeare's use of his material and what changes he worked on it.

> Pandosto, King of Bohemia, entertains at his Court his old friend, Egistus, King of Sicily. Pandosto's wife, Bellaria, treats Egistus with such friendly courtesy as to arouse her husband's jealousy. Accordingly he orders Franion, his cup-bearer, to poison Egistus. Franion, however, reveals the plot to him and the two escape to Sicily. Thereupon Pandosto throws his wife into prison, where she gives birth to a baby girl. Declaring the child a bastard, Pandosto has it turned adrift in a boat on the sea. He then brings Bellaria to trial, accusing her of adultery and of conspiracy with Franion to poison him. She appeals to the oracle on the island of Delphos, and the reply is returned: Bellaria is chaste; Pandosto treacherous; the babe an innocent; and the King shall live without an heir if that which is lost be not found. When this reply is read in court, the King is so confounded that he confesses his guilt and begs forgiveness. At this moment he hears that Gariner, his son by Bellaria, has suddenly died. On hearing this the Queen falls dead; Pandosto swoons, and later tries to kill himself. He buries the Queen and Garinter in a splendid tomb where he comes every day to mourn for them. Meanwhile the boat has drifted to Sicily, where the child is rescued by Porrus, a shepherd, who adopts her and calls her Fawnia. She grows up a girl as beautiful as Flora, and Dorastus, King Egistus' son, falls in love with her. After a long courtship she agrees to elope with him by sea. Porrus, disturbed by gossip about the Prince and Fawnia, sets out to tell the King that the girl is not his child, but a foundling. On his way he is seized by the Prince's friends and carried on board the ship to the young couple. A storm drives them to the coast of Bohemia. Here Pandosto, fired by the beauty of his unrecognized daughter, throws the Prince into prison and makes love to her. An

embassy now arrives from Egistus, who has heard of his son's whereabouts, asking Pandosto to free Dorastus and put Fawnia and Porrus to death. To save his life Porrus tells Pandosto how he found the child and shows a mantle and a chain that were with her in the boat. Pandosto recognizes Fawnia as his lost daughter, and they all go to Sicily, where Egistus welcomes them and marries his son to Fawnia. Pandosto, however, brooding over his past sins, falls into 'a melancholy fit' and, to quote Greene's words, 'to close up the comedy with a tragical stratagem' kills himself. Dorastus returns to reign with his wife in Bohemia.

In throwing this shapeless story into dramatic form, Shakespeare first shifts the emphasis. Greene devotes only a third of his novel to the unfortunate Queen and spends the rest on the love story of Dorastus and Fawnia. Shakespeare, on the contrary, takes the better part of three acts to deal with the accusation and trial of Hermione, and brings her back again in the denouement. He cuts out the long courtship; when we first meet Florizel and Perdita, they are already happy lovers. He keeps the King's recognition of his lost child off the stage to add greater effect to the Queen's return to life. If a proper name were to be chosen as a new title for this play, it would be Hermione, not Perdita.

Furthermore Shakespeare changes the whole tone of the story. It is not clear that Greene knew very well what he was doing; all he wanted was to write a romantic tale packed with situations giving occasion for his favorite long and euphuistic soliloquies. Shakespeare knew better than to 'close up a comedy with a tragical stratagem'; in fact he seems to have planned to convert Greene's story into a tragi-comedy where a near tragic beginning should be brought to a happy close. He retains the general outline of the novel, but he eliminates its most tragic incidents, the death of the Queen, Pandosto's unnatural passion for his daughter, and his final suicide. To add variety of interest he introduces several lifelike characters of whom Greene knows nothing, especially Paulina, the fearless defender of Hermione in the first part of the play, the agent of her restoration at the end. Along with her goes her husband Antigonus, invented by Shakespeare to serve as the reluctant exposer of the infant. Shakespeare may have thought that a Blackfriars audience would have balked at the notion that a lone baby could survive a stormy voyage from Bohemia to Sicily. In

the second part of the play, to give a realistic background to a romantic tale he brings in certain comic characters, the stupid Clown,
Perdita's foster-brother, with his rustic sweethearts, and the rogue,
Autolycus. There is no place for such characters in Greene's artificial
pastoral, but they are quite at home in an English rustic festival.

It may repay us to follow the action of the play and to observe
Shakespeare's use of the tragi-comic technique of surprise and spectacle. It opens gaily with the portrayal of the old friendship of the
two Kings and with Hermione's playful pressure on Polixenes to defer
his departure, but the first surprise comes swiftly with the revelation
of her husband's jealousy. No auditor, unless aware that Shakespeare
was dramatizing Greene's novel, could have expected this. The sudden
unmotivated passion of Leontes has often been denounced by critics,
but Shakespeare had no desire to write *Othello* over again. The jealousy of Leontes, unlike that of the Moor, is causeless, self-centered,
and recognized by all others in the action as morbid self-delusion. The
reader, like the spectator, is expected to take it as such and not to
argue about it. After the flight of Polixenes, Leontes turns against the
Queen and we have the spectacle of her trial and her death-like swoon.
In the source she really dies at this point, but in the play this would
violate the rules of tragi-comedy.[1]

The two parts of *The Winter's Tale* are linked by the speech of
Time as Chorus. This is a well-known device of early Elizabethan
drama, where an allegorical or historic figure acts as Presenter of the
play, like Gower in *Pericles*. It is artfully used here by Shakespeare
to persuade his audience to ignore the passage of years and the shift
of scene from Sicily to Bohemia. Orthodox believers in the classic
unities of time and space had long denounced the liberties taken with
these laws by contemporary playwrights. No doubt there were such
believers then in Blackfriars, Ben Jonson, perhaps, among them. Listen, says Shakespeare, Time is all-powerful, accept his ruling and see
what happens next. What happens next, after a brief expository reference to Prince Florizel and the shepherd's fair daughter, is 'Enter
Autolycus singing.' The near tragedy of the early acts has become
comedy, pushed here into broad farce by the 'cony-catching' trick

---

[1] It might be objected that the report of the Prince's death also breaks these
rules, but his death is necessary to fulfil the prediction of the oracle that the King
would live without an heir 'if that which is lost be not found.' And to give point
to this prediction, Shakespeare changes the name of the exposed child from
Greene's pastoral Fawnia to Perdita, the lost one. A word about the death of Antigonus will be said later.

Autolycus plays on the Clown, and the stately verse of the trial scene gives way to racy prose.

In the long scene that follows and concludes the act, prose alternates with some of Shakespeare's loveliest verse as he depicts the idyllic love of Florizel and Perdita set off against the patter of Autolycus as pedlar and ballad-singer and the squabbles of the Clown's sweethearts. At the very height of the feast, when Florizel invites the company to witness his formal betrothal to Perdita, Shakespeare springs another tragi-comic surprise. King Polixenes, present in disguise, reveals himself, rebukes his son, and threatens Perdita with a death as cruel as she is tender. There is too much of bluster in his speech to strike the tragic note, but it gives Perdita the chance to show herself her mother's own daughter:

> I was not much afeard; for once or twice
> I was about to speak and tell him plainly,
> The self-same sun that shines upon his court
> Hides not his visage from our cottage, but
> Looks on alike.

This highly effective situation is Shakespeare's invention; there is nothing like it in the source. That nothing serious need be feared from the King's threats is made plain by the broad comedy which closes the scene with the fooling of the Clown and the shepherd by Autolycus.

If the fourth act is Perdita's, the last reverts to Hermione; the charming girl of the rustic feast shrinks almost to a *persona muta* with less than a dozen lines to speak. The scene opens at the Court of the remorseful Leontes, where all the talk is of the dead Queen. His councilors would have the King wed again for the good of the state, but Paulina makes him swear never to marry but by her leave. Florizel and Perdita now arrive and are welcomed by Leontes, who, as he gazes on his unknown daughter, thinks of his lost wife. Their brief interview is interrupted by another surprise, the reported approach of Polixenes in chase of the lovers. On his way to Leontes he has encountered the shepherd and his son, and now, we know, the secret of Perdita's birth will be revealed. And so it is in the next scene, where a Nuntius-like Third Gentleman relates in courtly prose the joyful meeting of the two Kings and the recognition of Perdita as the lost heir to the throne. Included in his report is a statement that prepares the way for the last and most effective surprise: Perdita has heard of the lifelike statue of her mother, kept as in a shrine in Paulina's house, and all the court has gone to see it.

The final discovery is led up to with skill and delicate grace. Shakespeare keeps us in suspense while Paulina delays to draw the curtain before the statue. When at last she does, all present are struck with its living resemblance to the dead Queen. Perdita kneels to ask her blessing and would kiss her hand. Leontes is so moved by the sight of what he has lost that Paulina threatens to hide it from him. Recognizing, however, his true remorse and newly awakened love, she asserts that if he has faith she can make the statue move, descend, and take him by the hand. On her invocation and to the strains of music, Hermione, no longer a statue, descends and silently embraces the King. Shakespeare wisely omits a formal speech of forgiveness; the action suffices. The only words that Hermione speaks here are to her daughter, and in accordance with the religious tone of these last plays, they invoke the heavenly powers:

> You gods, look down,
> And from your sacred vials pour your graces
> Upon my daughter's head!

The transformation of a statue into a living woman goes back to the legend of Pygmalion and Galatea: the story had been told again and again since Ovid, but never with such dramatic effect. Yet we may well recognize in this *coup-de-théâtre* Shakespeare's ingenious adaptation of one of the devices of the Court Masque where a transformation scene discloses a group of statue-like and silent figures, who later come forward to take part in the action.

That the tragi-comedy of *The Winter's Tale* was a triumphant success with the audience at which it was aimed is shown by its repeated performances at Court. It was played there in November 1611, again in 1613 during the festivities celebrating the Princess Elizabeth's betrothal, thrice more before King James, and once at least before Charles I, when, Herbert says, it was 'likt' by the King. This compares most favorably with the one Court performance of *Cymbeline*.

It has seemed worth while to dwell upon the tragi-comic character of *The Winter's Tale*, since various adverse comments on this play spring, apparently, from a misconception of tragi-comedy. Coleridge, for example, held it 'mere indolence' on Shakespeare's part not to have provided 'some ground' for Hermione's 'seeming death and voluntary retirement.' This, he thinks, might have been effected by some 'obscure sentence' of the oracle.[2] But any hint that the Queen still lives would diminish, if not destroy, the effect of the surprise denouement at which Shakespeare was aiming from the beginning. After all this play is a 'winter's tale' to drive away the time; we should not demand reasonable grounds for belief in a fairy story. Quiller-Couch, in a recent edition of this play, echoes and enlarges on Johnson's opinion that 'it was only to spare his own labor' that Shakespeare put the recognition of Perdita into narrative. One might reply that in *Pericles* Shakespeare had already written a scene of a lost daughter's recognition by her father, a scene so admirable in form and expression that even he might have shrunk from an attempt to repeat it. Furthermore, we may note that this scene in *Pericles* quite eclipses a later one in which the hero regains his lost wife. Would not the dramatic value of Hermione's return to life have been impaired had it been preceded by a strong emotional scene between Leontes and Perdita? After all, *The Winter's Tale* is the tragi-comedy of Hermione; the love story of Perdita is only an idyllic interlude between the tragedy of the Queen's trial and her final happy reunion with a once lost husband and daughter.

Turning from the tragi-comic character of *The Winter's Tale* to the comic element in this play, we find first that there is a far larger proportion of comedy here than in *Cymbeline*. This may be due in part to the greater ease with which Shakespeare was working as he adjusted himself to the requirements of a novel genre; in part, also, to his freedom from the strain of inventing, as in *Cymbeline*, the various incidents of a complicated plot. The influence of the Court Masque, which regularly included the comic figures of the anti-masque to break the monotony of spectacle and formal dancing, naturally makes itself felt in the comedy of contemporary drama. The grotesque dance of Satyrs in *The Winter's Tale* seems to be directly borrowed from Jonson's *Masque of Oberon*. It has been suggested that the bear in the third act of *The Winter's Tale* also came from this Masque, in which the chariot of the fairy king is drawn by two white bears, but this is an error. Shakespeare's company had performed the popular old comedy of *Mucedorus* at Court nearly a year before Jonson's Masque, and in this play a bear provides a farcical act for Mouse, the Clown, who falls backwards over him, after which it chases a

---

[2] Coleridge actually invents a sentence which would have this desired effect, but it would be hard, if not impossible, to fit it into the oracle's prediction. It is always dangerous to tamper with the text of Shakespeare.

nobleman off the stage—compare 'Exit [Antigonus] pursued by a bear' (v. iii. 58). The successful performance of the well-trained beast at Court doubtless induced the company to borrow him again from the Beargarden for their new play at Blackfriars. Shakespeare must have been informed of this arrangement and consented to write in the necessary lines. To modern taste there is nothing at all comic in the plight of Antigonus, but an Elizabethan audience doubtless enjoyed the sight of a noble lord's hasty exit pursued by a lumbering bear. Even more repulsive to us is the Clown's gruesome report of the bear's tearing out the poor gentleman's shoulder bone while he roared for help, and the bear mocked him, roaring louder. Yet it is just such a mélange of the horrible and the ludicrous, as in contemporary scenes with mad folk, that provoked Elizabethan laughter. Shakespeare would not have written this speech for his comic Clown had he not expected just this reaction.

We are on surer ground when we come to deal with more familiar elements of comedy: speech, situation, and character. There is little in *The Winter's Tale* of Shakespeare's early delight in puns and word-play. The chatter of the boy-prince, Mamillius, is mildly amusing. In the scene where Paulina presents the new-born babe to the King, her blunt speech and the three-cornered scolding-match that breaks out between her, Leontes, and Antigonus, relieves the tragic tension, but only for a moment before the fateful order is given to expose the babe. It is only in the second part of the play that comedy appears in its true garb. Here we find one comic situation after another, grouped, naturally, about the comedy figures of the Clown and Autolycus. The first of these is the episode in which the rogue picks the pocket of the kindly Clown, who fondly thinks he is playing the good Samaritan. An added zest is given to this familiar trick of Elizabethan rogues by the thief's refusal of a loan from the man he just robbed. Later at the sheep-shearing feast when the Clown apologizes for his failure to bring back the promised gifts on the warrantable ground of having been cozened of all his money, the disguised thief standing by remarks with calm assurance: 'Indeed, sir, there are cozeners abroad.' A different situation arises at the end of this scene (IV. iv) when Autolycus, now sporting the dress Prince Florizel had worn at the feast, bullies the Clown and his frightened father in the character of a 'courtier cap-a-pe.' It is amusing that while writing this passage Shakespeare suddenly recalled the horrible punishment inflicted on the slanderer of woman's virtue in the story that had served as the source of *Cymbeline*. It could not be inflicted on Iachimo in that play; he, like all the others, must be pardoned, but here it runs off Shakespeare's pen into the mouth of Autolycus, as a warning of what awaits the son of the 'old sheep-whistling rogue,' who would wed his daughter to a royal prince.

There is a comic counterpart to this episode in the last act, when the Clown and his father again encounter Autolycus. The situation is now reversed. The country couple have not only escaped punishment; they have been promoted to the rank of gentlemen born—a social distinction that meant something to Shakespeare of Stratford. Swelling like a turkey-cock in his new clothes, the Clown brags of his connection with royalty: 'the Prince, my brother, and the Princess, my sister,' and lords it over Autolycus, now, apparently, shrunk to a poor servant of the Prince. The shepherd, who retains something of his old peasant's humility, admonishes his son that they must be gentle, now that they are gentlemen. Accordingly the Clown gives Autolycus his hand and promises him a good word to the Prince; he will even swear that Autolycus is a tall fellow of his hands and will not be drunk, even though he knows the contrary. The little episode is a neat bit of satire, no doubt appreciated by the gentle audience at Blackfriars, who had no love for the upstarts about King James's Court.

The close relationship of these two comic characters to stock figures in early English drama has never, it would seem, been fully realized. They are direct descendants of the country bumpkin and the Vice of the late Morals and the Interludes. Shakespeare, to be sure, took some pains to purge them before he introduced them to polite society. The Clown, whom he has not even troubled to christen, has had his face washed. He does not babble the almost unintelligible jargon which passed for rustic speech in the early drama; his language is not larded with the filth and profanity of his ancestors. Yet, though he has been cleaned up, the characteristic family features remain: the simple goodwill, the dense stupidity, and the blind self-conceit which make him the butt of the rogue. Shakespeare's Clown is, of course, a more distinct and recognizable individual than the typical boor of the old plays. Shakespeare has set him in his country environment and provided him with a father, a foster-sister, and a couple of sweethearts. He is apparently an old bachelor with something of an old boy's domineering manner, and he loves a ballad 'but even too well, if it be doleful matter merrily set down.'

The lineal descent of Autolycus from the Vice is, perhaps, even clearer. Like Merry-report in the *Play of the Weather* he is a singing, jesting figure. In the conventional manner of the Vice he immediately reveals his true character to the audience when he traces his ancestry back to Mercury, the god of thieves, through a father who was 'likewise a snapper-up of unconsidered trifles.' He is a mischief-maker and his first action is to rob the Clown. The exigencies of Shakespeare's borrowed plot prevent him from doing any real harm; the rural feast goes on in spite of his theft, and his trick in luring the Clown and the Shepherd on board Florizel's ship only secures a more opportune discovery of Perdita's parentage. Like the Vice he is an adept at changing his role; he appears in turn as a rambling rogue, a robbed traveler, a pedlar and ballad singer, a smart courtier, and a poor retainer. His assumed humble bearing to the Clown on his last appearance might even suggest the final discomfiture of the Vice in the stricter Morals. Yet Shakespeare has managed to transform the allegorical figure of the old drama into a living, very human character. Autolycus is the most amusing rogue in Shakespeare's plays. As amoral as Falstaff, he appeals like the fat Knight to a weak side of our common human nature through his hearty enjoyment of his own roguery and his shameless laughter at the 'fool Honesty and Trust his sworn brother.' He comes alive on the boards as none of Shakespeare's jesters since the Fool in *Lear* had done, but unlike that Fool he is not a mere commentator on the main action; he has his own part in it to play. The role of Autolycus must have been a brilliant one for Armin, who here, as in *Twelfth Night,* took over the part of a singing merrymaker.

All in all, *The Winter's Tale* is one of the most delightful plays of Shakespeare. And this for the reason that he seems to have found himself again. Freed from the incessant pressure of rehearsing, acting, and composing, back in his home town and living at ease a respected gentleman, he drinks in the familiar country sights and sounds, and marks the country characters. All things combine to liberate his spirit and restore his strength of hand. He shows in this play a grip on the development of plot and the portrayal of character that had not been his since he wrote *Coriolanus.* Above all he has regained his joy of life. He takes sheer delight in telling a winter's tale, excising all that is inconsistent with its tone and even heightening its unrealities. In the rural setting—so truly English—of the love story of Florizel and Perdita, he stands once more upon his native soil. The touch of mother earth unlocks his long-sealed spring of humor, and from this contact arise the traditional, yet transformed, comic figures of the Clown and Autolycus. The tragi-comedy of Hermione is lightened with bursts of hearty English laughter.

THE TEMPEST

The Tempest, perhaps the best loved of all Shakespeare's plays, occupies the position of honor as the first play in the Folio. It may have been placed there with the design of attracting prospective purchasers. Opening the large and expensive volume on the bookstall where it was exposed for sale, the customer would see at once the name of a play that had received the signal honor of repeated performances at Court; if at all acquainted with the contemporary theater he might know that *The Tempest* was the last play that Shakespeare had written without collaboration. And since it had never appeared before in print, here was his one chance to secure a copy of the famous play.

We are able, as it happens, to date the composition of *The Tempest* with sufficient accuracy. It was performed at Court on 1 November 1611, and had, no doubt, been seen more than once at Blackfriars before it was called to Court. On the other hand, there is conclusive evidence that it cannot have been written before the late autumn of 1610. In June 1609 a fleet of nine ships had set sail from Plymouth with additional settlers for Jamestown, Virginia, the first English colony beyond the seas. In mid-ocean the fleet was struck by a terrific storm in which the flagship, the *Sea Venture,* disappeared from sight. The other ships finally reached Jamestown, but the *Sea Venture,* with Sir Thomas Gates, the newly appointed governor, was given up for lost. Great was then the joy in England, when in the autumn of 1610 the news arrived that, while the flagship had indeed been wrecked, not a life had been lost, and that Gates and the crew were safe in Virginia. Separated from her consorts and driven before the wind, the *Sea Venture* had crashed on a coral reef off one of the Bermuda Islands. Luckily she stuck fast and did not sink, so that the crew got to shore unhurt. They were forced, however, to spend nine months or so in the islands, described by Strachey, one of the shipwrecked party, as 'so terrible to all that ever touched on them, and such tempests, thunders, and other fearful objects are seen and heard about them, that they be commonly called The Devil's Islands.' Yet in spite of their ill repute, the islands afforded a hospitable refuge to the castaways until, in the spring of 1610, the sailors built a couple of tiny vessels in which the whole party sailed across to Jamestown.

After this good news reached England, various accounts of the shipwreck, the stay on the Bermudas, and the arrival of the crew at Jamestown appeared in print. They were probably read by Shakespeare; certainly he read Strachey's 'letter to a lady,' which circulated in manuscript among the members of the Virginia council, to which, by the way, Shakespeare's friend Southampton belonged. Words and phrases describing the storm, the wreck, and the islands are so common to the letter and the play as to suggest that Shakespeare had it almost by heart. It is apparent, then, that *The Tempest* must have been written and staged between the late autumn of 1610 and that of 1611.

There is no direct source for *The Tempest* such as exists for *Cymbeline* and *The Winter's Tale*. There has been the usual talk of a lost play, and a Spanish novel has been searched for in vain. Probably no literary source was needed. Shakespeare's imagination may have been fired by the tale of the shipwreck and the sojourn of the crew on those Devil's Islands. He may even, as Kipling once suggested, have talked with a returned sailor and heard from him strange tales of the island sights and sounds. So the idea came to him of a new play for Blackfriars; the scene would be laid after a shipwreck in an enchanted island. Such an island naturally called for a magician as its lord, one who controlled the local demons, and came into conflict with the shipwrecked crew on whom he would practice his magic arts. This would furnish a fascinating background for an action, but what was the action itself to be? Here, we may suppose, the theme that haunted Shakespeare's mind during this last period, the theme of wrong done and redressed, of reconciliation and forgiveness, took control, and a simple plot, the simplest perhaps of all his plays since *Love's Labour's Lost*, began to shape itself in his mind. Let the shipwrecked party be guilty of an old crime against the magician, let them fall into his power on the island, and let him in the end use mercy rather than justice, forgiveness rather than revenge. It would add, of course, to the effect if the two parties were of high rank, a King and his courtiers on one side, a noble lord banished to the island, not a vulgar wizard, on the other. From his reading in Italian history Shakespeare got the names of Prospero of Milan, Alonso, King of Naples, and his son Ferdinand. A love story woven into the action would naturally heighten the interest, and so we get Ferdinand and Miranda, whose marriage unites the once hostile states of Naples and Milan, as that of Florizel and Perdita had linked Bohemia and Sicily. Surely such a build-up of a plot was not impossible for Shakespeare.

Incidental details, indeed, he may have caught up from various sources and woven together into his pattern. An old German play, *Die Schoene Sidea*, by Jakob Ayrer, who died in 1605, contains a princely magician who gets his enemy's son into his power and makes him carry logs. That is a bit of stage business which actors would be sure to remember, and English actors in Germany may have seen Ayrer's play at Nürnberg and carried its story back to England. It has further been suggested that Shakespeare borrowed the scenario of *The Tempest* from some version of the Arcadian plays of the Italian *commedia dell' arte*. In itself this is not impossible; Italian comedians gave repeated performances in England in the latter part of the sixteenth century. In some of the remaining versions of their plays we find a shipwreck and a magician ruling over an enchanted island; he plays tricks upon the shipwrecked strangers, but finally renounces his art and returns to Italy. All this is, indeed, like the action of *The Tempest*, as is also Shakespeare's unique observance in this play of the unity of time which characterizes Italian comedy. But to state that Shakespeare used the framework of an Italian scenario, 'elaborating the parts by literary borrowings,' seems to push the suggestion too far. The unity of time in *The Tempest* is a device adopted by Shakespeare to shorten the action in a play in which so much time was to be spent on masque-like effects of music, dance, and spectacle.

It is, in fact, to the Court Masque rather than to Italian comedy that *The Tempest* owes its distinguishing features as a stage play. These masque-like effects have been noted in Shakespeare's former plays for Blackfriars; it is in *The Tempest* that they culminate. Quite apart from the formal masque of the fourth act, stage directions from the beginning of the play imply effects that must have taxed all the resources of the theater. The very first of them calls for 'a tempestuous noise of thunder and lightning.' In the second act Ariel enters, 'playing solemn music,' dressed in a costume that is supposed to make him invisible. Later to 'solemn and strange music' there enter 'several strange Shapes, bringing in a banquet,' who 'dance about it with gentle actions of salutation . . . inviting the King to eat.' But when Alonso accepts this invitation, there is a crash of thunder, and Ariel, descending probably from above, 'like a harpy,' 'claps his wings upon the table; and with a quaint device, the banquet vanishes.' One would give something to know what the quaint device was which swept the banquet of wine, fruit, and confections off the table. Table and banquet could not have disappeared together down a trap, for a little later after Ariel has vanished in thunder, the 'Shapes' re-enter, this time with 'mocks and mows' to carry out the table.

At the end of the formal masque there is a still more puzzling stage direction. Certain nymphs and reapers are joining in a 'graceful dance' when Prospero 'starts suddenly, and speaks; after which, to a strange, hollow, and confused noise, they heavily [i.e. slowly] vanish.' There was some debate about this stage direction at the time of the 1916 New York production. The best conclusion seemed to be that it called for a discordant clash of instruments to divert the attention of the audience, and that a smoke rose through a trap from combustibles kindled beneath the stage, under cover of which goddesses, nymphs, and reapers slipped quietly away, or, to quote Shakespeare's own words, 'melted into air.' The recent Margaret Webster production avoided this difficulty by excising the entire masque.

Finally when the trio of drunken rascals is busy with Prospero's 'glistering apparel' a 'noise of hunters,' i.e. a flourish of horns, is heard, and there enter 'divers Spirits, in shape of hounds, and hunt them about.' Apparently the boys of Shakespeare's company were dressed and masked like dogs to play for a moment the role of Prospero's attendant spirits.

All these noises, transformations, and quaint costumes, to say nothing of the songs and music which pervade this play, are familiar features of the Court Masque and have been deliberately transferred into the drama by Shakespeare. There is some reason to believe that *The Tempest* was composed at Stratford and that, since Shakespeare was unable to direct the production at London, he wrote out these elaborate stage directions to serve as a guide for the performance at Blackfriars. What he planned, apparently, was to give his audience not only an entertaining play, but a taste of the special delights of the Court Masque.

That is what *The Tempest* was primarily meant to be, a good show. It would be absurd to call it great drama; there is no real dramatic conflict in it; the action is not determined by the interplay of characters; it is dominated from the storm at the beginning to the reunion at the end by one character of superhuman powers. On the other hand, how good a show it is only those can say who have been fortunate enough to attend one of its infrequent performances. The happy laughter of an audience of school children at a matinee many years ago was an unfeigned tribute to the magic of Shakespeare's art.

Yet for one who has seen *The Tempest* on the stage there are hundreds who know it only from the printed page. For them the original spectacular and musical effects have lost their appeal, and still the charm of the play remains, a baffling mysterious charm. Every reader of average intelligence instinctively feels that there is more in *The Tempest* than meets the eye at first glance; and this awareness of an inner meaning has led to the widest variety of interpretations. They vary from a conception of the play as Shakespeare's allegory of his own art to one in which it stands for a dramatic representation of 'the psychological experiences which mystics call Initiation.' To one critic Prospero represents the higher Reason; Ariel, Fancy; Caliban, brute Understanding; Miranda, Womanhood; and Ferdinand, Youth; to another it is 'a version of the universal epic of the soul's aspiration' and in the Epilogue Shakespeare invokes the spiritual aid of his readers to enforce the 'real and secret meaning' of his play. Common sense revolts against such interpretations; it is incredible that a practical playwright, composing, at the very end of his career, a play for Blackfriars and the Court, should consciously turn it into an allegory of his art or a cryptic version of the soul's aspiration.

There is, however, another interpretation of more general appeal, the autobiographic. The thought that forces itself upon the reader that Prospero resembles Shakespeare 'can hardly,' says Raleigh, 'have been absent from the mind of the author.' 'If there is no connection between Shakespeare's abandonment of the drama and the character of Prospero, which he sketched when his mind must have been full of the coming change,' says Morton Luce, 'we have a most astonishing literary coincidence,' and such a coincidence is most unlikely. So long as this view is not pushed too far, so long as we are content to think of Shakespeare pouring unconsciously a double measure of himself into *The Tempest*, we may accept this interpretation for what it may profit us in an understanding of the play. After all, no great dramatist has been wholly objective in his representation of human life. Shakespeare, the Elizabethan, and Shaw, the post-Victorian playwright, are far enough apart, but they have this in common, a recurrent urge to voice their own ideas through the mouths of their characters. It is most certainly Shakespeare's conception of the art of acting that Hamlet addresses to the strolling players at Elsinore, yet Hamlet is not Shakespeare. We dare not with Coleridge call Prospero 'the very

Shakespeare of *The Tempest*,' but it is impossible not to catch
Shakespeare's voice in the most famous lines of the play:

> We are such stuff
> As dreams are made on, and our little life
> Is rounded with a sleep

and in Prospero's abjuration of his art:

> I'll break my staff,
> Bury it certain fathoms in the earth,
> And, deeper than did ever plummet sound,
> I'll drown my book.

The Epilogue, spoken by Prospero, is no doubt in keeping with his
dramatic character; yet it seems, also, to have a special significance
as Shakespeare's last appeal to the audience he had so often enchanted.
It was not the first time that one of his characters had stepped forward to beg a favorable response to the play just presented. Puck
laughingly, Rosalind mockingly, had petitioned for applause, but
there is neither mockery nor mirth in Prospero's appeal, rather a sin-
cerity and depth of feeling that seems to carry beyond the immediate
object and to beg forgiveness, as his hearers would themselves be forgiven:

> As you from crimes would pardon'd be,
> Let your indulgence set me free.

It is hard to believe that Shakespeare wrote the Epilogue without a
backward glance at his long career as the magician of the theater, perhaps with a sigh for sins of omission and commission, and a prayer
for a final pardon.

It may be uncertain how fully Prospero represents Shakespeare, but
there can be no doubt that *The Tempest* as a whole expresses more
completely than any other play Shakespeare's final outlook on life.
The theme of forgiveness and reconciliation which runs like a golden
thread through the last plays finds here its ultimate and perfect expression. The tragic crime that starts the action in *Cymbeline* and in
The Winter's Tale is here reported only, as something that had happened in the dark backward and abysm of time. The action itself
begins years later, with the storm that delivers the criminals into the
hands of their former victim, and his power over them is exercised
only to bring them to repentance and to end the strife between Naples

and Milan in the marriage of their heirs. *The Tempest* possesses a unity, not only of time but of theme, that is wanting in the preceding plays. The union in the protagonist of supreme power and human benevolence, the exaltation in action of virtue over vengeance, mark this play as unique in Shakespeare's work, his fitting farewell to the stage which had so long been his world.

If there is so much, then, of Shakespeare's mind in *The Tempest* it follows naturally that there should be also in this play a goodly measure of that comic spirit which was his native birthright. And that is indeed what we discover. A strain of comedy runs through *The Tempest*, not as an underplot, but as an accompaniment of mirth to a serious action.

It begins, indeed, in the first scene. In spite of the imminent danger and the cries of the mariners: 'All lost!' 'Farewell, brother,' we cannot take the situation very seriously. It would be quite unlike Shakespeare to begin a play with a tragic catastrophe, and we learn in what immediately follows that not a hair of any creature in the vessel has been lost. In the scene itself there is a comic contrast between the frightened expostulations of the courtiers and the rough humor of the Boatswain, intent upon his duty and careless as the breakers for the name of King.

The second scene introduces, after the long expository narrative of Prospero, two of his attendants who in quite different ways contribute to the comedy. Ariel, the first of these, is the willing, if somewhat wilful, minister of Prospero's commands. We need not follow scholars into the derivation and original meaning of his name; certainly to Shakespeare's audience it suggested a spirit of the air, light, bright, playful, and fantastic. The part must have been played by one of the singing and dancing boys of the company; it was an impossible role for actor of Armin's age. The tricks that Ariel plays on Ferdinand and other members of the shipwrecked party and lastly on Caliban and his confederates are more calculated to provoke laughter when seen on the stage than in the study; they are, after all, the actions of a harmless fairy.

It is another matter with Caliban. His name is merely an anagram of Cannibal, a native of the West Indies, inhabited, according to popular belief, by man-eaters. Shakespeare, to be sure, does not attribute cannibalism to Caliban; to have done so would have destroyed the serio-comic effect he aimed at in this presentation of the savage Indian. For Caliban, on one side at least, represents Shakespeare's idea of the American Indian as he had gathered it from reports of voyagers. There is, however, another aspect of Caliban; he is the off-spring of the devil and a witch, a deformed sub-human monster, the reluctant slave of Prospero. As such he represents, in contrast to Ariel, the baser elements under the control of the magician; he is of the earth, earthy. Caliban has little to do in this scene except to exhibit his brutish and rebellious nature, but we may be sure that the audience were startled by this 'servant monster,' and looked forward to his next appearance and his part in the play; and they were not to be disappointed.

There is little of comedy either of action or character in the scene (II. i) that introduces the members of the shipwrecked party. It would seem as if Shakespeare took little interest in any of them except the honest and verbose Gonzalo. Into his mouth he puts a paraphrase of certain passages of Montaigne's essay, *Des Cannibales*, which may have amused the more literate members of his audience, but it is hardly a specimen of Shakespeare's own humor. Still less is the trivial word-play bandied back and forth between Sebastian and Antonio. It seems a strange reversion at this stage in Shakespeare's career to his early addiction to quips and puns. Possibly, indeed, he did not mean it to be laughed at, but rather used it as a quick method of characterizing men who in their distressing situation can think of nothing better than to mock Gonzalo and reproach the King. It can hardly have sur-prised the audience to find these mockers, before the end of the scene, on the verge of treason and of fratricide. Only Ariel's interposition prevents the perpetration of the crime of murder.

The next scene is one of the broadest bits of farce-comedy in Shake-speare. It brings Caliban together with two of the shipwrecked crew: Trinculo, the Jester, and Stephano, the drunken butler. It is a scene of lively comic action; Caliban first mistakes Trinculo for a spirit come to torment him, and hides under his outlandish gaberdine. Then Trinculo, to escape a cloud that looks about to fall in pailfuls —Shakespeare must have heard of rainstorms in Bermuda—also creeps under Caliban's cloak. Stephano enters to be startled by his discovery of a monster with four legs and two voices; but he has a universal panacea, liquor, which he presses first on Caliban and then on Trin-culo, whom he pulls out from under the gaberdine by the lesser legs, garbed, of course, in the parti-colored cloth of the professional Fool. Shakespeare, it seems, had learned of the Indians' partiality for the white man's fire-water, for Caliban at once takes Stephano for a god who bears celestial liquor, renounces his subjection to Prospero, kisses his new master's foot, and goes off with him, singing and shouting: 'Freedom, high-day! high-day, freedom!', in very truth 'a howling monster.'

After an intervening scene between Ferdinand and Miranda, the farce-comedy continues. Caliban and his new friends are 'red-hot with drinking,' but by no means in perfect amity. Trinculo mocks the monster as a natural, i.e. idiot; Caliban begs his master to beat him, and Stephano, now posing as lord of the island, threatens Trinculo with a mutineer's death, 'The poor monster's my subject, and he shall not suffer indignity.' Ariel enters, invisible, and by repeatedly whispering 'thou liest' provokes a quarrel in which Stephano strikes the Jester. This is a touch of the old-fashioned horseplay, but it soon passes, for the two mortals agree on Caliban's proposal to kill the magician in his sleep and seize his daughter. As they celebrate restored harmony in a drunken catch, Ariel strikes up the tune on a tabor and pipe, and leads them off bewitched, a comic counterpart to his graceful enchantment of Ferdinand in an earlier scene. We do not see them again till the next act when, after an elf-led progress through thorns and briers, they reach the mouth of the magician's cell.

Here, at the moment when they should fall upon Prospero, the attention of the two mortals is caught by the garments Ariel had hung out. True representatives of the London street-sweepings which England so often dispatched to her new colony, they fall greedily upon the prize, even as the first settlers in Virginia left their proper work to hunt for false gold in the streams. In spite of Caliban's appeals to drop it and get on with the murder—another touch, perhaps, of aboriginal savagery—they persist in loading him down with stuff to bear away, until Prospero and Ariel break in on them with a pack of spirit-hounds and chase them off the stage. They are rounded up for the last time to share in the final scene of forgiveness and dismissal. Stephano has consoled himself with more drink; Trinculo whimpers over the pickle he is in, and Caliban's eyes are opened to his folly in mistaking a drunkard for a god.

These comic scenes, so effective in action, lose some of their appeal in print, especially to a reader entranced by Shakespeare's poetry, or intent on discovering his secret meaning. Yet they are, in fact, an essential part of the play. The likeness of *The Tempest* to the Court Masque has already been pointed out, and the farcical behavior of Caliban and his companions bears the same relation to the poetic beauty and grave thought of the main action as the gamboling grotesque figures of the anti-masque bear to the splendid spectacle, the formal dancing, and, at times, the implied moral purpose of the typical Court Masque.

Yet these comic scenes have more significance than the pranks of the anti-masquers. The enchanted island is a little world that contains all sorts of men, from the almost superhuman magician, through the youth and innocence of Ferdinand and Miranda, and the wickedness of the brothers, down to the semi-bestial Caliban. There is a place above Caliban in this little world for such poor specimens of humanity as Trinculo and Stephano, as there had been for Nym and Pistol in the heroic war in France. And even for such characters Shakespeare retains his native kindliness. Trinculo, to be sure, is one of the feeblest of Shakespeare's Fools. That is due possibly to the situation in which he finds himself, shipwrecked on the island. At the Court of Naples he might have set the table in a roar; here, till he meets Stephano, he is a lonely and frightened man. There is something pathetically human in the cry with which he hails his shipmate: 'O Stephano, two Neapolitans scap'd!' Yet even after this meeting he plays a subordinate part, crushed, as it were, between the domineering butler and the brutish Caliban. His intense dislike of Caliban seems attributable in part to his jealousy of the hold the monster has so quickly acquired on Stephano, in part to the natural scorn an inmate of the royal Court would feel for this ignorant and credulous savage.

Stephano is a more firmly drawn and fully rounded character. He is described in the 'Names of the Actors' added to the Folio text as 'a drunken butler,' but he is more than that. He is a typical British seaman, temporarily, it seems, the King's butler during the voyage. He has a careless swagger, a fluent tongue, and a consuming thirst. He is not in the least alarmed at his situation; he has floated ashore upon a butt of sack, and while the liquor lasts nothing can subdue his mind. He enters roaring a sailor's song, passes the bottle to Trinculo and Caliban, and complacently accepts the monster's worship, asserting that he was once the man in the moon. Now that the King and all the rest are drowned, he proposes to inherit the island. There is nothing malicious about Stephano; it is Caliban who suggests the murder of Prospero, adding the savage details: 'batter his skull, or paunch him with a stake, or cut his wezand'; but he accepts the proposal without a qualm, especially as it will bring him the magician's lovely daughter to reign with him as queen—'save our Graces!' He is as easily diverted from bloody thoughts as he was led into them; the sight of the gay apparel puts murder quite out of his mind, the immediate booty means more than a future kingdom. Even at the end, as he reels back all one cramp from the pinches of Prospero's goblins, he retains something of his old swagger: 'Every man shift for all the rest,' he cries, 'and let no man take care for himself; for all is but fortune. Coragio, bully monster, coragio!' Shakespeare, one feels, had a real liking for this salty character. Stephano speaks always a racy idiomatic prose which contrasts, as it is meant to do, with the native poetry of Caliban. Compare, for example, Caliban's:

> Be not afeard: the isle is full of noises,
> Sounds and sweet airs, that give delight, and hurt not.
> Sometimes a thousand twangling instruments
> Will hum about mine ears,

with Stephano's reply: 'This will prove a brave kingdom to me, where I shall have my music for nothing.' It is this frank realism of characterization that permits Stephano to perform his essential function in the play. *The Tempest* like *A Midsummer Night's Dream* is a play of fantasy; the enchanted island corresponds to the fairy-haunted wood near Athens. Into both there enter characters who seem to have just stepped out of the daily humdrum of man's life, Bottom, the weaver, and Stephano, the swaggering sailor. Bottom's dream of a love affair with Titania is matched by Stephano's conceit of himself as King of the island. Both characters serve to link the imaginary with the real world; without the presence in *The Tempest* of such a figure as Stephano, the play would lose touch with ordinary human life and pass before us like an insubstantial pageant. Here, as elsewhere, it is Shakespeare's sense of humor that restrains his imagination from soaring, like Shelley's, into ethereal distance.

The Tempest is Shakespeare's last and loveliest utterance in romantic poetic drama, yet it still reflects, along with so much of his graver thought, his old sense of the comedy of human life, his old delight in the folly of mortal man.

13

Conclusion

It is no easy task to summarize Shakespeare's achievement in the field of comedy. This is partly because of the range and abundance of his work, extending as it does from *The Comedy of Errors* to *The Tempest,* including within these limits some three dozen plays. Into almost all of them comedy enters in some form and to some extent.

Also there is the extraordinary variety of comedy in Shakespeare's work. He did not limit himself to the comedy of humors, as did Jonson in his day, or to that of manners, as Congreve did after him. Shakespeare's comedy varies from such a patterned play as *Love's Labour's Lost,* where a King and three lords are paired off against a Princess and three ladies, to such a lively farce as *The Merry Wives of Windsor.* Yet into both of these the element of realism enters in the characters of Holofernes and Nathaniel, of Slender and Sir Hugh. We find an anticipation of the later comedy of manners in the duel of the sexes between Benedick and Beatrice, and this duel is thrust into a comedy of intrigue where the solution is provided by the intervention of a realistic Jack-in-Office. Or again we get comedy artfully blended with romance in *Twelfth Night,* where the old comic device of mistaken identity kindles the affection alike of the love-lorn Duke and the passionate Countess, while the carefree jests of Sir Toby and his mates keep sentiment from drifting into sentimentality. Here surely (as Dryden said of Chaucer) is God's plenty.

There is a like variety in Shakespeare's mode of expression. In his early work the young poet, not yet a master playwright, tends to throw even his comic scenes into verse, into rhyme for the most part, with spots of doggrel for broad jests and the Clown's patter, and patches of blank verse for higher characters. As he progresses he comes to realize that prose rather than verse is the true vehicle for comedy, at least so far as comedy is native, natural, and realistic. Whatever else Shakespeare's comedy may be, it is not the artificial comedy of the Restoration or the sentimental comedy of the eighteenth century. And it may be noted in passing that, though Shakespeare attains his greatest heights of expression in poetry, his prose, as a rule, is simpler and freer from conceits than his verse. The prose of Falstaff, Benedick, and Rosalind is unsurpassed in English literature.

One must reckon also with the great development of Shakespeare's art. He advances from a fairly close adherence to the Plautine pattern in *The Comedy of Errors* to independent invention in *The Tempest*. Nowhere, perhaps, is this advance more clearly seen than in his treatment of the fun-makers of his plays. In the early comedies they are such Clowns as Costard and Launce, holdovers from earlier tradition, boorish rustics whose uncouth speech and behavior provoke laughter. Later they become self-complacent citizens, Bottom, for example, and Dogberry, surely more complete and rounded characters. Later still Shakespeare introduces the professional Jester, Touchstone, or Lear's Fool, as a critic of the world in which he lives. And last of all we find characters like Autolycus and Stephano, who have few characteristics left of the traditional Clown and are yet a lively source of laughter.

Shakespearean comedy finds expression in action, speech, and character. The crudest form of action, physical violence, is an inheritance of Elizabethan Comedy from the old native drama where even Biblical characters like Noah and his wife exchange buffets to the delight of the on-lookers. It is comparatively rare in Shakespeare. We have, of course, the beaten slave in *The Errors*, but that is derived from the source. In the last of his comedies Stephano, to be sure, threatens and strikes the Jester, but that is rather a characterizing touch of the bullying sailor than an attempt to raise a laugh. Cases of physical violence off-stage are sometimes reported in a comic strain, such as the abuse of Dr. Pinch by Antipholus of Ephesus, and Dame Quickly's account of the Prince's breaking Falstaff's head. A report, of course, carries less conviction than an action seen on the stage; it would have been a fatal anticipation of Hal's rejection of his old companion to have seen him laying violent hands on the fat Knight. One form of physical violence, the kick, is altogether absent from Shakespeare's comedies, although it is not uncommon in contemporary plays. An instance may be noted in a Beaumont and Fletcher play where a gentle hero must be goaded by a kick into drawing his sword. Clearly the taste for this sort of fun was not extinct among the Elizabethans, but Shakespeare has little of it.

Action, however, if prolonged beyond the first moment, passes into situation, and in comic situation Shakespeare abounds. There is an admirable example in the early *Love's Labour's Lost*, where two lords and the King, each unconscious of the other's presence, confess themselves guilty of the crime of love. The second lord is rebuked by the first; both of them by the King; and the trio by Berowne, who, unseen, has overheard the whole; whereupon Berowne himself is exposed as a lover by the return of his amorous epistle to Rosaline. It is the one really comic situation in a play singularly devoid of action, and the prentice playwright seems to have been so pleased with it that he spun it out to unconscionable length; the episode covers over two hundred lines. That was not Shakespeare's manner as he perfected his art. Consider, for example, one of his best comic scenes, that in which Falstaff relates his adventure at Gadshill to Prince Hal. Here, surely, is an absurdly comic situation; Falstaff, as we know, had fled from the fray roaring for mercy. Yet now he describes the opponents he encountered, the blows he exchanged, the foes he overthrew, in one incredible exaggeration after another. He knows he is lying; the Prince knows it; and so does the audience; and all three rejoice together in the shameless lies. Yet Shakespeare does not linger too long over this delectable situation; almost before we know it we are confronted with another, perhaps even more amusing, that of the mock trial where Falstaff and Hal in turn impersonate the irate King and the accused Prince. So in *Twelfth Night* Malvolio's absurd courtship of his mistress is cut short by the arrival of the Duke's page, the steward's self-congratulatory soliloquy by the onslaught of Sir Toby, Fabian, and Maria who insist that he is possessed by a devil, and their enjoyment of their successful plot by the appearance of Sir Andrew with his foolish challenge to the page. This piling of one comic situation upon another springs from Shakespeare's inexhaustible fertility of invention. He was accustomed, of course, to borrow the outlines of his plots from old plays, histories, or romances, but having once borrowed he embroidered them with an endless variety of comic circumstance, and it will be found that nearly all these comic situations are of his own invention. Part of the fun of Shakespeare's comedies comes from this kaleidoscopic change of situation with which he gratified the desire of his audience for something fresh and new.

Further, Shakespeare's comedy finds expression in language, that is in the spoken words of his characters. Shakespeare is not a maker of witty phrases, like Congreve or Oscar Wilde. He seems, indeed, to have had a certain contempt for 'old fond paradoxes to make fools laugh i' the ale house'—or in the theater. His set wit-combats are often little better than slanging matches; witness, for example, the epithets with which Prince Hal and Falstaff pelt each other in the Boar's Head Tavern. Yet he was from the beginning a lover of language and knew how to wrest it for the ends of comedy. With the passage of time some, perhaps much, of the fun has gone out of his word-play. Here, as in so much else, Shakespeare was the child of his age, and the Elizabethans employed and enjoyed a license in the use of language that has never since been possible. Hence the quips, the puns, the running changes on a word, 'enough to crack the wind of the poor phrase.' On the other hand, the malapropisms, like 'comparisons are odorous,' which decorate the speech of many minor characters, are as amusing today as ever. They are, of course, an inheritance from the early native comedy, but Shakespeare uses them with a fine art as a means of characterization; a stumbling tongue often reveals a muddled mind, as in Elbow, that ineffectual officer of the law, or in the voluble and incoherent Quickly. Yet Shakespeare never lets this trick of speech degenerate into such a caricature as Sheridan's lady who only opens her mouth to vent the words, 'ingeniously misapplied,' from which she takes her name. The greatest delight, however, that we find in Shakespeare's language in the field of comedy springs neither from word-play nor malapropisms, but from the unchecked flood of speech which pours out of his characters when they are really moved to utterance, as in Berowne's defense of the lovers' perjury, in Falstaff's catechism of honor, or in Rosalind's admonitions to the enamoured Orlando and the foolish Phebe.

A word needs, perhaps, to be said on the occasional indecent speech of Shakespeare's comic characters. We of this age of popular four-letter-word fiction need not apologize for him as our Victorian ancestors were wont to do, on the ground of the freer and broader Elizabethan habit of speech. Attention was directed earlier in this work to the so-called 'humor of filth,' the delight in dirt for dirt's sake, that befouls much early comedy. Nothing of the sort is to be found in Shakespeare. The foul talk of Thersites is not comic, but satiric; the raving of Timon is a symptom of his misanthropic madness. Not averse at times to a broad jest, Shakespeare is incomparably the cleanest of Elizabethan playwrights; he avoids alike the wanton levity of Fletcher and the deliberate vulgarity of Jonson.

Yet it is neither in action nor in speech that Shakespeare attains the height of his art, but in character creation. And this holds good for comedy as for tragedy. It may be questioned, indeed, if Falstaff is not as divinely inspired a creation as Hamlet; Rosalind as Juliet or

Cordelia. Certainly Shakespeare's range of interest is wider in comedy than in tragedy. It extends, in fact, beyond the limit of human nature: on the one hand to Oberon and Puck, who sport with the mortals, on the other to the sub-human Caliban. And between these extremes what a wealth of comic characters, all sorts and conditions of men from the city handicraftsman to the country landlord, from Bottom to Justice Shallow! With all of these Shakespeare seems to be in perfect sympathy. Almost the only characters in his comedies for whom he seems, in fact, to have a certain aversion are complacent young gentlemen of rank and fashion, Claudio in *Much Ado,* Bertram in *All's Well.* For their opposites, for rogues and vagabonds, like Pompey and Autolycus, he certainly had a lurking fondness. Even for Shylock, usurer, miser, and, at that time generally detested Jew, Shakespeare had sufficient sympathy to keep him from degenerating into a monster like his prototype, the Jew of Malta.

Shakespeare reaches his height as a comic dramatist in the great trio of plays that overlap the end of the century. They are all dramatized love stories; the passion of young love had by this time become a fit theme for comic rather than satiric treatment. It is remarkable that in these plays the ladies rather than their lovers dominate the action. There is need for them to do so. The world in which they find themselves is no Arcadia where they may sit in peace to receive the vows of their worshipers. It is a working-day world and full of briers, where innocence is foully slandered, or driven into exile, or shipwrecked on a strange coast. There is need of all their courage, quick wit, sunny humor, and gentle patience to bring the ship of their fortunes to the desired haven. They are quite different characters, these three heroines, but they have one trait, at least, in common, an essential femininity. The firm faith of Beatrice in her cousin's innocence, when lover and father renounce her, is the woman's clear-eyed intuition of the truth; Rosalind's delight in the game she plays with Orlando is the woman's way of teasing whom she loves best; Viola's willingness to act as intercessor between the man she loves and the lady whom he fancies he loves shows the other side of woman's nature, the readiness to sacrifice self for the beloved. It is not surprising that these three plays went out of fashion in Restoration times when comedy usually presented woman either as a vixen or a puppet. They did not regain the stage till the spirit of Romance once more reigned in England. In these plays, as nowhere else, we discover Shakespeare's outlook on life from the standpoint of the comic dramatist.

It is easier to say what Shakespearean comedy is not than to formulate what it is. Certainly it is not satiric, neither personal nor social. This is not because there was no occasion for satire in Shakespeare's day; the period of his supreme comedies corresponds precisely to an outburst of satiric drama in the work of Marston, Jonson, and Chapman. Plays by Shakespeare's contemporaries were censored or suppressed because of alleged or actual attacks on private or public officials. The King himself was not immune; his broad Scotch accent, his profane oaths, were laughed at on the public stage. There is nothing of this sort in Shakespeare; not a single definite satiric personal [1] allusion, such as appears again and again in Aristophanes, the master of satiric comedy, can be found in Shakespeare. Nor can we find in Shakespeare's plays any trace of that satiric comment on the social abuses of his day which flourished so rankly in Elizabethan realistic comedy. Shakespeare was not troubled by the growing wealth and influence of the bourgeoisie; he belonged to that class himself and was very successfully making his way in the world. The sale of old landed estates to city merchants did not vex him; had he not bought the ruinous New Place in Stratford and rebuilt it handsomely? The false lights by which tradesmen sold their goods; the crushing rates of interest imposed upon reckless spendthrifts; the miseries of the debtors' prison: there is ample testimony to these abuses in contemporary plays, but not in Shakespeare's.

So far as we catch a note of satire in Shakespeare's comedy, it is general rather than specific. One exception might perhaps be made: Shakespeare loved his mother tongue and abhorred those who abused it, pedantically like Holofernes, or fashionably like Osric. Such defilers of the clear stream of English speech he was prompt to hold up to ridicule. For the rest, what we find of satire in Shakespeare is directed against the common failings of mankind: self-love, flattery, blind worship of false ideals. And he embodies these failings in characters who are not allegorical types, but human beings of flesh and blood; in Malvolio, Parolles, Troilus and the Greek chieftains.

Finally the comic genius of Shakespeare is not to be identified with

[1] The famous 'purge' he is supposed to have administered to Ben Jonson rests apparently on the wisecrack of a university playwright so ill-informed on theatrical affairs in London that he brought on Kempe and Burbage as fellow-actors some years after Kempe had deserted Shakespeare's company.

Meredith's 'Idea of Comedy,' that detached and supramundane spirit which looks down, 'humanely malign,' on mortal follies. Meredith, to be sure, places Shakespeare as a comic poet between the two great masters, Aristophanes and Molière; but if, as he asserts, 'the test of true comedy is that it shall awaken thoughtful laughter,' we begin to wonder how much of 'true comedy' Meredith really found in Shakespeare. Was it thoughtful laughter that shook the galleries of the Globe at Falstaff's flood of lies, 'gross as a mountain, open, palpable'? The truth is that the inspiring genius of Shakespeare's comedy is far removed from Meredith's 'Spirit overhead'; it walks upon solid ground and rubs elbows with men in crowded streets. Its motto might be that of Terence:

Homo sum: humani nihil a me alienum.

There can be nothing 'malign' in its glance at the follies of fellow mortals, it is a friendly genius, humane and beneficent. The words of the Latin comic poet are the final and perfect characterization of William Shakespeare, writer of immortal comedy.

Index

Nashe, Thomas, 68f., 77, 97, 120, 207;
  Pierce Penniless, 207
Nature, 15f., 23, 24
Nature of the Four Elements, 16, 23
Newington Butts, *see under* Theaters
Nice Wanton, The, 30f.
Noah, 5
North, Sir Thomas, 275f., 316, 322, 326,
  328f.

O'Neill, Eugene, *Mourning Becomes
  Electra*, 304
Old Wives' Tale, The, 68ff.
Orlando Furioso, 79, 155
Othello, 193, 272, 288-93, 294, 308, 310,
  316f., 318, 340, 347, 351, 356f., 380,
  384
Ovid, 62, 92f., 128, 386

Painfull Adventures of Pericles, The,
  369
Painter, William, 199; *Palace of Pleas-
  ure*, 199, 348
Palamon and Arcite, 47
Palsgrave's Company of Actors, *see un-
  der* Companies of Actors
Pandosto, the Triumph of Time, 77,
  381ff.
Pater Noster Play, 13
Patterne of Painefull Adventures, The,
  369ff.
Paul's Boys, *see under* Companies of
  Actors
Pecorone, Il, 135ff., 254, 258f.
Peele, George, 67-76, 97, 132, 210, 212,
  358
  Arraignment of Paris, The, 67ff., 76
  Battle of Alcazar, The, 68, 148
  David and Bethsabe, 68
  Edward I, 68ff.
  Farewell, A, 67
  Hunting of Cupid, The, 68, 83
  Mohamet and Hiren, 68
  Old Wives' Tale, The, 68 ff.
  Polyhymnia, 67
Peele, George, *The Gests of*, 68
Pembroke's Company, *see under* Com-
  panies of Actors
Pepys, Samuel, 284, 311f.
Pericles, Prince of Tyre, 103, 366-75,
  384, 387
Pernet qui va au vin, 35
Phelps, Samuel, 303

Philaster, 375
Pickford, Mary, 151
Pierce Penniless, 207
Plautus, 37f., 41, 49, 61, 100ff., 178, 180,
  191
  Amphitruo, 38, 102
  Menaechmi, 100ff., 178, 180
  Rudens, 49
Players' Club, 344
Plutarch, 128, 275ff., 306, 316, 322f.
  Advice to the Married, 275
  Antony, 276, 306, 316ff.
  Brutus, 276
  Caesar, 276
  Coriolanus, 328ff.
  Theseus, 128
Polo, Gil, 127
Polyhymnia, 67f.
Pope, Alexander, 371
Posidippus, *Didumoi*, 101
Pride of Life, The, 14f.
Prima Pastorum, 10
Problem Comedies, 337ff.
Processus Talentorum, 6f., 10f.
Promos and Cassandra, 51f., 358ff.

Queen Hester, 27f.
Queen's Company of Actors, *see under*
  Companies of Actors
Quem quaeritis, 4, 4n.
Quiller-Couch, Sir Arthur, 112f., 140,
  387

Rabelais, François, 24, 104f.
Radford, George, 238n.
Raleigh, Sir Walter (1552?-1618), 121
Raleigh, Sir Walter (1861-1922), 356,
  395
Ralph Roister Doister, 39f., 61
*Rare Triumphs of Love and Fortune,
  The*, 46f., 377
Rastell, John, 28, 29, 32, 48
Rastell, William, 16, 29, 32, 35
Ravenscroft, Edward, 191, 197
Redford, John, *Wit and Science*, 16f.,
  23, 42
Regularis Concordia, 4n.
Rehan, Ada, 171
Reinhardt, Max, 127
Respublica, 19f., 24, 36, 42
Richard II, 200, 228-32, 236, 244
Richard III, 53